THE BOOK ®

Fiat Punto
Service and Repair Manual

John S. Mead

Models covered
(4066-240-8AK1)

Hatchback with 1.2 litre (1242cc) petrol engine, including Speedgear models and special/limited editions

Does NOT cover Diesel or 1.8 litre (1747cc) petrol models
Does NOT cover 'new' range introduced August 2003

© Haynes Publishing 2006

A book in the **Haynes Service and Repair Manual Series**

ABCDE
FGHIJ
KLM

ISBN-10: **1 84425 066 0**
ISBN-13: **978 1 84425 066 0**

British Library Cataloguing in Publication Data
A catalogue record for this book is available from the British Library.

Printed in the USA

Haynes Publishing
Sparkford, Yeovil, Somerset BA22 7JJ, England

Haynes North America, Inc
861 Lawrence Drive, Newbury Park, California 91320, USA

Editions Haynes
4, Rue de l'Abreuvoir
92415 COURBEVOIE CEDEX, France

Haynes Publishing Nordiska AB
Box 1504, 751 45 UPPSALA, Sverige

Contents

Contents

REPAIRS & OVERHAUL

Advanced driving

Many people see the words 'advanced driving' and believe that it won't interest them or that it is a style of driving beyond their own abilities. Nothing could be further from the truth. Advanced driving is straightforward safe, sensible driving - the sort of driving we should all do every time we get behind the wheel.

An average of 10 people are killed every day on UK roads and 870 more are injured, some seriously. Lives are ruined daily, usually because somebody did something stupid. Something like 95% of all accidents are due to human error, mostly driver failure. Sometimes we make genuine mistakes - everyone does. Sometimes we have lapses of concentration. Sometimes we deliberately take risks.

For many people, the process of 'learning to drive' doesn't go much further than learning how to pass the driving test because of a common belief that good drivers are made by 'experience'.

Learning to drive by 'experience' teaches three driving skills:

☐ Quick reactions. (Whoops, that was close!)
☐ Good handling skills. (Horn, swerve, brake, horn).
☐ Reliance on vehicle technology. (Great stuff this ABS, stop in no distance even in the wet...)

Drivers whose skills are 'experience based' generally have a lot of near misses and the odd accident. The results can be seen every day in our courts and our hospital casualty departments.

Advanced drivers have learnt to control the risks by controlling the position and speed of their vehicle. They avoid accidents and near misses, even if the drivers around them make mistakes.

The key skills of advanced driving are **concentration,** effective all-round **observation, anticipation** and **planning.** When **good vehicle handling** is added to these skills, all driving situations can be approached and negotiated in a safe, methodical way, leaving nothing to chance.

Concentration means applying your mind to safe driving, completely excluding anything that's not relevant. Driving is usually the most dangerous activity that most of us undertake in our daily routines. It deserves our full attention.

Observation means not just looking, but seeing and seeking out the information found in the driving environment.

Anticipation means asking yourself what is happening, what you can reasonably expect to happen and what could happen unexpectedly. (One of the commonest words used in compiling accident reports is 'suddenly'.)

Planning is the link between seeing something and taking the appropriate action. For many drivers, planning is the missing link.

If you want to become a safer and more skilful driver and you want to enjoy your driving more, contact the Institute of Advanced Motorists at www.iam.org.uk, phone 0208 996 9600, or write to IAM House, 510 Chiswick High Road, London W4 5RG for an information pack.

Working on your car can be dangerous. This page shows just some of the potential risks and hazards, with the aim of creating a safety-conscious attitude.

General hazards

Scalding

• Don't remove the radiator or expansion tank cap while the engine is hot.
• Engine oil, automatic transmission fluid or power steering fluid may also be dangerously hot if the engine has recently been running.

Burning

• Beware of burns from the exhaust system and from any part of the engine. Brake discs and drums can also be extremely hot immediately after use.

Crushing

• When working under or near a raised vehicle, always supplement the jack with axle stands, or use drive-on ramps. *Never venture under a car which is only supported by a jack.*
• Take care if loosening or tightening high-torque nuts when the vehicle is on stands. Initial loosening and final tightening should be done with the wheels on the ground.

Fire

• Fuel is highly flammable; fuel vapour is explosive.
• Don't let fuel spill onto a hot engine.
• Do not smoke or allow naked lights (including pilot lights) anywhere near a vehicle being worked on. Also beware of creating sparks
(electrically or by use of tools).
• Fuel vapour is heavier than air, so don't work on the fuel system with the vehicle over an inspection pit.
• Another cause of fire is an electrical overload or short-circuit. Take care when repairing or modifying the vehicle wiring.
• Keep a fire extinguisher handy, of a type suitable for use on fuel and electrical fires.

Electric shock

• Ignition HT voltage can be dangerous, especially to people with heart problems or a pacemaker. Don't work on or near the ignition system with the engine running or the ignition switched on.

• Mains voltage is also dangerous. Make sure that any mains-operated equipment is correctly earthed. Mains power points should be protected by a residual current device (RCD) circuit breaker.

Fume or gas intoxication

• Exhaust fumes are poisonous; they often contain carbon monoxide, which is rapidly fatal if inhaled. Never run the engine in a confined space such as a garage with the doors shut.
• Fuel vapour is also poisonous, as are the vapours from some cleaning solvents and paint thinners.

Poisonous or irritant substances

• Avoid skin contact with battery acid and with any fuel, fluid or lubricant, especially antifreeze, brake hydraulic fluid and Diesel fuel. Don't syphon them by mouth. If such a substance is swallowed or gets into the eyes, seek medical advice.
• Prolonged contact with used engine oil can cause skin cancer. Wear gloves or use a barrier cream if necessary. Change out of oil-soaked clothes and do not keep oily rags in your pocket.
• Air conditioning refrigerant forms a poisonous gas if exposed to a naked flame (including a cigarette). It can also cause skin burns on contact.

Asbestos

• Asbestos dust can cause cancer if inhaled or swallowed. Asbestos may be found in gaskets and in brake and clutch linings. When dealing with such components it is safest to assume that they contain asbestos.

Special hazards

Hydrofluoric acid

• This extremely corrosive acid is formed when certain types of synthetic rubber, found in some O-rings, oil seals, fuel hoses etc, are exposed to temperatures above 400ºC. The rubber changes into a charred or sticky substance containing the acid. *Once formed, the acid remains dangerous for years. If it gets onto the skin, it may be necessary to amputate the limb concerned.*
• When dealing with a vehicle which has suffered a fire, or with components salvaged from such a vehicle, wear protective gloves and discard them after use.

The battery

• Batteries contain sulphuric acid, which attacks clothing, eyes and skin. Take care when topping-up or carrying the battery.
• The hydrogen gas given off by the battery is highly explosive. Never cause a spark or allow a naked light nearby. Be careful when connecting and disconnecting battery chargers or jump leads.

Air bags

• Air bags can cause injury if they go off accidentally. Take care when removing the steering wheel and/or facia. Special storage instructions may apply.

Diesel injection equipment

• Diesel injection pumps supply fuel at very high pressure. Take care when working on the fuel injectors and fuel pipes.

⚠ *Warning: Never expose the hands, face or any other part of the body to injector spray; the fuel can penetrate the skin with potentially fatal results.*

Remember...

DO

• Do use eye protection when using power tools, and when working under the vehicle.

• Do wear gloves or use barrier cream to protect your hands when necessary.

• Do get someone to check periodically that all is well when working alone on the vehicle.

• Do keep loose clothing and long hair well out of the way of moving mechanical parts.

• Do remove rings, wristwatch etc, before working on the vehicle – especially the electrical system.

• Do ensure that any lifting or jacking equipment has a safe working load rating adequate for the job.

DON'T

• Don't attempt to lift a heavy component which may be beyond your capability – get assistance.

• Don't rush to finish a job, or take unverified short cuts.

• Don't use ill-fitting tools which may slip and cause injury.

• Don't leave tools or parts lying around where someone can trip over them. Mop up oil and fuel spills at once.

• Don't allow children or pets to play in or near a vehicle being worked on.

Fiat Punto Dynamic

The new Fiat Punto range was introduced in October 1999 in 3-door and 5-door Hatchback layout. Although mechanically similar in some areas to the previous Punto range, the new version has been completely redesigned with significant improvements in comfort, handling and performance.

The Punto range is available with two sizes of petrol engines, and a turbocharged or normally-aspirated diesel engine. Covered in this manual are the popular 1.2 litre SOHC (8-valve) and DOHC (16-valve) petrol units. Both engines feature multi-point fuel injection and are equipped with an extensive range of emissions control systems. The engines are of a well-proven design and have been used extensively in a range of Fiat vehicles.

Fully-independent front suspension is fitted, with semi-independent torsion beam suspension used at the rear. Electrically-operated power steering is standard equipment on most models and is available as an option on others.

A five-speed manual transmission is fitted to all models except the Sporting and Speedgear versions. Sporting models are equipped with a six-speed manual transmission, whereas Speedgear models utilise a CVT automatic transmission which can also be operated manually with six-speed or seven-speed sequential gear selection.

A wide range of standard and optional equipment is available within the Punto range including central locking, electric windows, an electric sunroof, an anti-lock braking system with traction control and supplementary restraint system.

For the home mechanic, the Punto is a straightforward vehicle to maintain, and most of the items requiring frequent attention are easily accessible.

Your Fiat Punto Manual

The aim of this manual is to help you get the best value from your vehicle. It can do so in several ways. It can help you decide what work must be done (even should you choose to get it done by a garage), provide information on routine maintenance and servicing, and give a logical course of action and diagnosis when random faults occur. However, it is hoped that you will use the manual by tackling the work yourself. On simpler jobs, it may even be quicker than booking the car into a garage and going there twice, to leave and collect it. Perhaps most important, a lot of money can be saved by avoiding the costs a garage must charge to cover its labour and overheads.

The manual has drawings and descriptions to show the function of the various components, so that their layout can be understood. Then the tasks are described and photographed in a clear step-by-step sequence.

References to the 'left' or 'right' are in the sense of a person in the driver's seat, facing forward.

Acknowledgements

Thanks are due to Draper Tools Limited, who provided some of the workshop tools, and to all those people at Sparkford who helped in the production of this manual.

We take great pride in the accuracy of information given in this manual, but vehicle manufacturers make alterations and design changes during the production run of a particular vehicle of which they do not inform us. No liability can be accepted by the authors or publishers for loss, damage or injury caused by any errors in, or omissions from, the information given.

Fiat Punto Speedgear

The following pages are intended to help in dealing with common roadside emergencies and breakdowns. You will find more detailed fault finding information at the back of the manual, and repair information in the main chapters.

If your car won't start and the starter motor doesn't turn

☐ If it's a model with automatic transmission, make sure the selector is in P or N.
☐ Open the bonnet and make sure that the battery terminals are clean and tight.
☐ Switch on the headlights and try to start the engine. If the headlights go very dim when you're trying to start, the battery is probably flat. Get out of trouble by jump starting (see next page) using a friend's car.

If your car won't start even though the starter motor turns as normal

☐ Is there fuel in the tank?
☐ Is there moisture on electrical components under the bonnet? Switch off the ignition, then wipe off any obvious dampness with a dry cloth. Spray a water-repellent aerosol product (WD-40 or equivalent) on ignition and fuel system electrical connectors like those shown in the photos. Pay special attention to the ignition coil wiring connectors and HT leads.

A Check that the spark plug HT leads are securely connected at the spark plugs . . .

B . . . and at the ignition coils.

C Check the condition and security of critical wiring connectors such as those at the ignition coils . . .

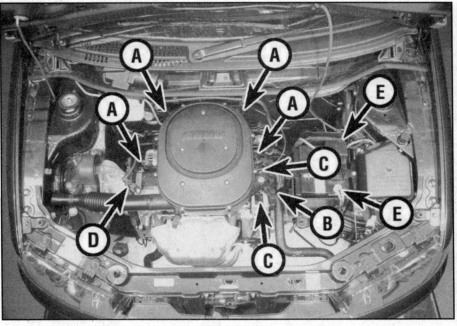

Check that electrical connections are secure (with the ignition switched off) and spray them with a water dispersant spray like WD-40 if you suspect a problem due to damp.

D . . . and camshaft position sensor.

E Check the condition and security of the battery terminals.

Jump starting

When jump-starting a car using a booster battery, observe the following precautions:

✔ Before connecting the booster battery, make sure that the ignition is switched off.

✔ Ensure that all electrical equipment (lights, heater, wipers, etc) is switched off.

✔ Take note of any special precautions printed on the battery case.

✔ Make sure that the booster battery is the same voltage as the discharged one in the vehicle.

✔ If the battery is being jump-started from the battery in another vehicle, the two vehicles MUST NOT TOUCH each other.

✔ Make sure that the transmission is in neutral (or PARK, in the case of automatic transmission).

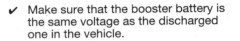

HAYNES HiNT *Jump starting will get you out of trouble, but you must correct whatever made the battery go flat in the first place. There are three possibilities:*

1 *The battery has been drained by repeated attempts to start, or by leaving the lights on.*

2 *The charging system is not working properly (alternator drivebelt slack or broken, alternator wiring fault or alternator itself faulty).*

3 *The battery itself is at fault (electrolyte low, or battery worn out).*

1 Connect one end of the red jump lead to the positive (+) terminal of the flat battery

2 Connect the other end of the red lead to the positive (+) terminal of the booster battery.

3 Connect one end of the black jump lead to the negative (-) terminal of the booster battery

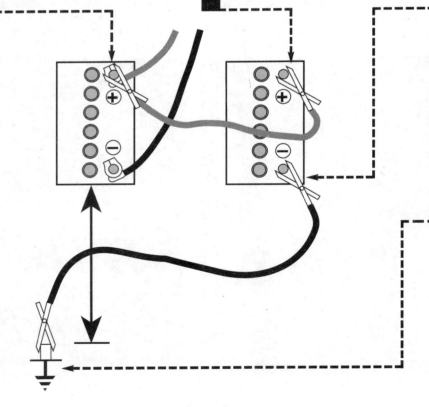

4 Connect the other end of the black jump lead to a bolt or bracket on the engine block, well away from the battery, on the vehicle to be started.

5 Make sure that the jump leads will not come into contact with the fan, drive-belts or other moving parts of the engine.

6 Start the engine using the booster battery and run it at idle speed. Switch on the lights, rear window demister and heater blower motor, then disconnect the jump leads in the reverse order of connection. Turn off the lights etc.

Wheel changing

Some of the details shown here will vary according to model. For instance, certain Punto models are supplied with a 'Fix & Go' puncture repair kit instead of a spare wheel. On models so equipped, follow the instructions supplied with the kit.

 Warning: Do not change a wheel in a situation where you risk being hit by another vehicle. On busy roads, try to stop in a lay-by or a gateway. Be wary of passing traffic while changing the wheel – it is easy to become distracted by the job in hand.

Preparation

- ☐ When a puncture occurs, stop as soon as it is safe to do so.
- ☐ Park on firm level ground, if possible, and well out of the way of other traffic.
- ☐ Use hazard warning lights if necessary.
- ☐ If you have one, use a warning triangle to alert other drivers of your presence.
- ☐ Apply the handbrake and engage first or reverse gear (or Park on models with automatic transmission).
- ☐ Chock the wheel diagonally opposite the one being removed – a couple of large stones will do for this.
- ☐ If the ground is soft, use a flat piece of wood to spread the load under the jack.

Changing the wheel

1 The spare wheel and tools (including the jack) are stored in the luggage compartment beneath the floor covering. Unscrew the central plastic nut to remove the tool holder.

2 Slacken each wheel bolt by a half turn.

3 Locate the jack under the triangular mark on the sill next to the wheel to be changed, on firm ground.

4 Turn the jack handle clockwise until the wheel is raised clear of the ground.

5 Unscrew the wheel bolts, withdraw the trim and remove the wheel.

6 Fit the space-saver spare wheel on the pins, and screw in the bolts. Lightly tighten the bolts with the wheelbrace then lower the vehicle to the ground.

7 Securely tighten the wheel bolts in the sequence shown, then stow the punctured tyre and wheel in the luggage compartment.

Finally...

- ☐ Remove the wheel chocks.
- ☐ Stow the jack and tools in the correct locations in the car.
- ☐ Check the tyre pressure on the wheel just fitted. If it is low, or if you don't have a pressure gauge with you, drive slowly to the nearest garage and inflate the tyre to the right pressure.
- ☐ When using the space-saver spare wheel, do not exceed 50 mph (80 kph).
- ☐ Have the damaged tyre or wheel repaired as soon as possible.

Identifying leaks

Puddles on the garage floor or drive, or obvious wetness under the bonnet or underneath the car, suggest a leak that needs investigating. It can sometimes be difficult to decide where the leak is coming from, especially if the engine bay is very dirty already. Leaking oil or fluid can also be blown rearwards by the passage of air under the car, giving a false impression of where the problem lies.

 Warning: Most automotive oils and fluids are poisonous. Wash them off skin, and change out of contaminated clothing, without delay.

HAYNES HiNT *The smell of a fluid leaking from the car may provide a clue to what's leaking. Some fluids are distinctively coloured. It may help to clean the car carefully and to park it over some clean paper overnight as an aid to locating the source of the leak.*
Remember that some leaks may only occur while the engine is running.

Sump oil

Engine oil may leak from the drain plug...

Oil from filter

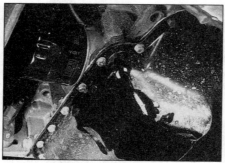

...or from the base of the oil filter.

Gearbox oil

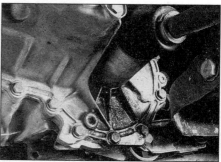

Gearbox oil can leak from the seals at the inboard ends of the driveshafts.

Antifreeze

Leaking antifreeze often leaves a crystalline deposit like this.

Brake fluid

A leak occurring at a wheel is almost certainly brake fluid.

Power steering fluid

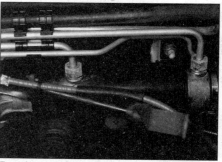

Power steering fluid may leak from the pipe connectors on the steering rack.

Towing

When all else fails, you may find yourself having to get a tow home – or of course you may be helping somebody else. Long-distance recovery should only be done by a garage or breakdown service. For shorter distances, DIY towing using another car is easy enough, but observe the following points:

☐ Use a proper tow-rope – they are not expensive. The vehicle being towed must display an ON TOW sign in its rear window.
☐ Always turn the ignition key to the MAR position when the vehicle is being towed, so that the steering lock is released, and that the direction indicator and brake lights will work.

☐ Only attach the tow-rope to the towing eyes provided.
☐ Before being towed, release the handbrake and select neutral on the transmission. **On models with automatic transmission, special precautions apply. If in doubt, do not tow, or transmission damage may result.**
☐ Note that greater-than-usual pedal pressure will be required to operate the brakes, since the vacuum servo unit is only operational with the engine running.
☐ On models with power steering, greater-than-usual steering effort will also be required.
☐ The driver of the car being towed must keep the tow-rope taut at all times to avoid snatching.

☐ Make sure that both drivers know the route before setting off.
☐ Only drive at moderate speeds and keep the distance towed to a minimum. Drive smoothly and allow plenty of time for slowing down at junctions.
☐ The towing eye is supplied as part of the tool kit stored in the luggage compartment. To fit the eye prise out the plastic cover from the front or rear bumper using a screwdriver, then screw the eye onto the threaded pin as tightly as possible.

 Warning: To prevent damage to the catalytic converter, a vehicle must not be push-started, or started by towing, when the engine is at operating temperature. Use jump leads (see Jump starting).

Introduction

There are some very simple checks which need only take a few minutes to carry out, but which could save you a lot of inconvenience and expense.

These *Weekly checks* require no great skill or special tools, and the small amount of time they take to perform could prove to be very well spent, for example:

☐ Keeping an eye on tyre condition and pressures, will not only help to stop them wearing out prematurely, but could also save your life.

☐ Many breakdowns are caused by electrical problems. Battery-related faults are particularly common, and a quick check on a regular basis will often prevent the majority of these.

☐ If your car develops a brake fluid leak, the first time you might know about it is when your brakes don't work properly. Checking the level regularly will give advance warning of this kind of problem.

☐ If the oil or coolant levels run low, the cost of repairing any engine damage will be far greater than fixing the leak, for example.

Underbonnet check points

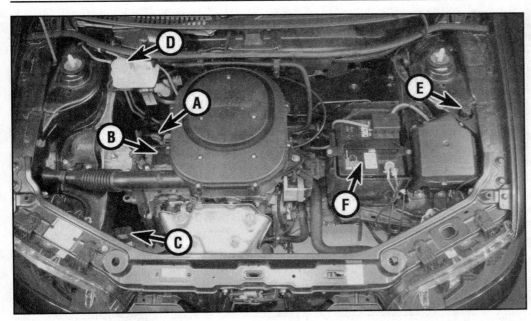

◀ SOHC (8-valve) engine

A *Engine oil level dipstick*
B *Engine oil filler cap*
C *Coolant expansion tank*
D *Brake fluid reservoir*
E *Screen washer fluid reservoir*
F *Battery*

◀ DOHC (16-valve) engine

A *Engine oil level dipstick*
B *Engine oil filler cap*
C *Coolant expansion tank*
D *Brake fluid reservoir*
E *Screen washer fluid reservoir*
F *Automatic transmission fluid level dipstick*
G *Battery*

Engine oil level

Before you start
✔ Make sure that your car is on level ground.
✔ Check the oil level before the car is driven, or at least 5 minutes after the engine has been switched off.

 HAYNES HiNT *If the oil level is checked immediately after driving the vehicle, some of the oil will remain in the upper engine components, resulting in an inaccurate reading on the dipstick.*

The correct oil
Modern engines place great demands on their oil. It is very important that the correct oil for your car is used (See *Lubricants and fluids*).

Car Care
● If you have to add oil frequently, you should check whether you have any oil leaks. Place some clean paper under the car overnight, and check for stains in the morning. If there are no leaks, the engine may be burning oil.

● Always maintain the level between the upper and lower dipstick marks (see photo 2). If the level is too low, severe engine damage may occur. Oil seal failure may result if the engine is overfilled by adding too much oil.

1 The dipstick is brightly-coloured for easy identification (see *Underbonnet check points*). Withdraw the dipstick from the tube.

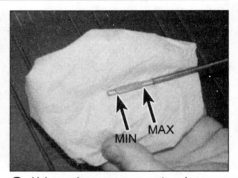

2 Using a clean rag or paper towel, remove all oil from the dipstick. Insert the clean dipstick into the tube as far as it will go, then withdraw it again. The level should be between the upper and lower marks.

3 If more oil is needed, remove the oil filler cap from the top of the engine.

4 Oil is added through the filler cap aperture. Add the oil a little at a time, checking the level on the dipstick often. Using a funnel will help to reduce spillage. Don't overfill (see *Car Care*).

Automatic transmission fluid level

Before you start
✔ Park the vehicle on level ground, and apply the handbrake firmly. Let the engine idle, and select P or N.

Safety First!
● The need for frequent topping-up indicates a leak, which should be investigated immediately.

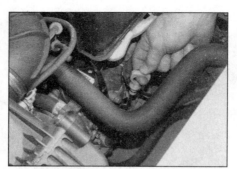

1 Open the bonnet, withdraw the transmission dipstick, and wipe it with a clean non-fluffy rag.

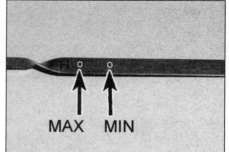

2 Re-insert the dipstick fully, withdraw it again and read the fluid level. It should be between the two level marks. There are two sets of marks. Use the C (cool) marks if the transmission is cold (20° to 40°C) or the H (hot) marks if it is hot (60° to 80°C). If topping-up is necessary, add the specified fluid via the dipstick tube, using a funnel with a fine mesh filter. Take great care not to introduce dirt into the transmission.

Coolant level

Warning: DO NOT attempt to remove the expansion tank pressure cap when the engine is hot, as there is a very great risk of scalding. Do not leave open containers of coolant about, as it is poisonous.

Car Care

● Adding coolant should not be necessary on a regular basis. If frequent topping-up is required, it is likely there is a leak. Check the radiator, all hoses and joint faces for signs of staining or wetness, and rectify as necessary.

● It is important that antifreeze is used in the cooling system all year round, not just during the winter months. Don't top-up with water alone, as the antifreeze will become too diluted.

1 The coolant level varies with engine temperature. The level is checked in the expansion tank, which is located at the front, right-hand side of the engine compartment. When the engine is cold, the coolant level should be between the MAX and MIN marks on the side of the tank.

2 If topping-up is necessary, **wait until the engine is cold** then turn the expansion tank cap slowly anti-clockwise, and pause until any pressure remaining in the system is released. Unscrew the cap and lift off.

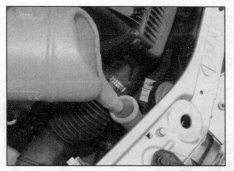

3 Add a mixture of water and antifreeze to the expansion tank, until the coolant level is up to the MAX level mark. Refit the cap, turning it clockwise as far as it will go until it is secure.

Brake fluid level

Warning:
● **Brake fluid can harm your eyes and will damage painted surfaces, so use extreme caution when handling and pouring it.**
● **Do not use fluid that has been standing open for some time, as it absorbs moisture from the air, which can cause a dangerous loss of braking effectiveness.**

HAYNES HiNT
● **Make sure that your car is on level ground.**
● **The fluid level in the reservoir will drop slightly as the brake pads or shoes wear down, but the fluid level must never be allowed to drop below the MIN mark.**

Safety First!

● If the reservoir requires repeated topping-up, this is an indication of a fluid leak somewhere in the system, which should be investigated immediately.
● If a leak is suspected, the car should not be driven until the braking system has been checked. Never take any risks where brakes are concerned.

1 The MIN and MAX marks are indicated on the side of the reservoir. The fluid level must be kept between the marks at all times.

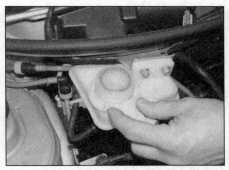

2 If topping-up is necessary, first wipe clean the area around the filler cap to prevent dirt entering the hydraulic system.

3 Unscrew the filler cap and lift it off the reservoir. Inspect the reservoir; if the fluid is dirty the hydraulic system should be drained and refilled (see Chapter 1).

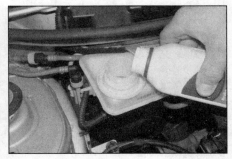

4 Carefully add fluid, taking care not to spill it onto the surrounding components. Use only the specified fluid; mixing different types can cause damage to the system. After topping-up to the correct level, securely refit the cap and wipe off any spilt fluid.

Tyre condition and pressure

It is very important that tyres are in good condition, and at the correct pressure - having a tyre failure at any speed is highly dangerous. Tyre wear is influenced by driving style - harsh braking and acceleration, or fast cornering, will all produce more rapid tyre wear. As a general rule, the front tyres wear out faster than the rears. Interchanging the tyres from front to rear ("rotating" the tyres) may result in more even wear. However, if this is completely effective, you may have the expense of replacing all four tyres at once!

Remove any nails or stones embedded in the tread before they penetrate the tyre to cause deflation. If removal of a nail does reveal that the tyre has been punctured, refit the nail so that its point of penetration is marked. Then immediately change the wheel, and have the tyre repaired by a tyre dealer.

Regularly check the tyres for damage in the form of cuts or bulges, especially in the sidewalls. Periodically remove the wheels, and clean any dirt or mud from the inside and outside surfaces. Examine the wheel rims for signs of rusting, corrosion or other damage. Light alloy wheels are easily damaged by "kerbing" whilst parking; steel wheels may also become dented or buckled. A new wheel is very often the only way to overcome severe damage.

New tyres should be balanced when they are fitted, but it may become necessary to re-balance them as they wear, or if the balance weights fitted to the wheel rim should fall off. Unbalanced tyres will wear more quickly, as will the steering and suspension components. Wheel imbalance is normally signified by vibration, particularly at a certain speed (typically around 50 mph). If this vibration is felt only through the steering, then it is likely that just the front wheels need balancing. If, however, the vibration is felt through the whole car, the rear wheels could be out of balance. Wheel balancing should be carried out by a tyre dealer or garage.

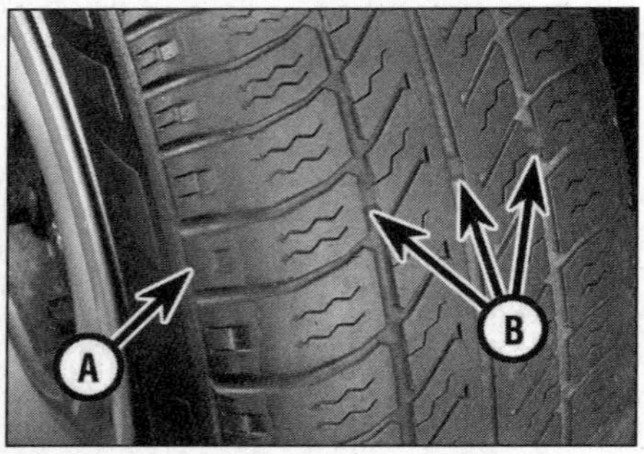

1 ***Tread Depth - visual check***
The original tyres have tread wear safety bands (B), which will appear when the tread depth reaches approximately 1.6 mm. The band positions are indicated by a triangular mark on the tyre sidewall (A).

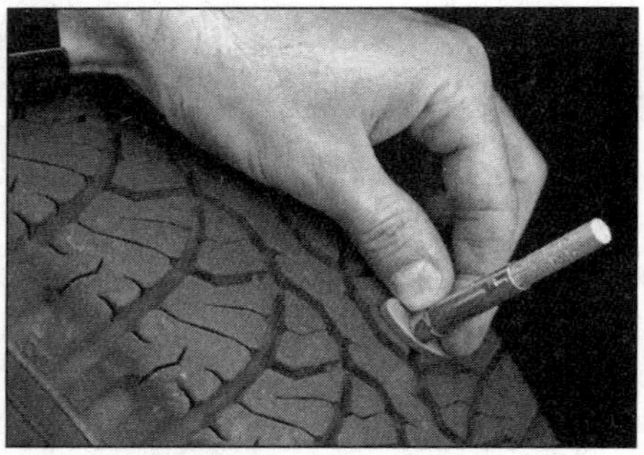

2 ***Tread Depth - manual check***
Alternatively, tread wear can be monitored with a simple, inexpensive device known as a tread depth indicator gauge.

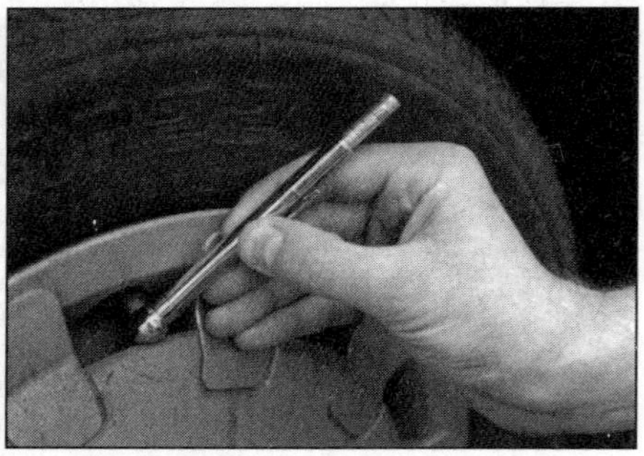

3 ***Tyre Pressure Check***
Check the tyre pressures regularly with the tyres cold. Do not adjust the tyre pressures immediately after the vehicle has been used, or an inaccurate setting will result.

Tyre tread wear patterns

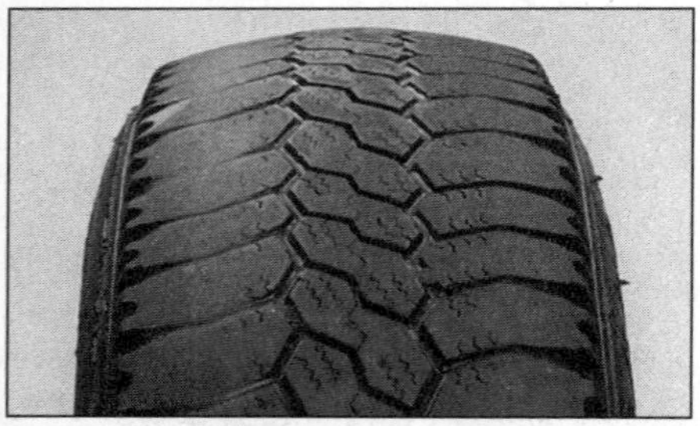

Shoulder Wear

Underinflation (wear on both sides)
Under-inflation will cause overheating of the tyre, because the tyre will flex too much, and the tread will not sit correctly on the road surface. This will cause a loss of grip and excessive wear, not to mention the danger of sudden tyre failure due to heat build-up.
Check and adjust pressures
Incorrect wheel camber (wear on one side)
Repair or renew suspension parts
Hard cornering
Reduce speed!

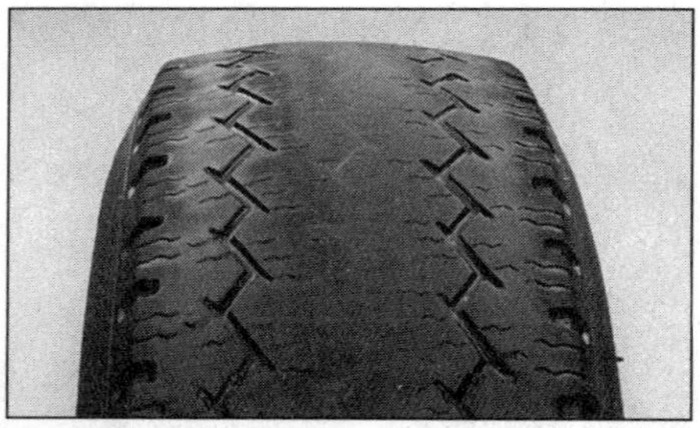

Centre Wear

Overinflation
Over-inflation will cause rapid wear of the centre part of the tyre tread, coupled with reduced grip, harsher ride, and the danger of shock damage occurring in the tyre casing.
Check and adjust pressures

If you sometimes have to inflate your car's tyres to the higher pressures specified for maximum load or sustained high speed, don't forget to reduce the pressures to normal afterwards.

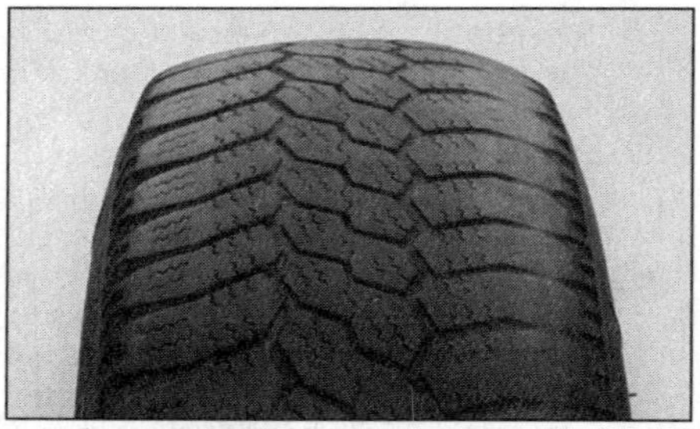

Uneven Wear

Front tyres may wear unevenly as a result of wheel misalignment. Most tyre dealers and garages can check and adjust the wheel alignment (or "tracking") for a modest charge.
Incorrect camber or castor
Repair or renew suspension parts
Malfunctioning suspension
Repair or renew suspension parts
Unbalanced wheel
Balance tyres
Incorrect toe setting
Adjust front wheel alignment
Note: *The feathered edge of the tread which typifies toe wear is best checked by feel.*

Electrical systems

✔ Check all external lights and the horn. Refer to the appropriate Sections of Chapter 12 for details if any of the circuits are found to be inoperative.

✔ Visually check all accessible wiring connectors, harnesses and retaining clips for security, and for signs of chafing or damage.

HAYNES HINT *If you need to check your brake lights and indicators unaided, back up to a wall or garage door and operate the lights. The reflected light should show if they are working properly.*

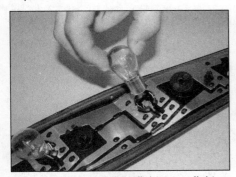

1 If a single indicator light, stop-light or headlight has failed, it is likely that a bulb has blown and will need to be renewed. Refer to Chapter 12 for details. If both stop-lights have failed, it is possible that the switch has failed (see Chapter 9).

2 If more than one indicator light or tail light has failed it is likely that either a fuse has blown or that there is a fault in the circuit (see Chapter 12). The main fuses are located in the fusebox under the facia on the driver's side, accessible after removing the cover panel.

3 Additional fuses are located in the fuse/relay box in the engine compartment; lift off the cover to gain access to the fuses and relays. To renew a blown fuse, simply pull it out using the special plastic tool and fit a new fuse of the correct rating (see Chapter 12). If the fuse blows again, it is important that you find out why – a complete checking procedure is given in Chapter 12.

Washer fluid level

● Screenwash additives not only keep the windscreen clean during foul weather, they also prevent the washer system freezing in cold weather – which is when you are likely to need it most. Don't top up using plain water as the screenwash will become too diluted, and will freeze during cold weather.

On no account use coolant antifreeze in the washer system – this could discolour or damage paintwork.

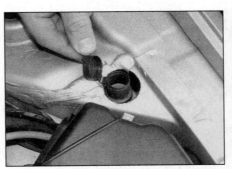

1 The screen washer fluid reservoir is located on the left-hand side of the engine compartment. Prise off the cap and pull out the telescopic filler.

2 When topping-up the reservoir, add a screenwash additive in the quantities recommended on the bottle.

Battery

Caution: Before carrying out any work on the vehicle battery, read the precautions given in 'Safety first!' at the start of this manual.

✔ Make sure that the battery tray is in good condition, and that the clamp is tight. Corrosion on the retaining clamp and the battery itself can be removed with a solution of water and baking soda. Thoroughly rinse all cleaned areas with water. Any metal parts damaged by corrosion should be covered with a zinc-based primer, then painted.

✔ Periodically (approximately every three months), check the charge condition of the battery as described in Chapter 5A.

✔ If the battery is flat, and you need to jump start your vehicle, see *Roadside Repairs*.

HAYNES HiNT

Battery corrosion can be kept to a minimum by applying a layer of petroleum jelly to the clamps and terminals after they are reconnected.

1 The exterior of the battery should be inspected periodically for damage such as a cracked case or cover, and the battery cable clamps should be checked for tightness to ensure good electrical connections.

2 If corrosion (white, fluffy deposits) is evident, remove the cables from the battery terminals, clean them with a small wire brush, then refit them. Automotive stores sell a tool for cleaning the battery post . . .

3 . . . as well as the battery cable clamps

Wiper blades

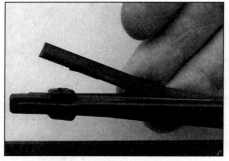

1 Check the condition of the wiper blades; if they are cracked or show any signs of deterioration, or if the glass swept area is smeared, renew them. Wiper blades should be renewed annually. Don't forget to check the tailgate wiper as well.

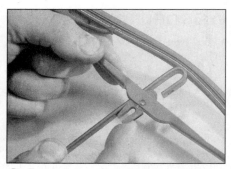

2 To remove a wiper blade, pull the arm fully away from the screen until it locks. Swivel the blade through 90°, press the locking tab with your fingers and slide the blade out of the arm's hooked end.

Lubricants and fluids

Engine . . . . Synthetic-based multigrade engine oil, viscosity SAE 5W/30 to 10W/40, to API SJ and ACEA A1, A3-96 or better

Cooling system . . . . Monothylene glycol-based antifreeze (Paraflu 11) and soft water

Manual gearbox . . . . Synthetic-based gear oil, viscosity SAE 75W-80 EP to API GL5 or better

Automatic transmission . . . . Tutela CVT N.G. transmission fluid

Braking system . . . . Hydraulic fluid to SAE J1703, DOT 4

Choosing your engine oil

Engines need oil, not only to lubricate moving parts and minimise wear, but also to maximise power output and to improve fuel economy.

HOW ENGINE OIL WORKS

• Beating friction

Without oil, the moving surfaces inside your engine will rub together, heat up and melt, quickly causing the engine to seize. Engine oil creates a film which separates these moving parts, preventing wear and heat build-up.

• Cooling hot-spots

Temperatures inside the engine can exceed 1000° C. The engine oil circulates and acts as a coolant, transferring heat from the hot-spots to the sump.

• Cleaning the engine internally

Good quality engine oils clean the inside of your engine, collecting and dispersing combustion deposits and controlling them until they are trapped by the oil filter or flushed out at oil change.

OIL CARE - FOLLOW THE CODE

To handle and dispose of used engine oil safely, always:

OIL CARE
FOLLOW THE CODE

OIL BANK LINE
0800 66 33 66
www.oilbankline.org.uk

• *Avoid skin contact with used engine oil. Repeated or prolonged contact can be harmful.*
• *Dispose of used oil and empty packs in a responsible manner in an authorised disposal site. Call 0800 663366 to find the one nearest to you. Never tip oil down drains or onto the ground.*

Tyre pressures (cold)

Note: *If the space-saver emergency spare tyre is fitted, it should be inflated to a pressure of 2.8 bars (41 psi).*

	Front	Rear
SOHC (8-valve) engine models:		
Normal use	2.0 bar (29 psi)	1.9 bar (28 psi)
Fully laden	2.2 bar (32 psi)	2.2 bar (32 psi)
DOHC (16-valve) engine models except Sporting:		
Normal use	2.0 bar (29 psi)	1.9 bar (28 psi)
Fully laden	2.2 bar (32 psi)	2.1 bar (30 psi)
DOHC (16-valve) engine Sporting models:		
Normal use	2.2 bar (32 psi)	2.1 bar (30 psi)
Fully laden	2.4 bar (35 psi)	2.3 bar (33 psi)

Chapter 1
Routine maintenance and servicing

Contents

Degrees of difficulty

Easy, suitable for novice with little experience

Fairly easy, suitable for beginner with some experience

Fairly difficult, suitable for competent DIY mechanic

Difficult, suitable for experienced DIY mechanic

Very difficult, suitable for expert DIY or professional

Lubricants and fluids

Refer to end of *Weekly checks*

Capacities

Engine oil (including filter)	2.80 litres
Cooling system	4.20 litres
Manual transmission	1.65 litres
Automatic transmission	1.98 litres
Fuel tank	47.0 litres

Engine

Auxiliary drivebelt tension:

Models without air conditioning	5.0 mm deflection midway between pulleys
Models with air conditioning	Controlled by automatic tensioner

Valve clearances (cold) – SOHC (8-valve) engines:

Inlet	0.40 ± 0.05 mm
Exhaust	0.45 ± 0.05 mm
Cam follower (tappet) shim sizes	3.20 to 4.70 mm in increments of 0.05 mm

Cooling system

Antifreeze mixture (50% antifreeze)	Protection down to –35°C

Note: *Refer to antifreeze manufacturer for latest recommendations.*

Fuel system

Engine idle speed	900 ± 50 rpm
CO%	0.35 maximum

Ignition system

Ignition timing ... Refer to Chapter 5B

Spark plugs:

	Type	Electrode gap
SOHC (8-valve) engines	Bosch FR 8 D+	0.8 mm
	NGK BKR5EZ	0.9 mm
DOHC (16-valve) engines	Bosch YR 7 DE	0.9 mm
	NGK DCPR8E-N	0.9 mm

Brakes

Brake pad lining minimum thickness	1.5 mm
Brake shoe friction material minimum thickness	2.0 mm

Torque wrench settings

	Nm	lbf ft
Automatic transmission fluid drain plug	25	18
Roadwheel bolts	86	63
Spark plugs	25	18
Sump drain plug	20	15

The maintenance intervals in this manual are provided with the assumption that you, not the dealer, will be carrying out the work. These are the minimum maintenance intervals recommended by us for vehicles driven daily. If you wish to keep your vehicle in peak condition at all times, you may wish to perform some of these procedures more often. We encourage frequent maintenance, because it enhances the efficiency, performance and resale value of your vehicle.

When the vehicle is new, it should be serviced by a factory-authorised dealer service department, in order to preserve the factory warranty.

Every 250 miles (400 km) or weekly

☐ Refer to *Weekly checks*

Every 6000 miles (10 000 km) or 6 months – whichever comes first

☐ Renew the engine oil and filter (Section 3).

Note: *Frequent oil and filter changes are good for the engine. We recommend changing the oil at the mileage specified here, or at least twice a year if the mileage covered is a less.*

Every 12 000 miles (20 000 km) or 12 months – whichever comes first

In addition to the items listed above, carry out the following:
☐ Check the condition and tension of the auxiliary drivebelt (Section 4).
☐ Hose and fluid leak check (Section 5).
☐ Check the front brake pads for wear (Section 6).
☐ Check the condition of the driveshaft gaiters (Section 7).
☐ Check the steering and suspension components for condition and security (Section 8).
☐ Check the underbody and sealant for damage (Section 9).
☐ Check the condition of the exhaust system and its mountings (Section 10).
☐ Check and if necessary adjust the handbrake (Section 11).
☐ Renew the pollen filter (Section 12).
☐ Lubricate all hinges and locks (Section 13).
☐ Carry out a road test (Section 14).

Every 24 000 miles (40 000 km) or 2 years – whichever comes first

In addition to the items listed above, carry out the following:
☐ Check and if necessary adjust the valve clearances – SOHC (8-valve) engines (Section 15).
☐ Renew the spark plugs (Section 16).
☐ Check the condition of the spark plug HT leads (Section 17).
☐ Renew the automatic transmission fluid and filter (Section 18).
☐ Check the engine management system (Section 19).
☐ Renew the brake fluid (Section 20).
☐ Renew the engine coolant (Section 21).

Every 36 000 miles (60 000 km) or 3 years – whichever comes first

In addition to the items listed above, carry out the following:
☐ Renew the air filter element (Section 22).
☐ Check the condition of the timing belt (Section 23).
☐ Check and if necessary top-up the manual transmission oil level (Section 24).
☐ Check the rear brake shoes for wear (Section 25).

Every 48 000 miles (80 000 km) or 4 years – whichever comes first

In addition to the items listed above, carry out the following:
☐ Renew the timing belt (Section 26)*.
☐ Check the operation of the evaporative loss system (Section 27).
☐ Check the condition and operation of the crankcase emission control system (Section 28).

*Note: *Although the normal interval for timing belt renewal is 72 000 miles (120 000 km), it is strongly recommended that the belt is renewed at 48 000 miles (80 000 km) on vehicles which are subjected to intensive use, ie, mainly short journeys or a lot of stop-start driving. The actual belt renewal interval is therefore very much up to the individual owner, but bear in mind that severe engine damage will result if the belt breaks.*

Underbonnet view – SOHC (8-valve) engine model

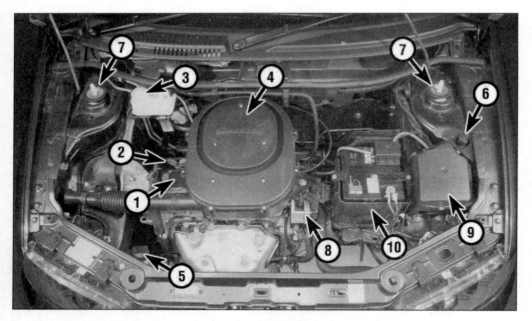

1 Engine oil filler cap
2 Engine oil dipstick
3 Brake fluid reservoir
4 Air cleaner cover
5 Coolant expansion tank
6 Windscreen washer fluid reservoir
7 Front suspension strut upper mounting
8 Ignition coils
9 Fuse/relay box
10 Battery

Underbonnet view – DOHC (16-valve) engine model

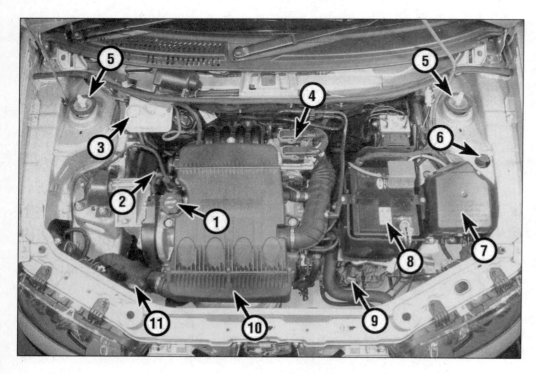

1 Engine oil filler cap
2 Engine oil dipstick
3 Brake fluid reservoir
4 ECU
5 Front suspension strut upper mounting
6 Windscreen washer fluid reservoir
7 Fuse/relay box
8 Battery
9 Automatic transmission fluid level dipstick
10 Air cleaner cover
11 Coolant expansion tank

Front underbody view (automatic transmission model shown)

1 Oil filter
2 Sump drain plug
3 Catalytic converter
4 Radiator electric cooling fan
5 Automatic transmission fluid drain plug
6 Left-hand driveshaft
7 Right-hand driveshaft
8 Front suspension lower arms
9 Front anti-roll bar
10 Exhaust front pipe
11 Front brake calipers
12 Rear engine mounting
13 Radiator bottom hose

Rear underbody view

1 Fuel tank
2 Exhaust tailpipe and silencer
3 Rear axle
4 Handbrake cables
5 Rear shock absorber lower mountings

1 Introduction

This Chapter is designed to help the home mechanic maintain his/her vehicle for safety, economy, long life and peak performance.

The Chapter contains a master maintenance schedule, and Sections dealing specifically with each task in the schedule. Visual checks, adjustments, component renewal and other helpful items are included. Refer to the accompanying illustrations of the engine compartment and the underside of the vehicle for the locations of the various components.

Servicing your vehicle in accordance with the mileage/time maintenance schedule and the following Sections will provide a planned maintenance programme, which should result in a long and reliable service life. This is a comprehensive plan, so maintaining some items but not others at the specified service intervals, will not produce the same results.

As you service your vehicle, you will discover that many of the procedures can, and should, be grouped together, because of the particular procedure being performed, or because of the proximity of two otherwise unrelated components to one another. For example, if the vehicle is raised for any reason, the exhaust can be inspected at the same time as the suspension and steering components.

The first step in this maintenance programme is to prepare yourself before the actual work begins. Read through all the Sections relevant to the work to be carried out, then make a list and gather all the parts and tools required. If a problem is encountered, seek advice from a parts specialist, or a dealer service department.

2 Regular maintenance

1 If, from the time the vehicle is new, the routine maintenance schedule is followed closely, and frequent checks are made of fluid levels and high-wear items, as suggested throughout this manual, the engine will be kept in relatively good running condition, and the need for additional work will be minimised.
2 It is possible that there will be times when the engine is running poorly due to the lack of regular maintenance. This is even more likely if a used vehicle, which has not received regular and frequent maintenance checks, is purchased. In such cases, additional work may need to be carried out, outside of the regular maintenance intervals.
3 If engine wear is suspected, a compression test (refer to the relevant Part of Chapter 2) will provide valuable information regarding the overall performance of the main internal components. Such a test can be used as a basis to decide on the extent of the work to

be carried out. If, for example, a compression test indicates serious internal engine wear, conventional maintenance as described in this Chapter will not greatly improve the performance of the engine, and may prove a waste of time and money, unless extensive overhaul work is carried out first.
4 The following series of operations are those usually required to improve the performance of a generally poor-running engine:

Primary operations

a) Clean, inspect and test the battery (See 'Weekly checks').
b) Check all the engine-related fluids (See 'Weekly checks').
c) Check the condition and tension of the auxiliary drivebelt(s) (Section 4).
d) Check the condition of all hoses, and check for fluid leaks (Section 5).
e) Renew the spark plugs (Section 16).
f) Inspect the ignition HT leads (Section 17).
g) Check the condition of the air filter, and renew if necessary (Section 22).
5 If the above operations do not prove fully effective, carry out the following secondary operations:

Secondary operations

All items listed under *Primary operations*, plus the following:

a) Check the charging system (Chapter 5A).
b) Check the ignition system (Chapter 5B).
c) Check the fuel system (Chapter 4A).
d) Renew the ignition HT leads (Section 17).

Every 6000 miles (10 000 km) or 6 months

3 Engine oil and filter renewal

1 Frequent oil and filter changes are the most important preventative maintenance which can be undertaken by the DIY owner. As engine oil ages, it becomes diluted and contaminated, which leads to premature engine wear.
2 Before starting this procedure, gather all the necessary tools and materials. Also make sure that you have plenty of clean rags and newspapers handy to mop-up any spills. Ideally, the engine oil should be warm, as it will drain better, and any impurities suspended in the oil will be removed with it. Take care, however, not to touch the exhaust or any other hot parts of the engine when working under the vehicle. To avoid any possibility of scalding, and to protect yourself from possible skin irritants and other harmful contaminants in used engine oils, it is advisable to wear gloves when carrying out this work. Access to the underside of the

vehicle will be greatly improved if it can be raised on a lift, driven onto ramps, or jacked up and supported on axle stands (see *Jacking and vehicle support*). Whichever method is chosen, make sure that the vehicle remains level, or if it is at an angle, that the drain plug is at the lowest point.
3 Slacken the drain plug about half a turn using an Allen key (see illustration). Position the draining container under the drain plug,

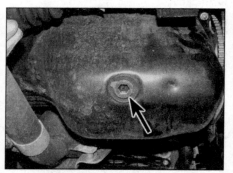

3.3 Engine oil drain plug location (arrowed)

then remove the plug completely (see Haynes Hint).
4 Allow some time for the old oil to drain, noting that it may be necessary to reposition

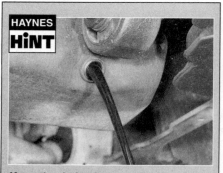

Keep the drain plug pressed into the sump while unscrewing it by hand the last couple of turns. As the plug releases, move it away sharply so that the stream of oil issuing from the sump runs into the container, not up your sleeve.

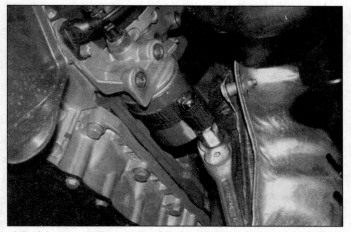

3.7 Using an oil filter removal tool to initially slacken the oil filter

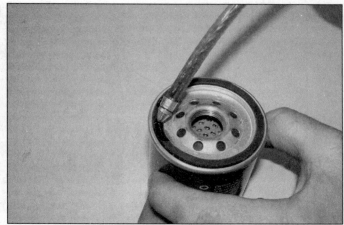

3.9 Apply a light coating of clean engine oil to the sealing ring on the new filter

the container as the oil flow slows to a trickle.

5 After all the oil has drained, wipe off the drain plug with a clean rag, then clean the area around the drain plug opening and refit the plug. Tighten the plug to the specified torque.

6 Move the container into position under the oil filter, which is located on the front right-hand side of the engine.

7 Using an oil filter removal tool if necessary, slacken the filter initially, then unscrew it by hand the rest of the way **(see illustration)**. Empty the oil in the old filter into the container.

8 Use a clean rag to remove all oil, dirt and sludge from the filter sealing area on the engine. Check the old filter to make sure that the rubber sealing ring has not stuck to the engine. If it has, carefully remove it.

9 Apply a light coating of clean engine oil to the sealing ring on the new filter, then screw it into position on the engine **(see illustration)**. Tighten the filter firmly by hand only – **do not** use any tools.

10 Remove the old oil and all tools from under the car then lower it to the ground (if applicable).

11 Withdraw the dipstick, and remove the oil filler cap from the cylinder head cover. Fill the engine, using the correct grade and type of oil (see *Lubricants and fluids*). An oil can spout or funnel may help to reduce spillage. Pour in half the specified quantity of oil first, then wait a few minutes for the oil to run to the sump. Continue adding oil a small quantity at a time until the level is up to the MAX mark on the dipstick. Refit the filler cap.

12 Start the engine and run it for a few

minutes; check for leaks around the oil filter seal and the sump drain plug. Note that there may be a delay of a few seconds before the oil pressure warning light goes out when the engine is first started, as the oil circulates through the engine oil galleries and the new oil filter before the pressure builds-up.

13 Switch off the engine, and wait a few minutes for the oil to settle in the sump once more. With the new oil circulated and the filter completely full, recheck the level on the dipstick, and add more oil as necessary.

14 Dispose of the used engine oil and filter safely, referring to *General repair procedures* in the Reference Chapter. Do not discard the old filter with domestic household waste. The facility for waste oil disposal provided by many local council refuse tips generally has a filter receptacle alongside.

Every 12 000 miles (20 000 km) or 12 months

| 4 | Auxiliary drivebelt check and renewal | |

Note: *On models with a manually-adjusted drivebelt, Fiat specify the use of a special tool to correctly set the drivebelt tension. If access to this equipment cannot be obtained, an approximate setting can be achieved using the method described below. If the method described is used, the tension should be checked using the special tool at the earliest possible opportunity.*

1 A single, multi-ribbed auxiliary drivebelt is used on all models. The belt drives the alternator, or alternator and air conditioning compressor according to equipment fitted. On models without air conditioning, the belt is adjusted manually, whereas on models with

air conditioning adjustment is by means of an automatic spring-loaded tensioning mechanism.

Checking

2 Firmly apply the handbrake, then jack up the front of the car and support it securely on axle stands (see *Jacking and vehicle support*). Remove the right-hand front wheel roadwheel.

3 Working under the right-hand wheel arch, undo the retaining screws and remove the wheel arch liner main and centre panels for access to the crankshaft pulley **(see illustration)**.

4 Using a socket on the crankshaft pulley bolt, rotate the crankshaft so that the full length of the drivebelt can be examined. Look for cracks, splitting and fraying on the surface of the belt; check also for signs of glazing

(shiny patches) and separation of the belt plies. If damage or wear is visible, the belt should be renewed.

5 If the condition of the belt is satisfactory,

4.3 Remove the wheel arch liner panels for access to the crankshaft pulley

4.7a Alternator lower pivot bolt (arrowed) . . .

4.7b . . . and upper adjustment bolts (arrowed)

where applicable check the drivebelt tension as described below.

Renewal

Models without air conditioning

6 If not already done, proceed as described in paragraphs 2 and 3.

7 Slacken the alternator lower pivot bolt and the upper adjustment bolts **(see illustrations)**. Swivel the alternator towards the engine and slip the drivebelt off the alternator pulley.

8 Unbolt and remove the crankshaft TDC sensor from the front of the engine (refer to Chapter 4A, Section 9 or 10 as appropriate, if necessary).

9 Remove the drivebelt from the crankshaft pulley.

10 When renewing a drivebelt, ensure that the correct type is used. Fit the belt around the two pulleys then swivel the alternator outwards to take up any slack in the belt.

11 Refit the crankshaft TDC sensor, then adjust the drivebelt tension correctly as described below.

Models with air conditioning

12 If not already done, proceed as described in paragraphs 2 and 3.

13 Undo the two bolts and remove the drivebelt guard from the air conditioning compressor.

14 Using a socket or spanner on the drivebelt tensioner pulley retaining bolt, rotate the tensioner against spring-pressure to release the tension from the belt. Hold the tensioner in this position and slip the drivebelt off the alternator and air conditioning compressor pulleys. Allow the tensioner to return to the released position.

15 Unbolt and remove the crankshaft TDC sensor from the front of the engine (refer to Chapter 4A, Section 9 or 10 as appropriate, if necessary).

16 Remove the drivebelt from the crankshaft pulley.

17 When renewing a drivebelt, ensure that the correct type is used.

18 Fit the belt around the pulleys, then rotate the tensioner until the belt can be slipped into place under the tensioner pulley.

19 Release the tensioner to allow the spring-loaded arm to automatically tension the belt.

20 Refit the crankshaft TDC sensor, then locate the drivebelt guard in position and secure with the two retaining bolts.

21 Refit the wheel arch liner panels and roadwheel, then lower the car to the ground.

Tensioning

22 Correct tensioning of the belt will ensure that it has a long life. A belt which is too slack will slip and perhaps squeal. Beware, however, of overtightening, as this can cause wear in the alternator bearings. On models equipped with air conditioning the correct belt tension is maintained automatically by means of the spring-loaded tensioning mechanism. On models without air conditioning, the tension must be adjusted manually as follows.

23 The belt should be tensioned so that, under firm thumb pressure, there is approximately 5.0 mm of free movement at the mid-point between the pulleys. To adjust the drivebelt, slacken the alternator pivot and

A leak in the cooling system will usually show up as white or rust-coloured deposits on the area adjoining the leak.

adjustment bolts (if not already done) then swivel the alternator outwards until the belt tension is correct. Hold the alternator in this position and fully tighten the adjustment bolts followed by the pivot bolt.

24 Refit the wheel arch liner panels and roadwheel, then lower the car to the ground.

5 Hose and fluid leak check

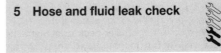

1 Visually inspect the engine joint faces, gaskets and seals for any signs of water or oil leaks. Pay particular attention to the areas around the camshaft cover, cylinder head, oil filter and sump joint faces. Bear in mind that, over a period of time, some very slight seepage from these areas is to be expected – what you are really looking for is any indication of a serious leak. Should a leak be found, renew the offending gasket or oil seal by referring to the appropriate Chapters in this manual.

2 Also check the security and condition of all the engine-related pipes and hoses. Ensure that all cable-ties or securing clips are in place and in good condition. Clips which are broken or missing can lead to chafing of the hoses, pipes or wiring, which could cause more serious problems in the future.

3 Carefully check the radiator hoses and heater hoses along their entire length. Renew any hose which is cracked, swollen or deteriorated. Cracks will show up better if the hose is squeezed. Pay close attention to the hose clips that secure the hoses to the cooling system components. Hose clips can pinch and puncture hoses, resulting in cooling system leaks.

4 Inspect all the cooling system components (hoses, joint faces etc.) for leaks. A leak in the cooling system will usually show up as white- or rust-coloured deposits on the area adjoining the leak **(see Haynes Hint)**. Where

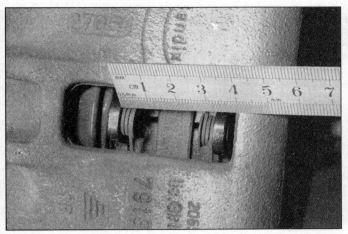

6.2 Check the thickness of the pad friction material through the hole on the front of the caliper

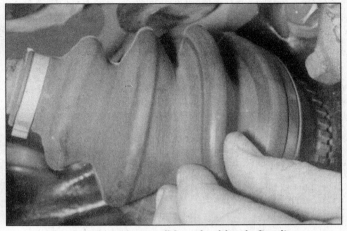

7.1 Checking the condition of a driveshaft gaiter

any problems of this nature are found on system components, renew the component or gasket with reference to Chapter 3.

5 Where applicable, inspect the automatic transmission fluid cooler hoses for leaks or deterioration.

6 With the vehicle raised, inspect the fuel tank and filler neck for punctures, cracks and other damage. The connection between the filler neck and tank is especially critical. Sometimes a rubber filler neck or connecting hose will leak due to loose retaining clamps or deteriorated rubber.

7 Carefully check all rubber hoses and metal fuel lines leading away from the fuel tank. Check for loose connections, deteriorated hoses, crimped lines, and other damage. Pay particular attention to the vent pipes and hoses, which often loop up around the filler neck and can become blocked or crimped. Follow the lines to the front of the vehicle, carefully inspecting them all the way. Renew damaged sections as necessary.

8 From within the engine compartment, check the security of all fuel hose attachments and pipe unions, and inspect the fuel hoses and vacuum hoses for kinks, chafing and deterioration.

6 Front brake pad check

1 Firmly apply the handbrake, then jack up the front of the car and support it securely on axle stands (see *Jacking and vehicle support*). Remove the front roadwheels.

2 Using a steel rule, measure the thickness of the friction material of the brake pads on both front brakes. This must not be less than 1.5 mm. Check the thickness of the pad friction material through the hole on the front of the caliper **(see illustration)**.

3 For a comprehensive check, the brake pads should be removed and cleaned. The

operation of the caliper can then also be checked, and the condition of the brake disc itself can be fully examined on both sides. Refer to Chapter 9 for further information.

4 If any pad's friction material is worn to the specified thickness or less, *all four pads must be renewed as a set.* Refer to Chapter 9.

5 On completion refit the roadwheels and lower the car to the ground.

7 Driveshaft gaiter check

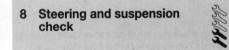

1 With the car raised and securely supported on stands (see *Jacking and vehicle support*), turn the steering onto full lock, then slowly rotate the roadwheel. Inspect the condition of the outer constant velocity (CV) joint rubber gaiters, squeezing the gaiters to open out the folds. Check for signs of cracking, splits or deterioration of the rubber, which may allow the grease to escape, and lead to water and grit entry into the joint. Also check the security and condition of the retaining clips. Repeat these checks on the inner CV joints **(see illustration)**. If any damage or deterioration is

8.3 Rocking a roadwheel to check for wear in the steering/suspension components

found, the gaiters should be renewed (see Chapter 8).

2 At the same time, check the general condition of the CV joints themselves by first holding the driveshaft and attempting to rotate the wheel. Repeat this check by holding the inner joint and attempting to rotate the driveshaft. Any appreciable movement indicates wear in the joints, wear in the driveshaft splines, or a loose driveshaft retaining nut.

8 Steering and suspension check

Front suspension and steering

1 Firmly apply the handbrake, then jack up the front of the car and support it securely on axle stands (see *Jacking and vehicle support*).

2 Inspect the balljoint dust covers and the steering rack and pinion gaiters for splits, chafing or deterioration. Any wear of these will cause loss of lubricant, together with dirt and water entry, resulting in rapid deterioration of the balljoints or steering gear.

3 Grasp the roadwheel at the 12 o'clock and 6 o'clock positions, and try to rock it **(see illustration)**. Very slight free play may be felt, but if the movement is appreciable, further investigation is necessary to determine the source. Continue rocking the wheel while an assistant depresses the footbrake. If the movement is now eliminated or significantly reduced, it is likely that the hub bearings are at fault. If the free play is still evident with the footbrake depressed, then there is wear in the suspension joints or mountings.

4 Now grasp the wheel at the 9 o'clock and 3 o'clock positions, and try to rock it as before. Any movement felt now may again be caused by wear in the hub bearings or the steering track rod balljoints. If the inner or outer balljoint is worn, the visual movement will be obvious.

5 Using a large screwdriver or flat bar, check for wear in the suspension mounting bushes by levering between the relevant suspension component and its attachment point. Some movement is to be expected as the mountings are made of rubber, but excessive wear should be obvious. Also check the condition of any visible rubber bushes, looking for splits, cracks or contamination of the rubber.

6 With the car standing on its wheels, have an assistant turn the steering wheel back-and-forth about an eighth of a turn each way. There should be very little, if any, lost movement between the steering wheel and roadwheels. If this is not the case, closely observe the joints and mountings previously described, but in addition check the steering column universal joints for wear, and the rack and pinion steering gear itself.

Strut/shock absorber check

7 Check for any signs of fluid leakage around the suspension strut/shock absorber body, or from the rubber gaiter around the piston rod. Should any fluid be noticed, the suspension strut/shock absorber is defective internally, and should be renewed. **Note:** *Suspension struts/shock absorbers should always be renewed in pairs on the same axle.*

8 The efficiency of the suspension strut/shock absorber may be checked by bouncing the vehicle at each corner. Generally speaking, the body will return to its normal position and stop after being depressed. If it rises and returns on a rebound, the suspension strut/shock absorber is probably suspect. Examine also the suspension strut/shock absorber upper and lower mountings for any signs of wear.

9 Underbody sealant check

1 Jack up the front and rear of the car and support it securely on axle stands (see *Jacking and vehicle support*). Alternatively position the car over an inspection pit.
2 Check the underbody, wheel housings and side sills for rust and/or damage to the underbody sealant. If evident, repair as necessary.

10 Exhaust system check

1 With the engine cold (at least an hour after the vehicle has been driven), check the complete exhaust system from the engine to the end of the tailpipe. The exhaust system is most easily checked with the car raised on a hoist, or suitably supported on axle stands (see *Jacking and vehicle support*), so that the exhaust components are readily visible and accessible.
2 Check the exhaust pipes and connections for evidence of leaks, severe corrosion and damage. Make sure that all brackets and mountings are in

good condition, and that all relevant nuts and bolts are tight. Leakage at any of the joints or in other parts of the system will usually show up as a black sooty stain in the vicinity of the leak.
3 Rattles and other noises can often be traced to the exhaust system, especially the brackets and mountings. Try to move the pipes and silencers. If the components are able to come into contact with the body or suspension parts, secure the system with new mountings. Otherwise separate the joints (if possible) and twist the pipes as necessary to provide additional clearance.

11 Handbrake check and adjustment

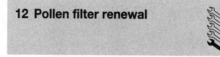

Apply the handbrake by pulling it through a maximum of five clicks of the ratchet mechanism and check that this locks the rear wheels, holding the vehicle stationary on an incline. In this position, there should be sufficient reserve travel in the handbrake lever to allow for brake shoe wear and cable stretching. If not, the handbrake mechanism should be adjusted as described in Chapter 9.

12 Pollen filter renewal

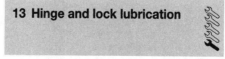

1 The pollen filter (where fitted) is located under the facia on the passenger's side, adjacent to the heater blower motor.
2 Undo the two retaining screws and lift off the access cover at the base of the filter housing.
3 Withdraw the filter from its housing.
4 Wipe clean the filter housing then fit the new filter. Refit the access cover and secure with the two screws.

13 Hinge and lock lubrication

1 Lubricate the hinges of the bonnet, doors and tailgate with a light general-purpose oil. Similarly, lubricate all latches, locks and lock strikers. At the same time, check the security and operation of all the locks, adjusting them if necessary (see Chapter 11).
2 Lightly lubricate the bonnet release mechanism and cable with a suitable grease.

14 Road test

Instruments and electrical equipment

1 Check the operation of all instruments and electrical equipment.

2 Make sure that all instruments read correctly, and switch on all electrical equipment in turn, to check that it functions properly.

Steering and suspension

3 Check for any abnormalities in the steering, suspension, handling or road feel.
4 Drive the vehicle, and check that there are no unusual vibrations or noises.
5 Check that the steering feels positive, with no excessive sloppiness, or roughness, and check for any suspension noises when cornering and driving over bumps.

Drivetrain

6 Check the performance of the engine, clutch (where applicable), transmission and driveshafts.
7 Listen for any unusual noises from the engine, clutch and gearbox/transmission.
8 Make sure that the engine runs smoothly when idling, and that there is no hesitation when accelerating.
9 Check that, where applicable, the clutch action is smooth and progressive, that the drive is taken up smoothly, and that the pedal travel is not excessive. Also listen for any noises when the clutch pedal is depressed.
10 On manual gearbox models, check that all gears can be engaged smoothly without noise, and that the gear lever action is smooth and not abnormally vague or notchy.
11 On automatic transmission models, check that all the gear positions can be selected with the vehicle at rest. If any problems are found, they should be referred to a Fiat dealer.
12 Listen for a metallic clicking sound from the front of the vehicle, as the vehicle is driven slowly in a circle with the steering on full lock. Carry out this check in both directions. If a clicking noise is heard, this indicates wear in a driveshaft joint, in which case renew the joint if necessary.

Braking system

13 Make sure that the vehicle does not pull to one side when braking, and that the wheels do not lock when braking hard.
14 Check that there is no vibration through the steering when braking.
15 Check that the handbrake operates correctly without excessive movement of the lever, and that it holds the vehicle stationary on a slope.
16 Test the operation of the brake servo unit as follows. With the engine off, depress the footbrake four or five times to exhaust the vacuum. Hold the brake pedal depressed, then start the engine. As the engine starts, there should be a noticeable give in the brake pedal as vacuum builds-up. Allow the engine to run for at least two minutes, and then switch it off. If the brake pedal is depressed now, it should be possible to detect a hiss from the servo as the pedal is depressed. After about four or five applications, no further hissing should be heard, and the pedal should feel considerably harder.

Every 24 000 miles (40 000 km) or 2 years

15 Valve clearance check and adjustment

Note: *The following procedure is not applicable to DOHC (16-valve) engines which utilise self-adjusting hydraulic tappets.*

1 The importance of having the valve clearances correctly adjusted cannot be overstressed, as they vitally affect the performance of the engine. Adjustment should only be necessary when the valve gear has become noisy, after engine overhaul, or when trying to trace the cause of power loss. The clearances are checked as follows. The engine must be cold for the check to be accurate.

2 Apply the handbrake then jack up the right-hand front of the car and support on an axle stand (*see Jacking and vehicle support*). Engage 4th gear. The engine can now be rotated by turning the right-hand front roadwheel.

3 Remove all spark plugs as described in Section 16.

4 Remove the camshaft cover as described in Chapter 2A.

5 Each valve clearance must be checked when the high point of the cam lobe is pointing directly upward away from the cam follower.

6 Check the clearances in the firing order

15.7 Checking a valve clearance with a feeler blade

15.11 Using a modified C-spanner and a screwdriver to remove a shim

1–3–4–2, No 1 cylinder being at the timing belt end of the engine. This will minimise the amount of crankshaft rotation required.

7 Insert the appropriate feeler blade between the heel of the cam and the cam follower shim of the first valve (**see illustration**). If necessary alter the thickness of the feeler blade until it is a stiff, sliding fit. Record the thickness, which will, of course, represent the valve clearance for this particular valve.

8 Turn the engine, check the second valve clearance and record it.

9 Repeat the operations on all the remaining valves, recording their respective clearances.

10 Remember that the clearance for inlet and exhaust valves differs – see *Specifications*. Counting from the timing belt end of the engine, the valve sequence is:

Inlet	2–4–5–7
Exhaust	1–3–6–8

11 Where clearances are incorrect, the particular shim will have to be changed. To remove the shim, turn the crankshaft until the high point of the cam is pointing directly upward. The cam follower will now have to be depressed so that the shim can be extracted. Special tools are commercially available to do the job, otherwise you will have to make up a forked lever to locate on the rim of the cam follower. This must allow room for the shim to be prised out by means of the cut-outs provided in the cam follower rim (**see illustration**).

12 Once the shim is extracted, establish its thickness and change it for a thicker or thinner one to bring the previously recorded clearance within specification. For example, if the measured valve clearance was 1.27 mm too great, a shim *thicker* by this amount will be required. Conversely, if the clearance was 1.27 mm too small, a shim *thinner* by this amount will be required.

13 Shims have their thickness (mm) engraved on them; although the engraved side should be fitted so as not to be visible, wear still occurs and often obliterates the number. In this case, measuring their thickness with a metric micrometer is the only method to establish their thickness (**see illustration**).

14 In practice, if several shims have to be

15.13 Shim thickness is marked on the lower face (here 4.20 mm)

changed, they can often be interchanged, so avoiding the necessity of having to buy more new shims than is necessary, but do not turn the engine with any shims missing.

15 If more than two or three valve clearances are found to be incorrect, it will be more convenient to remove the camshaft for easier removal of the shims.

16 Where no clearance can be measured, even with the thinnest available shim in position, the valve will have to be removed and the end of its stem ground off squarely. This will reduce its overall length by the minimum amount to provide a clearance. This job should be entrusted to an engine reconditioning specialist as it is important to keep the end of the valve stem square.

17 On completion, refit the camshaft cover as described in Chapter 2A, and the spark plugs as described in Section 16.

18 Lower the car to the ground.

16 Spark plug renewal

1 The correct functioning of the spark plugs is vital for the correct running and efficiency of the engine. It is essential that the plugs fitted are appropriate for the engine (a suitable type is specified at the beginning of this Chapter). If this type is used and the engine is in good condition, the spark plugs should not need attention between scheduled replacement intervals. Spark plug cleaning is rarely necessary, and should not be attempted unless specialised equipment is available, as damage can easily be caused to the firing ends.

2 To remove the plugs first remove the air cleaner assembly with reference to Chapter 4A. If the marks on the original-equipment spark plug (HT) leads cannot be seen, mark the leads 1 to 4, to correspond to the cylinder the lead serves (No 1 cylinder is at the timing belt end of the engine). Pull the leads from the plugs by gripping the end fitting, not the lead, otherwise the lead connection may be fractured (**see illustration**).

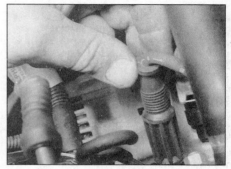

16.2 Disconnecting the HT leads from the spark plugs on 8-valve engines

16.4 Removing the spark plugs

16.9 Adjusting a spark plug electrode gap

It is very often difficult to insert spark plugs into their holes without cross-threading them. To avoid this possibility, fit a short length of 5/16 inch internal diameter rubber hose over the end of the spark plug. The flexible hose acts as a universal joint to help align the plug with the plug hole. Should the plug begin to cross-thread, the hose will slip on the spark plug, preventing thread damage to the cylinder head.

3 It is advisable to remove the dirt from the spark plug recesses using a clean brush, vacuum cleaner or compressed air before removing the plugs, to prevent dirt dropping into the cylinders.

4 Unscrew the plugs using a spark plug spanner, suitable box spanner or a deep socket and extension bar **(see illustration)**. Keep the socket aligned with the spark plug – if it is forcibly moved to one side, the ceramic insulator may be broken off. As each plug is removed, examine it as follows.

5 Examination of the spark plugs will give a good indication of the condition of the engine. If the insulator nose of the spark plug is clean and white, with no deposits, this is indicative of a weak mixture or too hot a plug (a hot plug transfers heat away from the electrode slowly, a cold plug transfers heat away quickly).

6 If the tip and insulator nose are covered with hard black-looking deposits, this indicates that the mixture is too rich. If the plug is black and oily, then it is likely that the engine is fairly worn, as well as the mixture being too rich.

7 If the insulator nose is covered with light tan to greyish-brown deposits, then the mixture is correct and it is likely that the engine is in good condition.

8 The spark plug electrode gap is of considerable importance as, if it is too large or too small, the size of the spark and its efficiency will be seriously impaired. The gap should be set to the value given in the *Specifications* at the beginning of this Chapter.

9 To set the gap, measure it with a feeler blade and then bend open, or closed, the outer plug electrode until the correct gap is achieved. The centre electrode should never be bent, as this may crack the insulator and cause plug failure, if nothing worse. If using feeler blades, the gap is correct when the appropriate-size blade is a firm sliding fit **(see illustration)**.

10 Special spark plug electrode gap adjusting tools are available from most motor accessory shops, or from some spark plug manufacturers.

11 Before fitting the spark plugs, check that the threaded connector sleeves are tight, and

that the plug exterior surfaces and threads are clean **(see Haynes Hint)**.

12 Remove the rubber hose (if used), and tighten the plug to the specified torque using the spark plug socket and a torque wrench. Refit the remaining spark plugs in the same manner.

13 Connect the HT leads in their correct order, and refit the air cleaner assembly.

17 Ignition system check

Warning: Due to the high voltages produced by the electronic ignition system, extreme care must be taken when working on the system with the ignition switched on. Persons with surgically-implanted cardiac pacemaker devices should keep well clear of the ignition circuits, components and test equipment.

1 The spark plug (HT) leads should be checked whenever new spark plugs are fitted.

2 Remove the air cleaner assembly as described in Chapter 4A.

3 Pull the leads from the plugs by gripping the end fitting, not the lead, otherwise the lead connection may be fractured.

HAYNES HINT *Ensure that the leads are numbered before removing them, to avoid confusion when refitting.*

4 Check inside the end fitting for signs of corrosion, which will look like a white crusty powder. Push the end fitting back onto the spark plug, ensuring that it is a tight fit on the plug. If not, remove the lead again and use pliers to carefully crimp the metal connector inside the end fitting until it fits securely on the end of the spark plug.

5 Using a clean rag, wipe the entire length of the lead to remove any built-up dirt and grease. Once the lead is clean, check for burns, cracks and other damage. Do not bend the lead

excessively, nor pull the lead lengthways – the conductor inside might break.

6 Disconnect the other end of the lead from the ignition coil. Again, pull only on the end fitting. Check for corrosion and a tight fit in the same manner as the spark plug end. Refit the lead securely on completion.

7 Check the remaining leads one at a time, in the same way.

8 If new spark plug (HT) leads are required, purchase a set for your specific car and engine.

9 Refit the air cleaner assembly on completion of the checks.

10 Even with the ignition system in first-class condition, some engines may still occasionally experience poor starting attributable to damp ignition components. To disperse moisture, a water-dispersant aerosol should be liberally applied.

18 Automatic transmission fluid and filter renewal

1 Take the car on a short run, to warm the transmission up to operating temperature. Park the car on level ground, then switch off the ignition.

2 Firmly apply the handbrake, then jack up the front of the car and support it securely on axle stands (see *Jacking and vehicle support*). Note that, when refilling and checking the fluid level, the car must be level to ensure accuracy.

3 Remove the dipstick, then position a suitable container under the transmission. Unscrew the drain plug at the rear of the sump pan and allow the fluid to drain for at least 10 minutes. Refit and tighten the drain plug when the fluid has completely drained.

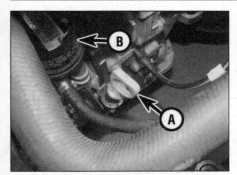

18.4 Automatic transmission fluid dipstick (A) and filter (B)

 Warning: The transmission fluid may be very hot and precautions must be taken to avoid scalding.

4 Move the container into position under the oil filter, which is located at the front of the transmission **(see illustration)**.

5 Using a filter removal tool if necessary, slacken the filter initially, then unscrew it by hand the rest of the way. Empty the fluid in the old filter into the container.

6 Use a clean rag to wipe the filter sealing area on the transmission.

7 Apply a light coating of clean transmission fluid to the sealing ring on the new filter, then screw it into position on the transmission. Tighten the filter firmly by hand only – **do not** use any tools.

8 Fill the transmission with the specified quantity of fluid via the dipstick tube, using a funnel with a fine mesh filter.

9 Run the engine to normal operating temperature, then check the fluid level as described in *Weekly checks*.

10 Dispose of the old fluid and filter safely.

19 Engine management system check

1 This check is part of the manufacturer's maintenance schedule, and involves testing the engine management system using special dedicated test equipment. Such testing will allow the test equipment to read any fault codes stored in the electronic control unit memory.

2 Unless a fault is suspected, this test is not essential, although it should be noted that it is recommended by the manufacturers.

3 If access to suitable test equipment is not possible, make a thorough check of all ignition, fuel and emission control system components, hoses, and wiring, for security and obvious signs of damage. Further details of the fuel system, emission control system and ignition system can be found in the relevant parts of Chapters 4 and 5.

20 Brake fluid renewal

 Warning: Brake hydraulic fluid can harm your eyes and damage painted surfaces, so use extreme caution when handling and pouring it. Do not use fluid that has been standing open for some time, as it absorbs moisture from the air. Excess moisture can cause a dangerous loss of braking effectiveness.

1 The procedure is similar to that for the bleeding of the hydraulic system as described in Chapter 9, except that the brake fluid reservoir should be emptied by syphoning, using a clean poultry baster or similar before starting, and allowance should be made for the old fluid to be expelled when bleeding a section of the circuit.

2 Working as described in Chapter 9, open the first bleed screw in the sequence, and pump the brake pedal gently until nearly all the old fluid has been emptied from the master cylinder reservoir.

3 Top-up to the MAX level with new fluid, and continue pumping until only the new fluid remains in the reservoir, and new fluid can be seen emerging from the bleed screw. Tighten the screw, and top the reservoir level up to the MAX level line.

4 Work through all the remaining bleed screws in the sequence until new fluid can be seen at all of them. Be careful to keep the master cylinder reservoir topped-up to above the MIN level at all times, or air may enter the system and greatly increase the length of the task.

5 When the operation is complete, check that all bleed screws are securely tightened, and that their dust caps are refitted. Wash off all traces of spilt fluid, and recheck the master cylinder reservoir fluid level.

6 Check the operation of the brakes before taking the car on the road.

21 Coolant renewal

 Warning: Wait until the engine is cold before starting this procedure. Do not allow antifreeze to come in contact with your skin, or with the painted surfaces of the vehicle. Rinse off spills immediately with plenty of water. Never leave antifreeze lying around in an open container, or in a puddle in the driveway or on the garage floor. Children and pets are attracted by its sweet smell, but antifreeze can be fatal if ingested.

Cooling system draining

1 With the engine completely cold, cover the expansion tank cap with a wad of rag, and slowly turn the cap anti-clockwise to relieve the pressure in the cooling system (a hissing sound will normally be heard). Wait until any pressure remaining in the system is released, then continue to turn the cap until it can be removed.

2 Position a suitable container beneath the radiator bottom hose connection, then release the retaining clip and ease the hose from the radiator stub. If the hose joint has not been disturbed for some time, it will be necessary to gently manipulate the hose to break the joint. Do not use excessive force, or the radiator stub could be damaged. Allow the coolant to drain into the container.

3 The cooling system bleed screws should be opened to aid the draining process and help prevent airlocks. These are located on the top left-hand edge of the radiator, and on the heater inlet hose **(see illustrations)**. If the coolant has been drained for a reason other than renewal, then provided it is clean and less than two years old, it can be re-used, though this is not recommended.

4 Once all the coolant has drained, reconnect the hose to the radiator and secure it in position with the retaining clip.

Cooling system flushing

5 If coolant renewal has been neglected, or if the antifreeze mixture has become diluted, then in time, the cooling system may gradually lose efficiency, as the coolant passages become restricted due to rust, scale deposits, and other sediment. The cooling system efficiency can be restored by flushing the system clean.

6 The radiator should be flushed independently of the engine, to avoid contamination.

21.3a Cooling system bleed screws located on the radiator (arrowed) . . .

21.3b . . . and heater inlet hose (arrowed)

Radiator flushing

7 To flush the radiator disconnect the top and bottom hoses and any other relevant hoses from the radiator, with reference to Chapter 3.
8 Insert a garden hose into the radiator top inlet. Direct a flow of clean water through the radiator, and continue flushing until clean water emerges from the radiator bottom outlet.
9 If after a reasonable period, the water still does not run clear, the radiator can be flushed with a good proprietary cooling system cleaning agent. It is important that their manufacturer's instructions are followed carefully. If the contamination is particularly bad, insert the hose in the radiator bottom outlet, and reverse-flush the radiator.

Engine flushing

10 To flush the engine, remove the thermostat housing as described in Chapter 3.
11 With the top and bottom hoses disconnected from the radiator, insert a garden hose into the radiator bottom hose. Direct a clean flow of water through the engine, and continue flushing until clean water emerges from the thermostat housing opening in the cylinder head.
12 On completion of flushing, refit the thermostat housing and reconnect the hoses with reference to Chapter 3.

Cooling system filling

13 Before attempting to fill the cooling system, make sure that all hoses and clips are in good condition, and that the clips are tight. Note that an antifreeze mixture must be used all year round, to prevent corrosion of the engine components (see below).
14 Remove the expansion tank filler cap, and fill the system by slowly pouring the coolant into the expansion tank to prevent airlocks from forming. Ensure that all bleed screws are open.
15 If the coolant is being renewed, begin by pouring in a couple of litres of water, followed by the correct quantity of antifreeze, then top-up with more water. Periodically squeeze the radiator top and bottom hoses to help expel any trapped air in the system.
16 Continue adding coolant until it is seen to emerge from the bleed screws. Close each bleed screw in turn as the coolant emerges.
17 Top-up the coolant level to the MAX mark and refit the expansion tank cap. Ensure that all bleed screws are closed.
18 Start the engine and run it at idling speed for two to three minutes. Allow the engine to continue running until the electric cooling fan operates, but during this time periodically increase the engine speed gradually to 2000 to 3000 rpm.
19 Stop the engine and allow it to cool down completely.
20 Check for leaks, particularly around disturbed components. Check the coolant level in the expansion tank, and top-up if necessary. Note that the system must be cold before an accurate level is indicated in the expansion tank.

Antifreeze mixture

21 The antifreeze should always be renewed at the specified intervals. This is necessary not only to maintain the antifreeze properties, but also to prevent corrosion which would otherwise occur as the corrosion inhibitors become progressively less effective.
22 Always use a monoethylene-glycol based antifreeze of the specified type (see *Lubricants and fluids*). The quantity of antifreeze and levels of protection are indicated in the *Specifications*.
23 Before adding antifreeze, the cooling system should be completely drained, preferably flushed, and all hoses checked for condition and security.
24 After filling with antifreeze, a label should be attached to the expansion tank, stating the type and concentration of antifreeze used, and the date installed. Any subsequent topping-up should be made with the same type and concentration of antifreeze.
25 Do not use engine antifreeze in the windscreen/tailgate washer system, as it will cause damage to the vehicle paintwork. A screenwash additive should be added to the washer system in the quantities stated on the bottle.

Every 36 000 miles (60 000 km) or 3 years

22 Air filter renewal

SOHC (8-valve) engines

1 Undo the retaining screws, lift off the air cleaner cover and take out the filter element **(see illustrations)**.
2 Remove any debris that may have collected inside the air cleaner and wipe the inner surfaces clean.
3 Fit a new air filter element in position, ensuring that the edges are securely seated.
4 Refit the air cleaner cover and secure with the retaining screws.

DOHC (16-valve) engines

5 Undo the three bolts securing the upper edge of the air cleaner cover to the main body. Tip the cover forward at the top

22.1a Undo the screws (arrowed) and lift off the air cleaner cover . . .

22.1b . . . then take out the filter element – SOHC (8-valve) engines

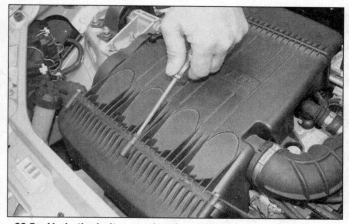

22.5a Undo the bolts securing the air cleaner cover to the main body . . .

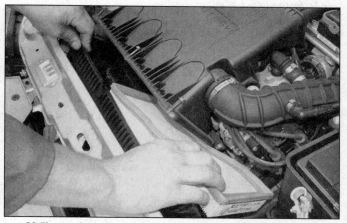

22.5b . . . then tip the cover forward and take out the filter element

and take out the filter element **(see illustrations)**.

6 Remove any debris that may have collected inside the air cleaner and wipe the inner surfaces clean.

7 Fit a new air filter element in position, ensuring that the edges are securely seated.

8 Refit the air cleaner cover and secure with the three bolts.

23 Timing belt inspection

1 The function of the timing belt is to drive the camshaft and coolant pump. Should the belt slip or break in service, the valve timing will be disturbed and piston-to-valve contact will occur, resulting in serious engine damage. It is therefore vitally important that the condition of the belt and surrounding components should be checked very carefully.

2 To gain access to the belt, remove the timing belt covers as described in the relevant Part of Chapter 2.

3 With the covers removed, inspect the timing belt for any signs of uneven wear, splitting, or oil contamination. Pay particular attention to the roots of the teeth. To enable the full length of the belt to be examined, turn the crankshaft using a spanner or socket on the crankshaft sprocket centre bolt.

4 Check for any signs of coolant leakage from the coolant pump or oil leakage from the crankshaft right-hand oil seal. If there is any doubt about the condition of the belt, it should be renewed as described in the relevant Part of Chapter 2. If any coolant or oil leakage is evident, trace the source of the leak and rectify it before fitting the new timing belt.

5 On completion of the inspection, refit the timing belt covers as described in the relevant Part of Chapter 2.

24 Manual transmission oil level check

1 Park the car on a level surface, if possible over an inspection pit or on a ramp as the filler/level plug is best reached from under the engine compartment. The oil level must be checked before the car is driven, or at least 5 minutes after the engine has been switched off. If the oil is checked immediately after driving the car, some of the oil will remain distributed around the transmission components, resulting in an inaccurate level reading.

2 Wipe clean the area around the filler/level plug, which is situated on the front of the transmission **(see illustration)**. Using an Allen key, unscrew the plug and clean it.

3 The oil level should reach the lower edge of the filler/level hole. A certain amount of oil will have gathered behind the filler/level plug, and will trickle out when it is removed; this does **not** necessarily indicate that the level is correct. To ensure that a true level is established, wait until the initial trickle has stopped, then add oil as necessary until a trickle of new oil can be seen emerging. The level will be correct when the flow ceases; use only good-quality oil of the specified type.

24.2 Manual transmission oil filler/level plug location (arrowed)

Make sure that the vehicle is completely level when checking the level and do not overfill.

4 When the level is correct refit and tighten the plug and wipe away any spilt oil.

25 Rear brake shoe check

1 Chock the front wheels then jack up the rear of the car and support it on axle stands (see *Jacking and Vehicle Support*). Remove the rear roadwheels.

2 Using the inspection hole at the edge of the brake drum, check that the linings are not worn below the minimum thickness given in the Specifications **(see illustration)**. If necessary use an electric torch.

3 If the friction material on any shoe is worn down to the specified minimum thickness or less, all four shoes must be renewed as a set.

4 At the same time check for signs of brake fluid leakage.

5 For a comprehensive check, the brake drum should be removed and cleaned. This will allow the wheel cylinders to be checked, and the condition of the brake drum itself to be fully examined (see Chapter 9).

6 On completion of the check, lower the car to the ground.

25.2 Check the thickness of the shoe friction material through the hole on the edge of the drum (arrowed)

Every 48 000 miles (80 000 km) or 4 years

26 Timing belt renewal

Refer to Chapter 2A or 2B.

27 Evaporative loss system check

Refer to Chapter 4B, Section 2, and check that all wiring and hoses are correctly connected to the evaporative loss system components.

28 Emission control system check

Refer to Chapter 4B. A full check of the emissions control systems must be made by a Fiat dealer.

Chapter 2 Part A:
SOHC (8-valve) engine in-car repair procedures

Contents

Degrees of difficulty

Easy, suitable for novice with little experience | **Fairly easy,** suitable for beginner with some experience | **Fairly difficult,** suitable for competent DIY mechanic | **Difficult,** suitable for experienced DIY mechanic | **Very difficult,** suitable for expert DIY or professional

Specifications

General

Engine code* 188 A4.000
Bore . . . . 70.80 mm
Stroke . . . . 78.86 mm
Capacity . . . . 1242 cc
Compression ratio 9.5:1
Firing order 1–3–4–2
No 1 cylinder location . . . . Timing belt end of engine
Timing belt tension . . . . See text
* Note: *See 'Vehicle identification' for the location of code marking on the engine.*

Camshaft

Drive . . . . Toothed belt
Camshaft bearing journal diameters:
  No 1 bearing . . . . 24.000 to 24.015 mm
  No 2 bearing . . . . 23.500 to 23.515 mm
  No 3 bearing . . . . 24.000 to 24.015 mm
Camshaft bearing journal running clearance . . . . 0.030 to 0.070 mm
Camshaft endfloat . . . . 0.10 to 0.20 mm

Lubrication system

Oil pump type . . . . By-rotor driven from front of crankshaft
Outer rotor-to-casing clearance . . . . 0.080 to 0.186 mm
Rotor endfloat . . . . 0.025 to 0.056 mm

Torque wrench settings

	Nm	lbf ft
Big-end bearing cap bolts:		
Stage 1	20	15
Stage 2	Angle-tighten a further 40°	
Camshaft bearing cap bolts:		
M6	10	7
M8	20	15
Camshaft cover bolts	8	6
Camshaft sprocket bolt	70	52
Crankshaft oil seal housing bolts	10	7
Crankshaft pulley bolts	22	16
Crankshaft sprocket centre bolt:		
Stage 1	20	15
Stage 2	Angle-tighten a further 90°	
Cylinder head bolts:		
Stage 1	30	22
Stage 2	Angle-tighten a further 90°	
Stage 3	Angle-tighten a further 90°	
Engine/transmission attachment bolts	80	59
Engine/transmission mountings:		
Left hand mounting-to-body bolts	25	18
Left-hand mounting bracket-to-transmission bolts	50	37
Left-hand mounting centre nut	90	66
Rear mounting-to-subframe bolt	120	89
Rear mounting-to-transmission bolt/nut	80	59
Right-hand mounting lower bracket-to-cylinder head bolts	22	16
Right-hand mounting upper bracket-to-lower bracket nuts	50	37
Right-hand mounting-to-body nuts	45	33
Flywheel bolts*	44	32
Main bearing cap bolts:		
Stage 1	20	15
Stage 2	Angle-tighten a further 90°	
Oil pump retaining bolts	10	7
Sump nuts/bolts	10	7
Timing belt tensioner nut	28	21

Use new bolts.

1 General information

Using this Chapter

This Part of Chapter 2 is devoted to in-car repair procedures for the SOHC (8-valve) engines. Similar information covering the DOHC (16-valve) engines will be found in Part B of this Chapter. Part C covers the removal of the engine/transmission as a unit, and describes the engine dismantling and overhaul procedures.

In Parts A and B, the assumption is made that the engine is installed in the car, with all ancillaries connected. If the engine has been removed for overhaul, the preliminary dismantling information which precedes each operation may be ignored.

Engine description

The engine covered in this Part of Chapter 2 is a water-cooled, single overhead camshaft (SOHC), in-line four-cylinder unit, with cast iron cylinder block and aluminium-alloy cylinder head. The engine is mounted transversely at the front of the car, with the transmission bolted to the left-hand end.

The cylinder head carries the camshaft which is driven by a toothed timing belt and runs in three bearings. It also houses the inlet and exhaust valves, which are closed by single coil springs, and which run in guides pressed into the cylinder head. The camshaft actuates the valves directly via cam followers mounted in the cylinder head. Adjustment of the valve clearances is by means of shims located on top of the followers. The cylinder head contains integral oilways which supply and lubricate the followers (tappets).

The crankshaft is supported by five main bearings, and endfloat is controlled by a thrust bearing fitted to the upper section of the centre main bearing.

Engine coolant is circulated by a pump, driven by the timing belt. For details of the cooling system, refer to Chapter 3.

Lubricant is circulated under pressure by a pump, driven from the front of the crankshaft. Oil is drawn from the sump through a strainer, and then forced through an externally-mounted, renewable screw-on filter. From there, it is distributed to the cylinder head, where it lubricates the camshaft journals and tappets, and also to the crankcase, where it lubricates the main bearings, connecting rod big and small-ends, gudgeon pins and cylinder bores.

Operations with engine in car

The following work can be carried out with the engine in the vehicle:

a) Compression pressure – testing.
b) Valve clearances – checking and adjustment.
c) Camshaft cover – removal and refitting.
d) Timing belt covers – removal and refitting.
e) Timing belt – removal, refitting and adjustment.
f) Timing belt tensioner and sprockets – removal and refitting.
g) Camshaft and cam followers – removal and refitting.
h) Cylinder head – removal and refitting.
i) Camshaft oil seal – renewal.
j) Crankshaft oil seals – renewal.
k) Flywheel – removal, inspection and refitting.
l) Engine mountings – inspection and renewal.
m) Sump – removal and refitting.
n) Oil pump and pick-up tube assembly – removal, inspection and refitting.

2 Top dead centre (TDC) for No 1 piston – locating

General information

1 The camshaft is driven by the crankshaft, by means of a timing belt and sprockets. Both sprockets rotate in phase with each other and this provides the correct valve timing as the engine rotates. When the timing belt is removed during servicing or repair, it is possible for the camshaft and crankshaft to rotate independently of each other and the correct valve timing is then lost.

2 The design of the engine is such that potentially damaging piston-to-valve contact may occur if the camshaft is rotated when any of the pistons are stationary at, or near, the top of their stroke.

3 For this reason it is important that the correct phasing between the camshaft and crankshaft is preserved whilst the timing belt is off the engine. This is achieved by setting the engine in a reference position (known as Top Dead Centre or TDC) before the timing belt is removed and then preventing the camshaft and crankshaft from rotating until the belt is refitted. Similarly, if the engine has been dismantled for overhaul, the engine can be set to TDC during reassembly to ensure that the correct shaft phasing is restored.

4 TDC is the highest point in the cylinder that each piston reaches as the crankshaft turns. Each piston reaches TDC at the end of the compression stroke and again at the end of the exhaust stroke. However, for the purpose of timing the engine, TDC refers to the position of No 1 piston at the end of its compression stroke. On all engines in this manual, No 1 piston (and cylinder) is at the timing belt end of the engine.

5 There are two different procedures for locating TDC on cylinder No 1, and it will be necessary to refer to the engine number to determine which procedure is to be followed. The engine number is stamped on the cylinder block, just below the cylinder head joint at the timing belt end.

6 With the engine number obtained, refer to procedure A or procedure B as follows:

Engine number outside the range 6.800.001 to 7.000.000 – refer to Procedure A
Engine number within the range 6.800.001 to 7.000.000 – refer to Procedure B

Procedure A

7 The camshaft sprocket is equipped with a marking which, when aligned with a reference notch on the cylinder head, indicates that the camshaft is correctly positioned with the piston of cylinder No 1 at TDC on its compression stroke.

8 The crankshaft sprocket is also equipped with a timing mark – when this is aligned with a reference marking on the oil pump cover, the engine is set with the pistons of cylinders

2.12a Camshaft sprocket and cylinder head TDC timing marks (arrowed) aligned

No 1 and 4 at TDC. Note that it is the camshaft positioning that determines whether a piston is on its compression or exhaust stroke.

9 Remove the timing belt upper and lower covers as described in Section 4.

10 Remove the spark plugs as described in Chapter 1.

11 Turn the engine in its normal direction of rotation (using a socket or spanner on the crankshaft sprocket centre bolt) until pressure can be felt at No 1 cylinder spark plug hole.

12 Continue turning the engine until the camshaft sprocket TDC timing mark is aligned with the notch on the cylinder head and the crankshaft sprocket timing mark is aligned with the mark on the oil pump casing **(see illustrations)**.

13 The engine is now set at TDC for No 1 cylinder on compression.

Procedure B

Note: *Fiat special tools 1.860.895.000 and 1.870.823.000 (or home-made alternatives) will be required for this procedure.*

14 The engines in the range covered by this procedure are not equipped with conventional timing marks and it is therefore necessary to use special tools to determine TDC for No 1 piston, and the correct corresponding position for the camshaft.

15 Remove the timing belt upper and lower covers as described in Section 4.

16 Remove the spark plugs as described in Chapter 1.

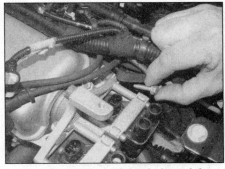

2.18a Undo the retaining bolt, and the upper and lower retaining nuts . . .

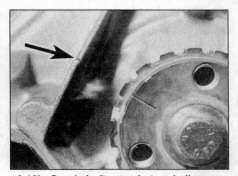

2.12b Crankshaft sprocket and oil pump casing TDC timing marks (arrowed) aligned

17 Identify the spark plug HT leads at their ignition coil connections, then disconnect the leads from the two coils. Also disconnect the LT wiring connector from each coil.

18 Undo the retaining bolt, and the upper and lower retaining nuts, and remove the ignition coils, complete with mounting bracket, from the end of the cylinder head **(see illustrations)**.

19 Turn the engine in its normal direction of rotation (using a socket or spanner on the crankshaft sprocket centre bolt) until pressure can be felt at No 1 cylinder spark plug hole.

20 It is now necessary to set up a dial test indicator so that the TDC position of No 1 piston can be determined. If Fiat special tool 1.860.895.000 (comprising an adaptor for the dial test indicator) is available, screw the adaptor into No 1 spark plug hole and mount the gauge on the adaptor. If the Fiat tool is not available, an alternative method is as follows.

21 Mount a conventional dial test indicator in a suitable position (using a piece of scrap metal as a mounting bracket, if necessary) so that the gauge probe is directly above No 1 spark plug location. Obtain a length of dowel rod to act as an extension to the gauge probe, and round off one end of the rod with a file.

22 To make a guide for the dowel rod, break off the ceramic upper section of an old spark plug and remove the centre electrode and earth tip. The easiest way to do this is to mount the spark plug in a vice (after removing the ceramic upper section) and drill a hole down through the centre of the plug. The

2.18b . . . and remove the ignition coils, complete with mounting bracket

2.23 Dial test indicator and probe set up for checking TDC on No 1 piston

diameter of the drill bit should be the same as the diameter of the dowel rod to be used.

23 Screw the spark plug guide into No 1 spark plug hole, then insert the dowel rod (round end first) through the plug into No 1 cylinder so that it contacts the piston. Move the dial test indicator into position with its probe contacting the dowel rod **(see illustration)**.

24 Turn the engine by means of the crankshaft sprocket until the highest reading is shown on the gauge, indicating that No 1 piston is at TDC. Take care when doing this as it is very easy for the dowel rod to jam in its guide.

25 At the other end of the engine, observe the position of the offset slot in the end of the camshaft, visible through the opening normally covered by the ignition coil mounting bracket. The camshaft slot should be horizontal, with the offset below the centreline **(see illustration)**. If this is the case, the engine is now correctly set at TDC for No 1 cylinder on compression.

26 If the camshaft slot offset is above the centreline, remove the dowel rod (to avoid jamming) then turn the crankshaft through one complete revolution, returning No 1 piston to the TDC position as described above.

27 To retain the camshaft in the correct position for all operations entailing removal of the timing belt, Fiat special tool 1.870.823.000, or a suitable alternative must be used. The Fiat tool consists of a metal plate which is secured to the two ignition coil mounting bracket studs on the cylinder head. A flange, welded to the inner face of the tool, engages with the offset slot in the camshaft and retains the camshaft in the set position. A home-made tool can be fabricated from steel strip of the same thickness as the camshaft slot. Bend the strip through 90°, mark and drill a mounting hole, then secure the tool using one of the studs on the cylinder head.

3 Compression test – description and interpretation

1 When engine performance is down, or if misfiring occurs which cannot be attributed to the ignition or fuel systems, a compression test can provide diagnostic clues as to the engine's condition. If the test is performed regularly, it can give warning of trouble before any other symptoms become apparent.

2 The engine must be fully warmed-up to normal operating temperature, the battery must be fully-charged, and all the spark plugs must be removed (see Chapter 1). The aid of an assistant will also be required.

3 Disable the ignition and fuel injection systems by disconnecting the two wiring multi-plug connectors at the engine management ECU, referring to Chapter 4A for further information.

4 Fit a compression tester to the No 1 cylinder spark plug hole – the type of tester which screws into the plug thread is to be preferred.

5 Have the assistant hold the throttle wide open, and crank the engine on the starter motor; after one or two revolutions, the compression pressure should build-up to a

maximum figure, and then stabilise. Record the highest reading obtained.

6 Repeat the test on the remaining cylinders, recording the pressure in each.

7 All cylinders should produce very similar pressures; a difference of more than 2 bars between any two cylinders indicates a fault. Note that the compression should build-up quickly in a healthy engine; low compression on the first stroke, followed by gradually-increasing pressure on successive strokes, indicates worn piston rings. A low compression reading on the first stroke, which does not build-up during successive strokes, indicates leaking valves or a blown head gasket (a cracked head could also be the cause). Deposits on the undersides of the valve heads can also cause low compression.

8 Although Fiat do not specify exact compression pressures, as a guide, any cylinder pressure of below 10 bars can be considered as less than healthy. Refer to a Fiat dealer or other specialist if in doubt as to whether a particular pressure reading is acceptable.

9 If the pressure in any cylinder is low, carry out the following test to isolate the cause. Introduce a teaspoonful of clean oil into that cylinder through its spark plug hole, and repeat the test.

10 If the addition of oil temporarily improves the compression pressure, this indicates that bore or piston wear is responsible for the pressure loss. No improvement suggests that leaking or burnt valves, or a blown head gasket, may be to blame.

11 A low reading from two adjacent cylinders is almost certainly due to the head gasket having blown between them; the presence of coolant in the engine oil will confirm this.

12 If the compression reading is unusually high, the combustion chambers are probably coated with carbon deposits. If this is the case, the cylinder head should be removed and decarbonised.

13 On completion of the test, refit the spark plugs and reconnect the engine management ECU wiring connectors.

4 Timing belt covers – removal and refitting

Removal

Upper cover

1 Disconnect the battery negative terminal (refer to *Disconnecting the battery* in the Reference Chapter).

2 Remove the air cleaner assembly as described in Chapter 4A.

3 If both the upper and lower timing belt covers are to be removed, firmly apply the handbrake, then jack up the front of the car and support it securely on axle stands (see *Jacking and vehicle support*). Remove the right-hand front roadwheel.

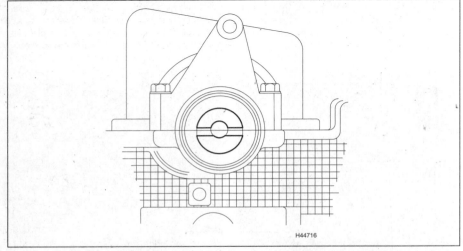

H44716

2.25 With No 1 piston at TDC on compression, the camshaft slot should be horizontal, with the offset below the centreline

4.5 Undo the retaining nuts and lift the right-hand engine mounting and upper bracket assembly off the studs

4.6 Undo the four bolts and remove the right-hand mounting lower bracket from the cylinder head

4.8 Disconnect and release the wiring harness from the upper timing cover

4 Place a trolley jack beneath the right-hand side of the engine, with a block of wood on the jack head. Raise the jack until it is supporting the weight of the engine.

5 Undo the three nuts securing the right-hand engine mounting to the body and the four nuts securing the mounting upper bracket to the lower bracket on the engine. Lift the mounting and upper bracket assembly off the studs and remove it from the car **(see illustration)**.

6 Undo the four bolts and remove the right-hand mounting lower bracket from the cylinder head **(see illustration)**.

7 Disconnect the wiring connector from the camshaft position sensor.

8 Disconnect the crankshaft TDC sensor wiring connector from the socket at the top of the timing cover, then release the wiring harness from the clip on the side of the cover **(see illustration)**.

9 Undo the retaining bolt at the rear of the cover, and the upper and lower retaining bolts at the front **(see illustrations)**.

10 Lift the cover upwards, slip the TDC sensor and oil pressure switch wiring out of the groove, and remove the upper cover from the engine **(see illustration)**.

Lower cover

11 Remove the upper cover as described previously.

12 Working under the right-hand wheel arch, undo the retaining screws and remove the wheel arch liner main and centre panels for access to the crankshaft pulley **(see illustration)**.

13 Remove the auxiliary drivebelt as described in Chapter 1.

14 Undo the three bolts and remove the crankshaft pulley from the sprocket.

15 Undo the retaining bolt in the centre of the lower timing cover **(see illustration)**.

16 Release the TDC sensor and oil pressure switch wiring from the periphery of the cover, and remove the cover from the engine **(see illustration)**.

4.9a Undo the retaining bolt (arrowed) at the rear of the upper timing cover . . .

4.9b . . . and the upper and lower retaining bolts (arrowed) at the front

4.10 Lift the cover upwards and slip the wiring out of the groove in the cover periphery

4.12 Undo the retaining screws and remove the wheel arch liner main and centre panels

4.15 Undo the retaining bolt (arrowed) in the centre of the lower timing cover

4.16 Release the wiring from the cover periphery and remove the lower cover from the engine

Refitting

17 Refitting is the reverse sequence to removal, bearing in mind the following points:
a) *Tighten the engine mounting and crankshaft pulley retaining nuts/bolts to the specified torque.*
b) *Refit and adjust the auxiliary drivebelt as described in Chapter 1.*
c) *Refit the air cleaner assembly as described in Chapter 4A.*

5 Timing belt –
removal and refitting

Note: *Fiat specify the use of special timing belt tension setting tools to correctly adjust the timing belt tension. As it is unlikely that this equipment will be available to the home mechanic, an approximate setting can be achieved using the method described below. If the method described is used, the tension must be checked using the special tools at the earliest possible opportunity. Do not drive the vehicle over large distances, or use high engine speeds, until the belt tension is known to be correct. Refer to a Fiat dealer for advice.*

General information

1 The function of the timing belt is to drive the camshaft and coolant pump. Should the belt slip or break in service, the valve timing will be disturbed and piston-to-valve contact will occur, resulting in serious engine damage.
2 The timing belt should be renewed at the specified intervals (see Chapter 1) or earlier if it is contaminated with oil, or if it is at all noisy in operation (a scraping noise due to uneven wear).
3 If the timing belt is being removed, it is a wise precaution to check the condition of the coolant pump at the same time (check for signs of coolant leakage). This may avoid the need to remove the timing belt again at a later stage, should the coolant pump fail.

Removal

4 Set the engine at TDC for No 1 piston as described in Section 2.
5 Release the nut on the timing belt

5.5 Undo the nut (arrowed) and move the timing belt tensioner pulley away from the belt

tensioner, move the tensioner pulley away from the belt and retighten the nut to hold the pulley in the retracted position **(see illustration)**.
6 If the timing belt is to be re-used, use white paint or chalk to mark the direction of rotation on the belt (if markings do not already exist), then slip the belt off the sprockets. Note that the crankshaft and camshaft must not be rotated whilst the belt is removed.
7 Check the timing belt carefully for any signs of uneven wear, splitting, or oil contamination. Pay particular attention to the roots of the teeth. Renew it if there is the slightest doubt about its condition. If the engine is undergoing an overhaul, renew the belt as a matter of course, regardless of its apparent condition. The cost of a new belt is nothing compared with the cost of repairs should the belt break in service. If signs of oil contamination are found, trace the source of the oil leak and rectify it. Wash down the engine timing belt area and all related components, to remove all traces of oil.

Refitting

8 Before refitting, thoroughly clean the timing belt sprockets. Check that the tensioner pulley rotates freely, without any sign of roughness. If necessary, renew the tensioner pulley as described in Section 6.
9 Referring to Section 2, make sure that the crankshaft and camshaft are still set at their correct TDC positions and, where applicable, the camshaft is locked in the correct position using the special tool.
10 On engines within the range 6.800.001 to 7.000.000 (see Section 2), slacken the camshaft sprocket retaining bolt, while

TOOL TIP

To make a camshaft sprocket holding tool, obtain two lengths of steel strip about 6 mm thick by 30 mm wide or similar, one 600 mm long, the other 200 mm long (all dimensions approximate). Bolt the two strips together to form a forked end, leaving the bolt slack so that the shorter strip can pivot freely. At the end of each 'prong' of the fork, secure a bolt with a nut and a locknut, to act as the fulcrums; these will engage with the cut-outs in the sprocket, and should protrude by about 30 mm.

holding the sprocket stationary using a suitable tool **(see Tool Tip)**.
11 With the arrows on the timing belt pointing in the direction of engine rotation, engage the timing belt with the crankshaft sprocket first, then place it around the coolant pump sprocket and the camshaft sprocket. Finally slip the belt around the tensioner pulley.
12 Release the tensioner nut and insert the jaws of a pair of right-angled circlip pliers (or similar) into the two holes on the front face of the tensioner pulley. Rotate the pulley anti-clockwise against the belt until the belt is quite taut **(see illustration)**. Check that the crankshaft and camshaft are still at their TDC positions and that, where applicable, the sprocket timing marks are still aligned.
13 Maintain the effort applied to the tensioner pulley, then tighten the retaining nut.
14 On engines within the range 6.800.001 to 7.000.000, tighten the camshaft sprocket retaining bolt to the specified torque, while holding the sprocket stationary using the method described previously. Remove the dial test indicator and the camshaft locking tool.
15 Turn the crankshaft through two complete turns in the normal direction of rotation and check that when the centre of the longest run of the belt is gripped between finger and thumb it can only just be twisted through 90°.
16 If the belt appears to be too slack or too tight, set the engine at the TDC position as described previously and repeat the complete tensioning procedure.
Caution: The above procedure serves only as a rough guide to setting the belt tension. The tension must be checked accurately by a Fiat dealer using the specialised checking equipment at the earliest opportunity.
17 Where applicable, refit the ignition coil mounting bracket to the cylinder head and secure with the bolt and nuts tightened securely. Reconnect the HT leads and the LT wiring connectors.
18 Refit the timing belt covers, the crankshaft pulley, auxiliary drivebelt, spark plugs and the air cleaner assembly. Adjust the tension of the auxiliary drivebelt as described in Chapter 1.
19 Refit the front wheel and lower the car to the ground.

5.12 Using right-angled circlip pliers, turn the tensioner pulley to fully tension the timing belt

6 Timing belt tensioner and sprockets – removal, inspection and refitting

Timing belt tensioner

Removal

1 Set the engine at TDC for No 1 piston as described in Section 2.
2 Loosen the nut on the timing belt tensioner and move the tensioner pulley away from the belt. Keep the belt engaged with the sprockets using a cable-tie or string.
3 Completely unscrew the nut and slide the tensioner off the mounting stud.

Inspection

4 Wipe the tensioner clean but do not use solvents that may contaminate the bearings. Spin the tensioner pulley on its hub by hand. Stiff movement or excessive freeplay is an indication of severe wear; the tensioner is not a serviceable component, and should be renewed.

Refitting

5 Slide the tensioner pulley over the mounting stud and fit the retaining nut.
6 Check and adjust the tension of the timing belt as described in Section 5.
7 Where applicable, refit the ignition coil mounting bracket to the cylinder head and secure with the bolt and nuts tightened securely. Reconnect the HT leads and the LT wiring connectors.
8 Refit the timing belt covers, the crankshaft pulley, auxiliary drivebelt, spark plugs and the air cleaner assembly. Adjust the tension of the auxiliary drivebelt as described in Chapter 1.
9 Refit the front wheel and lower the car to the ground.

Camshaft sprocket

Removal

10 Remove the timing belt as described in Section 5.
11 Slacken the camshaft sprocket retaining bolt while holding the sprocket stationary with a suitable tool (see Tool Tip in Section 5).
12 Unscrew and remove the retaining bolt and washer, then slide the sprocket from the end of the camshaft.

Inspection

13 With the sprocket removed, examine the camshaft oil seal for signs of leaking. If necessary, refer to Section 8 and renew it.
14 Check the sprocket teeth for damage.
15 Wipe clean the sprocket and camshaft mating surfaces.

Refitting

16 Locate the sprocket on the end of the camshaft, then refit the bolt and washer. On engines outside the range 6.800.001 to 7.000.000 (see Section 2), tighten the bolt to

the specified torque while holding the camshaft stationary using the method described previously. On all other engines, the retaining bolt is tightened during the timing belt refitting procedure.
17 Refit the timing belt as described in Section 5.

Crankshaft sprocket

Removal

18 Remove the timing belt as described in Section 5.
19 To prevent crankshaft rotation whilst the sprocket retaining bolt is being slackened, the flywheel ring gear must be locked using a suitable tool made from steel angle (see Tool Tip). Remove the cover plate from the base of the transmission bellhousing and bolt the tool to the lower bolt hole in the bellhousing flange so it engages with the ring gear teeth.
20 Using a suitable socket and extension bar, unscrew the crankshaft sprocket retaining bolt and slide the sprocket off the end of the crankshaft.

Inspection

21 With the sprocket removed, examine the crankshaft oil seal for signs of leaking. If necessary, refer to Section 9 and renew it.
22 Check the sprocket teeth for damage.
23 Wipe clean the sprocket and crankshaft mating surfaces.

Refitting

24 Slide the sprocket onto the crankshaft making sure the integral key engages with the slot on the end of the crankshaft. Refit the retaining bolt and tighten it to the specified torque. Hold the crankshaft stationary while the bolt is tightened using the method described in paragraph 19.
25 Refit the timing belt as described in Section 5.

7 Camshaft cover – removal and refitting

Removal

1 Remove the air cleaner assembly as described in Chapter 4A.
2 Disconnect the wiring connector from the camshaft position sensor located at the timing belt end of the camshaft cover.
3 Disconnect the accelerator inner cable end from the throttle cam and withdraw the outer cable from the grommet on the mounting bracket.
4 Disconnect the crankcase emission system hose from the outlet stub on the camshaft cover.
5 Release the clips and disconnect the fuel injector wiring duct from the slots on the camshaft cover.
6 Undo the timing belt upper cover retaining

TOOL TiP

H34034

A flywheel ring gear locking tool can be made from a short strip of steel bent to form a right-angle. Cut a slot in the upper part and bend this part up to engage with the ring gear teeth. File the edges to form a tooth profile. Drill a hole in the lower part to enable the tool to be bolted to the bellhousing flange.

bolt at the rear of the camshaft cover, and the upper retaining bolt at the front.
7 Progressively unscrew the mounting bolts from the top of the camshaft cover and lift off the cover – note the location of any supports on the bolts. If it sticks, do not attempt to lever it off – instead free it by working around the cover and tapping it lightly with a soft-faced mallet.
8 Recover the camshaft cover gasket. Inspect the gasket carefully, and renew it if damage or deterioration is evident.
9 Clean the mating surfaces of the cylinder head and camshaft cover thoroughly, removing all traces of oil and old gasket – take care to avoid damaging the surfaces as you do this.

Refitting

10 Locate a new gasket on the camshaft cover and make sure it is correctly seated (see illustration).
11 Lower the cover onto the cylinder head, making sure the gasket is not displaced.
12 Insert the cover retaining bolts and tighten them progressively to the specified torque.
13 The remainder of refitting is the reverse sequence to removal.

7.10 Ensure that the gasket is correctly seated in the camshaft cover groove

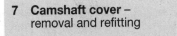

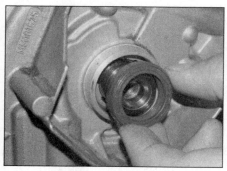

9.2 Carefully prise the crankshaft right-hand oil seal from the oil pump casing

9.4 Locate the new oil seal on the oil pump casing with the sealing lips facing inwards

9.5 Using a suitable tubular drift, drive the oil seal squarely into the casing

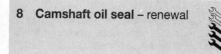

8 Camshaft oil seal – renewal

1 Remove the timing belt and camshaft sprocket as described in Sections 5 and 6.
2 Punch or drill a small hole in the oil seal. Screw a self-tapping screw into the hole, and pull on the screws with pliers to extract the seal.
3 Clean the seal housing, and polish off any burrs or raised edges, which may have caused the seal to fail in the first place.
4 Lubricate the lips of the new seal with clean engine oil, and drive it into position until it seats on its locating shoulder. Use a suitable tubular drift, such as a socket, which bears only on the hard outer edge of the seal. Take care not to damage the seal lips during fitting. Note that the seal lips should face inwards.
5 Refit the camshaft sprocket and timing belt as described in Sections 6 and 5.

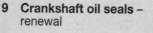

9 Crankshaft oil seals – renewal

Right-hand side oil seal

1 The front oil seal is located in the oil pump casing on the front of the crankshaft. Remove the timing belt as described in Section 5 and the crankshaft sprocket as described in Section 6.
2 Using a small screwdriver, carefully prise

the oil seal from the oil pump casing, taking care not to damage the surface of the crankshaft **(see illustration)**.
3 Clean the seating in the housing and the surface of the crankshaft. To prevent damage to the new oil seal as it is being fitted, wrap some adhesive tape around the end of the crankshaft and lightly oil it.
4 Lubricate the oil seal lip with clean engine oil then offer it up to the oil pump casing. Ensure that the sealing lip is facing inwards **(see illustration)**.
5 Using a suitable tubular drift, drive the oil seal squarely into the casing **(see illustration)**. Remove the adhesive tape.
6 Refit the crankshaft sprocket and timing belt as described in Sections 6 and 5.

Left-hand side oil seal

Note: *The following paragraphs describe renewal of the oil seal leaving the housing in position. Refer to Chapter 2C for details of removing the housing.*

7 Remove the flywheel as described in Section 12.
8 Using a suitable hooked instrument, remove the oil seal from the oil seal housing, taking care not to damage the surface of the crankshaft.
9 Clean the seating in the housing and the surface of the crankshaft. Check the crankshaft for burrs which may damage the sealing lip of the new seal, and if necessary use a fine file to remove them.
10 Dip the new seal in clean engine oil and

carefully locate it over the crankshaft flange making sure that it is the correct way round.
11 Progressively tap the oil seal into the housing keeping it square to prevent distortion. A block of wood is useful for this purpose.
12 Refit the flywheel with reference to Section 12.

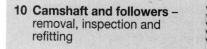

10 Camshaft and followers – removal, inspection and refitting

Removal

1 Remove the timing belt and camshaft sprocket as described in Sections 5 and 6.
2 Remove the camshaft cover as described in Section 7.
3 If not already done as part of the timing belt removal procedure, identify the spark plug HT leads at their ignition coil connections, then disconnect the leads from the two coils. Also disconnect the LT wiring connector from each coil.
4 Undo the retaining bolt, and the upper and lower retaining nuts, and remove the ignition coils, complete with mounting bracket, from the end of the cylinder head.
5 Mark the positions of the camshaft bearing caps, numbering them from the timing belt end.
6 Unbolt and remove the lubrication pipe (prise the oil feed stub out with a screwdriver). Unscrew the remaining bolts and take off the bearing caps **(see illustrations)**.

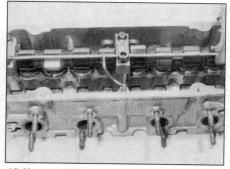

10.6a Prise out the feed stub of the camshaft lubrication pipe . . .

10.6b . . . and remove the lubrication pipe from the bearing caps

10.6c When removing the camshaft bearing caps, note the position of the long and short locating dowels

7 Lift the camshaft carefully from the cylinder head, checking that the valve clearance shims and cam followers are not withdrawn by the adhesion of the oil. Recover the oil seal from the end of the camshaft.

8 Remove the shims and cam followers, but keep them in their originally fitted order.

Inspection

9 Inspect the camshaft for wear on the surfaces of the lobes and journals. Normally their surfaces should be smooth and have a dull shine; look for scoring and pitting. Accelerated wear will occur once the hardened exterior of the camshaft has been damaged.

10 Examine the bearing cap and journal surfaces for signs of wear.

11 To measure the camshaft endfloat, temporarily refit the camshaft then push the camshaft to one end of the cylinder head as far as it will travel. Attach a dial test indicator to the cylinder head and zero it, then push the camshaft as far as it will go to the other end of the cylinder head and record the gauge reading. Verify the reading by pushing the camshaft back to its original position and checking that the gauge indicates zero again.

12 Where the camshaft and bearings are worn excessively, consider renewing the complete cylinder head, together with camshaft and cam followers. A reconditioned head may be available from engine overhaul specialists.

Refitting

13 Lubricate the cam followers and locate them in their correct positions in the cylinder head. Locate the shims in the cam followers making sure they are in their original positions.

14 Lubricate the journals then locate the camshaft in the cylinder head with the cam lobes of No 1 cylinder facing upwards (ie, No 1 piston at TDC).

15 Refit the bearing caps in their correct positions then locate the lubrication pipe over the bearing caps. Press in the oil feed stub then refit the bearing cap retaining bolts. Progressively tighten the bolts to the specified torque.

16 Lubricate the lips of the new seal with clean engine oil, and drive it into position until it seats on its locating shoulder. Use a suitable tubular drift, such as a socket, which bears only on the hard outer edge of the seal. Take care not to damage the seal lips during fitting. Note that the seal lips should face inwards.

17 Check the condition of the sealing O-ring on the ignition coil mounting bracket and renew the seal if necessary.

18 Unless the ignition coil mounting bracket was removed as part of the timing belt removal procedure, it can be refitted at this stage. Locate the bracket on the cylinder head and secure with the bolt and nuts tightened securely. Reconnect the HT leads and the LT wiring connectors.

19 Refit the camshaft sprocket and timing belt as described in Sections 6 and 5.

20 Check and if necessary adjust the valve clearances as described in Chapter 1, then refit the camshaft cover as described in Section 7.

11 Cylinder head – removal and refitting

Removal

1 Disconnect the battery negative terminal (refer to *Disconnecting the battery* in the Reference Chapter).

2 Drain the cooling system as described in Chapter 1.

3 Remove the inlet and exhaust manifolds as described in Chapter 4A.

4 Remove the timing belt as described in Section 5.

5 Remove the camshaft cover as described in Section 7.

6 Disconnect the radiator hose from the thermostat housing on the left-hand end of the cylinder head.

7 If not already done, disconnect the LT wiring connectors at the ignition coils.

8 Unscrew the cylinder head bolts half a turn at a time in the **reverse** order to that specified for tightening **(see illustration 11.21)**. When the bolts are free, remove them with their washers.

9 Lift the cylinder head from the block. If it is stuck tight insert pieces of wood into the exhaust or inlet ports, and use them as levers to rock the head off the block. On no account drive levers into the gasket joint, nor attempt to tap the head sideways, as it is located on positioning dowels.

10 Remove and discard the cylinder head gasket.

11 The cylinder head can be dismantled as described in Chapter 2C after removing the camshaft and cam followers as described in Section 10.

Preparation for refitting

12 The mating faces of the cylinder head and cylinder block must be perfectly clean before refitting the head. Use a hard plastic or wooden scraper to remove all traces of gasket and carbon; also clean the piston crowns. Take particular care when cleaning the piston crowns as the soft aluminium alloy is easily damaged. Make sure that the carbon is not allowed to enter the oil and water passages – this is particularly important for the lubrication system, as carbon could block the oil supply to the engine's components. Using adhesive tape and paper, seal the water, oil and bolt holes in the cylinder block. To prevent carbon entering the gap between the pistons and bores, smear a little grease in the gap. After cleaning each piston, use a small brush to remove all traces of grease and carbon from the gap, then wipe away the remainder with a clean rag. Clean all the pistons in the same way.

13 Check the mating surfaces of the cylinder block and the cylinder head for nicks, deep scratches and other damage. If slight, they may be removed carefully with a file, but if excessive, machining may be the only alternative to renewal. If warpage of the cylinder head gasket surface is suspected, use a straight-edge to check it for distortion. Refer to Part C of this Chapter if necessary.

14 Check the condition of the cylinder head bolts, and particularly their threads, whenever they are removed. Wash the bolts in a suitable solvent, and wipe them dry. Check each bolt for any sign of visible wear or damage, renewing them if necessary. Although Fiat do not specify that the bolts must be renewed, it is strongly recommended that the bolts should be renewed as a complete set whenever they are disturbed.

15 Refit the camshaft and followers as described in Section 10, then adjust the valve clearances as described in Chapter 1 before refitting the cylinder head to the block.

Refitting

16 Before refitting the assembled cylinder head, make sure that the head and block mating surfaces are perfectly clean, and that the bolt holes in the cylinder block have been mopped out to clear any oil.

17 Referring to Section 2, make sure that the crankshaft and camshaft are still set at their correct TDC positions and, where applicable, the camshaft is locked in the correct position using the special tool.

18 The new gasket should not be removed from its nylon cover until required for use. Fit the gasket dry, and make sure that the mating surfaces on the head and block are perfectly clean.

19 Place the gasket on the cylinder block so that the word ALTO can be read from above **(see illustration)**.

20 Lower the cylinder head onto the block so that it locates on the positioning dowels.

21 The cylinder head bolt threads must be clean and lightly lubricated. Screw the bolts in finger-tight then working progressively and in

11.19 Place the cylinder head gasket on the block so that the word ALTO can be read from above

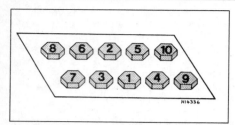

11.21 Cylinder head bolt tightening sequence

the sequence shown, tighten all the cylinder head bolts to the Stage 1 torque setting given in the Specifications, using a torque wrench and a suitable socket **(see illustration)**. With all the bolts tightened to their Stage 1 setting, working again in the specified sequence, first angle-tighten the bolts through the specified Stage 2 angle, then again through the Stage 3 angle, using a socket and extension bar. It is recommended that an angle-measuring gauge is used during this stage of tightening, to ensure accuracy.

22 Refit the inlet and exhaust manifolds as described in Chapter 4A.

23 Refit the camshaft cover as described in Section 7.

24 Refit the timing belt as described in Section 5.

25 Reconnect the LT wiring connectors at the ignition coils.

26 Reconnect the battery then fill and bleed the cooling system as described in Chapter 1.

12 Flywheel – removal, inspection and refitting

Removal

1 Remove the transmission as described in Chapter 7A, then remove the clutch assembly as described in Chapter 6.

2 The flywheel must now be held stationary while the bolts are loosened. A home-made locking tool may be fabricated from a piece of scrap metal and used to lock the ring gear **(see Tool Tip in Section 6)**. Bolt the tool to one of the transmission bellhousing mounting bolt holes on the cylinder block.

3 Mark the position of the flywheel with respect to the crankshaft using a dab of paint. Unscrew and remove the mounting bolts together with the spacer plate, then lift off the flywheel. Discard the flywheel bolts; new ones must be used on refitting.

Inspection

4 If the flywheel's clutch mating surface is deeply scored, cracked or otherwise damaged, the flywheel must be renewed. However, it may be possible to have it surface-ground; seek the advice of a Fiat dealer or engine reconditioning specialist.

5 If the ring gear is badly worn or has missing teeth, the flywheel must be renewed.

Refitting

6 Clean the mating surfaces of the flywheel and crankshaft. Remove any remaining locking compound from the threads of the crankshaft holes, using the correct-size tap, if available.

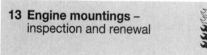

If a suitable tap is not available, cut two slots down the threads of one of the old bolts with a hacksaw, and use the bolt to remove the locking compound from the threads.

7 If the new retaining bolts are not supplied with their threads already precoated, apply a suitable thread-locking compound to the threads of each bolt.

8 Offer up the flywheel to the crankshaft, using the alignment marks made during removal, and fit the new retaining bolts together with the spacer plate.

9 Lock the flywheel using the method employed on removal, and tighten the retaining bolts to the specified torque.

10 Refit the clutch as described in Chapter 6, and the transmission as described in Chapter 7A.

13 Engine mountings – inspection and renewal

Inspection

1 Firmly apply the handbrake, then jack up the front of the car and support it securely on axle stands (see *Jacking and vehicle support*).

2 Check the mounting rubbers to see if they are cracked, hardened or separated from the metal at any point; renew the mounting if any such damage or deterioration is evident.

3 Check that all the mounting's fasteners are securely tightened; use a torque wrench to check if possible.

4 Using a large screwdriver or a crowbar, check for wear in the mounting by carefully levering against it to check for free play. Where this is not possible enlist the aid of an assistant to move the engine/transmission back-and-forth, or from side-to-side, while you watch the mounting. While some free play is to be

13.6 Right-hand engine mounting retaining nuts

expected, even from new components, excessive wear should be obvious. If excessive free play is found, check first that the fasteners are correctly secured, then renew any worn components as described below.

Renewal

Right-hand mounting

5 Place a trolley jack beneath the right-hand side of the engine, with a block of wood on the jack head. Raise the jack until it is supporting the weight of the engine.

6 Undo the three nuts securing the engine mounting to the body and the four nuts securing the mounting upper bracket to the lower bracket on the engine **(see illustration)**. Lift the mounting and upper bracket assembly off the studs and remove it from the car.

7 Undo the nut, withdraw the through-bolt and separate the mounting from the upper engine bracket.

8 Attach the new mounting to the upper engine bracket and secure with the nut and through-bolt. Do not fully tighten the nut at this stage.

9 Locate the mounting assembly on the body and lower engine bracket, refit the nuts and tighten them to the specified torque.

10 Securely tighten the through-bolt and nut securing the mounting to the upper engine bracket, then remove the trolley jack.

Left-hand mounting

11 Remove the battery and battery tray as described in Chapter 5A.

12 Place a trolley jack beneath the transmission, with a block of wood on the jack head. Raise the jack until it is supporting the weight of the engine/transmission.

13 Unscrew the bolts securing the left-hand mounting to the body **(see illustration)**.

14 Unscrew the nut securing the mounting to the transmission bracket and lift the mounting off the transmission bracket stud.

15 Locate the new mounting in the transmission bracket, refit the nut and tighten it to the specified torque.

16 Refit the mounting-to-body bolts and tighten the bolts to the specified torque.

17 Remove the trolley jack, then refit the battery tray and battery as described in Chapter 5A.

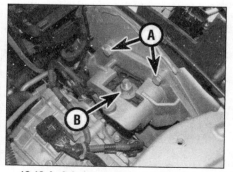

13.13 Left-hand engine mounting upper retaining bolts (A) and centre retaining nut (B)

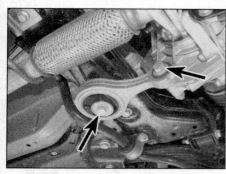

13.20 Rear engine mounting retaining bolts (arrowed)

15.8a Removing the oil pump pressure relief valve keeper plate

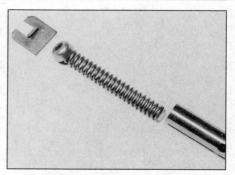

15.8b Oil pump pressure relief valve components

Rear mounting

18 Firmly apply the handbrake, then jack up the front of the car and support it securely on axle stands (see *Jacking and vehicle support*).
19 Temporarily support the weight of the engine/transmission using a trolley jack.
20 Working beneath the vehicle, unscrew the bolt securing the rear mounting assembly to the subframe **(see illustration)**.
21 Unbolt the rear mounting assembly from the transmission and withdraw from under the vehicle.
22 Fitting the new mounting is a reversal of the removal procedure, ensuring that all mounting bolts are tightened to the specified torque.

14 Sump –
removed and refitting

Removal

1 Firmly apply the handbrake, then jack up the front of the car and support it securely on axle stands (see *Jacking and vehicle support*). Drain the engine oil as described in Chapter 1.
2 Remove the exhaust manifold as described in Chapter 4A.
3 Unbolt and remove the cover plate from the base of the transmission bellhousing.
4 Unscrew the sump securing bolts and nuts then cut through as much of the joint sealant

as possible using a sharp knife. Pull the sump downwards to release it from the remaining sealant and remove it from under the car.
5 Thoroughly clean the sump and the cylinder block mating surfaces ensuring that all traces of old sealant are removed.

Refitting

6 Apply a 3.0 mm bead of RTV silicone sealant to the sump flange, then locate the sump in position. Refit the retaining bolts and nuts and tighten to the specified torque.
7 Refit the cover plate to the transmission bellhousing and tighten the retaining bolts securely.
8 Refit the exhaust manifold as described in Chapter 4A.
9 Lower the car to the ground and fill the engine with oil as described in Chapter 1.

15 Oil pump and pick-up tube –
removal, inspection and refitting

Removal

1 Remove the timing belt and crankshaft sprocket as described in Sections 5 and 6.
2 Drain the engine oil and remove the oil filter as described in Chapter 1.
3 Remove the sump as described in Section 14.
4 Remove the coolant pump as described in Chapter 3.
5 Disconnect the wiring connector from the

oil pressure switch on the side of the pump casing.
6 Undo the oil pump retaining bolts, noting the location of the longer bolt, and withdraw the pump assembly from the front of the engine. Recover the gasket.

Inspection

7 With the pump on the bench, undo the two bolts and remove the pick-up tube. Using a small screwdriver or similar tool, hook out the pick-up tube sealing O-ring from the pump body.
8 The pressure relief valve components can be removed for examination by depressing the spring and pulling out the keeper plate **(see illustrations)**.
9 If pump wear is suspected, check the rotors in the following way. Extract the fixing screws and remove the rear cover plate. The screws are very tight, and will probably require the use of an impact screwdriver **(see illustration)**.
10 Inspect the pump rotors, pump casing and cover for any signs of wear or damage. If satisfactory, refit the rotors to the pump casing ensuring that the orientation marks are facing upwards.
11 Check the clearance between the outer rotor and the pump casing using feeler blades. Check the rotor endfloat by placing a straight-edge across the pump casing, and checking the gap between the straight-edge and rotor face **(see illustrations)**. If the

15.9 Using an impact screwdriver to remove the oil pump rear cover plate screws

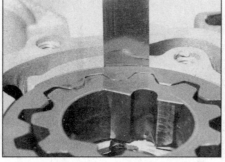

15.11a Measuring the oil pump outer rotor-to-pump casing clearance

15.11b Measuring oil pump rotor endfloat

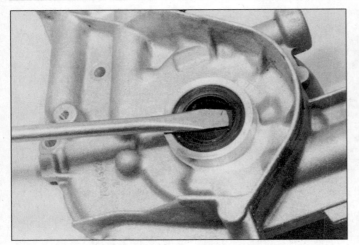

15.15a Removing the oil pump oil seal

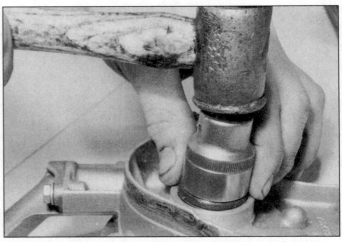

15.15b Using a socket to fit a new oil seal to the oil pump

clearances are outside the specified tolerance, renew the oil pump complete.

12 If the pump is unworn, lubricate the rotors with clean engine oil then place the cover plate in position. Apply thread locking compound to the retaining screws and tighten the screws securely.

13 Locate a new O-ring in the pump casing then refit the pick-up tube. Secure the tube with the two bolts tightened securely.

14 Lubricate the pressure relief valve components then refit the valve, spring and end cap, securing the assembly with the keeper plate.

15 Lever out the crankshaft oil seal and drive a new one squarely into the oil pump casing **(see illustrations)**. Lubricate the oil seal lips with clean engine oil.

16 Prior to refitting, prime the pump by pouring clean engine oil into its inlet duct, while at the same time turning the oil pump inner rotor.

Refitting

17 Ensure that the oil pump and cylinder block mating faces are clean, then place a new gasket on the pump casing. Retain the gasket in position by inserting two of the pump retaining bolts.

18 Locate the pump on the cylinder block, insert the retaining bolts and tighten them progressively to the specified torque.

19 Refit the coolant pump as described in Chapter 3.

20 Refit the sump as described in Section 14.

21 Refit the crankshaft sprocket and timing belt as described in Sections 6 and 5.

22 Reconnect the oil pressure switch wiring connector.

23 Fit a new oil filter then fill the engine with oil and coolant as described in Chapter 1.

Chapter 2 Part B:
DOHC (16-valve) engine in-car repair procedures

Contents

Degrees of difficulty

Easy, suitable for novice with little experience	Fairly easy, suitable for beginner with some experience	Fairly difficult, suitable for competent DIY mechanic	Difficult, suitable for experienced DIY mechanic	Very difficult, suitable for expert DIY or professional

Specifications

General

Engine code*	188 A5.000
Bore	70.80 mm
Stroke	78.86 mm
Capacity	1242 cc
Compression ratio	10.6:1
Firing order	1–3–4–2
No 1 cylinder location	Timing belt end of engine
Timing belt tension	See text

* Note: See 'Vehicle identification' for the location of the code marking on the engine.

Camshaft

Drive	Toothed belt
No of bearings	3
Camshaft bearing journal diameters:	
No 1 bearing	35.000 to 35.015 mm
No 2 bearing	48.000 to 48.015 mm
No 3 bearing	49.000 to 49.015 mm
Camshaft bearing journal running clearance	0.030 to 0.070 mm
Camshaft endfloat	0.15 to 0.34 mm

Cylinder head extension

Camshaft bearing diameters:	
No 1 bearing	35.045 to 35.070 mm
No 2 bearing	48.045 to 48.070 mm
No 3 bearing	49.045 to 49.070 mm
Cam follower (tappet) type	Hydraulic
Cam follower (tappet) diameter	28.353 to 28.370 mm
Cam follower (tappet) bore diameter in cylinder head extension	28.400 to 28.421 mm
Cam follower (tappet) running clearance	0.046 to 0.051 mm

Lubrication system

Oil pump type	Bi-rotor driven from front of crankshaft
Outer rotor-to-casing clearance	0.100 to 0.210 mm
Rotor endfloat	0.025 to 0.070 mm

Torque wrench settings

	Nm	lbf ft
Big-end bearing cap bolts:		
Stage 1	20	15
Stage 2	Angle-tighten a further 40°	
Camshaft drivegear bolts	120	89
Camshaft sprocket bolt	120	89
Crankshaft oil seal housing bolts	10	7
Crankshaft pulley bolts	22	16
Crankshaft sprocket centre bolt:		
Stage 1	20	15
Stage 2	Angle-tighten a further 90°	
Cylinder head bolts:		
Stage 1	30	22
Stage 2	Angle-tighten a further 90°	
Stage 3	Angle-tighten a further 90°	
Cylinder head extension to cylinder head	15	11
Engine/transmission attachment bolts	80	59
Engine/transmission mountings:		
Left hand mounting-to-body bolts	25	18
Left-hand mounting bracket-to-transmission bolts	50	37
Left-hand mounting centre nut	90	66
Rear mounting-to-subframe bolt	120	89
Rear mounting-to-transmission bolt/nut	80	59
Right-hand mounting lower bracket-to-cylinder head bolts	22	16
Right-hand mounting upper bracket-to-lower bracket nuts	50	37
Right-hand mounting-to-body nuts	45	33
Exhaust manifold-to-cylinder head nuts	25	18
Flywheel/driveplate bolts*	44	32
Lower crankcase-to-cylinder block bolts**:		
Stage 1	20	15
Stage 2	Angle-tighten a further 90°	
Oil pump retaining bolts	10	7
Sump nuts/bolts	10	7
Timing belt tensioner nut	25	18

* Use new bolts.

** At the time of writing there was conflicting information from the manufacturer concerning the lower crankcase retaining bolt torque setting. As it was not possible to confirm the validity of the figures given here, consult a Fiat dealer for latest information.

1 General information

Using this Chapter

This Part of Chapter 2 is devoted to in-car repair procedures for the DOHC (16-valve) engines. Similar information covering the SOHC (8-valve) engines will be found in Part A of this Chapter. Part C covers the removal of the engine/transmission as a unit, and describes the engine dismantling and overhaul procedures.

In Parts A and B, the assumption is made that the engine is installed in the car, with all ancillaries connected. If the engine has been removed for overhaul, the preliminary dismantling information which precedes each operation may be ignored.

Engine description

The engine covered in this Part of Chapter 2 is a water-cooled, double overhead camshaft (DOHC), in-line four-cylinder unit, with cast iron cylinder block and aluminium-alloy cylinder head. The engine is mounted transversely at the front of the car, with the transmission bolted to the left-hand end.

The cylinder head houses the eight inlet and eight exhaust valves, which are closed by single coil springs, and which run in guides pressed into the cylinder head. The two camshafts are housed in a cylinder head extension which is bolted to the top of the cylinder head. The exhaust camshaft is driven by a toothed timing belt and in turn drives the inlet camshaft via a pair of gears located at the left-hand end of the cylinder head extension. The camshafts actuate the valves directly via self-adjusting hydraulic cam followers mounted in the cylinder head extension.

The crankshaft is supported by five main bearings, and endfloat is controlled by a thrust bearing fitted to the upper section of the centre main bearing.

Engine coolant is circulated by a pump, driven by the timing belt. For details of the cooling system, refer to Chapter 3.

Lubricant is circulated under pressure by a pump, driven from the front of the crankshaft. Oil is drawn from the sump through a strainer, and then forced through an externally-mounted, renewable screw-on filter. From there, it is distributed to the cylinder head and cylinder head extension, where it lubricates the camshaft journals and cam followers, and also to the crankcase, where it lubricates the main bearings, connecting rod big and small-ends, gudgeon pins and cylinder bores. Oil jets are fitted to the base of each cylinder bore – these spray oil onto the underside of the pistons, to improve cooling.

Operations with engine in car

The following work can be carried out with the engine in the car:
a) Compression pressure – testing.
b) Timing belt covers – removal and refitting.
c) Timing belt – removal, refitting and adjustment.
d) Timing belt tensioner and sprockets – removal and refitting.
e) Cylinder head extension – removal and refitting.
f) Camshaft and cam followers – removal and refitting.
g) Cylinder head – removal and refitting.
h) Camshaft oil seal – renewal.
i) Crankshaft oil seals – renewal.
j) Sump – removal and refitting.
k) Oil pump and pick-up tube assembly – removal, inspection and refitting.
l) Flywheel/driveplate – removal, inspection and refitting.
m) Engine mountings – inspection and renewal.

Note: Many of the procedures in this Chapter entail the use of numerous special tools. Where possible, suitable alternatives are described with details of their fabrication. Before starting any operations on the engine, read through the entire procedure first to familiarise yourself with the work involved, tools to be obtained and new parts that may be necessary.

2 Engine assembly/valve timing holes – general information and usage

Note: Do not attempt to rotate the engine whilst the camshafts are locked in position. If the engine is to be left in this state for a long period of time, it is a good idea to place suitable warning notices inside the car, and in the engine compartment. This will reduce the possibility of the engine being accidentally cranked on the starter motor, which is likely to cause damage with the locking tools in place.

1 To accurately set the valve timing for all operations requiring removal and refitting of the timing belt, timing holes are drilled in the camshafts and cylinder head extension. The holes are used in conjunction with camshaft locking tools and crankshaft positioning rods to lock the camshafts when all the pistons are positioned at the mid-point of their stroke. This arrangement prevents the possibility of the valves contacting the pistons when refitting the cylinder head or timing belt, and also ensures that the correct valve timing can be obtained. The design of the engine is such that there are no conventional timing marks on the crankshaft or camshaft sprockets to indicate the normal TDC position. Therefore, for any work on the timing belt, camshafts or cylinder head the locking and positioning tools must be used.

2 The special Fiat tools for setting the camshafts and pistons consist of two rods which slide in sleeves that are screwed into No 1 and No 2 cylinder spark plug holes. The rods are pushed down to contact the pistons, and the crankshaft is then turned until both rods protrude from their sleeves by the same amount. With the crankshaft correctly set, two camshaft locking pins are used, one for the inlet camshaft and one for the exhaust camshaft. The pins are screwed into holes on each side of the cylinder head extension so that they engage with slots machined in the camshafts. The arrangement of the Fiat special tools are shown **(see illustrations)**. The tool numbers are as follows:

Camshaft locking tools   Tool No 1860985000
Piston positioning tool   Tool No 1860992000

3 Although the special Fiat tools are relatively inexpensive and should be readily available from Fiat dealers, it is possible to fabricate suitable alternatives, with the help of a local machine shop, as described below. Once the tools have been made up, their usage is described in the relevant Sections of this Chapter where the tools are required.

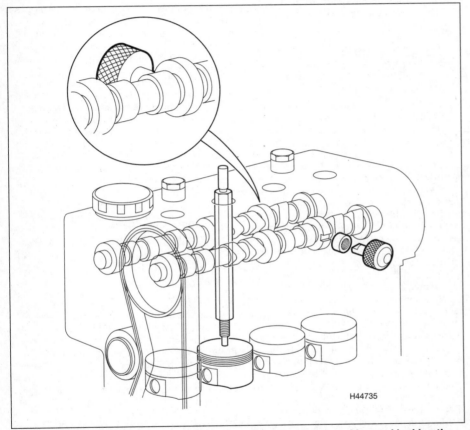

2.2a Arrangement of Fiat special tools for setting the piston position and locking the camshafts

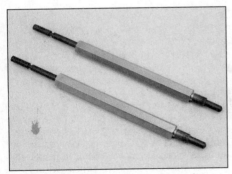

2.2b Fiat special tool for setting piston position . . .

2.2c . . . and locking the camshafts

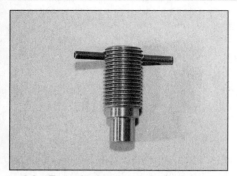

2.6a To make an alternative camshaft locking tool . . .

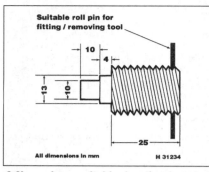

2.6b . . . have suitable dowel rods or bolts machined to the dimensions shown

Camshaft locking tool

4 Remove the air cleaner assembly as described in Chapter 4A.

5 Unscrew the sealing plug from the front face of the cylinder head extension.

6 Using the sealing plug as a pattern, obtain a length of threaded dowel rod or two suitable bolts to screw into the sealing plug hole. With the help of a machine shop or engineering works, make up the camshaft locking tools by having the dowel rod or bolts machined (see illustrations). Note that two will be needed, one for each camshaft.

Crankshaft setting tool

7 To make the crankshaft setting tools, four old spark plugs will be required, together with four lengths of dowel rod. The length of each dowel rod is not critical, but it must be long enough to protrude about 100 mm above the top of the cylinder head extension when resting on top of a piston located half-way down its bore. What is critical, however, is that all four dowel rods must be **exactly** the same length.

8 Break off the ceramic upper section of each plug and remove the centre electrode and earth tip. The easiest way to do this is to mount each spark plug in a vice (after removing the ceramic upper plug section) and drill a hole down through the centre of the plug. The diameter of the drill bit should be the same as the diameter of the dowel rod to be used. When finished you should have four spark plug bodies and four equal length dowel rods which will slide through the centre of the spark plugs.

3 Compression test – description and interpretation

1 When engine performance is down, or if misfiring occurs which cannot be attributed to the ignition or fuel systems, a compression test can provide diagnostic clues as to the engine's condition. If the test is performed regularly, it can give warning of trouble before any other symptoms become apparent.

2 The engine must be fully warmed-up to normal operating temperature, the battery must be fully-charged, and all the spark plugs must be removed (Chapter 1). The aid of an assistant will also be required.

3 Disable the ignition and fuel injection systems by disconnecting the wiring multi-plug connectors at the engine management ECU, referring to Chapter 4A for further information.

4 Fit a compression tester to the No 1 cylinder spark plug hole – the type of tester which screws into the plug thread is to be preferred.

5 Have the assistant hold the throttle wide open, and crank the engine on the starter motor; after one or two revolutions, the compression pressure should build-up to a maximum figure, and then stabilise. Record the highest reading obtained.

6 Repeat the test on the remaining cylinders, recording the pressure in each.

7 All cylinders should produce very similar pressures; any excessive difference indicates the existence of a fault. Note that the compression should build-up quickly in a healthy engine; low compression on the first stroke, followed by gradually-increasing pressure on successive strokes, indicates worn piston rings. A low compression reading on the first stroke, which does not build-up during successive strokes, indicates leaking valves or a blown head gasket (a cracked head could also be the cause).

8 If the pressure in any cylinder is very low, carry out the following test to isolate the cause. Introduce a teaspoonful of clean oil into that cylinder through its spark plug hole and repeat the test.

9 If the addition of oil temporarily improves the compression pressure, this indicates that bore or piston wear is responsible for the pressure loss. No improvement suggests that leaking or burnt valves, or a blown head gasket, may be to blame.

10 A low reading from two adjacent cylinders is almost certainly due to the head gasket having blown between them; the presence of coolant in the engine oil will confirm this.

11 If one cylinder is about 20 percent lower than the others and the engine has a slightly rough idle, a worn camshaft lobe could be the cause.

12 On completion of the test, refit the spark plugs and reconnect the ECU wiring connectors.

4 Timing belt covers – removal and refitting

Removal

Upper cover

1 Disconnect the battery negative terminal (refer to *Disconnecting the battery* in the Reference Chapter).

2 Remove the air cleaner assembly as described in Chapter 4A.

3 Undo the cover upper retaining bolt located above the engine mounting, and the front retaining bolt located behind the air cleaner intake duct (see illustrations).

4 Disconnect the crankshaft TDC sensor wiring connector, then release the sensor wiring socket from the clip on the timing cover (see illustration).

4.3a Undo the timing belt upper cover retaining bolt above the engine mounting . . .

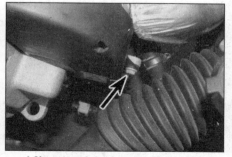

4.3b . . . and the front retaining bolt (arrowed) located behind the air cleaner intake duct

4.4 Disconnect the TDC sensor wiring connector, then release the wiring socket from the clip on the timing cover

4.5 Lift the cover upwards, slip the TDC sensor wiring out of the groove, and remove the upper cover from the engine

4.8 Remove the wheel arch liner centre panel for access to the crankshaft pulley

4.11 Undo the retaining bolt in the centre of the lower timing cover . . .

4.12 . . . release the wiring from the periphery of the cover, and manipulate the cover out from under the car

5 Lift the cover upwards, slip the TDC sensor wiring out of the groove, and remove the upper cover from the engine (**see illustration**).

Lower cover

6 Remove the upper cover as described previously.
7 Firmly apply the handbrake, then jack up the front of the car and support it securely on axle stands (see *Jacking and vehicle support*). Remove the right-hand front roadwheel.
8 Working under the right-hand wheel arch, undo the retaining screws and remove the wheel arch liner centre panel for access to the crankshaft pulley (**see illustration**).
9 Remove the auxiliary drivebelt as described in Chapter 1.

10 Undo the three bolts and remove the crankshaft pulley from the sprocket.
11 Undo the retaining bolt in the centre of the lower timing cover (**see illustration**).
12 Release the TDC sensor and oil pressure switch wiring from the periphery of the cover, and manipulate the cover out from under the car (**see illustration**).

Refitting

13 Refitting is the reverse sequence to removal. On completion, refit and adjust the auxiliary drivebelt as described in Chapter 1.

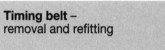

5 Timing belt –
removal and refitting

General information

1 The function of the timing belt is to drive the camshafts and coolant pump. Should the belt slip or break in service, the valve timing will be disturbed and piston-to-valve contact will occur, resulting in serious engine damage.
2 The timing belt should be renewed at the specified intervals (see Chapter 1) or earlier if it is contaminated with oil, or if it is at all noisy in operation (a scraping noise due to uneven wear).
3 If the timing belt is being removed, it is a wise precaution to check the condition of the coolant pump at the same time (check for signs of coolant leakage). This may avoid the

need to remove the timing belt again at a later stage, should the coolant pump fail.
4 Before carrying out this procedure, it will be necessary to obtain or fabricate suitable camshaft locking tools and piston positioning tools as described in Section 2. The procedures contained in this Section depict the use of the home-made alternative tools described in Section 2, which were fabricated in the Haynes workshop. If the manufacturer's tools are being used instead, the procedures are virtually identical. Do not attempt to remove the timing belt unless the special tools or their alternatives are available.

Removal

5 Remove the timing belt covers as described in Section 4.
6 Remove the inlet manifold as described in Chapter 4A.
7 Place a trolley jack beneath the right-hand side of the engine, with a block of wood on the jack head. Raise the jack until it is supporting the weight of the engine.
8 Undo the three nuts securing the right-hand engine mounting to the body and the four nuts securing the mounting upper bracket to the lower bracket on the engine. Lift the mounting and upper bracket assembly off the studs and remove it from the car (**see illustration**).
9 Undo the six bolts and remove the right-hand mounting lower bracket from the cylinder head (**see illustrations**).

5.8 Undo the retaining nuts and remove the right-hand engine mounting and upper bracket assembly

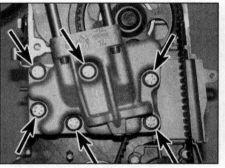

5.9a Undo the six bolts (arrowed) . . .

5.9b . . . and remove the right-hand mounting lower bracket from the cylinder head

5.12a Screw the spark plug bodies of the home-made piston positioning tools into each spark plug hole . . .

5.12b . . . place a suitable washer or similar into the recess to keep the dowel rod vertical . . .

5.12c . . . then insert the dowel rods

10 Remove the spark plugs as described in Chapter 1.

11 Unscrew the two sealing plugs from the front and rear of the cylinder head extension to enable the camshaft locking tools to be inserted.

12 Screw the spark plug bodies of the home-made piston positioning tools into each spark plug hole and insert the dowel rods into each body. To keep the dowel rods vertical, locate a suitable washer or similar over the rod and into the recess at the top of the spark plug hole. In the Haynes' workshop, an old valve stem oil seal housing was used but anything similar will suffice (see illustrations).

13 Using a socket on the crankshaft sprocket centre bolt, turn the crankshaft in the normal direction of rotation until all four dowel rods are protruding from the top of the cylinder head extension by the same amount. As the engine is turned, two of the rods will move up and two will move down until the position is reached where they are all at the same height. The best way to check this is to place a straight-edge along the top of the rods and turn the crankshaft very slowly until the straight-edge contacts all four rods (see illustration).

14 When all four rods are at the same height, all the pistons will be at the mid-point of their

stroke. Using a screwdriver or similar inserted into the front timing hole in the cylinder head extension, check that the timing slot in the exhaust camshaft is approximately aligned with the timing hole. If the camshaft slot cannot be felt, turn the crankshaft through one complete revolution and realign the dowel rods using the straight-edge. Check again for the camshaft slot. Note that although the pistons can be at the mid-point of their stroke twice for each cycle of the engine, the camshaft slots will only be positioned correctly once per cycle.

15 With the pistons correctly set, it should now be possible to screw in the camshaft locking tools into the timing holes in the cylinder head extension. To provide the necessary degree of timing accuracy, the machined end of the locking tools are a very close fit in the slots machined in the camshafts (see illustrations). To allow the tools to be screwed fully into engagement, it may be necessary to move the crankshaft in one direction or another *very slightly* until the tools are felt to engage fully.

16 Release the nut on the timing belt tensioner to release the tension on the belt (see illustration).

17 If the timing belt is to be re-used, use white paint or chalk to mark the direction of rotation on the belt (if markings do not already exist), then slip the belt off the sprockets (see

5.13 Place a straight-edge along the top of the rods and turn the crankshaft until the straight-edge contacts all four rods

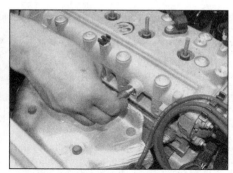

5.15a Screw the camshaft locking tools into the timing holes in the front . . .

5.15b . . . and rear of the cylinder head extension

5.15c The tools engage in the camshaft slots when fitted (shown removed for clarity)

5.16 Release the nut on the timing belt tensioner . . .

5.17 . . . then slip the timing belt off the sprockets

illustration). Note that the crankshaft must not be rotated whilst the belt is removed.

18 Check the timing belt carefully for any signs of uneven wear, splitting, or oil contamination. Pay particular attention to the roots of the teeth. Renew it if there is the slightest doubt about its condition. If the engine is undergoing an overhaul, renew the belt as a matter of course, regardless of its apparent condition. The cost of a new belt is nothing compared with the cost of repairs should the belt break in service. If signs of oil contamination are found, trace the source of the oil leak and rectify it. Wash down the engine timing belt area and all related components to remove all traces of oil.

Refitting

19 Before refitting, thoroughly clean the timing belt sprockets. Check that the tensioner pulley rotates freely, without any sign of roughness. If necessary, renew the tensioner pulley as described in Section 6.

20 The camshaft sprocket retaining bolt must now be slackened to allow the sprocket to move as the timing belt is refitted and tensioned. To hold the sprocket stationary while the retaining bolt is loosened, make up a tool and engage it with the holes in the sprocket (**see Tool Tip**). With the sprocket held, slacken the retaining bolt.

21 Check that the pistons are still correctly positioned at the mid-point of their stroke and that the camshafts are locked with the locking tools.

22 Ensuring that the direction markings on the timing belt point in the normal direction of

5.23 Using right-angled circlip pliers, turn the tensioner pulley to fully tension the belt

TOOL TiP

To make a camshaft sprocket holding tool, obtain two lengths of steel strip about 6 mm thick by 30 mm wide or similar, one 600 mm long, the other 200 mm long (all dimensions approximate). Bolt the two strips together to form a forked end, leaving the bolt slack so that the shorter strip can pivot freely. At the end of each 'prong' of the fork, secure a bolt with a nut and a locknut, to act as the fulcrums; these will engage with the cut-outs in the sprocket, and should protrude by about 30 mm.

engine rotation, engage the timing belt with the crankshaft sprocket first, then place it around the coolant pump sprocket and the camshaft sprocket. Finally slip the belt around the tensioner pulley.

23 Insert the jaws of a pair of right-angled circlip pliers (or similar) into the two holes on the front face of the tensioner pulley (**see illustration**). Rotate the pulley to tension the belt until the belt is quite taut. Maintain the effort applied to the tensioner pulley, then tighten the pulley retaining nut.

24 Tighten the camshaft sprocket retaining bolt to the specified torque while holding the camshaft stationary using the method described previously.

25 Remove the piston positioning tools and camshaft locking tools and turn the crankshaft through two complete turns in the normal direction of rotation.

26 Slacken the tensioner pulley retaining nut and reposition the tensioner to align the mobile indicator with the fixed reference mark

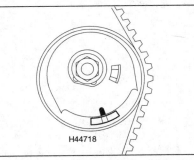

H44718

5.26 Position the tensioner so that the mobile indicator (1) is aligned with the fixed reference mark (2)

on the pulley face (**see illustration**). Hold the pulley in this position and tighten the retaining nut to the specified torque.

27 Turn the crankshaft through a further two complete turns in the normal direction of rotation. Check that the timing is correct by refitting the piston positioning tools and camshaft locking tools as described previously.

28 When all is correct, remove the setting and locking tools and refit the sealing plugs to the cylinder head extension, using new O-rings if necessary. Tighten the plugs securely.

29 Refit the spark plugs as described in Chapter 1.

30 Refit the engine mounting components and tighten the retaining bolts and nuts to the specified torque.

31 Refit the inlet manifold as described in Chapter 4A, then refit the timing belt covers as described in Section 4 of this Chapter.

6	Timing belt tensioner and sprockets – removal and refitting

Timing belt tensioner

Removal

1 Remove the timing belt as described in Section 5.

2 Completely unscrew the tensioner nut and slide the tensioner off the mounting stud.

Inspection

3 Wipe the tensioner clean but do not use solvents that may contaminate the bearings. Spin the tensioner pulley on its hub by hand. Stiff movement or excessive freeplay is an indication of severe wear; the tensioner is not a serviceable component, and should be renewed.

Refitting

4 Slide the tensioner pulley over the mounting stud and fit the securing nut.

5 Refit the timing belt as described in Section 5.

Camshaft sprocket

Removal

6 Remove the timing belt as described in Section 5.

7 Unscrew the bolt and slide the sprocket from the end of the camshaft.

Inspection

8 With the sprocket removed, examine the camshaft oil seal for signs of leaking. If necessary, refer to Section 7 and renew it.

9 Check the sprocket teeth for damage.

10 Wipe clean the sprocket and camshaft mating surfaces.

Refitting

11 Locate the sprocket on the end of the camshaft, then refit the retaining bolt finger tight only at this stage.

12 Refit the timing belt as described in Section 5.

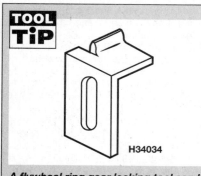

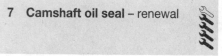

A flywheel ring gear locking tool can be made from a short strip of steel bent to form a right-angle. Cut a slot in the upper part and bend this part up to engage with the ring gear teeth. File the edges to form a tooth profile. Drill a hole in the lower part to enable the tool to be bolted to the bellhousing flange.

Crankshaft sprocket

Removal

13 Remove the timing belt as described in Section 5.
14 Remove the exhaust manifold as described in Chapter 4A.
15 Working beneath the engine, undo the bolts and remove the support brace linking the transmission to the cylinder block.
16 To prevent crankshaft rotation whilst the sprocket retaining bolt is being slackened, the flywheel/driveplate ring gear must be locked using a suitable tool made from steel angle **(see Tool Tip)**. Remove the cover plate from the base of the transmission bellhousing and bolt the tool to the lower bolt hole in the bellhousing flange so it engages with the ring gear teeth.
17 Using a suitable socket and extension bar, unscrew the crankshaft sprocket retaining bolt and slide the sprocket off the end of the crankshaft.

Inspection

18 With the sprocket removed, examine the crankshaft oil seal for signs of leaking. If necessary, refer to Section 8 and renew it.
19 Check the sprocket teeth for damage.
20 Wipe clean the sprocket and crankshaft mating surfaces.

Refitting

21 Slide the sprocket onto the crankshaft making sure the integral key engages with the slot on the end of the crankshaft. Refit the retaining bolt and tighten it to the specified torque, then through the specified angle. It is recommended that an angle-measuring gauge is used during this stage of tightening, to ensure accuracy. Hold the crankshaft stationary while the bolt is tightened using the method described in paragraph 16.
22 Refit the flywheel/driveplate cover plate and engine/transmission support brace.
23 Refit the exhaust manifold as described in Chapter 4A.
24 Refit the timing belt as described in Section 5.

7 Camshaft oil seal – renewal

1 Remove the timing belt and camshaft sprocket as described in Sections 5 and 6.
2 Punch or drill a small hole in the oil seal. Screw a self-tapping screw into the hole, and pull on the screws with pliers to extract the seal.
3 Clean the seal housing, and polish off any burrs or raised edges, which may have caused the seal to fail in the first place.
4 Lubricate the lips of the new seal with clean engine oil, and drive it into position until it seats on its locating shoulder. Use a suitable tubular drift, such as a socket, which bears only on the hard outer edge of the seal. Take care not to damage the seal lips during fitting. Note that the seal lips should face inwards.
5 Refit the camshaft sprocket and timing belt as described in Sections 6 and 5.

8 Crankshaft oil seals – renewal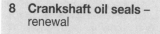

Right-hand side oil seal

1 The front oil seal is located in the oil pump casing on the front of the crankshaft. Remove the timing belt as described in Section 5 and the crankshaft sprocket as described in Section 6.
2 Using a small screwdriver, carefully prise the oil seal from the oil pump casing taking care not to damage the surface of the crankshaft **(see illustration)**.
3 Clean the seating in the housing and the surface of the crankshaft. To prevent damage to the new oil seal as it is being fitted, wrap some adhesive tape around the end of the crankshaft and lightly oil it.
4 Lubricate the oil seal lip with clean engine oil then offer it up to the oil pump casing. Ensure that the sealing lip is facing inwards **(see illustration)**.
5 Using a suitable tubular drift, drive the oil seal squarely into the casing **(see illustration)**. Remove the adhesive tape.
6 Refit the crankshaft sprocket and timing belt with reference to Sections 6 and 5.

Left-hand side oil seal

Note: *The left-hand side oil seal is integral with the oil seal housing.*
7 Remove the flywheel/driveplate as described in Section 12.
8 Remove the sump as described in Section 14.
9 Undo the six retaining bolts and remove the housing complete with integral oil seal **(see illustration)**.
10 Clean the cylinder block mating face and the seal contact surface on the crankshaft.

8.2 Carefully prise the crankshaft right-hand oil seal from the oil pump casing

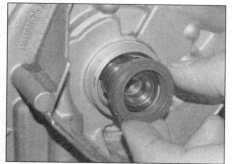

8.4 Locate the new oil seal on the oil pump casing with the sealing lips facing inwards

8.5 Using a suitable tubular drift, drive the oil seal squarely into the casing

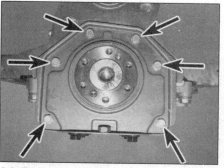

8.9 Undo the retaining bolts (arrowed) and remove the crankshaft left-hand oil seal housing complete with integral oil seal

9.3 Unscrew the protective caps covering the cylinder head extension retaining bolts

11 Lubricate the lip of the new seal, then locate the seal housing on the cylinder block. Refit the housing retaining bolts and tighten them to the specified torque.

12 Refit the sump as described in Section 14.

13 Refit the flywheel/driveplate as described in Section 12.

9 Cylinder head extension – removal and refitting

Removal

1 Remove the timing belt as described in Section 5.

2 Disconnect the LT wiring connector from the ignition coils.

3 Unscrew the protective caps covering the cylinder head extension retaining bolts **(see illustration)**.

4 To retain the cam followers in place as the cylinder head extension is removed, Fiat special tool No 1860988000 will be required. This tool consists of two strips of suitably-slotted thin metal angle which slip between the cylinder head extension and cylinder head mating faces as the extension is lifted off. The tool holds the cam followers in place in the extension allowing the assembly to be withdrawn without fouling the inlet and exhaust valves. The tools are relatively inexpensive and readily available from Fiat dealers. Suitable alternatives can be fabricated, if desired, using thin metal angle strip **(see Tool tip)**.

5 Progressively slacken and remove the bolts securing the cylinder head extension to the cylinder head.

6 Lift the cylinder head extension up very slightly, keeping it square to the cylinder head. Slip the tools in place to hold the cam followers, then lift the extension off the cylinder head **(see illustrations)**. Recover the gasket between the two assemblies.

7 Dismantling and inspection procedures for the cylinder head extension and camshafts are given in Section 10.

Refitting

8 Ensure that the mating faces of the cylinder head and extension are thoroughly cleaned,

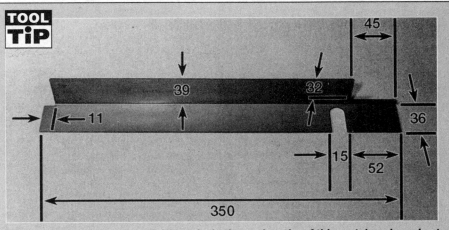

To make a cam follower retaining tool, obtain two lengths of thin metal angle and cut both to the dimensions (in mm) shown.

with all traces of old gasket removed, then locate a new gasket on the cylinder head **(see illustration)**.

9 Check that the pistons are still correctly positioned at the mid-point of their stroke and that the camshafts are locked with the locking tools. Locate the cam follower retaining tools in position and carefully lower the extension assembly over the valves and onto the cylinder head. When all the cam followers have engaged their respective valves, remove the tools.

10 Refit the retaining bolts and tighten them

progressively to pull the extension down onto the cylinder head. Do this slowly and carefully as the valve springs will be compressed during this operation and it is essential to keep the extension square and level as the bolts are tightened. Once all the bolts are initially tightened, progressively tighten them further to the specified torque.

11 If necessary renew the O-ring seals on the protective caps covering the cylinder head extension retaining bolts **(see illustration)**. Refit the caps and tighten them securely.

9.6a Lift the cylinder head extension slightly and insert the tools (shown with cylinder head extension removed for clarity) . . .

9.6b . . . then remove the cylinder head extension

9.8 Locate a new gasket on the cylinder head

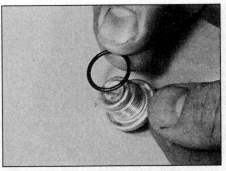

9.11 Renew the O-ring seals on the protective caps covering the cylinder head extension retaining bolts

10.3 Remove the cam followers from their locations in the cylinder head extension

10.5a Remove the camshaft sprocket . . .

10.5b . . . then undo the two bolts and remove the cover plate over the inlet camshaft

12 Reconnect the ignition coil wiring connector.
13 Refit the timing belt as described in Section 5.

10 Camshafts and cam followers – removal, inspection and refitting

Removal

1 Remove the cylinder head extension as described in Section 9.
2 Place the assembly upside-down on a bench and lift off the cam follower retaining tools.

10.7 Undo the two bolts securing the camshaft drivegears to the inlet and exhaust camshafts

10.10 Extract the exhaust camshaft oil seal . . .

3 Remove the cam followers from their locations in the cylinder head extension and place them in an oil-tight compartmented box labelled 1 to 8 (inlet) and 1 to 8 (exhaust) **(see illustration)**. Alternatively, place them into individual storage jars or containers suitably marked. Fill the box or the jars with clean engine oil until each cam follower is just submerged.
4 Undo the camshaft sprocket retaining bolt while holding the sprocket with a suitable tool, as described in Section 5.
5 Remove the camshaft sprocket, then undo the two bolts and remove the cover plate over the inlet camshaft **(see illustrations)**.
6 At the other end of the cylinder head extension, undo the nuts and remove the end

10.9 Carefully remove the inlet camshaft from the cylinder head extension

10.11 . . . then remove the exhaust camshaft from the cylinder head extension

cover, complete with ignition coils. Recover the gasket.
7 Undo the two bolts securing the camshaft drivegears to the inlet and exhaust camshafts **(see illustration)**. The camshaft locking tools used in the timing belt removal procedure (which should still be in place) are sufficient to prevent the camshafts rotating while the gear retaining bolts are undone. Remove the bolts and withdraw the camshaft gears.
8 Remove the camshaft locking tools.
9 Carefully remove the inlet camshaft from the cylinder head extension **(see illustration)**. Suitably mark the camshaft IN to avoid confusion when refitting.
10 Punch or drill a small hole in the exhaust camshaft oil seal. Screw a self-tapping screw into the hole, and pull on the screw with pliers to extract the seal **(see illustration)**.
11 Carefully remove the exhaust camshaft from the cylinder head extension **(see illustration)**. Suitably mark the camshaft EX to avoid confusion when refitting.

Inspection

12 Examine the camshaft bearing surfaces and cam lobes for signs of wear ridges and scoring. Renew the camshaft if any of these conditions are apparent. Examine the condition of the bearing surfaces, both on the camshaft journals and in the cylinder head extension. If the head extension bearing surfaces are worn excessively, the extension will need to be renewed. If suitable measuring equipment is available, camshaft bearing journal wear can be checked by direct measurement.
13 Examine the cam follower bearing surfaces which contact the camshaft lobes for wear ridges and scoring. Renew any follower on which these conditions are apparent. If a follower bearing surface is badly scored, also examine the corresponding lobe on the camshaft for wear, as it is likely that both will be worn. Renew worn components as necessary.

Refitting

14 Liberally lubricate the camshaft journals and cylinder head extension bearings, then locate both camshafts in position. Note that

10.15 Refit the camshaft locking tools

10.16 Fit a new exhaust camshaft oil seal

10.17 Tighten the inlet camshaft drivegear retaining bolt to the specified torque

the exhaust camshaft is nearest to the front facing side of the engine.

15 With the camshafts in position, rotate them as necessary until the camshaft locking tools can be re-inserted (see illustration).

16 Lubricate the lips of a new exhaust camshaft oil seal with clean engine oil, and drive it into position until it seats on its locating shoulder (see illustration). Use a suitable tubular drift, such as a socket, which bears only on the hard outer edge of the seal. Take care not to damage the seal lips during fitting. Note that the seal lips should face inwards.

17 Refit the inlet camshaft drivegear and retaining bolt then tighten the bolt to the specified torque (see illustration).

18 Refit the exhaust camshaft drivegear to the exhaust camshaft. As the gear is being

fitted, it will be necessary to align the anti-backlash inner gear teeth using a screwdriver to enable the teeth of both the gears to mesh (see illustration). Refit the drivegear retaining bolt and tighten it to the specified torque.

19 At this stage it is advisable to check the camshaft endfloat using a dial gauge mounted on the cylinder head extension, with its probe in contact with the camshaft being checked. Move the camshaft one way, zero the gauge, then move the camshaft as far as it will go the other way. Record the reading on the dial gauge and compare the figure with that given in the Specifications. Repeat on the other camshaft. If either of the readings exceeds the tolerance given, a new cylinder head extension will be required.

20 Locate a new gasket on the cylinder head extension end cover, then wrap round the

protruding tangs on the gasket to retain it in position (see illustrations).

21 Locate the end cover on the cylinder head extension and secure with the retaining nuts securely tightened.

22 Locate a new O-ring on the inlet camshaft cover plate, then apply RTV gasket sealant to the cover plate contact face (see illustrations). Fit the cover plate and secure with the two bolts securely tightened.

23 Refit the camshaft sprocket and secure with the retaining bolt tightened finger tight only at this stage.

24 Liberally lubricate the cam followers and place them in position in their respective cylinder head extension bores (see illustration).

25 Locate the cam follower retaining tools in position and refit the cylinder head extension as described in Section 9.

10.18 Refit the exhaust camshaft drivegear while aligning the anti-backlash inner gear teeth

10.20a Locate a new gasket on the cylinder head extension end cover . . .

10.20b . . . then wrap round the protruding tangs to retain the gasket

10.22a Locate a new O-ring on the inlet camshaft cover plate . . .

10.22b . . . then apply RTV gasket sealant to the cover plate contact face

10.24 Lubricate the cam followers and place them in position in their respective bores

11.2 Undo the upper and lower retaining bolts and remove the exhaust manifold heat shield

11.3 Undo the bolt (arrowed) securing the manifold downpipe support bracket to the transmission

11.4 Undo the retaining nuts and withdraw the exhaust manifold off the mounting studs

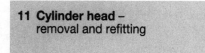

11 Cylinder head – removal and refitting

Note: *The cylinder head bolts are of special splined design and a Fiat tool should be obtained to unscrew them. A Torx key will not fit, although in practice it was found that a close-fitting Allen key could be used as an alternative.*

Removal

1 Remove the cylinder head extension as described in Section 9.

2 Undo the upper and lower retaining bolts and remove the heat shield from the exhaust manifold **(see illustration)**.

3 From under the car, undo the bolt securing the manifold downpipe support bracket to the transmission **(see illustration)**.

4 Undo the nuts securing the exhaust manifold to the cylinder head, noting that the engine lifting bracket is also secured by the two upper nuts at the timing belt end **(see illustration)**. Carefully withdraw the manifold off the mounting studs and collect the gasket.

5 Disconnect the radiator hose from the thermostat housing on the left-hand end of the cylinder head.

6 Check that nothing remains attached to the cylinder head likely to impede removal, then unscrew the cylinder head bolts half a turn at a time in the **reverse** order to the tightening sequence **(see illustration 11.17a)**. When the

bolts are free, remove them from their locations.

7 Lift the cylinder head from the block **(see illustration)**. If it is stuck tight rock the head to break the joint. On no account drive levers into the gasket joint, nor attempt to tap the head sideways, as it is located on positioning dowels.

8 Remove and discard the cylinder head gasket.

9 Refer to Chapter 2C for cylinder head dismantling and inspection procedures.

Preparation for refitting

10 The mating faces of the cylinder head and cylinder block must be perfectly clean before refitting the head. Use a hard plastic or wooden scraper to remove all traces of gasket and carbon; also clean the piston crowns. Take particular care when cleaning the piston crowns as the soft aluminium alloy is easily damaged. Make sure that the carbon is not allowed to enter the oil and water passages – this is particularly important for the lubrication system, as carbon could block the oil supply to the engine's components. Using adhesive tape and paper, seal the water, oil and bolt holes in the cylinder block. To prevent carbon entering the gap between the pistons and bores, smear a little grease in the gap. After cleaning each piston, use a small brush to remove all traces of grease and carbon from the gap, then wipe away the remainder with a clean rag. Clean all the pistons in the same way.

11 Check the mating surfaces of the cylinder block and the cylinder head for nicks, deep scratches and other damage. If slight, they may be removed carefully with a file, but if excessive, machining may be the only alternative to renewal. If warpage of the cylinder head gasket surface is suspected, use a straight-edge to check it for distortion. Refer to Part C of this Chapter if necessary.

12 Check the condition of the cylinder head bolts, and particularly their threads, whenever they are removed. Wash the bolts in a suitable solvent, and wipe them dry. Check each bolt for any sign of visible wear or damage, renewing them if necessary. Although Fiat do not specify that the bolts must be renewed, it is strongly recommended that the bolts should be renewed as a complete set whenever they are disturbed.

Refitting

13 Before refitting the assembled cylinder head, make sure that the head and block mating surfaces are perfectly clean, and that the bolt holes in the cylinder block have been mopped out to clear any oil.

14 The new gasket should not be removed from its protective cover until required for use. Fit the gasket dry, and make sure that the mating surfaces on the head and block are perfectly clean.

15 Place the gasket the correct way round on the cylinder block so that the words ALTO/TOP can be read from above **(see illustrations)**.

11.7 Undo the retaining bolts and lift the cylinder head from the block

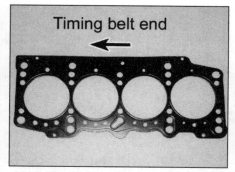

11.15a Place the cylinder head gasket the correct way round on the cylinder block . . .

11.15b . . . so that the words ALTO/TOP can be read from above

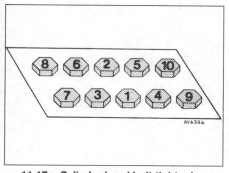

11.17a Cylinder head bolt tightening sequence

11.17b Tighten the cylinder head bolts to the Stage 1 torque setting . . .

11.17c . . . then through the Stage 2 and Stage 3 angle

16 Lower the cylinder head onto the block so that it locates on the positioning dowels.

17 The cylinder head bolt threads must be clean and lightly lubricated. Screw the bolts in finger-tight then working progressively and in sequence, tighten all the cylinder head bolts to the Stage 1 torque setting given in the Specifications, using a torque wrench and a suitable socket. With all the bolts tightened to their Stage 1 setting, working again in the specified sequence, first angle-tighten the bolts through the specified Stage 2 angle, then again through the Stage 3 angle, using a socket and extension bar. It is recommended that an angle-measuring gauge is used during this stage of tightening, to ensure accuracy **(see illustrations)**.

18 Ensure that the cylinder head and exhaust manifold mating surfaces are perfectly clean, then place a new manifold gasket over the mounting studs.

19 Engage the manifold with the mounting studs and refit the retaining nuts and the engine lifting bracket. Progressively tighten the nuts to the specified torque.

20 Refit the heat shield to the manifold and tighten the bolts securely.

21 Refit and tighten the bolt securing the manifold downpipe support bracket to the transmission.

22 Connect the radiator hose to the thermostat housing.

23 Refit the cylinder head extension as described in Section 9.

12 Flywheel/driveplate –
removal, inspection and refitting

Removal

1 Remove the transmission as described in Chapter 7A or 7B. On manual transmission models also remove the clutch (Chapter 6).

2 The flywheel/driveplate must now be held stationary while the bolts are loosened. A home-made locking tool may be fabricated from a piece of scrap metal and used to lock the ring gear **(see Tool Tip in Section 6)**. Bolt the tool to one of the transmission bellhousing mounting bolt holes on the cylinder block.

3 Mark the position of the flywheel/driveplate with respect to the crankshaft using a dab of paint. Unscrew and remove the mounting bolts together with the spacer plate, then lift off the flywheel/driveplate. Discard the bolts; new ones must be used on refitting.

Inspection

Flywheel

4 If the flywheel's clutch mating surface is deeply scored, cracked or otherwise damaged, the flywheel must be renewed. However, it may be possible to have it surface-ground; seek the advice of a Fiat dealer or engine reconditioning specialist.

5 If the ring gear is badly worn or has missing teeth, the flywheel must be renewed.

Driveplate

6 Check the driveplate for signs of damage and renew it if necessary. If the ring gear is badly worn or has missing teeth, the driveplate must be renewed.

Refitting

7 Clean the mating surfaces of the flywheel/driveplate and crankshaft. Remove any remaining locking compound from the threads of the crankshaft holes, using the correct-size tap, if available.

> **HAYNES HiNT**
>
> *If a suitable tap is not available, cut two slots down the threads of one of the old bolts with a hacksaw, and use the bolt to remove the locking compound from the threads.*

8 If the new retaining bolts are not supplied with their threads already precoated, apply a suitable thread-locking compound to the threads of each bolt.

9 Offer up the flywheel/driveplate to the crankshaft, using the alignment mark made during removal, and fit the new retaining bolts together with the spacer plate.

10 Lock the flywheel/driveplate using the method employed on dismantling, and tighten the retaining bolts to the specified torque.

11 Refit the clutch on manual transmission models as described in Chapter 6.

12 Refit the transmission as described in Chapter 7A or 7B.

13 Engine mountings –
inspection and renewal

Refer to Chapter 2A, Section 13.

14 Sump –
removal and refitting

Removal

1 Firmly apply the handbrake, then jack up the front of the car and support it securely on axle stands (see *Jacking and vehicle support*). Drain the engine oil as described in Chapter 1.

2 Remove the exhaust manifold as described in Chapter 4A.

3 Working beneath the engine, undo the bolts and remove the support brace linking the transmission to the cylinder block **(see illustration)**.

4 Unbolt and remove the cover plate from the base of the transmission bellhousing.

5 Unscrew the sump securing bolts and nuts then cut through as much of the joint sealant as possible using a sharp knife. Pull the sump downwards to release it from the remaining sealant and remove it from under the car.

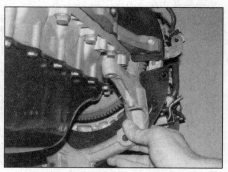

14.3 Undo the bolts and remove the support brace linking the transmission to the cylinder block

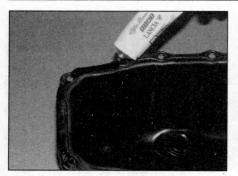

14.7 Apply a 3.0 mm bead of RTV silicone sealant to the sump flange, then locate the sump in position

15.7a Unbolt and remove the oil pump pick-up tube . . .

15.7b . . . then hook out the pick-up tube sealing O-ring from the pump body

6 Thoroughly clean the sump and the cylinder block mating surfaces ensuring that all traces of old sealant are removed.

Refitting

7 Apply a 3.0 mm bead of RTV silicone sealant to the sump flange, then locate the sump in position **(see illustration)**. Refit the retaining bolts and nuts and tighten to the specified torque.
8 Refit the cover plate to the transmission bellhousing, then refit the support brace. Tighten the retaining bolts securely.
9 Refit the exhaust manifold as described in Chapter 4A.

10 Lower the car to the ground and fill the engine with oil as described in Chapter 1.

15 Oil pump and pick-up tube – removal, inspection and refitting

Removal

1 Remove the crankshaft sprocket as described in Section 6.
2 Drain the engine oil and remove the oil filter as described in Chapter 1.
3 Remove the sump as described in Section 14.

4 Remove the coolant pump as described in Chapter 3.
5 Disconnect the wiring connector from the oil pressure switch on the side of the pump casing.
6 Undo the oil pump retaining bolts, noting the location of the longer bolt, and withdraw the pump assembly from the front of the engine. Recover the gasket.

Inspection

7 With the pump on the bench, undo the two bolts and remove the pick-up tube. Using a small screwdriver or similar tool, hook out the pick-up tube sealing O-ring from the pump body **(see illustrations)**.
8 The pressure relief valve can be removed for examination by unscrewing the end plug and withdrawing the spring and plunger **(see illustrations)**.
9 If pump wear is suspected, check the rotors in the following way. Extract the fixing screws and remove the rear cover plate **(see illustration)**. The screws are very tight, and will probably require the use of an impact screwdriver.
10 Inspect the pump rotors, pump casing and cover for any signs of wear or damage. If satisfactory, refit the rotors to the pump casing ensuring that the orientation marks are facing upwards **(see illustration)**.

15.8a Unscrew the oil pressure relief valve end plug . . .

15.8b . . . and withdraw the spring . . .

15.8c . . . and plunger

15.9 Extract the fixing screws and remove the oil pump rear cover plate

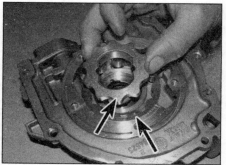

15.10 After inspection, refit the pump rotors with the orientation marks (arrowed) facing upwards

15.11a Checking the oil pump outer rotor-to-pump casing clearance

15.11b Checking the oil pump rotor endfloat

11 Check the clearance between the outer rotor and the pump casing using feeler blades. Check the rotor endfloat by placing a straight-edge across the pump casing, and checking the gap between the straight-edge and rotor face **(see illustrations)**. If the clearances are outside the specified tolerance, renew the oil pump complete.

12 If the pump is unworn, lubricate the rotors with clean engine oil then place the cover plate in position. Apply thread locking compound to the retaining screws and tighten the screws securely.

13 Locate a new O-ring in the pump casing then refit the pick-up tube. Secure the tube with the two bolts tightened securely.

14 Lubricate the pressure relief valve plunger then refit the plunger and spring. Apply thread-locking compound to the end plug then refit and securely tighten the plug.

15 Lever out the crankshaft oil seal and drive a new one squarely into the oil pump casing. Lubricate the oil seal lips with clean engine oil.

16 Prior to refitting, prime the pump by pouring clean engine oil into its inlet duct, while at the same time turning the oil pump inner rotor.

Refitting

17 Ensure that the oil pump and cylinder block mating faces are clean, then place a new gasket on the pump casing. Retain the gasket in position by inserting two of the pump retaining bolts.

18 Locate the pump on the cylinder block, insert the retaining bolts and tighten them progressively to the specified torque.

19 Refit the coolant pump as described in Chapter 3.

20 Refit the sump as described in Section 14.

21 Refit the crankshaft sprocket as described in Section 6.

22 Reconnect the oil pressure switch wiring connector.

23 Fit a new oil filter then fill the engine with oil and coolant as described in Chapter 1.

Notes

Chapter 2 Part C:
Engine removal and overhaul procedures

Contents

Degrees of difficulty

Easy, suitable for novice with little experience	**Fairly easy,** suitable for beginner with some experience	**Fairly difficult,** suitable for competent DIY mechanic	**Difficult,** suitable for experienced DIY mechanic	**Very difficult,** suitable for expert DIY or professional

Specifications

Cylinder head

Maximum gasket face distortion . . . . 0.10 mm

Valves

Valve stem diameter (inlet and exhaust):
  SOHC (8-valve) engines . . . . 6.982 to 7.000 mm
  DOHC (16-valve) engine . . . . 5.974 to 5.992 mm
Valve face angle . . . . 45° 30' ± 5'
Valve stem-to-guide clearance:
  SOHC (8-valve) engines . . . . 0.022 to 0.058 mm
  DOHC (16-valve) engine . . . . 0.030 to 0.066 mm

Cylinder block

Bore diameter:
  Nominal size . . . . 70.80 mm
  Oversizes available . . . . 0.4 mm

Pistons and piston rings

Piston diameter:
  Nominal size (measured 8.5 mm up from base of skirt) . . . . 70.76 to 70.77 mm
Piston-to-bore clearance . . . . 0.030 to 0.050 mm
Piston ring-to-groove clearance:
  Top compression ring:
    SOHC (8-valve) engines . . . . 0.040 to 0.080 mm
    DOHC (16-valve) engines . . . . 0 to 0.06 mm
  2nd compression ring:
    SOHC (8-valve) engines . . . . 0.020 to 0.055 mm
    DOHC (16-valve) engines . . . . 0 to 0.055 mm
  Oil scraper ring:
    SOHC (8-valve) engines . . . . 0.020 to 0.055 mm
    DOHC (16-valve) engines . . . . 0 to 0.055 mm
Piston ring end gap:
  Top compression ring . . . . 0.20 to 0.40 mm
  2nd compression ring . . . . 0.25 to 0.45 mm
  Oil scraper ring . . . . 0.20 to 0.45 mm

Crankshaft

Bearing journal diameters (standard):
   Main bearings (nominal) . . . . 47.98 mm
   Big-end bearings (nominal) . . . . 41.98 mm
Endfloat . . . . 0.05 to 0.26 mm

Torque wrench settings

SOHC (8-valve) engines
Refer to Chapter 2A Specifications.

DOHC (16-valve) engines
Refer to Chapter 2B Specifications.

1 General information

Included in this Part of Chapter 2 are details of removing the engine/transmission from the car and general overhaul procedures for the cylinder head, cylinder block/crankcase and all other engine internal components.

The information given ranges from advice concerning preparation for an overhaul and the purchase of new parts, to detailed step-by-step procedures covering removal, inspection, renovation and refitting of engine internal components.

After Section 5, all instructions are based on the assumption that the engine has been removed from the car. For information concerning in-car engine repair, as well as the removal and refitting of those external components necessary for full overhaul, refer to Part A or B of this Chapter (as applicable) and to Section 5. Ignore any preliminary dismantling operations described in Part A or B that are no longer relevant once the engine has been removed from the car.

2 Engine overhaul – general information

It is not always easy to determine when, or if, an engine should be completely overhauled, as a number of factors must be considered.

High mileage is not necessarily an indication that an overhaul is needed, while low mileage does not preclude the need for an overhaul. Frequency of servicing is probably the most important consideration. An engine which has had regular and frequent oil and filter changes, as well as other required maintenance, should give many thousands of miles of reliable service. Conversely, a neglected engine may require an overhaul very early in its life.

Excessive oil consumption is an indication that piston rings, valve seals and/or valve guides are in need of attention. Make sure that oil leaks are not responsible before deciding that the rings and/or guides are worn. Perform a compression test, as described in Part A or B of this Chapter, to determine the likely cause of the problem.

Check the oil pressure with a gauge fitted in place of the oil pressure switch. If it is extremely low, the main and big-end bearings, and/or the oil pump, are probably worn out.

Loss of power, rough running, knocking or metallic engine noises, excessive valve gear noise, and high fuel consumption may also point to the need for an overhaul, especially if they are all present at the same time. If a complete service does not remedy the situation, major mechanical work is the only solution.

An engine overhaul involves restoring all internal parts to the specification of a new engine. During an overhaul, the cylinders are rebored (where applicable), the pistons and the piston rings are renewed. New main and big-end bearings are generally fitted; if necessary, the crankshaft may be reground, to restore the journals. The valves are also serviced as well, since they are usually in less-than perfect condition at this point. The end result should be an as-new engine that will give many trouble-free miles.

Note: *Critical cooling system components such as the hoses, thermostat and coolant pump should be renewed when an engine is overhauled. The radiator should be checked carefully, to ensure that it is not clogged or leaking. Also, it is a good idea to renew the oil pump whenever the engine is overhauled.*

Before beginning the engine overhaul, read through the entire procedure, to familiarise yourself with the scope and requirements of the job. Check on the availability of parts and make sure that any necessary special tools and equipment are obtained in advance. Most work can be done with typical hand tools, although a number of precision measuring tools are required for inspecting parts to determine if they must be renewed. The services provided by an engineering machine shop or engine reconditioning specialist will almost certainly be required, particularly if major repairs such as crankshaft regrinding or cylinder reboring are necessary. Apart from carrying out machining operations, these establishments will normally handle the inspection of parts, offer advice concerning reconditioning or renewal and supply new components such as pistons, piston rings and bearing shells. It is recommended that the establishment used is a member of the Federation of Engine Re-Manufacturers, or a similar society.

Always wait until the engine has been completely dismantled, and until all components (especially the cylinder block and the crankshaft) have been inspected, before deciding what service and repair operations must be performed by an engineering works. The condition of these components will be the major factor to consider when determining whether to overhaul the original engine or to buy a reconditioned unit. Do not, therefore, purchase parts or have overhaul work done on other components until they have been thoroughly inspected.

As a final note, to ensure maximum life and minimum trouble from a reconditioned engine, everything must be assembled with care, in a spotlessly-clean environment.

3 Engine/transmission removal – methods and precautions

If you have decided that the engine must be removed for overhaul or major repair work, several preliminary steps should be taken.

Locating a suitable place to work is extremely important. Adequate work space, along with storage space for the car, will be needed. If a workshop or garage is not available, at the very least, a flat, level, clean work surface is required.

Cleaning the engine compartment and engine/transmission before beginning the removal procedure will help keep tools clean and organised.

An engine hoist will also be necessary. Make sure the equipment is rated in excess of the combined weight of the engine and transmission. Safety is of primary importance, considering the potential hazards involved in removing the engine/transmission from the car.

The help of an assistant is essential. Apart from the safety aspects involved, there are many instances when one person cannot simultaneously perform all of the operations required during engine/transmission removal.

Plan the operation ahead of time. Before starting work, arrange for the hire of or obtain all of the tools and equipment you will need.

4.5a Remove the fuse/relay box from its mounting bracket . . .

4.5b . . . and disconnect the three wiring connectors (arrowed)

Some of the equipment necessary to perform engine/transmission removal and installation safely (in addition to an engine hoist) is as follows: a heavy duty trolley jack, complete sets of spanners and sockets as described in the rear of this manual, wooden blocks, and plenty of rags and cleaning solvent for mopping-up spilled oil, coolant and fuel. If the hoist must be hired, make sure that you arrange for it in advance, and perform all of the operations possible without it beforehand. This will save you money and time.

Plan for the car to be out of use for quite a while. An engineering machine shop or engine reconditioning specialist will be required to perform some of the work which cannot be accomplished without special equipment. These places often have a busy schedule, so it would be a good idea to consult them before removing the engine, in order to accurately estimate the amount of time required to rebuild or repair components that may need work.

During the engine/transmission removal procedure, it is advisable to make notes of the locations of all brackets, cable ties, earthing points, etc, as well as how the wiring harnesses, hoses and electrical connections are attached and routed around the engine and engine compartment. An effective way of doing this is to take a series of photographs of the various components before they are disconnected or removed; the resulting photographs will prove invaluable when the engine/transmission is refitted.

Always be extremely careful when removing and refitting the engine/transmission. Serious injury can result from careless actions. Plan ahead and take your time, and a job of this nature, although major, can be accomplished successfully.

The engine and transmission assembly is removed downwards from the engine compartment on all models described in this manual.

4 Engine and transmission – removal, separation, connection and refitting

Note: The engine is lowered from the engine compartment as a complete unit with the transmission; the two are then separated for overhaul.

Removal

1 Remove the bonnet as described in Chapter 11.
2 Remove the battery and battery tray as described in Chapter 5A.
3 Carry out the following operations, using the information given in Chapter 4A:
  a) Remove the air cleaner assembly.
  b) Depressurise the fuel system, and disconnect the fuel feed hose at the quick-release connection on the fuel rail.
  c) On SOHC (8-valve) engines, disconnect the accelerator cable.
4 Remove the cover from the fuse/relay box on the left-hand side of the engine compartment.
5 Remove the fuse/relay box from its mounting bracket by disengaging the locating

lugs at each end. Disconnect the wiring multi-plug connector on the underside of the fuse relay box, and the two multi-plug connectors on the side of the fuse/relay box mounting bracket (see illustrations). Note that on certain models there is only one multi-plug connector on the fuse/relay box mounting bracket.
6 Prise out the grommet and disconnect the brake servo vacuum hose from the front of the servo unit. Release the hose from the retaining clip on the bulkhead.
7 Disconnect the evaporative emission control hose at the quick-release connection on the inlet manifold.
8 On DOHC (16-valve) engines, disconnect the wiring connector at the acceleration sensor, and release the sensor wiring from the cable clips (see illustration).

Manual transmission models

9 Disconnect the gearchange selector cable end fittings from the transmission lever ball-studs (see illustration). Undo the three bolts securing the selector cable support bracket to the transmission and move the bracket and cables to one side.
10 Unbolt the clutch slave cylinder from the top of the transmission then fit a cable-tie

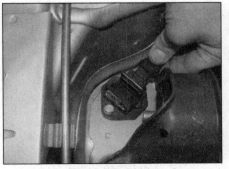

4.8 On DOHC (16-valve) engines, disconnect the wiring connector at the acceleration sensor (arrowed)

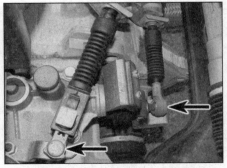

4.9 Disconnect the selector cable end fittings (arrowed) from the transmission lever ball-studs – manual transmission models

4.12a Disconnect the main wiring harness connector (arrowed) at the top of the transmission . . .

4.12b . . . then unscrew the bolt (arrowed) and disconnect the transmission earth lead – automatic transmission models

4.13 Extract the retaining clip (arrowed) and release the selector cable end fitting – automatic transmission models

around it to prevent the piston from being ejected. Position the cylinder to one side.

11 Disconnect the wiring connector from the reversing light switch on the front of the transmission, then unscrew the nut and disconnect the transmission earth lead from the top of the unit.

Automatic transmission models

12 Disconnect the main wiring harness connector at the top of the transmission, then unscrew the bolt and disconnect the transmission earth lead at the front of the unit **(see illustrations)**.

13 Extract the retaining clip and release the selector cable end fitting from the starter inhibitor/reversing light switch **(see illustration)**. Undo the two bolts securing the selector cable support bracket to the transmission and move the bracket and cable to one side.

All models

14 Firmly apply the handbrake, then jack up the front of the car and support it securely on axle stands (see *Jacking and vehicle support*). Remove both front roadwheels. In order to remove the engine/transmission assembly in an upright position from under the vehicle, there must be a minimum clearance of approximately 700 mm between the floor and the front crossmember. Additional height is necessary if the assembly is to be lowered onto a trolley.

15 Remove the right-hand wheel arch liner main and centre panels.

16 Carry out the following with reference to Chapter 1:

a) *Drain the engine oil.*
b) *Drain the cooling system.*
c) *On models with automatic transmission, drain the automatic transmission fluid.*
d) *On models with air conditioning, remove the auxiliary drivebelt.*

17 Identify the coolant heater hoses on the bulkhead for position, then loosen the clips and disconnect the hoses **(see illustration)**. Similarly disconnect the radiator top hose from the radiator and thermostat housing.

18 On models with air conditioning, unbolt the air conditioning compressor and secure it in a suitable position clear of the engine as far as the flexible hoses will allow. **Do not disconnect the air conditioning refrigerant pipes/hoses.**

19 On models with automatic transmission, remove the clips and disconnect the transmission fluid cooler hoses at their transmission connections.

20 Remove the exhaust manifold as described in Chapter 4A.

21 Undo the bolts securing the exhaust system mounting brackets to the underbody, then move the system to one side.

22 Unscrew the nuts retaining the track rod ends on the swivel hubs and use a balljoint separator tool to disconnect them.

23 Unscrew the two bolts securing the left-hand swivel hub assembly to the front suspension strut, then move the hub assembly outwards.

24 Remove the retaining clip securing the left-hand driveshaft inner CV joint gaiter to the joint body. Pull the driveshaft and spider out of the joint body and move the driveshaft clear of the engine/transmission **(see illustration)**. Suitably cover the joint body and the driveshaft spider to prevent the escape of grease.

25 Repeat paragraphs 23 and 24 to disconnect the right-hand driveshaft.

26 Using suitable spacers and washers, refit the engine right-hand lifting eye which was previously removed with the exhaust manifold.

27 Attach a suitable hoist to the engine right-hand lifting eye and the left-hand lifting eye on the transmission. To prevent the engine/transmission assembly tipping backward during removal, a third lifting eye, fabricated from scrap metal or similar should be secured to a suitable location in the vicinity of the alternator. Attach the hoist to the additional eye and evenly take the weight of the engine/transmission.

28 Working beneath the car, unscrew the bolts and nuts securing the rear engine mounting to the subframe and transmission, and withdraw the mounting.

29 In the engine compartment, unscrew the nuts securing the right-hand engine mounting to the body and to the bracket on the cylinder head. Lift the mounting assembly off the studs and remove it from the engine compartment.

30 Unscrew the centre nut securing the left-hand engine/transmission mounting stud to the bracket on the body.

31 Carefully lower the engine/transmission from the engine compartment taking care not to damage the surrounding components. Ideally lower the unit onto a low trolley so that it may be withdrawn from under the car. Disconnect the hoist from the engine/transmission assembly.

Separation

32 Rest the engine/transmission assembly on a firm, flat surface, and use wooden blocks as wedges to keep the unit steady.

4.17 Disconnect the coolant heater hoses (arrowed) at their bulkhead connections

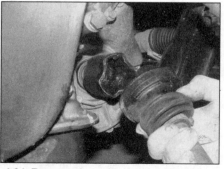

4.24 Remove the gaiter retaining clip and pull the driveshaft and spider out of the CV joint body

33 Disconnect all the individual wiring connectors from the various components on the engine and transmission to enable the main engine wiring harness to be removed. Make notes or attach labels to each connector to aid reconnection.

34 Detach the wiring harness support brackets and plastic ducting mountings, release the relevant cable ties and remove the complete harness assembly from the engine/transmission.

35 Remove the starter motor (Chapter 5A).

36 Undo the bolts and remove the support brace linking the transmission to the cylinder block.

37 Unbolt and remove the cover plate from the base of the transmission bellhousing.

Manual transmission models

38 Ensure that both engine and transmission are individually supported, then remove the remaining bolts securing the transmission bellhousing to the engine. Note the correct fitted positions of each bolt (and the relevant brackets) to aid refitting.

39 Withdraw the transmission from the engine, ensuring that the weight of the transmission is not allowed to hang on the input shaft while it is engaged with the clutch friction plate.

40 If they are loose, remove the locating dowels from the engine or transmission.

Automatic transmission models

41 Using a socket on the crankshaft sprocket centre bolt, turn the crankshaft in the normal direction of rotation until one of the four torque converter retaining bolts is accessible through the opening at the base of the transmission bellhousing **(see illustration)**. Undo the first retaining bolt, then turn the crankshaft as necessary and undo the remaining three bolts as they become accessible.

42 Ensure that both engine and transmission are individually supported, then remove the remaining bolts securing the transmission bellhousing to the engine. Note the correct fitted positions of each bolt (and the relevant brackets) to aid refitting.

43 Make sure that the torque converter is pushed fully onto the transmission shaft, then

4.41 Torque converter retaining bolt (arrowed) accessible through the bellhousing opening – automatic transmission models

carefully withdraw the transmission from the engine. If they are loose, remove the locating dowels from the engine or transmission.

44 With the transmission removed, secure the torque converter in position by bolting a length of metal bar to one of the bellhousing flange holes.

Connection

45 If the engine and transmission have not been separated, proceed to paragraph 56.

Manual transmission models

46 Apply a smear of high melting-point grease to the splines of the transmission input shaft. Do not apply too much, otherwise there is a possibility of the grease contaminating the clutch friction plate.

47 Ensure that the locating dowels are correctly positioned in the engine or transmission, and that the release bearing is correctly engaged with the fork.

48 Carefully offer the transmission to the engine, until the locating dowels are engaged. Ensure that the weight of the transmission is not allowed to hang on the input shaft as it is engaged with the clutch friction plate.

49 Refit the engine-to-transmission bolts, ensuring that all the necessary brackets are correctly positioned, and tighten them to the specified torque.

Automatic transmission models

50 Ensure that the torque converter is correctly engaged with the transmission, then carefully offer the transmission to the engine, and engage it on the locating dowels. Refit the engine-to-transmission bolts, ensuring that all the necessary brackets are correctly positioned, and tighten them to the specified torque settings.

51 Align the torque converter holes with the those in the driveplate, and install the retaining bolts. Tighten the torque converter retaining bolts to the specified torque (see Chapter 7B).

All models

52 Refit the cover plate to the base of the transmission bellhousing.

53 Locate the support brace linking the transmission to the cylinder block, then insert the bolts hand-tight. With all the bolts inserted, tighten them securely.

54 Refit the starter motor (see Chapter 5A).

55 Refit and reconnect the wiring harness to the components on the engine/transmission assembly making sure it is routed correctly.

Refitting

56 Locate the engine/transmission assembly beneath the engine compartment and attach the hoist to the lifting eyes.

57 Carefully lift the assembly up into the engine compartment taking care not to damage the surrounding components.

58 Engage the left-hand engine/transmission mounting stud with the mounting, then refit the retaining nut, moderately tightened.

59 Locate the right-hand engine/transmission mounting over the studs, refit the nuts and tighten them to the specified torque. With the engine/transmission assembly now supported, tighten the left-hand mounting nut to the specified torque.

60 Working beneath the vehicle, refit the rear engine mounting and tighten the bolts to the specified torque.

61 Disconnect the hoist from the engine and transmission lifting eyes and remove the hoist from under the vehicle.

62 The remainder of the refitting procedure is the direct reverse of the removal procedure, noting the following points:

a) Ensure that all hoses are correctly routed and are secured with the correct hose clips, where applicable. If the hose clips cannot be used again; proprietary worm-drive clips should be fitted in their place.

b) Refill the engine and automatic transmission with the correct quantity and type of lubricant, as described in Chapter 1.

c) Refill the cooling system as described in Chapter 1.

d) Where applicable, check and if necessary adjust the accelerator cable with reference to Chapter 4A.

e) When the engine is started for the first time, check for air, coolant, lubricant and fuel leaks from manifolds, hoses, etc. If the engine has been overhauled, read the notes in Section 19 before attempting to start it.

5 Engine overhaul – dismantling sequence

It is preferable to dismantle and work on the engine with it mounted on a portable engine stand. These stands can generally be hired from a tool hire shop. Before the engine is mounted on a stand, the flywheel/driveplate should be removed, so that the stand bolts can be tightened into the end of the cylinder block.

If a stand is not available, it is possible to dismantle the engine with it blocked up on a sturdy workbench, or on the floor. Be extra careful not to tip or drop the engine when working without a stand.

If a reconditioned engine is to be obtained, or if the original engine is to be overhauled, the external components in the following list must be removed first. These components can then be transferred to the reconditioned engine, or refitted to the existing engine after overhaul.

a) Alternator (including mounting brackets, where fitted) (Chapter 5A).

b) Engine mounting brackets (Chapter 2A and 2B).

c) The ignition system and HT components including all sensors, HT leads and spark plugs (Chapters 1 and 5B).

d) The fuel injection system components (Chapter 4A).

e) Inlet manifold (Chapter 4A).
f) All remaining electrical switches, actuators and sensors and the engine wiring harness (Chapters 4A and 5B).
g) Engine oil dipstick.
h) Oil filter (Chapter 1).
i) Cooling system components (Chapter 3).
j) Flywheel/driveplate (Chapter 2A and 2B).
k) Clutch components – manual transmission (Chapter 6).

Note: When removing the external components from the engine, pay close attention to details that may be helpful or important during refitting. Note the fitted position of gaskets, seals, spacers, pins, washers, bolts, and other small components.

If a 'short' engine is to be obtained (cylinder block, crankshaft, pistons and connecting rods all assembled), then the cylinder head, sump, oil pump, timing belt, sprockets and tensioner will have to be removed also.

If a complete overhaul of the existing engine is being undertaken, the engine can be dismantled, in the order given below.
a) Flywheel/driveplate.
b) Timing belt, sprockets, and tensioner.
c) Inlet manifold.
d) Cylinder head.
e) Sump.
f) Oil pump.
g) Pistons/connecting rods.
h) Crankshaft.

6 Cylinder head – dismantling

Note: New and reconditioned cylinder heads are available from the manufacturer, and from engine reconditioning specialists. Some specialist tools are required for dismantling and inspection, and new components may not be readily available. It may therefore be more practical and economical to obtain a reconditioned head, rather than overhaul the original head.

1 During dismantling, it is essential that each valve is stored together with its collets, retainer, spring, and spring seat. The valves should also be kept in their correct sequence,

6.1 Keep groups of components together in labelled bags or boxes

6.6b . . . and extract the two split collets from the top of the valve stem

unless they are so badly worn that they are to be renewed. If they are going to be kept and used again, place each valve assembly in a labelled polythene bag or similar small container **(see illustration)**. Number the bags or containers 1 to 8, or 1 to 8 inlet, and 1 to 8 exhaust, as applicable. Note that No 1 valve is at the timing belt end of the engine.
2 Remove the cylinder head as described in Part A or B of this Chapter (as applicable).
3 Undo the retaining nut and slide the timing belt tensioner off the mounting stud.
4 Undo the bolts and remove the thermostat housing from the left-hand end of the cylinder head. Recover the housing gasket.
5 On SOHC (8-valve) engines, if not already done, remove the camshaft and cam followers

6.6a Compress the valve spring using a valve spring compressor . . .

6.7a Release the compressor, and remove the spring retainer . . .

as described in Part A of this Chapter, and the spark plugs as described in Chapter 1.
6 Starting with valve No 1, compress the valve spring using a spring compressor and extract the two split collets from the top of the valve stem **(see illustrations)**. It may be necessary to tap the jaw of the compressor, directly over the spring, with a light hammer to free the spring retainer.
7 Release the compressor, and remove the spring retainer and spring **(see illustrations)**.
8 Using pliers, if necessary, extract the valve stem oil seal from the top of the guide, then lift off the spring seat **(see illustrations)**.
9 Withdraw the valve through the combustion chamber, then remove all the remaining valves in the same way.

6.7b . . . and valve spring

6.8a Extract the valve stem oil seal from the top of the guide . . .

6.8b . . . then lift off the spring seat

7 Cylinder head and valves – cleaning and inspection

Cleaning

1 Remove all traces of old gasket material from the cylinder head. Proprietary solvents are available for this purpose, but satisfactory results can be achieved by using a hard plastic or wood scraper to remove all traces of gasket and carbon.

2 Similarly, remove the carbon from the combustion chambers and ports, then wash the cylinder head thoroughly with paraffin or a suitable solvent.

3 Scrape off any heavy carbon deposits that may have formed on the valves, then use a power-operated wire brush to remove deposits from the valve heads and stems.

Inspection

Cylinder head

4 Inspect the head thoroughly for cracks, evidence of coolant leakage, and other damage. If significant defects are found, a new cylinder head should be obtained.

5 Use a straight-edge and feeler blade to check that the cylinder head gasket surface is not distorted. If it is, it may be possible to have it machined, provided that the cylinder head thickness is not excessively reduced. As no specifications of permissible distortion limits or cylinder head thickness tolerances are given by the manufacturer, seek the advice of an engine reconditioning specialist if distortion is apparent.

6 Examine the valve seats in each of the combustion chambers. If they are severely pitted, cracked, or burned, they will need to be renewed or recut by an engine reconditioning specialist. If they are only slightly pitted, this can be removed by grinding-in the valve heads and seats with fine valve-grinding compound, as described below.

7 Check the valve guides for wear by inserting the relevant valve, and checking for side-to-side motion of the valve. A very small amount of movement is acceptable. If the movement seems excessive, remove the valve. Measure the valve stem diameter (see below), and renew the valve if it is worn. If the valve stem is not worn, the wear must be in the valve guide, and the guide must be renewed. The renewal of valve guides should be carried out by an engine reconditioning specialist, who will have the necessary tools available.

8 If renewing the valve guides, the valve seats should be recut or reground only *after* the guides have been fitted.

Valves

9 Examine the head of each valve for pitting, burning, cracks, and general wear. Check the valve stem for scoring and wear ridges.

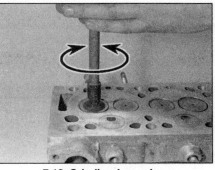

7.13 Grinding-in a valve

Rotate the valve, and check for any obvious indication that it is bent. Look for pits or excessive wear on the tip of each valve stem. Renew any valve that shows any such signs of wear or damage.

10 If the valve appears satisfactory at this stage, measure the valve stem diameter at several points using a micrometer. Any significant difference in the readings obtained indicates wear of the valve stem. Should any of these conditions be apparent, the valve(s) must be renewed.

11 If the valves are in satisfactory condition, they should be ground (lapped) into their respective seats, to ensure a smooth, gas-tight seal. If the seat is only lightly pitted, or if it has been recut, fine grinding compound *only* should be used to produce the required finish. Coarse valve-grinding compound should *not* be used, unless a seat is badly burned or deeply pitted. If this is the case, the cylinder head and valves should be inspected by a specialist, to decide whether seat recutting, or even the renewal of the valve or seat insert (where possible) is required.

12 Valve grinding is carried out as follows, with the head supported upside-down on blocks.

13 Smear a trace of (the appropriate grade of) valve-grinding compound on the seat face, and press a suction grinding tool onto the valve head. With a semi-rotary action, grind the valve head to its seat, lifting the valve occasionally to redistribute the grinding compound **(see illustration)**. A light spring

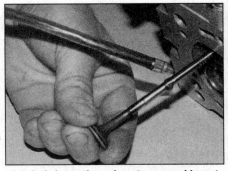

8.1 Lubricate the valve stems, and insert the valves into their original locations

placed under the valve head will greatly ease this operation.

14 If coarse grinding compound is being used, work only until a dull, matt even surface is produced on both the valve seat and the valve, then wipe off the used compound, and repeat the process with fine compound. When a smooth unbroken ring of light grey matt finish is produced on both the valve and seat, the grinding operation is complete. *Do not* grind-in the valves any further than absolutely necessary, or the seat will be prematurely sunk into the cylinder head.

15 When all the valves have been ground-in, carefully wash off *all* traces of grinding compound using paraffin or a suitable solvent, before reassembling the cylinder head.

Valve components

16 Examine the valve springs for signs of damage and discoloration. Stand each spring on a flat surface, and check it for squareness. If any of the springs are damaged, distorted or have lost their tension, obtain a complete new set of springs. It is normal to fit new springs as a matter of course if a major overhaul is being carried out.

17 Renew the valve stem oil seals regardless of their apparent condition.

8 Cylinder head – reassembly

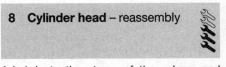

1 Lubricate the stems of the valves, and insert the valves into their original locations **(see illustration)**. If new valves are being fitted, insert them into the locations to which they have been ground.

2 Refit the spring seat then, working on the first valve, dip the new valve stem seal in fresh engine oil. Carefully locate it over the valve and onto the guide. Take care not to damage the seal as it is passed over the valve stem. Use a suitable socket or metal tube to press the seal firmly onto the guide **(see illustration)**.

3 Locate the valve spring on top of its seat, then refit the spring retainer.

4 Compress the valve spring, and locate the

8.2 Use a suitable socket or metal tube to press the valve stem oil seal firmly onto the guide

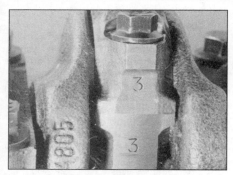

9.4 Connecting rod and big-end cap identification numbers

9.6 Unscrew the retaining bolts and remove the big-end cap and bearing shell

10.5 Main bearing cap identification markings – SOHC (8-valve) engines

split collets in the recess in the valve stem. Release the compressor, then repeat the procedure on the remaining valves.

 HAYNES HiNT *Use a dab of grease to hold the collets in position on the valve stem while the spring compressor is released.*

5 With all the valves installed, place the cylinder head on blocks on the bench and, using a hammer and interposed block of wood, tap the end of each valve stem to settle the components.
6 Refit the thermostat housing as described in Chapter 3.
7 Locate the timing belt tensioner on the mounting stud and refit the retaining nut.
8 On SOHC (8-valve) engines, refit the camshaft and cam followers as described in Part A of this Chapter, and the spark plugs as described in Chapter 1.
9 The cylinder head can then be refitted as described in Part A or B of this Chapter, as applicable.

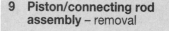
9 Piston/connecting rod assembly – removal

1 Remove the sump and cylinder head as described in Part A or B of this Chapter, as applicable.
2 Undo the two bolts and remove the oil pump pick-up tube.
3 If there is a pronounced wear ridge at the top of any bore, it may be necessary to remove it with a scraper or ridge reamer, to avoid piston damage during removal. Such a ridge indicates excess bore wear.
4 Check to see if the big-end caps and connecting rods are numbered **(see illustration)**. If no numbers are visible, use quick-drying paint, or similar, to mark each connecting rod and big-end cap with its respective cylinder number on the flat machined surface provided. Note that No 1 cylinder is at the timing belt end of the engine.

5 Turn the crankshaft to bring pistons 1 and 4 to BDC (bottom dead centre).
6 Unscrew the bolts from No 1 piston big-end bearing cap, and remove the big-end cap and bearing shell **(see illustration)**. If the bearing shells are to be re-used, tape the cap and the shell together.
7 Using a hammer handle, push the piston up through the bore, and remove it from the top of the cylinder block. Recover the bearing shell, and tape it to the connecting rod for safe-keeping.
8 Loosely refit the big-end cap to the connecting rod, and secure with the bolts – this will help to keep the components in their correct order.
9 Remove No 4 assembly in the same way.
10 Turn the crankshaft through 180° to bring pistons 2 and 3 to BDC (bottom dead centre), and remove them in the same way.

10 Crankshaft – removal

1 Remove the sump, oil pump and pick-up tube, and flywheel/driveplate with reference to the relevant Sections of Chapter 2A or 2B.
2 Remove the pistons and connecting rods, as described in Section 9. If no work is to be done on the pistons and connecting rods there is no need to remove the cylinder head, or to push the pistons out of the cylinder bores. The pistons should just be pushed far enough up the bores that they are positioned clear of the crankshaft journals.
3 Unbolt the crankshaft oil seal housing from the cylinder block and recover the gasket, where fitted.
4 Check the crankshaft endfloat as described in Section 13, then proceed as follows.

SOHC (8-valve) engines

5 Note the identification markings on the main bearing caps which should be as follows. One line on the cap nearest the timing belt end, two on the second cap, C on the centre cap, then three and four lines on the

remaining caps **(see illustration)**. If no markings are visible, mark them using quick-drying paint.
6 Slacken and remove the main bearing cap retaining bolts, and lift off each bearing cap. Recover the lower bearing shells, and tape them to their respective caps for safe-keeping.
7 Lift the crankshaft from the crankcase and remove the upper bearing shells from the crankcase. Note that the centre main bearing shell incorporates thrustwashers to control crankshaft endfloat **(see illustration)**. If the shells are to be used again, keep them identified for position.

DOHC (16-valve) engines

8 Working in the **reverse** of the tightening sequence **(see illustration 17.16a)**, progressively slacken and remove the ten outer bolts securing the lower crankcase to the cylinder block.
9 Again, working in the reverse of the tightening sequence, progressively slacken and remove the ten inner (main bearing) bolts.
10 With all the retaining bolts removed, tap around the outer periphery of the lower crankcase using a mallet to break the seal between the lower crankcase and cylinder block. Once the seal is released and the crankcase is clear of the locating dowels, lift it

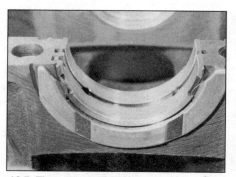

10.7 Thrustwashers located on the centre main bearing shell – SOHC (8-valve) engines

10.10 Removing the lower crankcase from the cylinder block – DOHC (16-valve) engines

up and off the crankshaft and cylinder block (see illustration). Recover the lower main bearing shells, and tape them to their respective locations in the lower crankcase. If the two locating dowels are a loose fit, remove them and store them with the lower crankcase.

11 Lift out the crankshaft, recover the upper main bearing shells, and store them along with the relevant lower bearing shells. Note that the centre main bearing shell incorporates thrustwashers to control crankshaft endfloat.

11 Cylinder block/crankcase – cleaning and inspection

Cleaning

1 Remove all remaining external components and electrical switches/sensors from the block.

2 Where applicable, undo the retaining bolts and remove the piston oil jet spray tubes from inside the cylinder block.

3 Remove all traces of gasket/sealant from the cylinder block, and from the lower crankcase on DOHC (16-valve) engines, taking care not to damage the gasket/sealing surfaces.

4 Remove all oil gallery plugs (where fitted). The plugs are usually very tight – they may have to be drilled out, and the holes retapped.

11.8 To clean the cylinder block threads, run a correct-size tap into the holes

Use new plugs when the engine is reassembled.

5 If any of the castings are extremely dirty, all should be steam-cleaned, or cleaned with a suitable de-greasing agent.

6 After cleaning, clean all oil holes and oil galleries one more time. Flush all internal passages with warm water until the water runs clear. Dry thoroughly, and apply a light film of oil to the cylinder bores to prevent rusting. If possible, use compressed air to speed up the drying process, and to blow out all the oil holes and galleries.

⚠ **Warning: Wear eye protection when using compressed air.**

7 If the castings are not very dirty, they can be cleaned with very hot, soapy water and a stiff brush. Take plenty of time, and do a thorough job. Regardless of the cleaning method used, be sure to clean all oil holes and galleries very thoroughly, and to dry all components well. Protect the cylinder bores as described above, to prevent rusting.

8 All threaded holes must be clean, to ensure accurate torque readings during reassembly. To clean the threads, run the correct-size tap into each of the holes to remove rust, corrosion, thread sealant or sludge, and to restore damaged threads (see illustration). If possible, use compressed air to clear the holes of debris produced by this operation.

⚠ **Warning: Wear eye protection when using compressed air.**

Inspection

9 Visually check the castings for cracks and corrosion. Look for stripped threads in the threaded holes. If there has been any history of internal water leakage, it may be worthwhile having an engine reconditioning specialist check the cylinder block with special equipment. If defects are found, have them repaired if possible, or renew the assembly.

10 Check each cylinder bore for scuffing and scoring. Check for signs of a wear ridge at the top of the cylinder, indicating that the bore is excessively worn.

11 Accurate measuring of the cylinder bores requires specialised equipment and experience. We recommend having the bores measured by an engine reconditioning specialist who will also be able to supply appropriate pistons should a rebore be necessary.

12 If the cylinder bores and pistons are in reasonably good condition, and not worn beyond the specified limits, and if the piston-to-bore clearances can be maintained, then it will only be necessary to renew the piston rings. If this is the case, the cylinder bores must be honed to allow the new piston rings to bed-in correctly and provide the best possible seal. An engine reconditioning specialist will carry out this work at moderate cost.

13 If the engine is not going to be reassembled right away, cover it with a large plastic bag to keep it clean and prevent rusting. If the engine is ready for reassembly Apply suitable sealant to the new oil gallery plugs, and insert them into the holes in the block. Tighten the plugs securely.

14 Where applicable, refit the piston oil jet spray tubes to the cylinder block, and securely tighten the retaining bolts. Bend over the tabs to lock the bolts.

15 Refit all the external components and electrical switches/sensors removed prior to cleaning.

12 Piston/connecting rod assembly – inspection

1 Before the inspection process can begin, the piston/connecting rod assemblies must be cleaned, and the original piston rings removed from the pistons. **Note:** *Always use new piston rings when the engine is reassembled.*

2 Carefully expand the old rings over the top of the pistons. The use of two or three old feeler blades will be helpful in preventing the rings dropping into empty grooves. Be careful not to scratch the piston with the ends of the ring. The rings are brittle, and will snap if they are spread too far. They are also very sharp – protect your hands and fingers.

3 Scrape away all traces of carbon from the top of the piston. A hand-held wire brush (or a piece of fine emery cloth) can be used, once the majority of the deposits have been scraped away.

4 Remove the carbon from the ring grooves in the piston, using an old ring. Break the ring in half to do this (be careful not to cut your fingers – piston rings are sharp). Be careful to remove only the carbon deposits – do not remove any metal, and do not nick or scratch the sides of the ring grooves.

5 Once the deposits have been removed, clean the piston/connecting rod assembly with paraffin or a suitable solvent, and dry thoroughly. Make sure that the oil return holes in the ring grooves are clear.

6 If the pistons and cylinder bores are not damaged or worn excessively, and if the cylinder block does not need to be rebored, the original pistons can be refitted. Normal piston wear shows up as even vertical wear on the piston thrust surfaces, and slight looseness of the top ring in its groove. New piston rings, however, should always be used when the engine is reassembled.

7 Carefully inspect each piston for cracks around the skirt, around the gudgeon pin holes, and at the piston ring lands (between the ring grooves).

8 Look for scoring and scuffing on the piston skirt, holes in the piston crown, and burned areas at the edge of the crown. If the skirt is scored or scuffed, the engine may have been suffering from overheating, and/or abnormal

combustion which caused excessively high operating temperatures. The cooling and lubrication systems should be checked thoroughly. Scorch marks on the sides of the pistons show that blow-by has occurred. A hole in the piston crown, or burned areas at the edge of the piston crown, indicates that abnormal combustion has been occurring. If any of the above problems exist, the causes must be investigated and corrected, or the damage will occur again.

9 Corrosion of the piston, in the form of pitting, indicates that coolant has been leaking into the combustion chamber and/or the crankcase. Again, the cause must be corrected, or the problem may persist in the rebuilt engine.

10 Examine each connecting rod carefully for signs of damage, such as cracks around the big-end and small-end bearings. Check that the rod is not bent or distorted. Damage is highly unlikely, unless the engine has been seized or badly overheated. Detailed checking of the connecting rod assembly can only be carried out by an engine reconditioning specialist with the necessary equipment.

11 On all engines, the gudgeon pins are an interference fit in the connecting rod small-end bearing. Therefore, piston and/or connecting rod renewal should be entrusted to an engine reconditioning specialist who will have the necessary tooling to remove and install the gudgeon pins.

12 Although not specified by Fiat, it is highly recommended that the big-end cap bolts are renewed as a complete set prior to refitting.

---

13 Crankshaft – inspection

Checking endfloat

1 If the crankshaft endfloat is to be checked, this must be done when the crankshaft is still installed in the cylinder block/crankcase, but is free to move.

2 Check the endfloat using a dial gauge in contact with the end of the crankshaft. Push the crankshaft fully one way, and then zero the gauge. Push the crankshaft fully the other way, and check the endfloat. The result can be compared with the figures given in the Specifications, and will give an indication as to whether new thrustwashers are required **(see illustration)**.

3 If a dial gauge is not available, feeler blades can be used. First push the crankshaft fully towards the flywheel end of the engine, then use feeler blades to measure the gap between the crankpin web and the main bearing thrustwasher.

Inspection

4 Clean the crankshaft using paraffin or a suitable solvent, and dry it, preferably with compressed air if available. Be sure to clean

the oil holes with a pipe cleaner or similar probe, to ensure that they are not obstructed.

> ⚠️ **Warning: Wear eye protection when using compressed air.**

5 Check the main and big-end bearing journals for uneven wear, scoring, pitting and cracking.

6 Big-end bearing wear is accompanied by distinct metallic knocking when the engine is running (particularly noticeable when the engine is pulling from low speed) and some loss of oil pressure.

7 Main bearing wear is accompanied by severe engine vibration and rumble – getting progressively worse as engine speed increases – and again by loss of oil pressure.

8 Check the bearing journal for roughness by running a finger lightly over the bearing surface. Any roughness (which will be accompanied by obvious bearing wear) indicates that the crankshaft requires regrinding (where possible) or renewal.

9 Accurate measurement of the crankshaft requires specialised equipment and experience. We recommend having the crankshaft measured by an engine reconditioning specialist who will also be able to supply appropriate bearing shells should a regrind be necessary.

10 If the crankshaft has been reground, check for burrs around the crankshaft oil holes (the holes are usually chamfered, so burrs should not be a problem unless regrinding has been carried out carelessly). Remove any burrs with a fine file or scraper, and thoroughly clean the oil holes as described previously.

---

14 Main and big-end bearings – inspection

Inspection

1 Even though the main and big-end bearings should be renewed during the engine overhaul, the old bearings should be retained for close examination, as they may reveal valuable information about the condition of the engine. Main and big-end bearings are

13.2 Using a dial gauge to check the crankshaft endfloat

available in standard sizes and a range of undersizes to suit reground crankshafts. The engine reconditioner will select the correct bearing shells for a standard or machined crankshaft.

2 Bearing failure can occur due to lack of lubrication, the presence of dirt or other foreign particles, overloading the engine, or corrosion. Regardless of the cause of bearing failure, the cause must be corrected (where applicable) before the engine is reassembled, to prevent it from happening again **(see illustration)**.

3 When examining the bearing shells, remove them from the cylinder block/crankcase, the main bearing caps, the connecting rods and the connecting rod big-end caps. Lay them out on a clean surface in the same general position as their location in the engine. This will enable you to match any bearing problems with the corresponding crankshaft journal. *Do not* touch any shell's bearing surface with your fingers while checking it.

4 Dirt and other foreign matter gets into the engine in a variety of ways. It may be left in the engine during assembly, or it may pass through filters or the crankcase ventilation system. It may get into the oil, and from there into the bearings. Metal chips from machining operations and normal engine wear are often present. Abrasives are sometimes left in engine components after reconditioning, especially when parts are not thoroughly cleaned using the proper cleaning methods. Whatever the source, these foreign objects often end up embedded in the soft bearing material, and are easily recognised. Large particles will not embed in the bearing, and will score or gouge the bearing and journal. The best prevention for this cause of bearing failure is to clean all parts thoroughly, and keep everything spotlessly-clean during

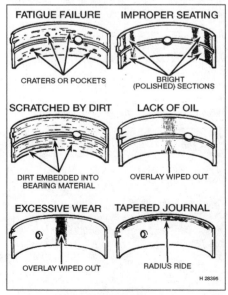

14.2 Typical bearing failures

engine assembly. Frequent and regular engine oil and filter changes are also recommended.

5 Lack of lubrication (or lubrication breakdown) has a number of interrelated causes. Excessive heat (which thins the oil), overloading (which squeezes the oil from the bearing face) and oil leakage (from excessive bearing clearances, worn oil pump or high engine speeds) all contribute to lubrication breakdown. Blocked oil passages, which can be the result of misaligned oil holes in a bearing shell, will also oil-starve a bearing, and destroy it. When lack of lubrication is the cause of bearing failure, the bearing material is wiped or extruded from the steel backing of the bearing. Temperatures may increase to the point where the steel backing turns blue from overheating.

6 Driving habits can have a definite effect on bearing life. Full-throttle, low-speed operation (labouring the engine) puts very high loads on bearings, tending to squeeze out the oil film. These loads cause the bearings to flex, which produces fine cracks in the bearing face (fatigue failure). Eventually, the bearing material will loosen in pieces, and tear away from the steel backing.

7 Short-distance driving leads to corrosion of bearings, because insufficient engine heat is produced to drive off the condensed water and corrosive gases. These products collect in the engine oil, forming acid and sludge. As the oil is carried to the engine bearings, the acid attacks and corrodes the bearing material.

8 Incorrect bearing installation during engine assembly will lead to bearing failure as well. Tight-fitting bearings leave insufficient bearing running clearance, and will result in oil starvation. Dirt or foreign particles trapped behind a bearing shell result in high spots on the bearing, which lead to failure.

9 Do not touch any shell's bearing surface with your fingers during reassembly; there is a risk of scratching the delicate surface, or of depositing particles of dirt on it.

10 As mentioned at the beginning of this Section, the bearing shells should be renewed as a matter of course during engine overhaul; to do otherwise is false economy.

15 Engine overhaul – reassembly sequence

Before reassembly begins, ensure that all new parts have been obtained, and that all necessary tools are available. Read through the entire procedure to familiarise yourself with the work involved, and to ensure that all items necessary for reassembly of the engine are at hand. In addition to all normal tools and materials, thread-locking compound will be needed. A suitable tube of sealant will also be required for the joint faces that are fitted without gaskets. It is recommended that Fiat's own products are used, which are specially formulated for this purpose.

In order to save time and avoid problems, engine reassembly can be carried out in the following order:

a) Crankshaft (Section 17).
b) Piston/connecting rod assemblies (Section 18).
c) Oil pump (see Part A or B of this Chapter – as applicable).
d) Sump (see Part A or B of this Chapter – as applicable).
e) Flywheel/driveplate (see Part A or B of this Chapter – as applicable).
f) Cylinder head (see Part A or B of this Chapter – as applicable).
g) Coolant pump (see Chapter 3).
h) Timing belt tensioner and sprockets, and timing belt (See Part A or B of this Chapter – as applicable).
i) Engine external components.

At this stage, all engine components should be absolutely clean and dry, with all faults repaired. The components should be laid out on a completely clean work surface.

16 Piston rings – refitting

1 Before fitting new piston rings, the ring end gaps must be checked as follows.
2 Lay out the piston/connecting rod assemblies and the new piston ring sets, so that the ring sets will be matched with the same piston and cylinder during the end gap measurement and subsequent engine reassembly.
3 Insert the top ring into the first cylinder, and push it down the bore using the top of the piston. This will ensure that the ring remains square with the cylinder walls. Position the ring near the bottom of the cylinder bore, at the lower limit of ring travel. Note that the top and second compression rings are different. The second ring is easily identified by the step on its lower surface, and by the fact that its outer face is tapered.
4 Measure the end gap using feeler blades.
5 Repeat the procedure with the ring at the top of the cylinder bore, at the upper limit of its travel and compare the measurements with the figures given in the Specifications.
6 If the gap is too small (unlikely if reputable parts are used), it must be enlarged, or the ring ends may contact each other during engine operation, causing serious damage. Ideally, new piston rings providing the correct end gap should be fitted. As a last resort, the end gap can be increased by filing the ring ends very carefully with a fine file. Mount the file in a vice equipped with soft jaws, slip the ring over the file with the ends contacting the file face, and slowly move the ring to remove material from the ends. Take care, as piston rings are sharp, and are easily broken.
7 With new piston rings, it is unlikely that the end gap will be too large. If the gaps are too large, check that you have the correct rings for the engine and for the cylinder bore size.

8 Repeat the checking procedure for each ring in the first cylinder, and then for the rings in the remaining cylinders. Remember to keep rings, pistons and cylinders matched up.
9 Once the ring end gaps have been checked and if necessary corrected, the rings can be fitted to the pistons. Note: Always follow any instructions supplied with the new piston ring sets – different manufacturers may specify different procedures. Do not mix up the top and second compression rings, as they have different cross-sections.
10 Fit the piston rings using the same technique as for removal. Fit the bottom (oil control) ring first, and work up. Ensure that the second compression ring is fitted the correct way up, with its identification mark (either a dot of paint or the word TOP stamped on the ring surface) at the top.
11 Position the rings so that the end gaps are 180° apart and are offset from the gudgeon pin centreline.

17 Crankshaft – bearing selection and refitting

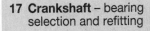

Bearing selection

1 Main bearings for the engines described in this Chapter are available in standard sizes and a range of undersizes to suit reground crankshafts. Refer to your Fiat dealer or engine reconditioning specialist for details.

Refitting

2 Clean the backs of the bearing shells, and the bearing locations in both the cylinder block and the main bearing caps or lower crankcase.
3 Press the bearing shells into their locations, ensuring that the tab on each shell engages in the notch in the cylinder block or bearing cap/lower crankcase. Note that the bearing shell incorporating the thrustwashers is fitted to the centre main bearing shell location in the cylinder block. Take care not to touch any shell's bearing surface with your fingers.
4 Wipe dry the shells with a lint-free cloth, then liberally lubricate each bearing shell in the cylinder block with clean engine oil.
5 Lower the crankshaft into position so that Nos 2 and 3 cylinder crankpins are at TDC; Nos 1 and 4 cylinder crankpins will be at BDC, ready for fitting No 1 piston. Proceed as follows according to engine type.

SOHC (8-valve) engines

6 Lubricate the lower bearing shells in the main bearing caps with clean engine oil.
7 Fit the main bearing caps to their correct locations, ensuring that they are fitted the correct way round (the bearing shell tab recesses in the block and caps must be on the same side). Insert the bolts loosely.
8 Tighten the main bearing cap bolts to the specified Stage 1 torque wrench setting. Once

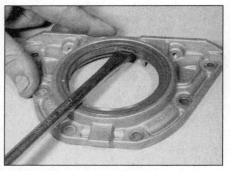

17.10a Use a screwdriver to prise out the oil seal . . .

17.10b . . . locate the new oil seal in the housing . . .

17.10c . . . and use a block of wood to drive it in – SOHC (8-valve) engines

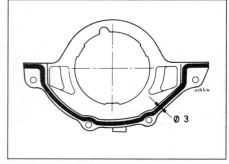

17.11 Application area for silicone sealant on crankshaft oil seal housing – SOHC (8-valve) engines

17.13 Apply a 2.0 mm bead of silicone sealant to the lower crankcase mating surface – DOHC (16-valve) engines

all the bolts have been tightened to the Stage 1 setting, angle-tighten the bolts through the specified Stage 2 angle, using a socket and extension bar. It is recommended that an angle-measuring gauge is used during this stage of the tightening, to ensure accuracy.

9 Check that the crankshaft rotates freely.

10 Prise out the crankshaft oil seal and fit a new seal to the housing (see illustrations).

11 Lubricate the oil seal lips then carefully locate the oil seal housing into position, using a new gasket. If the oil seal housing was originally fitted without a gasket, apply a 3.0 mm bead of RTV silicone sealant to the housing flange (see illustration). Refit the retaining bolts and tighten them securely.

12 Continue with engine reassembly in the sequence given in Section 15.

DOHC (16-valve) engines

Note: At the time of writing there was conflicting information from the manufacturer concerning the lower crankcase retaining bolt torque setting. As it was not possible to confirm the validity of the figures given in the Specifications, consult a Fiat dealer for latest information.

13 Thoroughly degrease the mating surfaces of the cylinder block and the lower crankcase. Apply a 2.0 mm bead of RTV silicone sealant to the lower crankcase mating surface (see illustration).

14 Lubricate the lower bearing shells with clean engine oil, then refit the lower crankcase, ensuring that the shells are not displaced, and that the locating dowels engage correctly.

15 Install the ten inner (main bearing) bolts, and the ten outer bolts securing the lower crankcase to the cylinder block. Screw all the bolts in until they are just making contact with the lower crankcase.

16 Working in sequence, tighten the ten inner (main bearing) bolts to the Stage 1 torque setting given in the Specifications. Once all the ten inner bolts have been tightened to the Stage 1 setting, angle-tighten the bolts through the specified Stage 2 angle, using a socket and extension bar. It is recommended that an angle-measuring gauge is used during this stage of the tightening, to ensure accuracy (see illustrations).

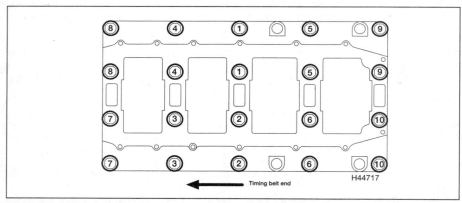

17.16a Lower crankcase retaining bolt tightening sequence – DOHC (16-valve) engines

17.16b Tighten the ten inner lower crankcase bolts to the Stage 1 torque setting using a torque wrench . . .

17.16c . . . then through the Stage 2 angle using an angle-measuring gauge – DOHC (16-valve) engines

17 Working in the same sequence as for the inner (main bearing) bolts, tighten the ten outer bolts to the Stage 1 torque setting, then through the Stage 2 angle.

18 With the lower crankcase in place, check that the crankshaft rotates freely.

19 Lubricate the oil seal lips then carefully locate a new oil seal housing into position **(see illustration)**. Refit the retaining bolts and tighten them securely.

20 Continue with engine reassembly in the sequence given in Section 15.

18 Piston/connecting rod assembly – bearing selection and refitting

Bearing selection

1 Big-end bearings for the engines described in this Chapter are available in standard sizes and a range of undersizes to suit reground crankshafts. Refer to your Fiat dealer or engine reconditioning specialist for details.

Refitting

2 Clean the backs of the bearing shells, and the bearing locations in both the connecting rods and bearing caps.

3 Press the bearing shells into their locations, ensuring that the tab on each shell engages in the notch in the connecting rod and cap. Take care not to touch any shell's bearing surface with your fingers.

4 Note that the following procedure assumes that the crankshaft and main bearing caps/lower crankcase are in place (see Section 17).

5 Wipe dry the shells and connecting rods with a lint-free cloth.

6 Lubricate the cylinder bores, the pistons, and piston rings, then lay out each piston/connecting rod assembly in its respective position.

17.19 Lubricate the oil seal lips then locate a new rear oil seal housing into position – DOHC (16-valve) engines

7 Start with assembly No 1. Position the piston ring gaps as described in Section 16, then clamp them in position with a piston ring compressor.

8 Insert the piston/connecting rod assembly into the top of cylinder No 1, ensuring that the arrow on the piston crown is pointing towards the timing belt end of the engine **(see illustrations)**.

9 Using a block of wood or hammer handle against the piston crown, tap the assembly into the cylinder until the piston crown is flush with the top of the cylinder **(see illustration)**.

10 Ensure that the bearing shell is still correctly installed. Liberally lubricate the crankpin and both bearing shells. Taking care not to mark the cylinder bores, tap the piston/connecting rod assembly down the bore and onto the crankpin.

11 Refit the big-end bearing cap, tightening its retaining bolts finger-tight at first. Note that the faces with the identification marks must match (which means that the bearing shell locating tabs abut each other).

12 Tighten the bearing cap retaining bolts evenly and progressively to the Stage 1 torque setting, then angle-tighten them to the specified Stage 2 angle using an angle-measuring gauge.

13 Once the bearing cap retaining bolts have been correctly tightened, rotate the crankshaft. Check that it turns freely; some stiffness is to be expected if new components have been fitted, but there should be no signs of binding or tight spots.

14 Refit the remaining three piston/connecting rod assemblies in the same way.

15 Continue with engine reassembly in the sequence given in Section 15.

19 Engine – initial start-up after overhaul

1 With the engine refitted in the car, double-check the engine oil and coolant levels. Make a final check that everything has been reconnected, and that there are no tools or rags left in the engine compartment.

2 Start the engine, noting that this may take a little longer than usual, due to the fuel system components having been disturbed. Make sure that the oil pressure warning light goes out then allow the engine to idle.

3 While the engine is idling, check for fuel, water and oil leaks. Don't be alarmed if there are some odd smells and smoke from parts getting hot and burning off oil deposits.

4 Assuming all is well, keep the engine idling until hot water is felt circulating through the top hose, then switch off the engine.

5 After a few minutes, recheck the oil and coolant levels as described in *Weekly checks*, and top-up as necessary.

6 Note that there is no need to retighten the cylinder head bolts once the engine has first run after reassembly.

7 If new pistons, rings or crankshaft bearings have been fitted, the engine must be treated as new, and run-in for the first 500 miles (800 km). *Do not* operate the engine at full-throttle, or allow it to labour at low engine speeds in any gear. It is recommended that the oil and filter be changed at the end of this period.

18.8a Insert the piston/connecting rod assembly into the top of cylinder No 1 . . .

18.8b . . . ensuring that the arrow on the piston crown is pointing towards the timing belt end of the engine

18.9 Tap the assembly into the cylinder using a block of wood or hammer handle

Notes

Chapter 3
Cooling, heating and air conditioning systems

Contents

Degrees of difficulty

Easy, suitable for novice with little experience	Fairly easy, suitable for beginner with some experience	Fairly difficult, suitable for competent DIY mechanic	Difficult, suitable for experienced DIY mechanic	Very difficult, suitable for expert DIY or professional

Specifications

General
Expansion tank relief valve opening pressure .... 0.99 bar

Thermostat
Opening temperature:
   Starts to open .... 85 to 89°C
   Fully open .... 100°C

Coolant temperature sensor
Resistance:
   At 0°C .... 5.97 k ohms
   At 10°C .... 3.81 k ohms
   At 20°C .... 2.50 k ohms
   At 40°C .... 1.15 k ohms
   At 50°C .... 0.80 k ohms
   At 60°C .... 0.57 k ohms
   At 80°C .... 0.30 k ohms
   At 90°C .... 0.24 k ohms
   At 100°C .... 0.17 k ohms

Torque wrench settings	Nm	lbf ft
Coolant pump securing nut/bolts	10	7
Coolant temperature sensor	34	25
Thermostat housing bolts	10	7

1 General information and precautions

General information

The engine cooling system is of pressurised type, comprising a coolant pump driven by the timing belt, a crossflow radiator, a coolant expansion tank, an electric cooling fan, a thermostat, heater matrix, and all associated hoses and switches.

The system functions as follows: the coolant pump circulates cold water around the cylinder block and head passages, and through the inlet manifold, heater matrix and throttle body to the thermostat housing.

When the engine is cold, the thermostat remains closed and prevents coolant from circulating through the radiator. When the coolant reaches a predetermined temperature, the thermostat opens, and the coolant passes through the top hose to the radiator. As the coolant circulates through the radiator, it is cooled by the in-rush of air when the car is in forward motion. The airflow is supplemented by the action of the electric cooling fan, when necessary.

When the engine is at normal operating temperature, the coolant expands, and some of it is displaced into the expansion tank integrated into the side of the radiator. Coolant collects in the tank, and is returned to the radiator when the system cools.

The two-speed electric cooling fan is mounted on the radiator and controlled by the engine management electronic control unit in conjunction with the engine coolant temperature sensor.

Precautions

• *Do not attempt to remove the expansion tank pressure cap, or to disturb any part of the cooling system while the engine is hot, as there is a high risk of scalding. If the expansion tank pressure cap must be removed before the engine and radiator have fully cooled (even though this is not recommended), the pressure in the cooling system must first be relieved. Cover the cap with a thick layer of cloth, to avoid scalding, and slowly unscrew the pressure cap until a hissing sound is heard. When the hissing stops, indicating that the pressure has reduced, slowly unscrew the pressure cap until it can be removed; if more hissing sounds are heard, wait until they have stopped before unscrewing the cap completely. At all times, keep your face well away from the pressure cap opening, and protect your hands.*
• *Do not allow antifreeze to come into contact with your skin, or with the painted surfaces of the vehicle. Rinse off spills immediately, with plenty of water. Never leave antifreeze lying around in an open container, or in a puddle in the driveway or on the garage floor. Children and pets are attracted by its sweet smell, but antifreeze can be fatal if ingested.*
• *If the engine is hot, the electric cooling fan may start rotating even if the engine and ignition are switched off. Be careful to keep your hands, hair, and any loose clothing well clear when working in the engine compartment.*

2 Cooling system hoses – disconnection and renewal

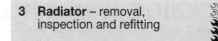

1 The number, routing and pattern of hoses will vary according to model, but the same basic procedure applies. Before commencing work, make sure that the new hoses are to hand, along with new hose clips if needed. It is good practice to renew the hose clips at the same time as the hoses.
2 Drain the cooling system, as described in Chapter 1, saving the coolant if it is fit for re-use. Apply a little penetrating oil onto the hose clips if they are corroded.
3 Release the hose clips from the hose concerned. Three types of clip are used; worm-drive, spring, and crimped. The worm-drive clip is released by turning its screw anti-clockwise. The spring clip is released by squeezing its tags together with pliers, at the same time working the clip away from the hose stub. The crimped clips are not re-usable, and are best cut off with snips or side-cutters.
4 Unclip any wires, cables or other hoses which may be attached to the hose being removed. Make notes for reference when reassembling if necessary.
5 Release the hose from its stubs with a twisting motion. Be careful not to damage the stubs on delicate components such as the radiator, or thermostat housings. If the hose is stuck fast, the best course is often to cut it off

using a sharp knife, but again be careful not to damage the stubs.
6 Before fitting the new hose, smear the stubs with washing-up liquid or a suitable rubber lubricant to aid fitting. Do not use oil or grease, which may attack the rubber.
7 Fit the hose clips over the ends of the hose, then fit the hose over its stubs. Work the hose into position. When satisfied, locate and tighten the hose clips.
8 Refill the cooling system as described in Chapter 1 then run the engine and check that there are no leaks.
9 Recheck the tightness of the hose clips on any new hoses after a few hundred miles.
10 Top-up the coolant level if necessary.

3 Radiator – removal, inspection and refitting

Note: *If leakage is the reason for removing the radiator, bear in mind that minor leaks can often be cured using proprietary radiator sealing compound, with the radiator in situ.*

Removal

1 Disconnect the battery negative terminal (refer to *Disconnecting the battery* in the Reference Chapter).
2 Drain the cooling system as described in Chapter 1.
3 Remove the electric cooling fan assembly as described in Section 5.
4 Undo the bolt securing the horn mounting bracket to the front body panel. Disconnect the wiring connectors and remove the horn.

Models with automatic transmission

5 Remove the front bumper as described in Chapter 11.
6 Working through the bumper aperture, undo the bolts securing the automatic transmission fluid cooler pipes to the front of the radiator **(see illustrations)**.
7 Undo the bolt securing the automatic

3.6a Undo the bolts (arrowed) securing the automatic transmission fluid cooler pipes to the right-hand . . .

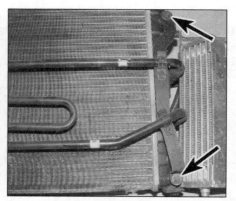

3.6b . . . and left-hand sides of the radiator (shown with radiator removed)

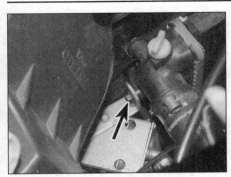

3.7 Undo the bolt (arrowed) securing the automatic transmission fluid heat exchanger to the radiator

3.11 Carefully manoeuvre the radiator up and out of the engine compartment

4.6 Unscrew the bolts, and remove the thermostat housing from the cylinder head

transmission fluid heat exchanger to the left-hand side of the radiator **(see illustration)**.

8 Lift the heat exchanger upward to disengage the lower mounting lug from the grommet on the crossmember. Move the heat exchanger and fluid cooler pipes forward just sufficiently to allow removal of the radiator.

Models with air conditioning

9 Remove the front bumper as described in Chapter 11.

10 Working through the bumper aperture, undo the bolts securing the air conditioning condenser to the front of the radiator. Suitably tie or support the condenser to avoid straining the refrigerant pipes.

All models

11 Tip the top of the radiator toward the engine and lift it upward to disengage the lower mounting lugs from the grommets on the crossmember. Carefully manoeuvre the radiator up and out of the engine compartment **(see illustration)**. Recover the lower mounting grommets if they are loose.

Inspection

12 If the radiator has been removed due to suspected blockage, it may be flushed out as described in Chapter 1. Clean dirt and debris from the radiator fins, using an air line (in which case, wear eye protection) or a soft brush. Be careful, as the fins are sharp, and can also be easily damaged.

13 If necessary, a radiator specialist can perform a flow test on the radiator, to establish whether an internal blockage exists.

14 A leaking radiator must be referred to a specialist for permanent repair. Do not attempt to weld or solder a leaking radiator, as damage to the plastic components may result.

15 Inspect the radiator rubber mounting grommets, and renew them if necessary.

Refitting

16 Refitting is a reversal of removal, bearing in mind the following points:
  a) *Ensure that the radiator lower lugs engage correctly with the lower mounting grommets.*

  b) *On completion, refill the cooling system as described in Chapter 1.*

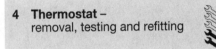

4 Thermostat –
removal, testing and refitting

General

1 The thermostat housing is bolted to the left-hand end of the cylinder head. The thermostat itself cannot be separated from the housing and can only be renewed as part of a complete assembly.

Removal

2 Drain the cooling system as described in Chapter 1.

3 Remove the air cleaner assembly as described in Chapter 4A.

4 Remove the battery and battery tray as described in Chapter 5A.

5 Remove the clip and detach the radiator top hose from the thermostat housing.

6 Unscrew the two securing bolts, and remove the thermostat housing from the cylinder head **(see illustration)**. If it sticks, tap it gently first on one side and then the other to free it – do not lever between the mating faces. Recover the remains of the old gasket.

Testing

7 A rough test of the thermostat may be made by suspending it with a piece of string in a container full of water. Heat the water to bring it to the boil and observe the movement of the valve shaft through the inlet port.

8 The thermostat valve must be fully open by the time the water boils. If not, renew the complete thermostat/housing assembly.

9 If a thermometer is available, the precise opening temperature of the thermostat may be determined; compare with the figures given in the Specifications. The opening temperature is also marked on the thermostat housing.

10 Note that a thermostat which fails to close completely as the water cools must also be renewed.

Refitting

11 Ensure that the cylinder head and thermostat housing mating surfaces are completely clean and free from all traces of the old gasket material.

12 Lay a new gasket in position on the cylinder head, then fit the thermostat housing and insert retaining bolts. Tighten the bolts to the specified torque.

13 Refit the radiator top hose to the thermostat housing and secure with a new retaining clip.

14 Refit the battery tray and battery as described in Chapter 5A.

15 Refit the air cleaner assembly as described in Chapter 4A.

16 Refill the cooling system as described in Chapter 1.

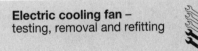

5 Electric cooling fan –
testing, removal and refitting

Testing

1 Detailed fault diagnosis should be carried out by a Fiat dealer using dedicated test equipment, but basic diagnosis can be carried out as follows.

2 If the fan does not appear to work, run the engine until normal operating temperature is reached, then allow it to idle. The fan should cut in within a few minutes (before the warning light illuminates, or the temperature gauge needle enters the red section). If not, switch off the engine and disconnect the cooling fan motor wiring connector.

3 The motor can be tested by disconnecting it from the wiring loom, and connecting a 12 volt supply directly to it. The motor should operate – if not, the motor, or the motor wiring, is faulty.

4 If the motor operates when tested as described, the fault is likely to be in one of the cooling fan relays, the relay fuse, or the engine wiring harness. If these components are satisfactory any further fault diagnosis should be referred to a suitably-equipped Fiat dealer – **do not** attempt to test the engine management electronic control unit.

5.8 Disconnect the wiring connector (arrowed) from the electric fan motor

5.9a Undo the bolt (arrowed) below the bonnet lock . . .

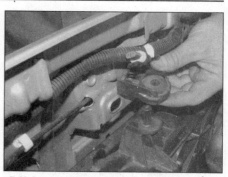

5.9b . . . and remove the upper mounting bracket from the top of the fan shroud

5.10a Undo the bolts (arrowed) securing the fan shroud to the right-hand . . .

5.10b . . . and left-hand sides of the radiator . . .

5.10c . . . then lift out the cooling fan assembly

Removal

5 Disconnect the battery negative terminal (refer to *Disconnecting the battery* in the Reference Chapter).

6 On DOHC (16-valve) engines, remove the air cleaner assembly as described in Chapter 4A.

7 Where applicable, disconnect the wiring connectors from the fan motor resistor.

8 Disconnect the fan motor wiring connector (see illustration). Release the wiring harness from the clips on the fan shroud.

9 Undo the bolt located below the bonnet lock assembly, and lift the upper mounting bracket off the top of the fan shroud (see illustrations).

10 Undo the four bolts securing the fan shroud to the radiator, then lift out the cooling fan assembly (see illustrations).

Refitting

11 Refitting is a reversal of removal.

6 Coolant temperature sensor – testing, removal and refitting

Testing

1 The sensor is located at the left-hand end of the inlet manifold, and can be identified by its green wiring connector (see illustration).

2 The unit contains a thermistor – an electronic component whose electrical resistance decreases at a predetermined rate as its temperature rises.

3 The engine management ECU supplies the sensor with a set voltage and then, by measuring the current flowing in the sensor circuit, it determines the engine temperature. This information is then used, in conjunction with other inputs, to control the engine management system and associated components. The sensor signal is also used to operate the temperature gauge and/or warning light on the instrument panel.

4 If the sensor circuit should fail to provide plausible information, the ECU back-up facility will override the sensor signal. In this event, the ECU assumes a predetermined setting which will allow the engine management system to operate, albeit at reduced efficiency. When this occurs, the engine warning light on the instrument panel will illuminate, and the advice of a Fiat dealer should be sought. The sensor itself can be tested by removing it, and checking the resistances at various temperatures using an ohmmeter (heat the sensor in a container of water, and monitor the temperature with a thermometer). The resistance values are given in the Specifications.

5 Refer to Chapter 4A for further details of the engine management system.

Removal

6 Remove the air cleaner assembly as described in Chapter 4A.

7 Remove the battery and battery tray as described in Chapter 5A.

8 Partially drain the cooling system to just below the level of the sensor (see Chapter 1). Alternatively, have ready a suitable bung to plug the aperture in the housing when the sensor is removed.

9 Disconnect the wiring connector from the sensor.

10 Carefully unscrew the sensor and recover the sealing ring. If the system has not been drained, plug the sensor aperture to prevent further coolant loss.

Refitting

11 Check the condition of the sealing ring and renew it if necessary.

6.1 Engine coolant temperature sensor location (arrowed) on the left-hand end of the inlet manifold

12 Refitting is a reversal of removal, tightening the sensor to the specified torque. Refill (or top-up) the cooling system as described in Chapter 1 and *Weekly checks*.
13 On completion, start the engine and run it until it reaches normal operating temperature. Continue to run the engine until the cooling fan cuts in and out correctly.

7 Coolant pump – removal, inspection and refitting

Removal

1 Disconnect the battery negative terminal (refer to *Disconnecting the battery* in the Reference Chapter).
2 Drain the cooling system and remove the auxiliary drivebelt as described in Chapter 1.
3 Remove the timing belt as described in Chapter 2A or 2B, as applicable.
4 Unscrew the retaining nut and the three bolts and withdraw the coolant pump (**see illustration**). If the pump is stuck, tap it gently using a soft-faced mallet – **do not** lever between the pump and cylinder block mating faces.

Inspection

5 Check the pump body and impeller for signs of excessive corrosion or evidence of coolant leakage. Turn the impeller, and check for stiffness due to corrosion, or roughness due to excessive end play. If any of these conditions are apparent, the pump must be renewed as a complete assembly.

Refitting

6 Commence refitting by thoroughly cleaning all traces of sealant from the mating faces of the pump and cylinder block.
7 Apply a continuous bead of RTV sealant to the cylinder block mating face of the pump, taking care not to apply excessive sealant, which may enter the pump itself (**see illustration**).
8 Place the pump in position in the cylinder block, then refit and tighten the nut and bolts to the specified torque.
9 Refit the timing belt as described in Chapter 2A or 2B.
10 Refit the auxiliary drivebelt and refill the cooling system as described in Chapter 1.
11 Reconnect the battery negative terminal.

8 Heater/ventilation components – removal and refitting

Complete heater assembly

 Warning: On models equipped with air conditioning, do not attempt to remove the complete heater assembly as this entails

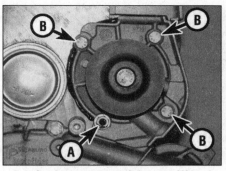

7.4 Coolant pump retaining nut (A) and retaining bolts (B)

disconnection of refrigerant lines. Entrust this work to a Fiat dealer, or air conditioning specialist.
Note: *This is an involved procedure, and it is recommended that the following Section is read thoroughly before commencing work. Plenty of time should be allowed to complete the operation. During dismantling, make notes on the routing of all wiring and cables, and the locations of all fixings, to aid reassembly.*

Removal

1 Disconnect the battery negative terminal (refer to *Disconnecting the battery* in the Reference Chapter).
2 Drain the cooling system as described in Chapter 1.
3 Remove the complete facia assembly as described in Chapter 11.
4 Undo the bolts and remove the tubular support beam from the front of the heater assembly (**see illustration**).
5 Working in the engine compartment, remove the clips and detach the heater coolant hoses from their bulkhead connections.
6 From within the engine compartment, remove the protective plastic caps to expose the two heater assembly mounting studs. Unscrew and remove the nuts from the studs.
7 Label the electrical connections to the heater assembly, to aid correct refitting later, and then unplug them at their connectors. Release the wiring harness from the clips and cable ties on the heater casing.

8.4 Remove the tubular support beam (arrowed) from the front of the heater assembly

7.7 Apply a continuous bead of RTV sealant to the coolant pump mating face

8 Remove the rubber sleeve connecting the heater assembly air duct to the floor air duct (**see illustration**).
9 Slacken and remove the three nuts at the top of the unit and lift the heater assembly off its mounting studs.

Refitting

10 Refitting is a reversal of removal, bearing in mind the following points:
 a) *Make sure that all wiring and cables are routed as noted during dismantling.*
 b) *Make sure that all air ducts are securely reconnected.*
 c) *Refit the facia assembly with reference to Chapter 11.*
 d) *On completion, refill the cooling system as described in Chapter 1.*

Heater matrix

Removal

11 Remove the complete heater assembly as described previously in this Section.
12 Undo the upper and lower retaining bolts and separate the two halves of the heater assembly casing.
13 Undo the bolt and remove the support bracket for the matrix pipes.
14 Undo the bolts and lift off the side cover panel over the matrix pipes.
15 Carefully lift out the matrix, complete with pipes from the heater casing.

Refitting

16 Refitting is a reversal of removal.

8.8 Remove the rubber sleeve (arrowed) between the heater and floor air ducts

Heater blower motor

Removal

17 Working under the facia on the passenger's side, undo the three screws securing the blower motor to the underside of the heater assembly **(see illustration)**.

18 Withdraw the motor from the heater assembly and disconnect the wiring connector **(see illustration)**.

Refitting

19 Refitting is a reversal of removal.

Heater blower motor resistor

Removal

20 The resistor is located on the underside of the heater assembly, adjacent to the blower motor.

21 Working under the facia on the passenger's side, disconnect the wiring connector from the resistor.

22 Undo the two screws and remove the resistor from the heater assembly **(see illustration)**.

Refitting

23 Refitting is a reversal of removal.

Heater/ventilation control unit

Removal

24 Remove the complete facia assembly as described in Chapter 11.

25 Release the retaining clips or cable clamps and disconnect the three control cables, either at the control unit or at their respective levers on the heater assembly **(see illustration)**.

26 Disconnect the control unit wiring connector and remove the unit from the car.

Refitting

27 Reconnect the wiring connector, then reconnect control cables to the control unit or heater assembly as applicable.

28 Check that the operating levers on the heater assembly move through their full range of travel when moving the respective knobs on the control unit. If necessary, reposition the outer cables in their clips or clamps as required.

29 Refit the facia assembly as described in Chapter 11.

---

9 Air conditioning system – general information and precautions

General information

An air conditioning system is available on certain models. It enables the temperature of incoming air to be lowered, and also dehumidifies the air, which allows rapid demisting and increased comfort.

The cooling side of the system works in the same way as a domestic refrigerator. Refrigerant gas is drawn into a belt-driven compressor where the increase in pressure causes the refrigerant gas to turn to liquid. It then passes through a condenser mounted on the front of the radiator, where it is cooled. The liquid then passes through an expansion valve to an evaporator, where it changes from liquid under high pressure to gas under low pressure. This change is accompanied by a drop in temperature, which cools the evaporator and hence the air passing over it. The refrigerant returns to the compressor, and the cycle begins again.

The air blown through the evaporator passes to the air distribution unit where it is mixed, if required, with hot air blown through the heater matrix to achieve the desired temperature in the passenger compartment.

The heating side of the system works in the same way as on models without air conditioning.

The system is electronically-controlled. Any problems with the system should be referred to a Fiat dealer.

Precautions

With an air conditioning system, it is necessary to observe special precautions whenever dealing with any part of the system, or its associated components. If for any reason the system must be disconnected, it is essential that you entrust this task to your Fiat dealer or air conditioning specialist.

⚠ **Warning: The refrigeration circuit contains a liquid refrigerant and it is dangerous to disconnect any part of the system without specialist knowledge and equipment.**

The refrigerant is potentially dangerous, and should only be handled by qualified persons. If it is splashed onto the skin, it can cause severe frostbite. It is not itself poisonous, but in the presence of a naked flame (including a cigarette), it forms a poisonous gas. Uncontrolled discharging of the refrigerant is dangerous and potentially damaging to the environment.

8.17 Undo the three screws (arrowed) securing the blower motor to the underside of the heater assembly

8.18 Withdraw the blower motor and disconnect the wiring connector

---

10 Air conditioning system components – removal and refitting

Note: *Do not operate the air conditioning system if it is known to be short of refrigerant, as this may damage the compressor.*

1 The only operation which can be carried out easily without discharging the refrigerant is renewal of the auxiliary (compressor) drivebelt – this procedure is described in Chapter 1. All other operations must be referred to a Fiat dealer or an air conditioning specialist.

2 If necessary for access to other components, the compressor can be unbolted and moved aside, *without disconnecting its flexible hoses*, after removing the drivebelt.

⚠ *Warning: Do not attempt to open the refrigerant circuit. Refer to the precautions given in Section 9.*

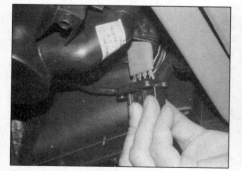

8.22 Undo the two screws and remove the blower motor resistor from the heater assembly

8.25 Control cable retaining clamps (arrowed) on the top of the heater/ventilation control unit

Chapter 4 Part A:
Fuel and exhaust systems

Contents

Degrees of difficulty

Easy, suitable for novice with little experience	**Fairly easy,** suitable for beginner with some experience	**Fairly difficult,** suitable for competent DIY mechanic	**Difficult,** suitable for experienced DIY mechanic	**Very difficult,** suitable for expert DIY or professional

Specifications

System type
SOHC (8-valve) engines . . . . Weber-Marelli 59F multi-point fuel injection/ignition system
DOHC (16-valve) engines . . . . Bosch Motronic ME 7.3 H4 multi-point fuel injection/ignition system

Fuel system data
Engine idle speed . . . . 900 ± 50 rpm*
CO% . . . . 0.35 maximum*
Fuel pump type . . . . Electric, immersed in fuel tank
Fuel pump delivery rate:
   SOHC (8-valve) engines . . . . 120 litres/hour minimum
   DOHC (16-valve) engines . . . . 110 litres/hour minimum
Regulated fuel pressure:
   SOHC (8-valve) engines . . . . 3.5 bars
   DOHC (16-valve) engines . . . . 3.0 bars
Crankshaft TDC sensor resistance at 20°C . . . . 1134 to 1386 ohms
Injector electrical resistance:
   SOHC (8-valve) engines . . . . 13.8 to 15.2 ohms
   DOHC (16-valve) engines . . . . 14.0 to 15.0 ohms
Not adjustable – controlled by ECU

Recommended fuel
Minimum octane rating . . . . 95 RON unleaded

Torque wrench settings

	Nm	lbf ft
Exhaust manifold downpipe support bracket bolt	30	22
Exhaust manifold to cylinder head	25	18
Exhaust system flange joint	25	18
Exhaust system mounting bracket bolts	30	22
Inlet manifold to cylinder head:		
SOHC (8-valve) engines	27	20
DOHC (16-valve) engines	15	11

1 General information and precautions

General information

The fuel supply system consists of a fuel tank (which is mounted under the centre of the car, with an electric fuel pump immersed in it) and fuel feed line. The fuel pump supplies fuel to the fuel rail, which acts as a reservoir for the four fuel injectors which inject fuel into the inlet tracts.

The fuel injection and ignition functions are combined into a single engine management system. The systems fitted are manufactured by Weber-Marelli and Bosch, and are very similar in terms of construction and operation. The only significant differences being in the software contained in the system Electronic Control Unit (ECU), and certain specific component variations according to engine type. Each system incorporates a closed-loop catalytic converter and an evaporative emission control system, and complies with the latest emission control standards. Refer to Chapter 5B for information on the ignition side of each system; the fuel side of the system operates as follows.

The fuel pump supplies fuel from the tank to the fuel rail (mounted directly above the fuel injectors) by means of a 'returnless' system. With this arrangement, the fuel filter and fuel pressure regulator are an integral part of the fuel pump assembly located in the fuel tank. The regulator maintains a constant fuel pressure in the supply line to the fuel rail and allows excess fuel to recirculate in the fuel tank, by means of a bypass channel, if the regulated fuel pressure is exceeded. As the fuel filter is an integral part of the pump assembly, fuel filter renewal is no longer necessary as part of the maintenance and servicing schedule.

The fuel injectors are electromagnetic pintle valves which spray atomised fuel into the combustion chambers under the control of the ECU. There are four injectors, one per cylinder, mounted in the inlet manifold close to the cylinder head. Each injector is mounted at an angle that allows it to spray fuel directly onto the back of the inlet valve(s). The ECU controls the volume of fuel injected by varying the length of time for which each injector is held open. The fuel injection systems are of the sequential type, whereby each injector operates individually in cylinder sequence.

The electrical control system consists of the ECU, along with the following sensors:
a) *Throttle potentiometer – informs the ECU of the throttle valve position, and the rate of throttle opening/closing.*
b) *Engine coolant temperature sensor – informs the ECU of engine temperature (refer to Chapter 3).*
c) *Intake air temperature/pressure sensor – informs the ECU of intake air temperature*

and load on the engine (expressed in terms of inlet manifold vacuum).
d) *Lambda sensors – inform the ECU of the oxygen content of the exhaust gases (explained in greater detail in Part B of this Chapter).*
e) *Crankshaft TDC sensor – informs the ECU of engine speed and crankshaft angular position.*
f) *Vehicle speed sensor – informs the ECU of the vehicle speed.*
g) *Knock sensor – informs the ECU of pre-ignition (detonation) within the cylinders (refer to Chapter 5B).*
h) *Camshaft position sensor – informs the ECU of which cylinder is on the firing stroke.*

On the Bosch system, the following additional sensors are also used:
a) *Acceleration sensor – enables the ECU to distinguish between engine roughness caused by pre-ignition (detonation) within the cylinders, or engine shake caused by abnormal road conditions.*
b) *Accelerator pedal potentiometer – informs the ECU of accelerator pedal position so that a specific throttle opening can be determined by the throttle valve actuator.*

Signals from each of the sensors are compared by the ECU and, based on this information, the ECU selects the response appropriate to those values, and controls the fuel injectors (varying the pulse width – the length of time the injectors are held open – to provide a richer or weaker air/fuel mixture, as appropriate). The air/fuel mixture is constantly varied by the ECU, to provide the best settings for cranking, starting (with either a hot or cold engine) and engine warm-up, idle, cruising and acceleration.

The ECU also has full control over the engine idle speed, via a stepper motor or throttle valve actuator fitted to the throttle body. On the Weber-Marelli system, the stepper motor controls the amount of air passing through a bypass drilling at the side of the throttle. When the throttle valve is closed (accelerator pedal released), the ECU uses the motor to open or close an air passage, controlling the amount of air bypassing the throttle valve and so controlling the idle speed. The ECU also carries out 'fine tuning' of the idle speed by varying the ignition timing to increase or reduce the torque of the engine as it is idling. This helps to stabilise the idle speed when electrical or mechanical loads (such as headlights, air conditioning, etc) are switched on and off. On the Bosch system, the ECU has total control over the full range of throttle valve movement by means of a throttle valve actuator. The accelerator pedal potentiometer informs the ECU of accelerator pedal position and from this data, the ECU controls the throttle valve actuator so that a corresponding throttle opening can be obtained. This arrangement is often termed 'drive-by-wire' as there is no direct accelerator cable connection between the accelerator pedal and throttle valve.

The exhaust and evaporative loss emission control systems are described in more detail in Chapter 4B.

If there is any abnormality in any of the readings obtained from the main engine sensors, the ECU enters its 'back-up' mode. If this happens, the erroneous sensor signal is overridden, and the ECU assumes a preprogrammed 'back-up' value, which will allow the engine to continue running, albeit at reduced efficiency. If the ECU enters this mode, the warning lamp on the instrument panel will be illuminated, and the relevant fault code will be stored in the ECU memory.

If the warning light illuminates, the vehicle should be taken to a Fiat dealer at the earliest opportunity. Once there, a complete test of the engine management system can be carried out, using a special electronic diagnostic test unit which is plugged into the system's diagnostic connector.

Precautions

Warning: Many of the procedures in this Chapter require the removal of fuel lines and connections, which may result in some fuel spillage. Before carrying out any operation on the fuel system, refer to the precautions given in 'Safety first!' at the beginning of this manual, and follow them implicitly. Petrol is a highly dangerous and volatile liquid, and the precautions necessary when handling it cannot be overstressed. Note that residual pressure will remain in the fuel lines long after the vehicle was last used. When disconnecting any fuel line, first depressurise the fuel system as described in Section 5.

2 Air cleaner assembly – removal and refitting

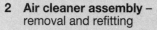

Removal

SOHC (8-valve) engines

1 Disconnect the air inlet air duct from the retaining clip adjacent to the right-hand engine mounting **(see illustration)**.

2.1 On SOHC (8-valve) engines, disconnect the air inlet air duct from the clip adjacent to the engine mounting

2.2 Release the spring-tensioned clasp at the front of the air cleaner casing

2.3 Undo the retaining bolts located on each side of the air cleaner casing

2.4 Lift the air cleaner casing off the throttle body and disconnect the crankcase ventilation hose

2 Release the spring-tensioned clasp at the front of the air cleaner casing **(see illustration)**.

3 Undo the two retaining bolts, one located on each side of the air cleaner casing **(see illustration)**.

4 Lift the air cleaner casing off the throttle body and disconnect the crankcase ventilation hose from the air cleaner base **(see illustration)**.

5 Recover the sealing ring. Check the ring for condition and renew it if necessary.

DOHC (16-valve) engines

6 Disconnect the vacuum hose from the air cleaner-to-throttle body inlet duct **(see illustration)**.

7 Release the clips securing the inlet duct to the air cleaner and throttle body **(see illustration)**.

8 Release the crankcase breather hose clip, disconnect the hose and lift out the inlet duct **(see illustration)**.

9 Undo the three bolts securing the air cleaner casing to the cylinder head extension and inlet manifold **(see illustration)**.

10 Release the clip and detach the cold air intake duct, then lift the air cleaner casing off the engine **(see illustrations)**.

11 If required, the cold air intake duct can be removed after undoing the end fitting retaining screw **(see illustration)**.

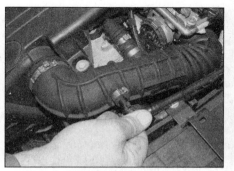

2.6 On DOHC (16-valve) engines, disconnect the vacuum hose from the air cleaner-to-throttle body inlet duct

2.7 Release the clips securing the inlet duct to the air cleaner and throttle body

2.8 Release the clip, disconnect the breather hose (arrowed) and lift out the inlet duct

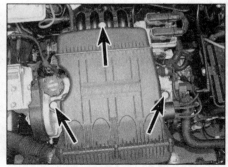

2.9 Undo the air cleaner casing retaining bolts (arrowed)

2.10a Detach the cold air intake duct . . .

2.10b . . . then lift the air cleaner casing off the engine

2.11 The cold air intake duct can be removed after undoing the end fitting retaining screw

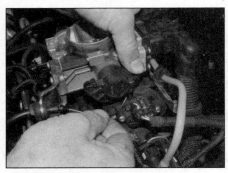

3.2a Disengage the accelerator inner cable from the throttle cam . . .

3.2b . . . and withdraw the outer cable from the rubber grommet on the mounting bracket

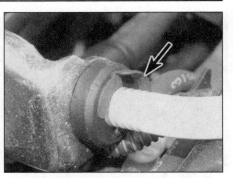

3.9 Accelerator outer cable retaining clip (arrowed)

Refitting

12 Refitting is a reversal of removal but renew the air cleaner filter element, as described in Chapter 1, if necessary.

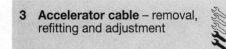

3 Accelerator cable – removal, refitting and adjustment

Note: *An accelerator cable is only used on SOHC (8-valve) engines. On DOHC (16-valve) engines, a 'drive-by-wire' system is employed, whereby the throttle valve is operated by a throttle valve actuator incorporated in the throttle body. The system is controlled by the engine management ECU using signal inputs from the accelerator pedal potentiometer.*

Removal

1 Remove the air cleaner assembly as described in Section 2.
2 Disengage the inner cable from the throttle cam, and withdraw the outer cable from the rubber grommet on the mounting bracket **(see illustrations)**.
3 Working back along the length of the cable, free it from any retaining clips or ties, noting its correct routing.
4 From under the facia, inside the car, unhook the cable from the fork at the top of the pedal arm.

4.3 Accelerator pedal retaining bolts (arrowed) – DOHC (16-valve) engines

5 Release the bulkhead grommet and withdraw the accelerator cable from inside the engine compartment.

Refitting

6 Feed the accelerator cable through the bulkhead grommet, then return to the car and locate the inner cable end fitting in the pedal arm.
7 From within the engine compartment, work along the cable, securing it in position with the retaining clips and ties, and ensuring that the cable is correctly routed.
8 Pass the outer cable through its throttle body mounting bracket grommet, and reconnect the inner cable to the throttle cam. Adjust the cable as described below.

Adjustment

9 Extract the retaining clip from its groove in the outer cable **(see illustration)**.
10 Ensuring that the throttle cam is fully against its stop, gently pull the cable out of its grommet until all free play is removed from the inner cable.
11 With the cable held in this position, refit the retaining clip to the last exposed outer cable groove in front of the rubber grommet. When the clip is refitted and the outer cable is released, there should be only a small amount of free play in the inner cable.
12 Have an assistant depress the accelerator pedal, and check that the throttle cam opens fully and returns smoothly to its stop.
13 On completion, refit the air cleaner assembly as described in Section 2.

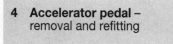

4 Accelerator pedal – removal and refitting

Removal

SOHC (8-valve) engines

1 From under the facia inside the car, unhook the accelerator cable from the fork at the top of the pedal arm.

2 Release the two retaining lugs and lift the pedal off the mounting bracket.

DOHC (16-valve) engines

3 From under the facia inside the car, undo the two bolts securing the pedal and potentiometer assembly to the mounting bracket **(see illustration)**.
4 Withdraw the pedal from its location, disconnect the potentiometer wiring connector, and remove the assembly from the car.

Refitting

5 Refitting is a reversal of removal. On SOHC (8-valve) engines check, and if necessary adjust, the accelerator cable as described in Section 3.

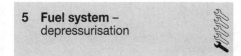

5 Fuel system – depressurisation

Note: *Refer to the warning given in Section 1 before proceeding.*

⚠️ *Warning: The following procedure will merely relieve the pressure in the fuel system – remember that fuel will still be present in the system components and take precautions accordingly before disconnecting any of them.*

1 The fuel system referred to in this Section is defined as the tank-mounted fuel pump, the fuel rail, the fuel injectors, and the metal pipes and flexible hoses of the fuel lines between these components. All these contain fuel which will be under pressure while the engine is running and/or while the ignition is switched on. The pressure will remain for some time after the ignition has been switched off, and must be relieved before any of these components are disturbed for servicing work.
2 Disconnect the battery negative terminal (refer to *Disconnecting the battery* in the Reference Chapter).
3 Remove the air cleaner assembly as described in Section 2.
4 Locate the Schrader valve situated at the

5.4a Fuel system depressurisation Schrader valve location (arrowed) on SOHC (8-valve) engines ...

5.4b ... and on DOHC (16-valve) engines

5.5 Withdraw the plastic cap from the top of the Schrader valve ...

right-hand end of the fuel rail **(see illustrations)**. The Schrader valve works like a tyre valve whereby on depressing the central plunger, the system fuel pressure will be released.

5 Withdraw the protective plastic cap from the top of the valve **(see illustration)**.

6 Place an absorbent rag around the valve then, using a small screwdriver, slowly depress the central plunger to allow the pressure to be released **(see illustration)**. Ensure that the rag completely covers the valve to catch the fuel spray which will be expelled.

7 On completion of the operations for which system depressurisation was necessary, refit the Schrader valve cap and reconnect the battery negative terminal. Refit the air cleaner assembly as described in Section 2.

6 Fuel pump and fuel gauge sender unit – removal and refitting

Note 1: *Refer to the warning given in Section 1 before proceeding.*
Note 2: *A new sealing O-ring will be required for refitting.*

Removal

1 Disconnect the battery negative terminal (refer to *Disconnecting the battery* in the Reference Chapter).
2 Depressurise the fuel system as described in Section 5.
3 Lift up the rear seat cushion and the floor covering for access to the fuel pump cover.
4 Undo the three screws and lift the cover

from the aperture in the floor panel **(see illustration)**.
5 Release the locking catch and disconnect the wiring connector from the top of the fuel pump **(see illustration)**.
6 Bearing in mind the warning given in Section 1, disconnect the fuel supply line quick-release fitting from the pump unit by pressing the tabs **(see illustration)**. Plug the end of the supply line or cover it with adhesive tape.
7 Unscrew the large locking ring and remove it from the tank. This is best accomplished by making up a simple tool from two strips of metal, suitably drilled and bolted together with two lengths of threaded bar and locknuts. Engage the tool with the ribs of the locking ring, and turn the ring anti-clockwise until it can be unscrewed by hand **(see illustrations)**.

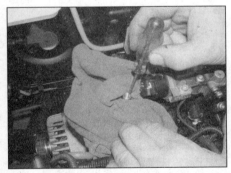

5.6 ... then depress the central plunger to allow the fuel pressure to be released

6.4 Remove the fuel pump cover from the aperture in the floor panel

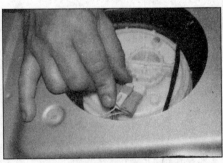

6.5 Release the locking catch and disconnect the wiring connector from the fuel pump

6.6 Disconnect the fuel line quick-release fitting by pressing the tabs

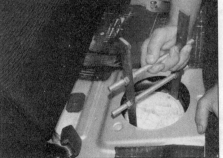

6.7a Using a home-made tool, slacken the fuel pump locking ring ...

6.7b ... then remove the ring from the tank

6.8a Lift the fuel pump and sender unit assembly out of the fuel tank . . .

6.8b . . . and recover the sealing O-ring

8 Lift the fuel pump and sender unit assembly out of the fuel tank, taking great care not to damage the float arm. Recover the sealing O-ring and discard it – a new one must be used on refitting **(see illustrations)**.

9 Note that the fuel pump and sender unit is only available as a complete assembly – no components are available separately.

Refitting

10 Refitting is a reversal of the removal procedure using a new sealing ring. Prior to refitting the access cover, reconnect the battery, then start the engine and check the fuel line for signs of leakage.

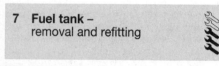

7 Fuel tank – removal and refitting

Note: *Refer to the warning given in Section 1 before proceeding.*

Removal

1 Before removing the fuel tank, all fuel must be drained from the tank. Since a fuel tank drain plug is not provided, it is therefore preferable to carry out the removal operation when the tank is nearly empty. Before proceeding, disconnect the battery negative terminal (refer to *Disconnecting the battery* in the Reference Chapter), and syphon or hand-pump the remaining fuel from the tank.

2 Working as described in Section 6,

disconnect the fuel pump wiring connector and the fuel supply line from the top of the pump.

3 Chock the front wheels, then jack up the rear of the car and securely support it on axle stands (see *Jacking and vehicle support*). Remove both rear roadwheels.

4 Disconnect the handbrake cables from the rear brake shoes as described in Chapter 9. Release the handbrake cables from their retaining clips on the rear axle mountings, exhaust heat shields, fuel tank support brackets and fuel tank **(see illustrations)**.

5 With reference to Section 13, disconnect the exhaust system from the catalytic converter downpipe and from its mountings on the underbody. Move the complete system to one side, for access to the fuel tank heat shield.

6 Undo the retaining nuts, extract the spring clip and remove the heat shield from under the fuel tank.

7 Loosen the clips and disconnect the filler pipe and vent pipe from the right-hand side of the fuel tank. Disconnect the roll-over valve hoses at the quick-release fittings adjacent to the filler pipe.

8 Place a trolley jack with an interposed block of wood beneath the tank, then raise the jack until it is supporting the weight of the tank.

9 Undo the four fuel tank mounting strap bolts, then carefully lower the tank from its location. Move the exhaust system as far as possible to one side to provide the necessary clearance for removal.

10 If the tank is contaminated with sediment or water, remove the fuel pump/fuel gauge sender unit as described in Section 6, and swill the tank out with clean fuel. The tank is injection-moulded from a synthetic material – if seriously damaged, it should be renewed. However, in certain cases, it may be possible to have small leaks or minor damage repaired. Seek the advice of a specialist before attempting to repair the fuel tank.

Refitting

11 Refitting is a reversal of the removal procedure, bearing in mind the following points:
  a) *Ensure that all pipes hoses are correctly routed and securely reconnected.*
  b) *Refit the exhaust system with reference to Section 13.*
  c) *Reconnect the handbrake cables and adjust the handbrake as described in Chapter 9.*

8 Fuel injection system – testing and adjustment

Testing

1 If a fault appears in the fuel injection/engine management system, first ensure that all the system wiring connectors are securely connected and free of corrosion. Ensure that the fault is not due to poor maintenance; ie, check that the air cleaner filter element is clean, the spark plugs are in good condition and correctly gapped, the valve clearances are correctly adjusted (where applicable), the cylinder compression pressures are correct, and that the engine breather hoses are clear and undamaged, referring to the relevant Parts of Chapters 1 and 2 for further information.

2 If these checks fail to reveal the cause of the problem, the vehicle should be taken to a Fiat dealer or suitably-equipped garage for testing. A diagnostic socket is located below the passenger compartment fusebox in which a fault code reader or other suitable test equipment can be connected. By using the

7.4a Release the handbrake cables from their clips on the rear axle mountings (arrowed) . . .

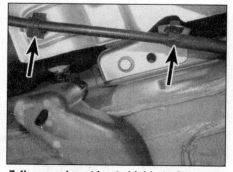

7.4b . . . exhaust heat shields and support brackets (arrowed) . . .

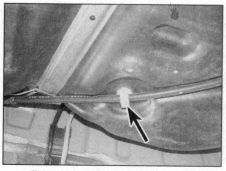

7.4c . . . and fuel tank (arrowed)

9.5 Disconnect the wiring connectors from the throttle potentiometer and the idle control stepper motor (arrowed)

9.6 Disconnect the ECU earth lead (arrowed) from the throttle body

9.7 Throttle body retaining bolts (arrowed)

code reader or test equipment, the engine management ECU (and the various other vehicle system ECUs) can be interrogated, and any stored fault codes can be retrieved. This will allow the fault to be quickly and simply traced, alleviating the need to test all the system components individually, which is a time-consuming operation that carries a risk of damaging the ECU.

Adjustment

3 Experienced home mechanics with a considerable amount of skill and equipment (including a tachometer and an accurately calibrated exhaust gas analyser) may be able to check the exhaust CO level and the idle speed. However, if these are found to be outside the specified tolerance, the car must be taken to a suitably-equipped garage for further testing. Neither the mixture adjustment (exhaust gas CO level) nor the idle speed are adjustable, and should either be incorrect, a fault may be present in the engine management system.

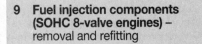

9 Fuel injection components (SOHC 8-valve engines) – removal and refitting

Note: *Refer to the warning given in Section 1 before proceeding.*

Throttle body assembly

Removal

1 Disconnect the battery negative terminal (refer to *Disconnecting the battery* in the Reference Chapter).
2 Remove the air cleaner assembly as described in Section 2.
3 Disengage the accelerator inner cable from the throttle cam, and withdraw the outer cable from the rubber grommet on the mounting bracket.
4 Remove the electronic control unit as described later in this Section.
5 Disconnect the wiring connectors from the throttle potentiometer and the idle control stepper motor **(see illustration)**.
6 Undo the retaining screw and disconnect the ECU earth lead from the front of the throttle body **(see illustration)**.
7 Slacken and remove the three bolts securing the throttle body assembly to the inlet manifold, then remove the assembly and collect the sealing O-ring **(see illustration)**.

Refitting

8 Refitting is a reversal of the removal procedure, bearing in mind the following points:
  a) Ensure the throttle body and inlet manifold mating surfaces are clean and dry, then fit the throttle body with a new

O-ring, and securely tighten the retaining bolts.
  b) Refit the electronic control unit as described later in this Section.
  c) Adjust the accelerator cable as described in Section 3.

Fuel rail and injectors

Removal

9 Disconnect the battery negative terminal (refer to *Disconnecting the battery* in the Reference Chapter).
10 Remove the air cleaner assembly as described in Section 2.
11 Depressurise the fuel system as described in Section 5.
12 Disconnect the wiring connectors at the fuel injectors **(see illustration)**.
13 Disconnect the fuel supply pipe at the quick-release connector on the left-hand end of the fuel rail **(see illustration)**.
14 Unscrew the two bolts securing the fuel rail assembly to the inlet manifold, then carefully pull the injectors from their manifold locations **(see illustration)**. Remove the assembly from the engine and remove the injector lower O-ring seals.
15 The injectors can be removed individually from the fuel rail by extracting the relevant metal clip and easing the injector out of the rail. Remove the injector upper O-ring seals.

9.12 Disconnect the wiring connectors at the fuel injectors

9.13 Disconnect the fuel supply pipe at the fuel rail quick-release connector

9.14 Unscrew the two bolts (arrowed) securing the fuel rail assembly to the inlet manifold

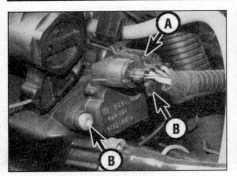

9.22 Intake air temperature/pressure sensor wiring connector (A) and retaining screws (B)

9.26 Crankshaft TDC sensor location (arrowed)

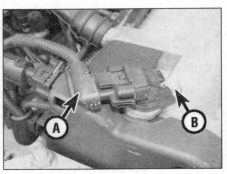

9.34 Camshaft position sensor wiring connector (A) and retaining bolt (B)

16 Check the electrical resistance of the injector using a multimeter and compare it with the Specifications. **Note:** *If a faulty injector is suspected, before condemning the injector it is worth trying the effect of one of the proprietary injector-cleaning treatments.*

Refitting

17 Refitting is a reversal of the removal procedure, bearing in mind the following points:
  a) *Renew the injector O-ring seals, and smear them with a little petroleum jelly before assembling. Take care when fitting the injectors to the fuel rail and do not press them in further than required to fit the retaining clip otherwise the O-ring seal may be damaged.*
  b) *Ensure that the injector retaining clips are securely seated.*
  c) *On completion check the fuel rail and injectors for fuel leaks.*

Idle control stepper motor

18 The idle control stepper motor is an integral part of the throttle body and cannot be individually renewed.

Throttle potentiometer

19 The idle control stepper motor is an integral part of the throttle body and cannot be individually renewed.

Intake air temperature/pressure sensor

Removal

20 Disconnect the battery negative terminal (refer to *Disconnecting the battery* in the Reference Chapter).
21 Remove the air cleaner assembly as described in Section 2.
22 Disconnect the wiring connector, undo the two retaining screws and remove the sensor from the left-hand end of the inlet manifold **(see illustration)**.

Refitting

23 Refitting is a reversal of the removal procedure.

Coolant temperature sensor
24 Refer to Chapter 3.

Lambda sensors
25 Refer to Chapter 4B.

Crankshaft TDC sensor

Removal

26 The crankshaft TDC sensor is located adjacent to the front facing side of the crankshaft pulley **(see illustration)**.
27 Disconnect the battery negative terminal (refer to *Disconnecting the battery* in the Reference Chapter).
28 Remove the timing belt upper and lower covers as described in Chapter 2A.
29 Undo the bolt securing the sensor to the oil pump casing and remove the sensor from its location.

Refitting

30 Locate the sensor in position and secure with the retaining bolt.
31 Engage the sensor wiring harness with the upper and lower timing belt covers, then refit the covers as described in Chapter 2A.

Knock sensor
32 Refer to Chapter 5B.

Camshaft position sensor

Removal

33 Disconnect the battery negative terminal (refer to *Disconnecting the battery* in the Reference Chapter).
34 Disconnect the wiring connector from the camshaft position sensor located at the timing belt end of the camshaft cover **(see illustration)**.
35 Undo the retaining bolt and withdraw the sensor from the camshaft cover.

Refitting

36 Refitting is a reversal of the removal procedure.

Electronic control unit (ECU)

Removal

37 The electronic control unit is attached to the rear of the throttle body.
38 Disconnect the battery negative terminal (refer to *Disconnecting the battery* in the Reference Chapter).
39 Remove the air cleaner assembly as described in Section 2.
40 Rotate the wiring connector locking catches and disconnect the two wiring connectors from the top of the ECU **(see illustrations)**.
41 Undo the two mounting bolts and remove the ECU from the throttle body **(see illustrations)**.

9.40a Rotate the ECU wiring connector locking catches . . .

9.40b . . . and disconnect the two wiring connectors from the ECU

9.41a Undo the two mounting bolts (arrowed) . . .

9.41b . . . and remove the ECU from the throttle body

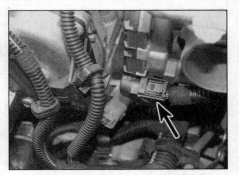

10.3 Throttle valve actuator wiring connector (arrowed)

Refitting

42 Refitting is a reversal of the removal procedure.

Inertia safety switch

Removal

43 Disconnect the battery negative terminal (refer to *Disconnecting the battery* in the Reference Chapter).

44 Working under the facia on the right-hand side, move away the floor covering and side trim for access to the switch.

45 Disconnect the wiring connector, then undo the two bolts and remove the switch from its location.

Refitting

46 Refitting is a reversal of the removal procedure.

Vehicle speed sensor

Note: *On cars equipped with ABS, the vehicle speed sensor signal is supplied to the ECU by the ABS wheel speed sensors.*

Removal

47 The vehicle speed sensor is located on the top of the transmission differential housing.

48 Disconnect the battery negative terminal (refer to *Disconnecting the battery* in the Reference Chapter).

49 Firmly apply the handbrake, then jack up

the front of the car and support it securely on axle stands (see *Jacking and vehicle support*).

50 Disconnect the sensor wiring connector then unscrew the sensor from the differential housing.

Refitting

51 Refitting is a reversal of the removal procedure.

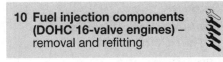

10 Fuel injection components (DOHC 16-valve engines) – removal and refitting

Note: *Refer to the warning given in Section 1 before proceeding.*

Throttle body assembly

Removal

1 Disconnect the battery negative terminal (refer to *Disconnecting the battery* in the Reference Chapter).

2 Remove the air cleaner assembly as described in Section 2.

3 Disconnect the wiring connector for the throttle valve actuator **(see illustration)**.

4 Remove the electronic control unit as described later in this Section.

5 Slacken and remove the four bolts securing the throttle body assembly to the inlet manifold. Move the ECU mounting bracket

aside, then remove the assembly and collect the sealing O-ring **(see illustration)**.

Refitting

6 Refitting is a reversal of the removal procedure, bearing in mind the following points:

a) *Ensure the throttle body and inlet manifold mating surfaces are clean and dry, then fit the throttle body with a new O-ring, and securely tighten the retaining bolts.*

b) *Refit the electronic control unit as described later in this Section.*

Fuel rail and injectors

Removal

7 Disconnect the battery negative terminal (refer to *Disconnecting the battery* in the Reference Chapter).

8 Remove the air cleaner assembly as described in Section 2.

9 Depressurise the fuel system as described in Section 5.

10 Disconnect the fuel supply pipe at the quick-release connector in the centre of the fuel rail **(see illustration)**.

11 Disconnect the wiring connectors at the fuel injectors. Release the injector wiring harness from the retaining clips on the fuel rail and move the harness to one side **(see illustration)**.

12 Unscrew the two bolts securing the fuel rail

10.5 Throttle body retaining bolts (arrowed) – shown with inlet manifold removed

10.10 Fuel supply pipe quick-release connector (arrowed)

10.11 Fuel injector wiring connectors (A) harness clips (B) and fuel rail retaining bolts (C) – shown with inlet manifold removed

10.21 Disconnect the wiring connector at the intake air temperature/pressure sensor

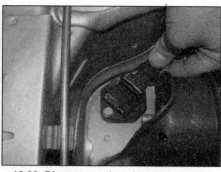

10.38 Disconnect the wiring connector from the acceleration sensor

10.44 Rotate the locking catches and disconnect the two wiring connectors from the top of the ECU

assembly to the inlet manifold, then carefully pull the injectors from their manifold locations. Remove the assembly from the engine and remove the injector lower O-ring seals.

13 The injectors can be removed individually from the fuel rail by extracting the relevant metal clip and easing the injector out of the rail. Remove the injector upper O-ring seals.

14 Check the electrical resistance of the injector using a multimeter and compare it with the Specifications. **Note:** *If a faulty injector is suspected, before condemning the injector it is worth trying the effect of one of the proprietary injector-cleaning treatments.*

Refitting

15 Refitting is a reversal of the removal procedure, bearing in mind the following points:

a) *Renew the injector O-ring seals, and smear them with a little petroleum jelly before assembling. Take care when fitting the injectors to the fuel rail and do not press them in further than required to fit the retaining clip otherwise the O-ring seal may be damaged.*

b) *Ensure that the injector retaining clips are securely seated.*

c) *On completion check the fuel rail and injectors for fuel leaks.*

Throttle valve actuator

16 The throttle valve actuator is an integral part of the throttle body and cannot be individually renewed.

Throttle potentiometer

17 The throttle potentiometer is incorporated in the throttle valve actuator and cannot be individually renewed.

Accelerator pedal potentiometer

18 The accelerator pedal potentiometer is an integral part of the accelerator pedal assembly and cannot be individually renewed. Refer to Section 4 for accelerator pedal removal and refitting procedures.

Intake air temperature/pressure sensor

Removal

19 Disconnect the battery negative terminal

(refer to *Disconnecting the battery* in the Reference Chapter).

20 Remove the air cleaner assembly as described in Section 2.

21 Disconnect the wiring connector, then undo the retaining bolt and remove the sensor from the right-hand end of the inlet manifold **(see illustration)**.

Refitting

22 Refitting is a reversal of the removal procedure.

Coolant temperature sensor

23 Refer to Chapter 3.

Lambda sensors

24 Refer to Chapter 4B.

Crankshaft TDC sensor

Removal

25 The crankshaft TDC sensor is located adjacent to the front facing side of the crankshaft pulley **(see illustration 9.26)**.

26 Disconnect the battery negative terminal (refer to *Disconnecting the battery* in the Reference Chapter).

27 Remove the timing belt upper and lower covers as described in Chapter 2B.

28 Undo the bolt securing the sensor to the oil pump casing and remove the sensor from its location.

Refitting

29 Locate the sensor in position and secure with the retaining bolt.

30 Engage the sensor wiring harness with the upper and lower timing belt covers, then refit the covers as described in Chapter 2B.

Knock sensor

31 Refer to Chapter 5B.

Camshaft position sensor

Removal

32 Disconnect the battery negative terminal (refer to *Disconnecting the battery* in the Reference Chapter).

33 Remove the air cleaner assembly as described in Section 2.

34 Disconnect the wiring connector from the

camshaft position sensor located in the centre of the cylinder head extension.

35 Undo the retaining bolt and withdraw the sensor from its location.

Refitting

36 Refitting is a reversal of the removal procedure.

Acceleration sensor

Removal

37 Disconnect the battery negative terminal (refer to *Disconnecting the battery* in the Reference Chapter).

38 Disconnect the wiring connector from the acceleration sensor located adjacent to the right-hand engine mounting **(see illustration)**.

39 Undo the retaining bolt and remove the sensor from its location.

Refitting

40 Refitting is a reversal of the removal procedure.

Electronic control unit (ECU)

Removal

41 The electronic control unit is attached to the top of the throttle body.

42 Disconnect the battery negative terminal (refer to *Disconnecting the battery* in the Reference Chapter).

43 Remove the air cleaner assembly as described in Section 2.

44 Rotate the wiring connector locking catches and disconnect the two wiring connectors from the top of the ECU **(see illustration)**.

45 Undo the four nuts securing the ECU to the throttle body, noting the location of the earth lead under the front left-hand nut. Lift the unit up and off the throttle body.

Refitting

46 Refitting is a reversal of the removal procedure.

Inertia safety switch

47 Refer to Section 9.

Vehicle speed sensor

48 Refer to Section 9.

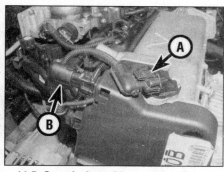

11.5 Camshaft position sensor (A) and crankshaft TDC sensor (B) wiring connectors – SOHC (8-valve) engines

11.6 Intake air temperature/pressure sensor wiring connector (arrowed) – SOHC (8-valve) engines

11.7a Disconnect the wiring connector . . .

11 Inlet manifold – removal and refitting

Note: *Refer to the warning given in Section 1 before proceeding.*

SOHC (8-valve) engines

Removal

1 Disconnect the battery negative terminal (refer to *Disconnecting the battery* in the Reference Chapter).
2 Remove the air cleaner assembly as described in Section 2.
3 Drain the cooling system as described in Chapter 1.
4 Prise out the grommet and disconnect the brake servo vacuum hose from the front of the servo unit. Release the hose from the retaining clip on the bulkhead.
5 Disconnect the wiring connectors from the camshaft position sensor and crankshaft TDC sensor **(see illustration)**.
6 Disconnect the wiring connectors from the intake air temperature/pressure sensor, and engine coolant temperature sensor **(see illustration)**.
7 Disconnect the wiring connector and fuel vapour hose from the evaporative emission control solenoid **(see illustrations)**.

8 Release the retaining clip and disconnect the coolant hose from the rear of the manifold.
9 Disconnect the crankcase ventilation system hose from the right-hand side of the manifold **(see illustration)**.
10 Remove the throttle body assembly as described in Section 9.
11 Remove the fuel rail and injectors as described in Section 9.
12 Release the clips and disconnect the fuel injector wiring duct from the slots on the camshaft cover. Move the wiring duct and associated cables clear of the inlet manifold.
13 Release the wiring harness from the clips at the rear of the manifold.
14 Undo the manifold retaining nuts bolts, and remove the manifold from the cylinder head. Remove the sealing rings and obtain new rings for refitting.

Refitting

15 Refitting is a reverse of the removal procedure, noting the following points:
a) *Ensure that the manifold and cylinder head mating surfaces are clean and dry, and fit new manifold sealing rings. Refit the manifold and securely tighten its retaining nuts.*
b) *Ensure all relevant hoses and wiring are*

reconnected to their original positions and are securely held (where necessary) by the retaining clips.
c) *Refit the fuel rail and injectors, and the throttle body assembly with reference to Section 9.*
d) *On completion, refill the cooling system as described in Chapter 1.*

DOHC (16-valve) engines

Removal

16 Disconnect the battery negative terminal (refer to *Disconnecting the battery* in the Reference Chapter).
17 Remove the air cleaner assembly as described in Section 2.
18 Drain the cooling system as described in Chapter 1.
19 Depressurise the fuel system as described in Section 5.
20 Disconnect the fuel supply pipe at the quick-release connector in the centre of the fuel rail. Release the fuel supply pipe from the retaining clips on the manifold and move it to one side.
21 Disconnect the evaporative emission control system fuel vapour hose at the quick-release connector on the manifold right-hand side **(see illustration)**.
22 Release the clip and disconnect the

11.7b . . . and fuel vapour hose from the evaporative emission control solenoid – SOHC (8-valve) engines

11.9 Disconnect the crankcase ventilation system hose from the right-hand side of the manifold – SOHC (8-valve) engines

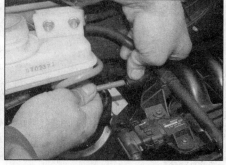

11.21 Disconnect the evaporative emission control vapour hose at the quick-release connector – DOHC (16-valve) engines

11.22 Release the clip and disconnect the vacuum hose from the rear of the manifold – DOHC (16-valve) engines

11.24 Open the clip and free the ECU wiring harness from the throttle body – DOHC (16-valve) engines

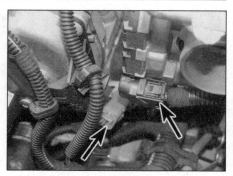

11.25a Disconnect the wiring connectors at the engine coolant temperature sensor and throttle valve actuator (arrowed) . . .

11.25b . . . and at the evaporative emission control solenoid and fuel injector harness (arrowed) – DOHC (16-valve) engines

11.27 Disconnect the crankcase breather hose from the pipe stub behind the throttle body – DOHC (16-valve) engines

vacuum hose from the rear of the inlet manifold **(see illustration)**.

23 Rotate the wiring connector locking catches and disconnect the two wiring connectors from the top of the ECU. Undo the nut and release the earth lead from the ECU front mounting stud.

24 Open the cable clip and free the ECU wiring harness from the throttle body **(see illustration)**.

25 Disconnect the wiring connectors from the engine coolant temperature sensor, throttle valve actuator, evaporative emission control solenoid and fuel injector harness **(see illustrations)**.

26 At the right-hand end of the manifold, disconnect the wiring connector from the intake air temperature/pressure sensor.

27 Disconnect the crankcase breather hose from the pipe stub behind the throttle body **(see illustration)**.

28 Release the clip and disconnect the coolant hose from the rear of the manifold **(see illustration)**.

29 Release the spark plug HT leads from the manifold upper support bracket, then undo the bolt securing the support bracket to the cylinder head extension **(see illustration)**.

30 Detach the engine wiring harness from the two clips at the rear of the manifold.

31 Undo the eight retaining bolts and remove the manifold from the cylinder head **(see illustrations)**.

32 Remove the sealing rings and obtain new rings for refitting **(see illustration)**.

11.28 Release the clip and disconnect the coolant hose from the rear of the manifold – DOHC (16-valve) engines

11.29 Undo the bolt securing the inlet manifold support bracket to the cylinder head extension – DOHC (16-valve) engines

11.31a Undo the eight retaining bolts (arrowed) . . .

11.31b . . . and remove the inlet manifold from the cylinder head – DOHC (16-valve) engines

11.32 Renew the inlet manifold sealing rings prior to refitting – DOHC (16-valve) engines

Refitting

33 Refitting is a reverse of the removal procedure, noting the following points:

a) *Ensure that the manifold and cylinder head mating surfaces are clean and dry, and fit new manifold sealing rings. Refit the manifold and securely tighten its retaining bolts.*

b) *Ensure all relevant hoses and wiring are reconnected to their original positions and are securely held (where necessary) by the retaining clips.*

c) *On completion, refill the cooling system as described in Chapter 1.*

12 Exhaust manifold – removal and refitting

Removal

1 Disconnect the battery negative terminal (refer to *Disconnecting the battery* in the Reference Chapter).

2 Remove the air cleaner assembly as described in Section 2.

3 Firmly apply the handbrake, then jack up the front of the car and support it securely on axle stands (see *Jacking and vehicle support*).

4 Undo the four bolts securing the heat shield to the exhaust manifold.

5 From under the car, undo the three nuts securing the heat shield to the catalytic converter, then remove the heat shield from the manifold **(see illustration)**.

6 Disconnect the wiring for the 'upstream' and 'downstream' lambda sensors at the connectors on the transmission bellhousing **(see illustrations)**.

7 Unscrew the nuts and disconnect the exhaust system front pipe flange from the manifold downpipe **(see illustration)**. Recover the gasket.

8 Undo the bolt securing the manifold downpipe support bracket to the transmission.

9 Undo the nuts securing the exhaust manifold to the cylinder head, noting that the engine lifting bracket is also secured by the two upper nuts at the timing belt end. Carefully withdraw the manifold off the mounting studs and collect the gasket.

Refitting

10 Refitting is a reversal of the removal procedure but use a new manifold gasket, and new front pipe flange gasket. Tighten all mounting and attachment nuts/bolts to the specified torque.

13 Exhaust system – general information and component renewal

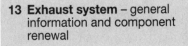

General information

1 A one-piece exhaust system is fitted comprising a front pipe, intermediate silencer and rear silencer. The front pipe is connected

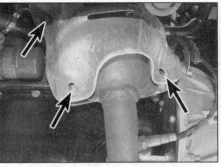

12.5 Exhaust manifold heat shield lower retaining nuts (arrowed)

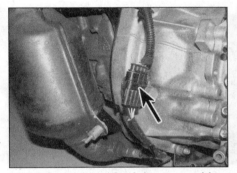

12.6b Downstream lambda sensor wiring connector (arrowed)

to the exhaust manifold downpipe by means of a flange joint, and contains a flexible section to cater for engine movement. A catalytic converter is fitted to all models, and is an integral part of the exhaust manifold.

2 The system is suspended throughout its entire length by rubber mountings.

3 The intermediate and rear silencers can be individually renewed by cutting the original system at a specified distance from the front pipe flange joint. The new section is then secured by a clamping sleeve which is supplied as part of the new front or rear section.

Component renewal

Exhaust manifold and catalytic converter

4 Refer to Section 12.

Intermediate and rear silencers

5 Firmly apply the handbrake, then jack up the front and rear of the car and support it securely on axle stands (see *Jacking and vehicle support*).

6 Using a tape measure, measure rearwards from the flat surface of the front pipe-to-manifold downpipe flange, and suitably mark the system 1974.0 mm from the flange. This will be the cutting point for renewal of the intermediate or rear silencer.

7 Unscrew the nuts and disconnect the front pipe flange from the manifold downpipe. Recover the gasket.

8 Undo the bolts securing the front and rear exhaust system mounting brackets to the

12.6a Upstream lambda sensor wiring connector (arrowed)

12.7 Exhaust system front pipe flange retaining nuts (arrowed)

underbody. Lower the system and suitably support it.

9 Using a hacksaw, cut through the system at the point previously marked, then remove the front pipe and intermediate silencer or the tailpipe and rear silencer, as applicable.

10 Remove any burrs from the remaining section at the cutting point, then slide the clamping sleeve into position. Locate the new section in place in the clamping sleeve.

11 Refit the bolts securing the front and rear mounting brackets to the underbody and tighten them to the specified torque.

12 Reconnect the front pipe flange to the manifold downpipe using a new gasket, and tighten the nuts to the specified torque.

13 Align the two exhaust system sections so that there is adequate clearance between the system and vehicle underbody, then securely tighten the clamping sleeve nut.

14 On completion, lower the car to the ground.

Heat shields

15 Undo the bolts securing the front and rear exhaust system mounting brackets to the underbody. Lower the system and suitably support it.

16 The heat shields are secured to the underbody by an assortment of nuts, bolts and retaining clips. Remove the relevant attachments and withdraw the heat shield(s) from their location.

17 Refit the heat shield(s), and exhaust system mounting brackets, tightening the bracket retaining bolts to the specified torque.

Notes

Chapter 4 Part B:
Emission control systems

Contents

Degrees of difficulty

Easy, suitable for novice with little experience	**Fairly easy,** suitable for beginner with some experience	**Fairly difficult,** suitable for competent DIY mechanic	**Difficult,** suitable for experienced DIY mechanic	**Very difficult,** suitable for expert DIY or professional

Specifications

Torque wrench setting	Nm	lbf ft
Lambda sensor to manifold	45	33

1 General information

All models use unleaded petrol and are controlled by engine management systems that are 'tuned' to give the best compromise between driveability, fuel consumption and exhaust emission production. In addition, a number of systems are fitted that help to minimise other harmful emissions: a crankcase emission-control system that reduces the release of pollutants from the crankcase, an evaporative loss emission control system to reduce the release of hydrocarbons from the fuel tank, and a catalytic converter to reduce exhaust gas pollutants.

Crankcase emission control

To reduce the emission of unburned hydrocarbons from the crankcase into the atmosphere, the engine is sealed and the blow-by gases and oil vapour are drawn from inside the crankcase, into the inlet tract to be burned by the engine during normal combustion.

Under conditions of high manifold depression (idling, deceleration) the gases will by sucked positively out of the crankcase. Under conditions of low manifold depression (acceleration, full-throttle running) the gases are forced out of the crankcase by the (relatively) higher crankcase pressure; if the engine is worn, the raised crankcase pressure (due to increased blow-by) will cause some of the flow to return under all manifold conditions.

Exhaust emission control

To minimise the amount of pollutants which escape into the atmosphere, a catalytic converter is fitted integrally into the exhaust manifold. The fuel system is of the closed-loop type, in which two lambda (or oxygen) sensors in the exhaust system provide the engine management system ECU with constant feedback, enabling the ECU to adjust the air/fuel mixture to optimise combustion. One lambda sensor is fitted 'upstream' of the catalytic converter, and the second sensor is fitted 'downstream' of the converter. The ECU compares the voltage signals from the two sensors to obtain the optimum inlet air/fuel ratio.

The lambda sensors have a heating element built-in that is controlled by the ECU to quickly bring the sensor's tip to its optimum operating temperature. The sensor's tip is sensitive to oxygen and provides a voltage signal to the ECU that varies according on the amount of oxygen in the exhaust gas. If the inlet air/fuel mixture is too rich, the exhaust gases are low in oxygen so the sensor sends a low-voltage signal, the voltage rising as the mixture weakens and the amount of oxygen rises in the exhaust gases. Peak conversion efficiency of all major pollutants occurs if the

2.6a Disconnect the wiring connector . . .

2.6b . . . and fuel vapour hose from the control solenoid – SOHC (8-valve) engines

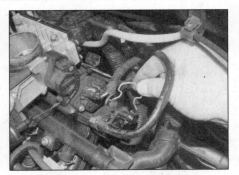

2.7a Extract the retaining spring clip . . .

inlet air/fuel mixture is maintained at the chemically-correct ratio for the complete combustion of petrol of 14.7 parts (by weight) of air to 1 part of fuel (the stoichiometric ratio). The sensor output voltage alters in a large step at this point, the ECU using the signal change as a reference point and correcting the inlet air/fuel mixture accordingly by altering the fuel injector pulse width.

Evaporative emission control

To minimise the escape of unburned hydrocarbons into the atmosphere, an evaporative loss emission control system is fitted. The fuel tank filler cap is sealed and a charcoal canister is mounted underneath the right-hand wheel arch to collect the petrol vapours released from the fuel contained in the fuel tank. It stores them until they can be drawn from the canister (under the control of the engine management system ECU) via the evaporative emission control solenoid valve into the inlet tract, where they are then burned by the engine during normal combustion.

To ensure that the engine runs correctly when it is cold and/or idling and to protect the catalytic converter from the effects of an over-rich mixture, the solenoid valve is not opened by the ECU until the engine has warmed-up, and the engine is under load; the solenoid valve is then modulated on and off to allow the stored vapour to pass into the inlet tract.

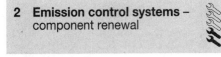

2 Emission control systems – component renewal

Crankcase emission control

1 The crankcase emission control system consists of a hose from the camshaft cover/cylinder head extension to the air cleaner (or inlet duct).
2 The system requires no attention other than to check at regular intervals that the hose is free of blockages and undamaged.

Evaporative emission control

3 The evaporative loss emission control system consists of the control solenoid, the activated charcoal filter canister and connecting fuel vapour hoses.

Control solenoid renewal

SOHC (8-valve) engines

4 Disconnect the battery negative terminal (refer to *Disconnecting the battery* in the Reference Chapter).
5 Remove the air cleaner assembly as described in Chapter 4A.
6 Disconnect the wiring connector and fuel vapour hose from the control solenoid (**see illustrations**).
7 Extract the retaining spring clip, and

remove the solenoid from the inlet manifold (**see illustrations**).
8 Refitting is a reversal of removal.

DOHC (16-valve) engines

9 Disconnect the battery negative terminal (refer to *Disconnecting the battery* in the Reference Chapter).
10 Remove the air cleaner assembly as described in Chapter 4A.
11 Disconnect the wiring connector and fuel vapour hose from the control solenoid (**see illustration**).
12 Undo the two retaining screws and remove the solenoid from the inlet manifold (**see illustration**).
13 Refitting is a reversal of removal.

Charcoal canister renewal

14 Firmly apply the handbrake, then jack up the front of the car and support it securely on axle stands (see *Jacking and vehicle support*). Remove the right-hand front roadwheel.
15 Working under the right-hand wheel arch, undo the retaining screws and remove the wheel arch liner main and centre panels for access to the charcoal canister.
16 From within the engine compartment, disconnect the two fuel vapour hoses at their quick-release fittings adjacent to the right-hand suspension strut tower.
17 Working under the wheel arch, undo the retaining nut and bolt, and remove the

2.7b . . . and remove the solenoid from the inlet manifold – SOHC (8-valve) engines

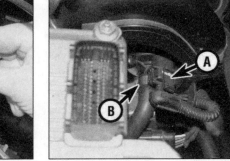

2.11 Disconnect the wiring connector (A) and fuel vapour hose (B) from the control solenoid – DOHC (16-valve) engines

2.12 Undo the two retaining screws (arrowed) and remove the solenoid from the inlet manifold – DOHC (16-valve) engines

canister and vapour hoses from under the car.

18 Refitting is a reversal of removal.

Exhaust emission control

Catalytic converter renewal

19 The catalytic converter is an integral part of the exhaust manifold. Refer to Chapter 4A, Section 12, for exhaust manifold removal and refitting procedures.

Lambda sensors renewal

Note: *The lambda sensors are delicate and will not work if dropped or knocked, if their power supply is disrupted, or if any cleaning materials are used on them.*

20 The two sensors are threaded into the exhaust manifold – one 'upstream' and one 'downstream' of the catalytic converter.

21 Disconnect the battery negative terminal (refer to *Disconnecting the battery* in the Reference Chapter).

22 Remove the air cleaner assembly as described in Chapter 4A.

23 Firmly apply the handbrake, then jack up the front of the car and support it securely on axle stands (see *Jacking and vehicle support*).

24 Undo the four bolts securing the heat shield to the exhaust manifold.

25 From under the car, undo the three nuts securing the heat shield to the catalytic converter, then remove the heat shield from the manifold.

26 Disconnect the relevant sensor wiring connector located on the transmission bellhousing **(see illustrations)**.

27 Unscrew the sensor, taking care to avoid damaging the sensor probe as it is removed. **Note:** *As a flying lead remains connected to the sensor after it has been disconnected, if the correct spanner is not available, a slotted socket will be required to remove the sensor.*

28 Apply a little anti-seize grease to the sensor threads – avoid contaminating the probe tip.

29 Refit the sensor to the downpipe,

2.26a Upstream lambda sensor wiring connector (arrowed)

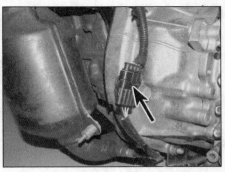

2.26b Downstream lambda sensor wiring connector (arrowed)

tightening it to the specified torque. Reconnect the wiring connector.

30 Refit the heat shield and air cleaner assembly, then reconnect the battery and lower the car to the ground.

---

3 Catalytic converter – general information and precautions

The catalytic converter is a reliable and simple device which needs no maintenance in itself, but there are some facts of which an owner should be aware if the converter is to function properly for its full service life.

a) *DO NOT use leaded petrol or LRP in a car equipped with a catalytic converter – the lead will coat the precious metals, reducing their converting efficiency and will eventually destroy the converter.*

b) *Always keep the ignition and fuel systems well-maintained in accordance with the manufacturer's schedule.*

c) *If the engine develops a misfire, do not drive the car at all (or at least as little as possible) until the fault is cured.*

d) *DO NOT push- or tow-start the car – this will soak the catalytic converter in*

unburned fuel, causing it to overheat when the engine does start.

e) *DO NOT switch off the ignition at high engine speeds.*

f) *DO NOT use fuel or engine oil additives – these may contain substances harmful to the catalytic converter.*

g) *DO NOT continue to use the car if the engine burns oil to the extent of leaving a visible trail of blue smoke.*

h) *Remember that the catalytic converter operates at very high temperatures. DO NOT, therefore, park the car in dry undergrowth, over long grass or piles of dead leaves after a long run.*

i) *Remember that the catalytic converter is FRAGILE – do not strike it with tools during servicing work.*

j) *In some cases a sulphurous smell (like that of rotten eggs) may be noticed from the exhaust. This is common to many catalytic converter-equipped cars and once the car has covered a few thousand miles the problem should disappear.*

k) *The catalytic converter, used on a well-maintained and well-driven car, should last for between 50 000 and 100 000 miles – if the converter is no longer effective it must be renewed.*

Chapter 5 Part A:
Starting and charging systems

Contents

Degrees of difficulty

Easy, suitable for novice with little experience	**Fairly easy,** suitable for beginner with some experience	**Fairly difficult,** suitable for competent DIY mechanic	**Difficult,** suitable for experienced DIY mechanic	**Very difficult,** suitable for expert DIY or professional

Specifications

General
System type .... 12 volt, negative earth

Battery
Charge condition:
Poor	12.5 volts
Normal	12.6 volts
Good	12.7 volts

Torque wrench settings

	Nm	lbf ft
Alternator:		
M10 nuts/bolts	50	37
M12 nuts/bolts	80	59
Starter motor	27	20

1 General information and precautions

General information

The engine electrical system consists mainly of the charging and starting systems. Because of their engine-related functions, these components are covered separately from the body electrical devices such as the lights, instruments, etc (which are covered in Chapter 12). Information on the ignition system is covered in Part B of this Chapter.

The electrical system is of 12 volt negative earth type.

The battery fitted as original equipment is of maintenance-free (sealed for life) type and is charged by the alternator, which is belt-driven from the crankshaft pulley. If a non-original battery is fitted it may be of standard or low maintenance type.

The starter motor is of the pre-engaged type incorporating an integral solenoid. On starting, the solenoid moves the drive pinion into engagement with the flywheel ring gear before the starter motor is energised. Once the engine has started, a one-way clutch prevents the motor armature being driven by the engine until the pinion disengages from the flywheel.

Precautions

Further details of the various systems are given in the relevant Sections of this Chapter. While some repair procedures are given, the usual course of action is to renew the component concerned. The owner whose interest extends beyond mere component renewal should obtain a copy of the *Automotive Electrical & Electronic Systems Manual*, available from the publishers of this manual.

It is necessary to take extra care when working on the electrical system to avoid damage to semi-conductor devices (diodes and transistors), and to avoid the risk of personal injury. In addition to the precautions given in *Safety first!* at the beginning of this manual, observe the following when working on the system:

• *Always remove rings, watches, etc before working on the electrical system.* Even with the battery disconnected, capacitive discharge could occur if a component's live terminal is earthed through a metal object. This could cause a shock or nasty burn.

• *Do not reverse the battery connections.* Components such as the alternator, electronic control units, or any other components having semi-conductor circuitry could be irreparably damaged.

• If the engine is being started using jump leads and a slave battery, connect the batteries *positive-to-positive* and *negative-to-negative* (see *Jump starting*). This also applies when connecting a battery charger but in this case both of the battery terminals should first be disconnected.

• Never disconnect the battery terminals, the alternator, any electrical wiring or any test instruments when the engine is running.
• Do not allow the engine to turn the alternator when the alternator is not connected.
• Never test for alternator output by flashing the output lead to earth.
• Never use an ohmmeter of the type incorporating a hand-cranked generator for circuit or continuity testing.
• Always ensure that the battery negative lead is disconnected when working on the electrical system.
• Before using electric-arc welding equipment on the car, disconnect the battery, alternator and components such as the fuel injection/ignition electronic control unit to protect them from the risk of damage.

Several systems fitted to the vehicle require battery power to be available at all times, either to ensure their continued operation (such as the clock) or to maintain control unit memories or security codes which would be wiped if the battery were to be disconnected. To ensure that there are no unforeseen consequences of this action, Refer to *Disconnecting the battery* in the Reference Chapter for further information.

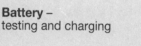

2 Battery – testing and charging

Testing

Standard and low maintenance battery

1 If the vehicle covers a small annual mileage, it is worthwhile checking the specific gravity of the electrolyte every three months to determine the state of charge of the battery. Use a hydrometer to make the check and compare the results with the following table. Note that the specific gravity readings assume an electrolyte temperature of 15°C (60°F); for every 10°C (18°F) below 15°C (60°F) subtract 0.007. For every 10°C (18°F) above 15°C (60°F) add 0.007.

	Ambient temperature	
	Above 25°C	Below 25°C
Charged	1.210 to 1.230	1.270 to 1.290
70% charged	1.170 to 1.190	1.230 to 1.250
Discharged	1.050 to 1.070	1.110 to 1.130

2 If the battery condition is suspect, first check the specific gravity of electrolyte in each cell. A variation of 0.040 or more between any cells indicates loss of electrolyte or deterioration of the internal plates.
3 If the specific gravity variation is 0.040 or more, the battery should be renewed. If the cell variation is satisfactory but the battery is discharged, it should be charged as described later in this Section.

Maintenance-free battery

4 In cases where a sealed for life maintenance-free battery is fitted, topping-up and testing of the electrolyte in each cell is not

possible. The condition of the battery can therefore only be tested using a battery condition indicator or a voltmeter.
5 Certain models may be fitted with a maintenance-free battery with a built-in charge condition indicator. The indicator is located in the top of the battery casing, and indicates the condition of the battery from its colour. If the indicator shows green, then the battery is in a good state of charge. If the indicator turns darker, eventually to black, then the battery requires charging, as described later in this Section. If the indicator shows clear/yellow, then the electrolyte level in the battery is too low to allow further use, and the battery should be renewed. **Do not** attempt to charge, load or jump start a battery when the indicator shows clear/yellow.
6 If testing the battery using a voltmeter, connect the voltmeter across the battery and compare the result with those given in the *Specifications* under 'charge condition'. The test is only accurate if the battery has not been subjected to any kind of charge for the previous six hours. If this is not the case, switch on the headlights for 30 seconds, then wait four to five minutes before testing the battery after switching off the headlights. All other electrical circuits must be switched off, so check that the doors and tailgate are fully shut when making the test.
7 If the voltage reading is less than 12.2 volts, then the battery is discharged, whilst a reading of 12.2 to 12.4 volts indicates a partially discharged condition.
8 If the battery is to be charged, remove it from the vehicle (Section 3) and charge it as described later in this Section.

Charging

Note: *The following is intended as a guide only. Always refer to the manufacturer's recommendations (often printed on a label attached to the battery) before charging a battery.*

Standard and low maintenance battery

9 Charge the battery at a rate of 3.5 to 4 amps and continue to charge the battery at this rate until no further rise in specific gravity is noted over a four hour period.
10 Alternatively, a trickle charger charging at the rate of 1.5 amps can safely be used overnight.
11 Specially rapid boost charges which are claimed to restore the power of the battery in 1 to 2 hours are not recommended, as they can cause serious damage to the battery plates through overheating.
12 While charging the battery, note that the temperature of the electrolyte should never exceed 37.8°C (100°F).

Maintenance-free battery

13 This battery type takes considerably longer to fully recharge than the standard type, the time taken being dependent on the extent of discharge, but it can take anything up to three days.

14 A constant voltage type charger is required, to be set, when connected, to 13.9 to 14.9 volts with a charger current below 25 amps. Using this method, the battery should be usable within three hours, giving a voltage reading of 12.5 volts, but this is for a partially discharged battery and, as mentioned, full charging can take considerably longer.
15 If the battery is to be charged from a fully discharged state (condition reading less than 12.2 volts), have it recharged by your Fiat dealer or local automotive electrician, as the charge rate is higher and constant supervision during charging is necessary.

3 Battery and battery tray – removal and refitting

Note: *Refer to 'Disconnecting the battery' in the Reference Chapter before proceeding.*

Battery

Removal

1 Slacken the clamp bolt and disconnect the clamp from the battery negative (earth) terminal **(see illustration)**.
2 Remove the insulation cover and disconnect the positive terminal lead(s) in the same way.
3 Undo the two retaining bolts and lift off the battery retaining strap.
4 Lift the battery up and out of the tray and remove it from the engine compartment.

Refitting

5 Refitting is a reversal of removal but make sure that the positive terminal is connected first followed by the negative terminal.

Battery tray

Removal

6 With the battery removed, undo the three bolts securing the battery tray to the body platform **(see illustration)**.
7 Release the wiring harness from the clips on the side of the battery tray, then lift the tray from its location.

Refitting

8 Refitting is a reversal of removal.

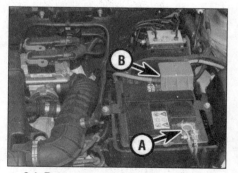

3.1 Battery negative terminal (A) and positive terminal (B)

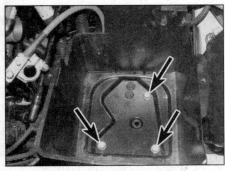

3.6 Battery tray retaining bolts (arrowed)

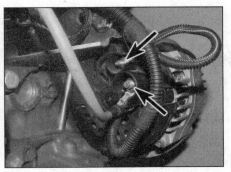

5.4 Disconnect the cables (arrowed) from the rear of the alternator

Models without air conditioning

4 Undo the retaining nuts and disconnect the cables from the rear of the alternator **(see illustration)**.

5 Slacken the alternator lower pivot bolt and the upper adjustment bolts **(see illustrations)**. Swivel the alternator towards the engine and slip the auxiliary drivebelt off the alternator pulley.

6 Unscrew and remove the pivot and adjustment bolts and withdraw the alternator from the engine.

Models with air conditioning

7 Working as described in Chapter 1, release the auxiliary drivebelt automatic tensioner and slip the drivebelt off the alternator pulley.

8 From under the car, undo the two nuts securing the exhaust manifold downpipe to the front pipe flange. Separate the front pipe from the downpipe **(see illustration)**.

9 Unscrew the bolt securing the rear engine mounting assembly to the subframe.

10 Undo the retaining nuts and disconnect the cables from the rear of the alternator.

11 Unscrew the alternator upper and lower mounting bolts and withdraw the alternator from the engine. Note that it will be necessary to tip the engine forward slightly to gain access to the upper mounting bolt.

Refitting

12 Refitting is a reversal of removal, bearing in mind the following points:

a) *Refer to Chapter 1 for details of tensioning the auxiliary drivebelt.*

b) *On models with air conditioning, tighten the exhaust front pipe flange nuts and rear engine mounting bolt to the specified torque (see Chapters 4A and 2B respectively).*

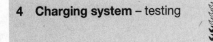

4 Charging system – testing

Note: *Refer to the warnings given in 'Safety first!' and in Section 1 of this Chapter before starting work.*

1 If the ignition warning light fails to illuminate when the ignition is switched on, first check the alternator wiring connections for security. If satisfactory, check that the warning light bulb has not blown, and that the bulbholder is secure in its location in the instrument panel. If the light still fails to illuminate, check the continuity of the warning light feed wire from the alternator to the bulbholder. If all is satisfactory, the alternator is at fault and should be renewed or taken to an auto-electrician for testing and repair.

2 If the ignition warning light illuminates when the engine is running, stop the engine and check that the drivebelt is correctly tensioned (see Chapter 1) and that the alternator connections are secure. If all is so far satisfactory, have the alternator checked by an auto-electrician.

3 If the alternator output is suspect even though the warning light functions correctly, the regulated voltage may be checked as follows.

4 Connect a voltmeter across the battery terminals and start the engine.

5 Increase the engine speed until the voltmeter reading remains steady; the reading should be approximately 12 to 13 volts, and no more than 14 volts.

6 Switch on as many electrical accessories (eg, the headlights, heated rear window and heater blower) as possible, and check that the alternator maintains the regulated voltage at around 13 to 14 volts.

7 If the regulated voltage is not as stated, the fault may be due to worn brushes, weak brush springs, a faulty voltage regulator, a faulty diode, a severed phase winding or worn or damaged slip-rings. The alternator should be renewed or taken to an auto-electrician for testing and repair.

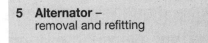

5 Alternator – removal and refitting

Removal

1 Disconnect the battery negative terminal (refer to *Disconnecting the battery* in the Reference Chapter).

2 Firmly apply the handbrake, then jack up the front of the car and support it securely on axle stands (see *Jacking and vehicle support*). Remove the right-hand front roadwheel.

3 Working under the right-hand wheel arch, undo the retaining screws and remove the wheel arch liner main and centre panels for access to the alternator lower mounting bolt.

6 Alternator – testing and overhaul

If the alternator is thought to be suspect, it should be removed from the car and taken to an auto-electrician for testing. Most auto-

5.5a Slacken the alternator lower pivot bolt (arrowed) . . .

5.5b . . . and upper adjustment bolts (arrowed), then swivel the alternator towards the engine to remove the drivebelt

5.8 On models with air conditioning, undo the nuts (arrowed) and separate the exhaust manifold downpipe from the front pipe

electricians will be able to supply and fit new parts at a reasonable cost. However, check on the cost of repairs before proceeding as it may prove more economical to obtain a new or exchange alternator.

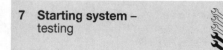

7 Starting system – testing

Note: *Refer to the precautions given in 'Safety first!' and in Section 1 of this Chapter before starting work.*

1 If the starter motor fails to operate when the ignition key is turned to the appropriate position, the following possible causes may be to blame.
   a) *The battery is faulty.*
   b) *The electrical connections between the switch, solenoid, battery and starter motor are somewhere failing to pass the necessary current from the battery through the starter to earth.*
   c) *The solenoid is faulty.*
   d) *The starter motor is mechanically or electrically defective.*

2 To check the battery, switch on the headlights. If they dim after a few seconds, this indicates that the battery is discharged – recharge (see Section 2) or renew the battery. If the headlights glow brightly, operate the ignition switch and observe the lights. If they dim, then this indicates that current is reaching the starter motor, therefore the fault

must lie in the starter motor. If the lights continue to glow brightly (and no clicking sound can be heard from the starter motor solenoid), this indicates that there is a fault in the circuit or solenoid – see following paragraphs. If the starter motor turns slowly when operated, but the battery is in good condition, then this indicates that either the starter motor is faulty, or there is considerable resistance somewhere in the circuit.

3 If a fault in the circuit is suspected, disconnect the battery leads (including the earth connection to the body), the starter/solenoid wiring and the engine/transmission earth strap. Thoroughly clean the connections, and reconnect the leads and wiring, then use a voltmeter or test lamp to check that full battery voltage is available at the battery positive lead connection to the solenoid, and that the earth is sound. Smear petroleum jelly around the battery terminals to prevent corrosion – corroded connections are amongst the most frequent causes of electrical system faults.

4 If the battery and all connections are in good condition, check the circuit by disconnecting the wire from the solenoid blade terminal. Connect a voltmeter or test lamp between the wire end and a good earth (such as the battery negative terminal), and check that the wire is live when the ignition switch is turned to the start position. If it is, then the circuit is sound – if not, the circuit wiring can be checked as described in Chapter 12, Section 2.

5 The solenoid contacts can be checked by connecting a voltmeter or test lamp across the solenoid. When the ignition switch is turned to the start position, there should be a reading or lighted bulb, as applicable. If there is no reading or lighted bulb, the solenoid is faulty and should be renewed.

6 If the circuit and solenoid are proved sound, the fault must lie in the starter motor. In this event, it may be possible to have the starter motor overhauled by a specialist, but check on the cost of spares before proceeding, as it may prove more economical to obtain a new or exchange motor.

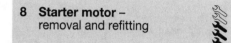

8 Starter motor – removal and refitting

Removal

1 Disconnect the battery negative terminal (refer to *Disconnecting the battery* in the Reference Chapter).

2 Firmly apply the handbrake, then jack up the front of the car and support it securely on axle stands (see *Jacking and vehicle support*).

3 Remove the air cleaner assembly as described in Chapter 4A.

4 Unscrew and remove the starter motor upper mounting bolt located at the top of the transmission bellhousing **(see illustration)**.

5 From under the car, raise the plastic cover over the starter solenoid wiring terminals **(see illustration)**.

6 Unscrew the two nuts and disconnect the wiring from the solenoid terminal studs **(see illustration)**.

7 Unscrew the lower mounting bolt(s), then withdraw the starter motor from the transmission **(see illustration)**.

Refitting

8 Refitting is a reversal of removal.

9 Starter motor – testing and overhaul

If the starter motor is thought to be suspect, it should be removed from the car and taken to an auto-electrician for testing. Most auto-electricians will be able to supply and fit new parts at a reasonable cost. However, check on the cost of repairs before proceeding as it may prove more economical to obtain a new or exchange motor.

10 Ignition switch – removal and refitting

The ignition switch is integral with the steering column lock and can be removed as described in Chapter 10.

8.4 Unscrew and remove the starter motor upper mounting bolt (arrowed)

8.5 Raise the plastic cover over the starter solenoid wiring terminals

8.6 Unscrew the nuts (arrowed) and disconnect the wiring from the solenoid terminal studs

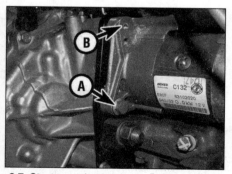

8.7 Starter motor lower mounting bolt (A) and, on certain models, the additional bolt at (B)

Chapter 5 Part B:
Ignition system

Contents

Degrees of difficulty

Easy, suitable for novice with little experience	Fairly easy, suitable for beginner with some experience	Fairly difficult, suitable for competent DIY mechanic	Difficult, suitable for experienced DIY mechanic	Very difficult, suitable for expert DIY or professional

Specifications

General

System type	Static (distributorless) ignition system controlled by engine management ECU
Firing order	1–3–4–2 (No 1 cylinder at timing belt end of engine)
Spark plugs	See Chapter 1 Specifications
Ignition timing	Controlled by engine management ECU

Ignition coil

Resistances (at 20° C):

Primary windings	0.52 to 0.62 ohms
Secondary windings	6.83 to 7.83 k ohms

Torque wrench setting	Nm	lbf ft
Knock sensor securing bolt	20	15

1 General information

The ignition system is integrated with the fuel injection system to form a combined engine management system under the control of one ECU (see Chapter 4A for further information).

The ignition side of the system is of the static (distributorless) type, consisting only of two twin-output ignition coils located on the left-hand side of the cylinder head. Each ignition coil supplies two cylinders (one coil supplies cylinders 1 and 4, and the other cylinders 2 and 3). Under the control of the ECU, the ignition coils operate on the wasted spark principle, ie, each spark plug sparks twice for every cycle of the engine, once on the compression stroke and once on the exhaust stroke. The spark voltage is greatest in the cylinder which is under compression, the other cylinder having a very weak spark which has no effect on the exhaust gases. The ECU uses its inputs from the various sensors to calculate the required ignition advance setting and coil charging time depending on engine temperature, load and speed.

A knock sensor is also incorporated into the ignition system. Mounted onto the cylinder block, the sensor detects the high-frequency vibrations caused when the engine starts to pre-ignite, or 'pink'. Under these conditions, the knock sensor sends an electrical signal to the ECU which in turn retards the ignition advance setting in small steps until the 'pinking' ceases.

2 Ignition system – testing

Warning: Due to the high voltages produced by the electronic ignition system, extreme care must be taken when working on the system with the ignition switched on. Persons with surgically-implanted cardiac pacemaker devices should keep well clear of the ignition circuits, components and test equipment.

1 If a fault appears in the engine management (fuel injection/ignition) system first ensure that the fault is not due to a poor electrical connection or poor maintenance; ie, check that the air cleaner filter element is clean, the spark plugs are in good condition and correctly gapped, that the engine breather hoses are clear and undamaged, referring to Chapter 1 for further information. On SOHC (8-valve) engines, also check that the accelerator cable is correctly adjusted as described in Chapter 4A. If the engine is running very roughly, check the compression pressures and the valve clearances as described in Chapters 1 and 2.

2 If these checks fail to reveal the cause of the problem, the vehicle should be taken to a suitably-equipped Fiat dealer for testing. A diagnostic connector is incorporated in the engine management wiring circuit into which a special electronic diagnostic tester can be plugged. The tester will locate the fault quickly and simply alleviating the need to test all the system components individually which is a time-consuming operation that carries a high risk of damaging the ECU.

3 The only ignition system checks which can be carried out by the home mechanic are those described in Chapter 1, relating to the spark plugs, and the ignition coil test described in this Chapter. If necessary, the system wiring and wiring connectors can be checked as described in Chapter 12, ensuring that the ECU wiring connectors have first been disconnected.

3 Ignition HT coils – removal, testing and refitting

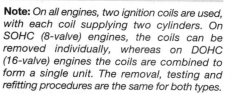

Note: *On all engines, two ignition coils are used, with each coil supplying two cylinders. On SOHC (8-valve) engines, the coils can be removed individually, whereas on DOHC (16-valve) engines the coils are combined to form a single unit. The removal, testing and refitting procedures are the same for both types.*

Removal

1 Remove the air cleaner assembly as described in Chapter 4A.

2 Disconnect the LT wiring plug(s) from the top of the ignition coil **(see illustration)**.

3 Identify the HT leads for position then disconnect them from the coil HT terminals **(see illustration)**.

4 Unscrew the mounting bolts and remove the relevant ignition coil from the end of the cylinder head **(see illustrations)**.

Testing

5 Testing of the coil consists of using a multimeter set to its resistance function, to check the primary and secondary windings for continuity and resistance. Compare the results obtained to those given in the Specifications at the start of this Chapter. Note the resistance of the coil windings varies slightly according to the coil temperature and the figures in the Specifications are values for the coil at 20ºC.

6 Check that there is no continuity between the HT lead terminals and the coil body/mounting bracket.

7 Note that with the ignition switched on and the engine stationary, voltage will only be supplied to the ignition coils for approximately 2 seconds. However, when the engine is being cranked or running, voltage will be continually supplied.

8 If faulty, the coil should be renewed.

Refitting

9 Refitting is a reversal of the removal procedure ensuring that the wiring and HT leads are correctly reconnected.

4 Ignition timing – checking and adjustment

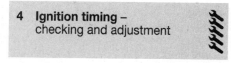

1 The ignition timing is constantly being monitored and adjusted by the engine management ECU, and nominal values cannot be given. Therefore, it is not possible for the home mechanic to check the ignition timing.

2 The only way in which the timing can be checked is using special electronic test equipment, connected to the engine management system diagnostic connector (refer to Chapter 4A for further information).

5 Knock sensor – removal and refitting

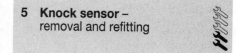

Removal

1 The knock sensor is screwed into the rear face of the cylinder block, behind the alternator rear mounting bracket.

2 Firmly apply the handbrake, then jack up the front of the car and support it securely on axle stands (see *Jacking and vehicle support*).

3 Trace the wiring back from the sensor to its wiring connector, and disconnect it from the main loom.

4 From under the car, disconnect the knock sensor wiring connector.

5 Undo the sensor securing bolt and remove the sensor from the cylinder block.

Refitting

6 Refitting is a reversal of the removal procedure, ensuring that the sensor securing bolt is tightened to the specified torque.

3.2 Disconnect the ignition coil LT wiring plug(s)

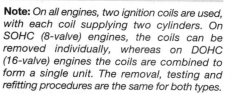

3.3 Identify the HT leads for position then disconnect them from the coil terminals

3.4a Unscrew the mounting bolts . . .

3.4b . . . and remove the relevant ignition coil from the end of the cylinder head

Chapter 6
Clutch

Contents

Degrees of difficulty

Easy, suitable for novice with little experience		**Fairly easy,** suitable for beginner with some experience		**Fairly difficult,** suitable for competent DIY mechanic		**Difficult,** suitable for experienced DIY mechanic		**Very difficult,** suitable for expert DIY or professional	

Specifications

General
Type . . . . Single dry plate with diaphragm spring, hydraulically-operated

Friction plate diameter
SOHC (8-valve) engines . . . . 180.0 mm
DOHC (16-valve) engines . . . . 190.0 mm

Torque wrench setting	Nm	lbf ft
Pressure plate retaining bolts	16	12

1 General information

The clutch assembly consists of a friction plate, a pressure plate, a release bearing and release fork; all of these components are contained in the large cast-aluminium alloy bellhousing, sandwiched between the engine and the transmission. The release mechanism is hydraulic, utilising a master cylinder and slave cylinder.

The friction plate is fitted between the engine flywheel and the clutch pressure plate, and is allowed to slide on the transmission input shaft splines.

The pressure plate assembly is bolted to the engine flywheel. When the engine is running, drive is transmitted from the crankshaft, via the flywheel, to the friction plate (these components being clamped securely together by the pressure plate assembly) and from the friction plate to the transmission input shaft.

To interrupt the drive, the spring pressure must be relaxed. This is done by means of the clutch release bearing, fitted concentrically around the transmission input shaft. The bearing is pushed onto the pressure plate assembly by means of the release fork actuated by the slave cylinder pushrod.

The clutch pedal is connected to the clutch master cylinder by a short pushrod. The master cylinder is mounted on the engine side of the bulkhead in front of the driver and receives its hydraulic fluid supply from the brake master cylinder reservoir. Depressing the clutch pedal moves the piston in the master cylinder forwards, so forcing hydraulic fluid through the clutch hydraulic pipe to the slave cylinder. The piston in the slave cylinder moves forward on the entry of the fluid and actuates the clutch release fork by means of a short pushrod. The release fork pivots on its mountings, and the other end of the fork then presses the release bearing against the pressure plate spring fingers. This causes the springs to deform and releases the clamping force on the pressure plate.

The clutch operating mechanism is self-adjusting, and no manual adjustment is required.

2 Clutch hydraulic system – bleeding

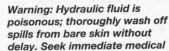

Warning: Hydraulic fluid is poisonous; thoroughly wash off spills from bare skin without delay. Seek immediate medical advice if any fluid is swallowed or gets into the eyes. Certain types of hydraulic fluid

are inflammable and may ignite when brought into contact with hot components; when servicing any hydraulic system, it is safest to assume that the fluid IS inflammable, and to take precautions against the risk of fire as though it were petrol that was being handled. Hydraulic fluid is an effective paint stripper and will also attack many plastics. If spillage occurs onto painted bodywork or fittings it should be washed off immediately, using copious quantities of fresh water. It is also hygroscopic – it can absorb moisture from the air, which then renders it useless. Old fluid may have suffered contamination, and should never be re-used. When topping-up or renewing the fluid, always use the recommended grade, and ensure that it comes from a new sealed container.

General information

1 Whenever the clutch hydraulic lines are disconnected for service or repair, a certain amount of air will enter the system. The presence of air in any hydraulic system will introduce a degree of elasticity, and in the clutch system this will translate into poor pedal feel and reduced travel, leading to inefficient gearchanges and even clutch system failure. For this reason, after reconnection of the hydraulic lines, the system must be topped-up and bled to remove any air bubbles.

2 The most effective way of bleeding the clutch hydraulic system is to use a pressure brake bleeding kit. These are readily available in motor accessories shops and are extremely effective. The following procedure describes bleeding the clutch system using such a kit. The alternative method is to bleed the system by depressing the clutch pedal – refer to the brake hydraulic system bleeding procedures contained in Chapter 9 for details of this method.

3 Two different types of clutch slave cylinder are used on Punto models and it is necessary to identify the type fitted as the bleeding procedure differs between types.

4 Remove the battery and battery tray as described in Chapter 5A, then observe the slave cylinder which is located on the top of the transmission housing. Check whether the cylinder incorporates a conventional bleed nipple which can be unscrewed using a spanner. If a bleed nipple cannot be seen there will be a hydraulic fluid outlet stub in its place. On this type of cylinder there is an internal bleed valve which is opened by partially releasing the hydraulic fluid supply hose.

5 Having identified the type of slave cylinder fitted, proceed as follows according to type.

Bleeding

6 Remove the protective cap from the slave cylinder bleed nipple, or from the fluid outlet stub. Connect a length of clear plastic hose over the nipple or outlet and insert the other end into a clean container. Pour hydraulic fluid into the container, such that the end of the hose is covered.

7 Following the manufacturer's instructions, pour hydraulic fluid into the bleeding kit vessel.

8 Unscrew the brake fluid reservoir filler cap, then connect the bleeding kit fluid supply hose to the reservoir.

9 Connect the pressure hose to a supply of compressed air – a spare tyre is a convenient source. **Caution: Check that the pressure in the tyre does not exceed the maximum supply pressure quoted by the kit manufacturer, let some air escape to reduce the pressure, if necessary. Gently open the air valve and allow the air and fluid pressures to equalise. Check that there are no leaks before proceeding.**

10 Where a bleed nipple is fitted, slacken the nipple approximately half a turn. If a bleed nipple is not fitted, extract the retaining clip securing the hydraulic fluid hose to the slave cylinder. With the clip removed, carefully pull the hose out of the slave cylinder by one click, to open the internal bleed valve.

11 Allow the hydraulic fluid to flow from the slave cylinder, through the plastic hose and into the container. Maintain a steady flow until the emerging fluid is free of air bubbles; keep a watchful eye on the level of fluid in the bleeding kit vessel and the brake fluid reservoir – if it is allowed to drop too low, air may be forced into the system, defeating the object of the exercise. To refill the vessel, turn off the compressed air supply, remove the lid and pour in an appropriate quantity of fresh fluid – do not re-use the fluid collected in the receiving container. Repeat as necessary until the ejected fluid is bubble-free.

12 When clean hydraulic fluid, free from air bubbles, emerges from the plastic hose, tighten the slave cylinder bleed nipple, or push in the hydraulic fluid hose and secure with the retaining clip, as applicable.

13 Pump the clutch pedal several times to assess its feel and travel. If firm, constant pedal resistance is not felt throughout the pedal stroke, it is probable that air is still present in the system – repeat the bleeding procedure until the pedal feel is restored.

14 Depressurise the bleeding kit and remove the kit, plastic hose and receiving container from the vehicle. Refit the protective cap to the bleed nipple or outlet stub. Discard the fluid expelled from the hydraulic system as it will be contaminated with moisture, air and dirt, making it unfit for further use.

15 Check the fluid level in the reservoir. At this point, the reservoir may be over-full; the excess should be removed using a *clean* pipette to reduce the level to the MAX mark.

16 Refit the battery and tray with reference to Chapter 5A.

17 Finally, road test the vehicle and check the operation of the clutch system whilst changing up and down through the gears, whilst pulling away from a standstill and from a hill start.

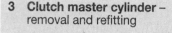

3 Clutch master cylinder – removal and refitting

Note: *Refer to the warning at the beginning of Section 2 regarding the hazards of working with hydraulic fluid.*

Removal

1 Disconnect the battery negative terminal (refer to *Disconnecting the battery* in the Reference Chapter).

2 Remove the air cleaner assembly as described in Chapter 4A.

3 Working inside the vehicle, depress the clutch pedal fully, then release the plastic retainer securing the master cylinder pushrod to the clutch pedal.

4 To minimise hydraulic fluid loss, remove the brake master cylinder reservoir filler cap, then tighten it down onto a piece of polythene to obtain an airtight seal. Alternatively, fit a brake hose clamp to the hose between the hydraulic fluid reservoir and the clutch master cylinder.

5 Place absorbent rags beneath the master cylinder and be prepared for hydraulic fluid loss.

6 Disconnect the fluid supply hose at the master cylinder, then extract the retaining clip and disconnect the hydraulic pipe from the cylinder outlet.

7 Unscrew the mounting bolts and withdraw the master cylinder from the bulkhead.

8 It is not possible to obtain an overhaul kit from Fiat, however some motor factors may be able to supply one. Follow the instructions with the repair kit if obtained.

Refitting

9 Refitting is the reverse of the removal procedure, but bleed the clutch hydraulic system as described in Section 2 on completion.

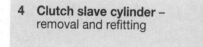

4 Clutch slave cylinder – removal and refitting

Note: *Refer to the warning at the beginning of Section 2 regarding the hazards of working with hydraulic fluid.*

Removal

1 Remove the battery and battery tray as described in Chapter 5A.

2 To minimise hydraulic fluid loss, remove the brake master cylinder reservoir filler cap, then tighten it down onto a piece of polythene to obtain an airtight seal.

3 Place absorbent rags around the slave cylinder, and be prepared for hydraulic fluid loss.

4.5 Clutch slave cylinder retaining bolts (arrowed)

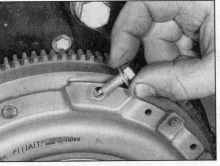

5.3 Removing the clutch pressure plate bolts

5.16 Using a clutch friction plate centralising tool

4 Extract the retaining clip and disconnect the hydraulic hose from the slave cylinder.

5 Unscrew the slave cylinder mounting bolts, release the cylinder pushrod from the release arm on the transmission, then remove the unit from the engine compartment **(see illustration)**.

6 It is not possible to obtain an overhaul kit from Fiat, however some motor factors may be able to supply one. Follow the instructions with the repair kit if obtained.

Refitting

7 Refitting is the reverse of the removal procedure, but bleed the clutch hydraulic system as described in Section 2 on completion.

5 Clutch assembly – removal, inspection and refitting

Warning: Dust created by clutch wear and deposited on the clutch components may contain asbestos, which is a health hazard. DO NOT blow it out with compressed air, or inhale any of it. DO NOT use petrol or petroleum-based solvents to clean off the dust. Brake system cleaner or methylated spirit should be used to flush the dust into a suitable receptacle. After the clutch components are wiped clean with rags, dispose of the contaminated rags and cleaner in a sealed, marked container.

Removal

1 Unless the complete engine/transmission is to be removed from the car and separated for major overhaul (see Chapter 2C), the clutch can be reached by removing the transmission as described in Chapter 7A.

2 Before disturbing the clutch, use chalk or a marker pen to mark the relationship of the pressure plate assembly to the flywheel.

3 Working in a diagonal sequence, slacken the pressure plate bolts by half a turn at a time, until spring pressure is released and the bolts can be unscrewed by hand **(see illustration)**.

4 Prise the pressure plate assembly off its locating dowels, and collect the friction plate, noting which way round the friction plate is fitted.

Inspection

Note: *Due to the amount of work necessary to remove and refit clutch components, it is usually considered good practice to renew the clutch friction plate, pressure plate assembly and release bearing as a matched set, even if only one of these is actually worn enough to require renewal. It is also worth considering the renewal of the clutch components on a preventative basis if the engine and/or transmission have been removed for some other reason.*

5 When cleaning clutch components, read first the warning at the beginning of this Section; remove dust using a clean, dry cloth, and working in a well-ventilated atmosphere. **Note:** *Although some friction materials may no longer contain asbestos, it is safest to assume that they DO, and to take precautions accordingly.*

6 Check the friction plate facings for signs of wear, damage or oil contamination. If the friction material is cracked, burnt, scored or damaged, or if it is contaminated with oil or grease (shown by shiny black patches), the friction plate must be renewed.

7 If the friction material is still serviceable, check that the centre boss splines are unworn, that the torsion springs are in good condition and securely fastened, and that all the rivets are tight. If any wear or damage is found, the friction plate must be renewed.

8 If the friction material is fouled with oil, this must be due to an oil leak from the crankshaft left-hand oil seal, from the sump-to-cylinder block joint, or from the transmission input shaft. Renew the seal or repair the joint, as appropriate, before installing the new friction plate.

9 Check the pressure plate assembly for obvious signs of wear or damage; shake it to check for loose rivets or worn or damaged fulcrum rings, and check that the drive straps securing the pressure plate to the cover do not show signs (such as a deep yellow or blue discoloration) of overheating. If the diaphragm spring is worn or damaged, or if its pressure is in any way suspect, the pressure plate assembly should be renewed.

10 Examine the machined bearing surfaces of the pressure plate and of the flywheel; they should be clean, completely flat, and free from scratches or scoring. If either is discoloured from excessive heat, or shows signs of cracks, it should be renewed – although minor damage of this nature can sometimes be polished away using emery paper.

11 Check that the release bearing contact surface rotates smoothly and easily, with no sign of noise or roughness. Also check that the surface itself is smooth and unworn, with no signs of cracks, pitting or scoring. If there is any doubt about its condition, the bearing must be renewed.

Refitting

12 On reassembly, ensure that the bearing surfaces of the flywheel and pressure plate are completely clean, smooth, and free from oil or grease. Use solvent to remove any protective grease from new components.

13 Fit the friction plate so that its spring hub assembly faces away from the flywheel; there may also be a marking showing which way round the plate is to be refitted.

14 Refit the pressure plate assembly, aligning the marks made on dismantling (if the original pressure plate is re-used), and locating the pressure plate on its locating dowels. Fit the pressure plate bolts, but tighten them only finger-tight, so that the friction plate can still be moved.

15 The friction plate must now be centralised, so that when the transmission is refitted, its input shaft will pass through the splines at the centre of the friction plate.

16 Centralisation can be achieved by passing a screwdriver or other long bar through the friction plate and into the hole in the crankshaft; the friction plate can then be moved around until it is centred on the crankshaft hole. Alternatively, a clutch-aligning tool can be used to eliminate the guesswork; these can be obtained from most accessory shops **(see illustration)**. A home-made aligning tool can be fabricated from a length of metal rod or wooden dowel which fits closely inside the crankshaft hole, and has

insulating tape wound around it to match the diameter of the friction plate splined hole.

17 When the friction plate is centralised, tighten the pressure plate bolts evenly and in a diagonal sequence to the specified torque setting.

18 Apply a thin smear of molybdenum disulphide grease to the splines of the friction plate and the transmission input shaft, and also to the release bearing bore and release fork shaft.

19 Refit the transmission as described in Chapter 7A.

---

6 Clutch release mechanism – removal, inspection and refitting

Removal

1 Unless the complete engine/transmission is to be removed from the car and separated for major overhaul (see Chapter 2C), the clutch release mechanism can be reached by removing the transmission as described in Chapter 7A.

2 Unhook the release bearing from the fork and slide it off the guide tube.

3 Using circlip pliers extract the circlip from the top of the release fork shaft.

4 Note the position of the arm then slide it off the splines.

5 Using a small drift, tap out the upper release shaft bush from the transmission casing **(see illustration)**.

6 Lift the release shaft from the lower bush then remove it from inside the transmission casing.

7 Extract the lower bush from the casing.

Inspection

8 Check the release mechanism, renewing any worn or damaged parts. Carefully check all bearing surfaces and points of contact.

9 When checking the release bearing itself, note that it is often considered worthwhile to renew it as a matter of course. Check that the contact surface rotates smoothly and easily, with no sign of roughness, and that the surface itself is smooth and unworn, with no signs of cracks, pitting or scoring. If there is any doubt about its condition, the bearing must be renewed.

Refitting

10 Apply a smear of molybdenum disulphide grease to the shaft pivot bushes and the contact surfaces of the release fork.

6.5 Clutch release shaft (1) and upper shaft bush (2)

11 Tap the lower bush into the casing and refit the release fork and shaft.

12 Slide the upper bush down the shaft and tap it into the casing making sure that the ridge engages with the cut-out, then slide the arm on the splines the correct way round.

13 Refit the circlip in the shaft groove.

14 Slide the release bearing onto the guide tube and engage it with the fork.

15 Refit the transmission as described in Chapter 7A.

Chapter 7 Part A:
Manual transmission

Contents

Degrees of difficulty

Easy, suitable for novice with little experience	Fairly easy, suitable for beginner with some experience	Fairly difficult, suitable for competent DIY mechanic	Difficult, suitable for experienced DIY mechanic	Very difficult, suitable for expert DIY or professional

Specifications

General
Type .... Transversely-mounted, front wheel drive layout with integral transaxle differential/final drive. 5 or 6 forward speeds, 1 reverse speed
Designation .... C.514.5.10 (5-speed) or C.514.6.10 (6-speed)

Lubrication
Recommended oil type .... Refer to *Lubricants and fluids*
Capacity .... 1.65 litres

Torque wrench settings

	Nm	lbf ft
Engine/transmission attachment bolts	80	59
Engine/transmission mountings:		
Left-hand mounting bracket-to-transmission bolts	50	37
Left hand mounting-to-body bolts	25	18
Rear mounting-to-subframe bolt	120	89
Rear mounting-to-transmission bolt/nut	80	59
Gear lever housing retaining bolts:		
Upper bolt(s)	25	18
Lower bolts	30	22
Transmission oil drain and filler/level plugs	25	18

2.2 Transmission oil drain plug location (arrowed)

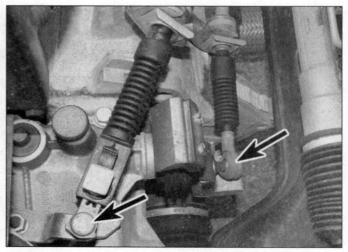

3.2 Disconnect the selector cable end fittings (arrowed) from the transmission selector levers

1 General information

The transmission is contained in a cast-aluminium alloy casing bolted to the engine's left-hand end, and consists of the gearbox and final drive differential.

Drive is transmitted from the crankshaft via the clutch to the input shaft, which has a splined extension to accept the clutch friction plate and rotates in roller bearings at its right-hand end and ball-bearings at its left-hand end (on 6-speed versions the left-hand extension rotates in a roller bearing). From the input shaft, drive is transmitted to the output shaft which rotates in roller bearings at its right-hand end and ball-bearings at its left-hand end (on 6-speed versions the left-hand extension rotates in ball-bearings). From the output shaft, the drive is transmitted to the differential crownwheel which rotates with the differential case and gears in taper roller bearings, thus driving the sun gears and driveshafts. The rotation of the differential gears on their shaft allows the inner roadwheel to rotate at a slower speed than the outer roadwheel when the car is cornering.

The input and output shafts are arranged side-by-side, parallel to the crankshaft and driveshafts, so that their gear pinion teeth are in constant mesh. In the neutral position, the relevant input shaft and output shaft gear pinions rotate freely, so that drive cannot be transmitted to the output shaft and crownwheel.

Gear selection is via a floor-mounted lever and twin selector cable mechanism. The selector cables cause the appropriate selector fork to move its respective synchro-sleeve along the shaft, to lock the gear to the synchro-hub. Since the synchro-hubs are

splined to the input and output shafts, this locks the gear to the shaft so that drive can be transmitted. To ensure that gearchanging can be made quickly and quietly, a synchromesh system is fitted to all forward gears.

2 Manual transmission oil – draining and refilling

1 Park the vehicle on a level surface, if possible over an inspection pit or on a ramp as the filler/level and drain plugs are accessed from under the engine compartment. If necessary jack up the vehicle and support on axle stands (see Jacking and vehicle support).
2 Wipe clean the area around the filler/level and drain plugs, which are on the front and bottom of the transmission (see illustration).
3 Using an Allen key, unscrew the filler/level plug and clean it.
4 Position a suitable container beneath the transmission, then use the Allen key to unscrew the drain plug. Allow the oil to completely drain.
5 Wipe clean the drain plug then refit and tighten it to the specified torque.
6 Fill the transmission with the correct grade and quantity of oil, referring to Chapter 1 when checking the level. Refit and tighten the filler/level plug.
7 Where applicable lower the vehicle to the ground.

3 Gearchange selector cables – removal and refitting

Removal

1 Disconnect the battery negative terminal

(refer to Disconnecting the battery in the Reference Chapter).
2 Disconnect the selector cable end fittings from their attachments at the transmission selector levers (see illustration).
3 Extract the retaining clip securing each selector cable to the transmission support bracket, then withdraw both cables from the bracket (see illustration).
4 Firmly apply the handbrake, then jack up the front of the car and support it securely on axle stands (see Jacking and vehicle support).
5 Unscrew the nuts and disconnect the exhaust front pipe flange from the manifold downpipe. Recover the gasket.
6 Undo the bolts securing the front and rear exhaust system mounting brackets to the underbody. Lower the system and suitably support it.
7 Where an exhaust system front heat shield is fitted, undo the retaining bolts and remove the heat shield.
8 Undo the bolts and remove the cover from

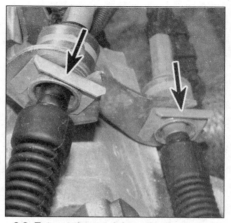

3.3 Extract the retaining clips (arrowed) securing the selector cables to the transmission support bracket

the base of the gear lever housing (see illustration).

9 Disconnect the selector cable end fittings from their attachments at the gear lever linkage.

10 Extract the two retaining clips securing the selector cables to the front of the gear lever housing. Withdraw the two cables from the housing.

11 Release the selector cables from the support clip above the front subframe, then remove the cables from under the car (see illustration).

Refitting

12 Refitting is a reversal of removal, bearing in mind the following points:

a) *Reconnect the exhaust system flange joint using a new gasket and tighten the mounting nuts to the specified torque (see Chapter 4A).*

b) *On completion, check that all gears can be selected without stiffness or binding. If necessary, adjust the position of the cable end fitting at the transmission end to improve gear selection quality.*

---

4 Gearchange lever assembly – removal and refitting

Removal

1 Disconnect the battery negative terminal (refer to *Disconnecting the battery* in the Reference Chapter).

2 From inside the car, release the gear lever gaiter from the centre console and slide the gaiter up the lever.

3 Undo the retaining bolt(s) at the front of the gear lever housing.

4 Firmly apply the handbrake, then jack up the front of the car and support it securely on axle stands (see *Jacking and vehicle support*).

5 Unscrew the nuts and disconnect the exhaust front pipe flange from the manifold downpipe. Recover the gasket.

6 Undo the bolts securing the front and rear exhaust system mounting brackets to the underbody. Lower the system and suitably support it.

7 Where an exhaust system front heat shield is fitted, undo the retaining bolts and remove the heat shield.

8 Undo the bolts and remove the cover from the base of the gear lever housing.

9 Disconnect the selector cable end fittings from their attachments at the gear lever linkage.

10 Extract the two retaining clips securing the selector cables to the front of the gear lever housing. Withdraw the two cables from the housing and position them to one side.

11 Undo the bolts securing the gear lever housing to the underbody and remove the housing from under the car.

3.8 Undo the bolts and remove the cover (arrowed) from the base of the gear lever housing

Refitting

12 Refitting is a reversal of removal, bearing in mind the following points:

a) *Tighten the gear lever housing retaining bolts to the specified torque.*

b) *Reconnect the exhaust system flange joint using a new gasket and tighten the mounting nuts to the specified torque (see Chapter 4A).*

---

5 Manual transmission – removal and refitting

Removal

1 Firmly apply the handbrake, then jack up the front of the car and support it securely on axle stands (see *Jacking and vehicle support*).

2 Remove both front wheels, then remove the left-hand wheel arch liner main and centre panels.

3 Remove the air cleaner assembly as described in Chapter 4A.

4 Remove the battery, battery tray and starter motor as described in Chapter 5A.

5 Disconnect the gearchange selector cable end fittings from the transmission lever ball-studs. Undo the three bolts securing the selector cable support bracket to the transmission and move the bracket and cables to one side.

6 Unbolt the clutch slave cylinder from the top of the transmission then fit a cable-tie around it to prevent the piston from being ejected. Position the cylinder to one side.

7 Disconnect the wiring connector from the reversing light switch on the front of the transmission, then unscrew the nut and disconnect the transmission earth lead from the top of the unit.

DOHC (16-valve) engine models

8 Remove the exhaust manifold as described in Chapter 4A.

9 Undo the bolts securing the engine

3.11 Release the selector cables from the support clip (arrowed) above the front subframe

management ECU mounting bracket to the throttle body and move the ECU to one side.

All models

10 Undo the bolts and remove the support brace linking the transmission to the cylinder block.

11 Unbolt and remove the cover plate from the base of the transmission bellhousing.

12 Disconnect the wiring from the vehicle speed sensor located on the top of the transmission differential housing.

13 Unscrew the nuts retaining the track rod ends on the swivel hubs and use a balljoint separator tool to disconnect them.

14 Unscrew the two bolts securing the right-hand swivel hub assembly to the front suspension strut, then move the hub assembly outwards.

15 Remove the retaining clip securing the right-hand driveshaft inner CV joint gaiter to the joint body. Pull the driveshaft and spider out of the joint body and move the driveshaft clear of the engine/transmission. Suitably cover the joint body and the driveshaft spider to prevent the escape of grease.

16 Undo the two bolts securing the left-hand brake caliper mounting bracket to the swivel hub. Slide the caliper and mounting bracket off the brake disc and suitably support it clear of the work area.

17 On models equipped with ABS, undo the retaining bolt securing the left-hand wheel speed sensor to the swivel hub. Withdraw the sensor from the swivel hub and position it clear of the work area.

18 Unscrew the two bolts securing the left-hand swivel hub assembly to the front suspension strut, and separate the hub assembly from the strut.

19 Slacken and remove the nut and clamp bolt then lift the left-hand swivel hub off the suspension lower arm balljoint.

20 Remove the retaining clip securing the left-hand driveshaft inner CV joint gaiter to the joint body. Pull the driveshaft and spider out of the joint body and remove the driveshaft and swivel hub assembly from the car.

Suitably cover the joint body and the driveshaft spider to prevent the escape of grease.

21 Working beneath the car, unscrew the bolts and nuts securing the rear engine mounting to the subframe and transmission, and withdraw the mounting.

22 Support the weight of the engine using a hoist attached to home-made brackets secured to suitable positions at the left-hand end of the engine.

23 Support the weight of the transmission on a trolley jack then unscrew the engine-to-transmission retaining bolts. Move aside all wiring and support brackets secured by the retaining bolts.

24 Unscrew the bolts securing the left-hand engine/transmission mounting to the body then unscrew the bolts from the transmission and remove the mounting.

25 Check that all pipes, hoses and wiring are moved clear then carefully pull the transmission away from the engine. Lower the trolley jack and remove the transmission from under the car.

⚠️ *Warning: Support the transmission to ensure that it remains steady on the jack head. Keep the transmission level until the input shaft is fully withdrawn from the clutch friction plate.*

Refitting

26 Refitting is a reversal of the removal procedure, bearing in mind the following points.
a) *Apply a smear of high-melting-point grease to the clutch friction plate splines; take care to avoid contaminating the friction surfaces.*
b) *Tighten all bolts to the specified torque, referring to the Chapters indicated for components not covered in this Chapter.*
c) *Use new clips to secure the driveshaft gaiters to their respective joint bodies.*

6 Reversing light switch – testing, removal and refitting

Testing

1 The reversing light circuit is controlled by a plunger-type switch screwed into the front of the transmission casing **(see illustration)**. If a fault develops, first ensure that the circuit fuse has not blown.

2 To test the switch, disconnect the wiring connector, and use a multimeter (set to the resistance function) or a battery-and-bulb test circuit to check that there is continuity between the switch terminals only when reverse gear is selected. If this is not the case, and there are no obvious breaks or other damage to the wires, the switch is faulty, and must be renewed.

Removal

3 Working in the engine compartment, disconnect the wiring connector, then unscrew the switch from the transmission casing.

Refitting

4 Refit and securely tighten the switch, then reconnect the wiring.

7 Manual transmission overhaul – general information

Overhauling a manual transmission is a difficult and involved job for the DIY home mechanic. In addition to dismantling and reassembling many small parts, clearances must be precisely measured and, if necessary, changed by selecting shims and spacers. Internal transmission components are also often difficult to obtain, and in many instances,

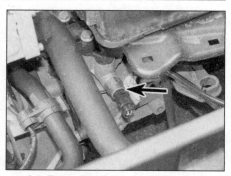

6.1 Reversing light switch location (arrowed)

extremely expensive. Because of this, if the transmission develops a fault or becomes noisy, the best course of action is to have the unit overhauled by a specialist repairer, or to obtain an exchange reconditioned unit.

Nevertheless, it is not impossible for the more experienced mechanic to overhaul the transmission, provided the special tools are available, and the job is done in a deliberate step-by-step manner, so that nothing is overlooked.

The tools necessary for an overhaul include internal and external circlip pliers, bearing pullers, a slide hammer, a set of pin punches, a dial test indicator, and possibly a hydraulic press. In addition, a large, sturdy workbench and a vice will be required.

During dismantling of the transmission, make careful notes of how each component is fitted, to make reassembly easier and more accurate.

Before dismantling the transmission, it will help if you have some idea what area is malfunctioning. Certain problems can be closely related to specific areas in the transmission, which can make component examination and replacement easier. Refer to the *Fault finding* in the Reference Chapter for more information.

Chapter 7 Part B:
Automatic transmission

Contents

Degrees of difficulty

Easy, suitable for novice with little experience	**Fairly easy,** suitable for beginner with some experience	**Fairly difficult,** suitable for competent DIY mechanic	**Difficult,** suitable for experienced DIY mechanic	**Very difficult,** suitable for expert DIY or professional

Specifications

General

Type .... ECVT (Electronic Continuously Variable Transmission)

Torque wrench settings	Nm	lbf ft
Engine/transmission attachment bolts	80	59
Engine/transmission mountings:		
Left-hand mounting bracket-to-transmission bolts	50	37
Left hand mounting-to-body bolts	25	18
Rear mounting-to-subframe bolt	120	89
Rear mounting-to-transmission bolt/nut	80	59
Gear selector lever housing retaining bolts	25	18
Torque converter retaining bolts:		
Stage 1	25	18
Stage 2	32	24

1 General information

The automatic transmission is of the ECVT (Electronic Continuously Variable Transmission) type, which can also be operated manually with six-speed or seven-speed sequential gear selection. The main components of the transmission are a torque converter, a variable-ratio coupling, an epicyclic geartrain, hydraulically-operated clutches, a final drive/differential unit, and the associated control mechanisms.

The variable-ratio coupling consists of two pulleys and a flexible metal drivebelt. When the transmission is in automatic mode, the effective diameter of the two pulleys is automatically varied to provide different transmission ratios between them. During normal driving, the transmission automatically selects the appropriate ratio, according to engine and vehicle speed, that provides the best compromise between economy and performance. An economy function is also available which enables the transmission to select ratios that provide greater fuel economy with a slight loss of performance. When the transmission is in manual mode, the epicyclic geartrain provides six or seven fixed ratios (according to model) which can be selected sequentially by the driver.

2.3a Extract the selector cable end fitting retaining clip (arrowed) . . .

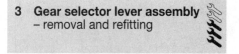

2.3b . . . and release the end fitting from the starter inhibitor/reversing light switch lever

Driver control of the transmission is by a floor-mounted selector lever, and an economy (E) button. The control positions in automatic mode are as follows:

P (Parking)   *The transmission is mechanically locked internally.*

R (Reverse)   *Reverse gear is engaged.*

N (Neutral)   *The transmission is in neutral.*

D (Drive)   *Normal driving position. Transmission ratio is varied automatically to suit prevailing speed and load. With the economy function selected, the transmission ratios will sacrifice performance to improve economy.*

L (Low)   *Prevents the transmission moving into high ratios. Provides maximum acceleration and maximum engine braking.*

With the transmission in manual mode, the selector lever is used to manually shift up or down sequentially through the six, or seven, fixed ratios provided by the epicyclic geartrain.

The transmission is electronically-controlled by means of an electronic control unit (ECU) located in the passenger's footwell. The transmission ECU receives signals from various sensors and is able to communicate with the engine management system ECU.

From the inputs received, the ECU is able to calculate vehicle speed and load and alter the transmission ratio accordingly.

Due to the complexity of the automatic transmission, any repair or overhaul work must be left to a Fiat dealer with the necessary special equipment for fault diagnosis and repair. The contents of the following Sections are therefore confined to supplying general information, and any service information and instructions that can be used by the owner.

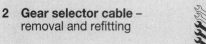

2 Gear selector cable – removal and refitting

Removal

1 Remove the air cleaner assembly as described in Chapter 4A.

2 Remove the battery and battery tray as described in Chapter 5A.

3 Extract the retaining clip and release the selector cable end fitting from the starter inhibitor/reversing light switch lever **(see illustrations)**.

4 Undo the nut securing the selector outer cable to the transmission support bracket and withdraw the cable from the bracket **(see illustration)**.

5 Firmly apply the handbrake, then jack up the front of the car and support it securely on axle stands (see *Jacking and vehicle support*).

6 Unscrew the nuts and disconnect the exhaust front pipe flange from the manifold downpipe. Recover the gasket.

7 Undo the bolts securing the front and rear exhaust system mounting brackets to the underbody. Lower the system and suitably support it.

8 Undo the retaining bolts and remove the exhaust system front heat shield.

9 Undo the bolts and remove the cover from the base of the selector lever housing.

10 Disconnect the selector cable end fitting from the base of the selector lever.

11 Extract the retaining clip securing the

selector cable to the front of the selector lever housing. Withdraw the cable from the housing and remove it from under the car.

Refitting

12 Reconnect the cable end fitting to the selector lever and secure the outer cable to the lever housing. Refit the cover to the base of the housing.

13 Feed the cable up over the transmission and secure the outer cable to the transmission support bracket.

14 Refit the heat shield and exhaust system, using a new gasket at the front pipe flange joint. Tighten the exhaust system fastenings to the specified torque settings as given in Chapter 4A.

15 Move the gear selector lever to the P (Park) position and rotate the starter inhibitor/reversing light switch lever fully clockwise to the end of its travel.

16 The cable end fitting should now be aligned with the peg on the switch lever and the end fitting should slide directly over the peg without binding. If this is not the case, slacken the end fitting locknut and rotate the end fitting as necessary. Tighten the locknut when the end fitting is correctly positioned.

17 Locate the cable end fitting over the starter inhibitor/reversing light switch lever and secure with the retaining clip.

18 Refit the battery tray and battery as described in Chapter 5A, then lower the car to the ground.

3 Gear selector lever assembly – removal and refitting

Removal

1 Disconnect the battery negative terminal (refer to *Disconnecting the battery* in the Reference Chapter).

2 Using a small screwdriver, carefully prise the selector lever knob locking collar downward to disengage the internal grooves on the collar from the external lugs on the

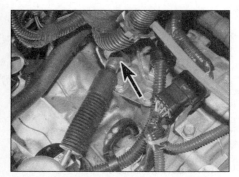

2.4 Undo the nut (arrowed) and withdraw the selector cable from the support bracket

3.2a Carefully prise the selector lever knob locking collar downward to disengage it from the knob . . .

3.2b . . . slide the knob off the selector lever . . .

3.2c . . . then remove the locking collar

knob base. Slide the knob off the selector lever, then remove the locking collar **(see illustrations)**.

3 Release the selector lever cover from the centre console and lift the cover up and off the selector lever **(see illustration)**.

4 Release the wiring harness from the selector lever housing and disconnect the wiring connector **(see illustration)**.

5 Firmly apply the handbrake, then jack up the front of the car and support it securely on axle stands (see *Jacking and vehicle support*).

6 Unscrew the nuts and disconnect the exhaust front pipe flange from the manifold downpipe. Recover the gasket.

7 Undo the bolts securing the front and rear exhaust system mounting brackets to the underbody. Lower the system and suitably support it.

8 Undo the retaining bolts and remove the exhaust system front heat shield.

9 Undo the bolts and remove the cover from the base of the selector lever housing.

10 Disconnect the selector cable end fitting from the base of the selector lever.

11 Extract the retaining clip and withdraw the selector cable from the housing.

12 Undo the bolts securing the selector lever housing to the underbody and remove the housing from under the car.

Refitting

13 Refitting is a reversal of removal, bearing in mind the following points:

4.2 Prise out the protective caps, then unbolt and remove the ECU cover

3.3 Release the selector lever cover from the console and lift the cover off the selector lever

a) Tighten the gear selector lever housing retaining bolts to the specified torque.

b) Reconnect the exhaust system flange joint using a new gasket and tighten the mounting nuts to the specified torque (see Chapter 4A).

---

4   Electronic control unit –
removal and refitting

Removal

1 Disconnect the battery negative terminal (refer to *Disconnecting the battery* in the Reference Chapter).

2 Working in the passenger's footwell, prise

4.3 Undo the mounting bolts and remove the ECU mounting bracket (arrowed)

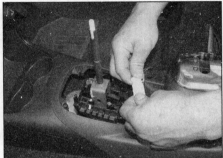

3.4 Release the wiring harness from the housing and disconnect the wiring connector

out the protective caps, undo the three bolts and lift off the ECU cover **(see illustration)**.

3 Undo the mounting bolts securing the ECU mounting bracket to the floor, noting the location of the earth lead **(see illustration)**.

4 Lift up the mounting bracket, disconnect the ECU wiring connectors and remove the assembly from the car.

5 Undo the four nuts securing the ECU to the mounting bracket and remove the ECU.

Refitting

6 Refitting is a reversal of removal.

---

5   Automatic transmission fluid cooler/heat exchanger –
removal and refitting

Removal

1 Remove the radiator as described in Chapter 3.

2 Remove the clips and disconnect the transmission fluid cooler/heat exchanger hoses at their connections on the transmission.

3 Lift the fluid cooler/heat exchanger from its location and remove it from the car.

Refitting

4 Referring to the procedures described in Chapter 3, refit the radiator, together with the fluid cooler/heat exchanger. Reconnect the hoses to the transmission and secure with new clips.

6 Automatic transmission – removal and refitting

Removal

1 Firmly apply the handbrake, then jack up the front of the car and support it securely on axle stands (see *Jacking and vehicle support*).
2 Remove both front wheels, then remove the left-hand wheel arch liner main and centre panels.
3 Remove the air cleaner assembly as described in Chapter 4A.
4 Remove the battery, battery tray and starter motor as described in Chapter 5A.
5 Drain the automatic transmission fluid as described in Chapter 1.
6 Disconnect the main wiring harness connector at the top of the transmission, then unscrew the bolt and disconnect the transmission earth lead at the front of the unit.
7 Extract the retaining clip and release the selector cable end fitting from the starter inhibitor/reversing light switch. Undo the two bolts securing the selector cable support bracket to the transmission and move the bracket and cable to one side.
8 Remove the clips and disconnect the transmission fluid cooler hoses at their transmission connections.
9 Remove the exhaust manifold as described in Chapter 4A.
10 Undo the bolts securing the engine management ECU mounting bracket to the throttle body and move the ECU to one side.
11 Undo the bolts and remove the support brace linking the transmission to the cylinder block.
12 Unbolt and remove the cover plate from the base of the transmission bellhousing.
13 Disconnect the wiring from the vehicle speed sensor located on the top of the transmission differential housing.
14 Unscrew the nuts retaining the track rod ends on the swivel hubs and use a balljoint separator tool to disconnect them.
15 Unscrew the two bolts securing the right-hand swivel hub assembly to the front suspension strut, then move the hub assembly outwards.
16 Remove the retaining clip securing the right-hand driveshaft inner CV joint gaiter to the joint body. Pull the driveshaft and spider out of the joint body and move the driveshaft clear of the engine/transmission. Suitably cover the joint body and the driveshaft spider to prevent the escape of grease.

17 Undo the two bolts securing the left-hand brake caliper mounting bracket to the swivel hub. Slide the caliper and mounting bracket off the brake disc and suitably support it clear of the work area.
18 On models equipped with ABS, undo the retaining bolt securing the left-hand wheel speed sensor to the swivel hub. Withdraw the sensor from the swivel hub and position it clear of the work area.
19 Unscrew the two bolts securing the left-hand swivel hub assembly to the front suspension strut, and separate the hub assembly from the strut.
20 Slacken and remove the nut and clamp bolt then lift the left-hand swivel hub off the suspension lower arm balljoint.
21 Remove the retaining clip securing the left-hand driveshaft inner CV joint gaiter to the joint body. Pull the driveshaft and spider out of the joint body and remove the driveshaft and swivel hub assembly from the car. Suitably cover the joint body and the driveshaft spider to prevent the escape of grease.
22 Using a socket on the crankshaft sprocket centre bolt, turn the crankshaft in the normal direction of rotation until one of the four torque converter retaining bolts is accessible through the opening at the base of the transmission bellhousing **(see illustration)**. Undo the first retaining bolt, then turn the crankshaft as necessary and undo the remaining three bolts as they become accessible.
23 Unscrew the bolts and nuts securing the rear engine mounting to the subframe and transmission, and withdraw the mounting.
24 Support the weight of the engine using a hoist attached to home-made brackets secured to suitable positions at the left-hand end of the engine.
25 Support the weight of the transmission on a trolley jack then unscrew the engine-to-transmission retaining bolts. Note the correct fitted positions of each bolt (and the relevant brackets) to aid refitting. Move aside all wiring and support brackets secured by the retaining bolts.
26 Unscrew the bolts securing the left-hand engine/transmission mounting to the body then unscrew the bolts from the transmission and remove the mounting.
27 Make sure that the torque converter is pushed fully onto the transmission shaft, then carefully withdraw the transmission from the engine. If they are loose, remove the locating dowels from the engine or transmission.
28 Lower the trolley jack and remove the transmission from under the car.

6.22 Torque converter retaining bolt (arrowed) accessible through the bellhousing opening

 Warning: Keep the transmission well supported to ensure that it remains steady on the jack head.

29 With the transmission removed, secure the torque converter in position by bolting a length of metal bar to one of the bellhousing flange holes.

Refitting

30 Refitting is a reversal of the removal procedure, bearing in mind the following points.
  a) Tighten all bolts to the specified torque, referring to the Chapters indicated for components not covered in this Chapter.
  b) Tighten the torque converter retaining bolts to the Stage 1 torque setting, then turn the crankshaft through one complete revolution and tighten the bolts to the Stage 2 torque setting.
  c) Use new clips to secure the driveshaft gaiters to their respective joint bodies.
  d) Refill the transmission with the specified type and quantity of fluid as described in Chapter 1.

7 Automatic transmission – overhaul

In the event of a fault occurring on the transmission, it is first necessary to determine whether it is of an electrical, mechanical or hydraulic nature, and to do this special test equipment is required. It is therefore essential to have the work carried out by a Fiat dealer if a transmission fault is suspected.

Do not remove the transmission from the car for possible repair before professional fault diagnosis has been carried out, since most tests require the transmission to be in the vehicle.

Chapter 8
Driveshafts

Contents

Degrees of difficulty

Easy, suitable for novice with little experience	Fairly easy, suitable for beginner with some experience	Fairly difficult, suitable for competent DIY mechanic	Difficult, suitable for experienced DIY mechanic	Very difficult, suitable for expert DIY or professional

Specifications

General
Type .... Unequal-length, solid steel shafts, splined to inner and outer constant velocity joints

Lubrication
Lubricant type .... Fiat specification grease (Tutela MRM 2) or equivalent

Torque wrench settings	Nm	lbf ft
Driveshaft nut*	240	177
Roadwheel bolts	85	63
Suspension strut-to-swivel hub bolts	75	55
Track rod end-to-swivel hub nut	40	30

* Use a new nut.

1 General information

Power is transmitted from the differential to the roadwheels by the driveshafts, via inner and outer constant velocity (CV) joints.

The outer ball-and-cage type CV joints allow smooth transmission of drive to the wheels at all steering and suspension angles.

Drive is transmitted by means of a number of radially static steel balls that run in grooves between the two halves of the joint.

The inner CV joints are of the tripod type. Drive is transmitted across the joint by means of three rollers, mounted on the driveshaft in a tripod arrangement, that are radially static but are free to slide in the grooved joint body.

The joints are protected by rubber gaiters, and are packed with grease to provide permanent lubrication. If wear is detected in the joint, it can be detached from the

driveshaft and renewed. Normally, the CV joints do not require additional lubrication, unless they have been overhauled or the rubber gaiters have been damaged, allowing the grease to become contaminated. Refer to Chapter 1 for guidance in checking the condition of the driveshaft gaiters.

Both driveshafts are splined at their outer ends, to accept the wheel hubs, and are threaded so that the hubs can be fastened to the driveshafts by means of a staked nut.

2 Driveshafts – removal and refitting

Note: *A balljoint separator tool will be required for this operation. A new driveshaft retaining nut and inner CV joint gaiter retaining clip will be required for refitting.*

Removal

1 Firmly apply the handbrake, then jack up the front of the car and support it securely on axle stands (see *Jacking and vehicle support*). Remove the appropriate roadwheel(s).

2 Using a hammer and chisel or similar tool, tap up the staking securing the driveshaft retaining nut in position **(see illustration)**.

3 The front wheel hub must be held stationary in order to loosen the driveshaft nut. Ideally, the hub should be held by a suitable tool bolted into place using two of the roadwheel bolts **(see Tool Tip)**. Alternatively, have an assistant firmly apply the foot brake to prevent the hub from rotating. Using a socket and extension bar, slacken and remove the driveshaft retaining nut.

⚠ **Warning: The nut is extremely tight. Discard the nut – a new one must be used on refitting.**

4 Release the brake caliper hydraulic hose (and, where applicable, the ABS wheel speed sensor cable) from the brackets at the base of the suspension strut.

2.2 Tap up the staking securing the driveshaft retaining nut in position

5 Unscrew the nut securing the track rod end to the swivel hub. Release the track rod end tapered shank using a balljoint separator tool.

6 Unscrew the two nuts and remove the bolts securing the top of the swivel hub to the base of the suspension strut.

7 Pull the swivel hub outwards at the top and withdraw the driveshaft outer constant velocity joint from the hub assembly **(see illustrations)**. If necessary, the joint can be tapped out of the hub using a soft-faced mallet. Support the end of the driveshaft – do not allow the end of the driveshaft to hang down as this will strain the joint components and gaiters.

8 Remove the rubber gaiter retaining clip from the inner CV joint, then pull the driveshaft and tripod out of the joint body **(see illustration)**.

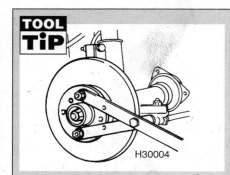

H30004

A tool to hold the front hub stationary whilst the driveshaft nut is slackened can be fabricated from two lengths of steel strip (one long, one short) and a nut and bolt; the nut and bolt forming the pivot of a forked tool.

9 Remove the driveshaft from under the vehicle. Cover the open CV joint body remaining on the transmission to prevent the ingress of dirt; use a plastic bag secured with elastic bands.

10 Loosely refit one of the strut lower mounting bolts to support the swivel hub while the driveshaft is removed.

Refitting

11 After removing the temporarily-fitted bolt from the strut mounting, pivot the swivel hub away from the car and engage the outer CV joint into the hub.

12 Screw on the new driveshaft retaining nut, but do not tighten it at this stage.

13 Support the driveshaft with one hand and push the swivel hub back towards the car.

14 Re-engage the tripod at the inner end of the driveshaft with the CV joint body on the transmission. Slide the gaiter into position over the joint and briefly lift the lip of the gaiter to expel any air trapped inside. Ensure that the gaiter is seated squarely over the joint body.

15 Refit the suspension strut-to-swivel hub bolts and tighten them to the specified torque.

16 Engage the track rod end with the swivel hub, refit the retaining nut and tighten the nut to the specified torque.

17 Refit the brake caliper hydraulic hose (and, where applicable, the ABS wheel speed sensor cable) to the bracket on the base of the suspension strut.

18 Locate a new retaining clip over the rubber gaiter on the inner CV joint. Ensure that the clip is seated squarely on the gaiter then secure the clip in place by compressing the raised portion.

19 Using the method employed on removal to prevent rotation of the hub, tighten the driveshaft retaining nut to the specified torque. Secure the nut by tapping the staking into the two grooves in the end of the CV joint using a hammer and chisel **(see illustration)**.

20 Refit the roadwheel and lower the car to the ground.

2.7a Pull the swivel hub outwards at the top . . .

2.7b . . . and withdraw the driveshaft outer constant velocity joint from the hub assembly

2.8 Remove the gaiter retaining clip, then pull the driveshaft and tripod out of the inner joint body

2.19 Secure the driveshaft retaining nut by tapping the staking into the two grooves in the CV joint

3.2 Release the rubber gaiter retaining clips by cutting them off with side-cutters

3.3a Sharply strike the edge of the outer CV joint to release it from the internal circlip . . .

3.3b . . . then withdraw the outer joint from the driveshaft

3 Driveshaft overhaul and rubber gaiter renewal

Outer joint

1 Remove the driveshaft as described in Section 2.

2 Release the rubber gaiter retaining clips by cutting them off with a pair of side-cutters **(see illustration)**. Remove the clips and slide the gaiter down the driveshaft away from the CV joint.

3 Using a mallet, sharply strike the edge of the outer joint to drive it off the end of the driveshaft **(see illustrations)**. The joint is retained on the driveshaft by an internal circlip, and striking the joint in this manner forces the circlip into its groove, so allowing the joint to slide off.

4 Remove the circlip from the groove in the driveshaft splines, and discard it **(see illustration)**. A new circlip must be fitted on reassembly.

5 Slide the old gaiter off the end of the driveshaft.

6 With the constant velocity joint removed from the driveshaft, thoroughly clean the joint using paraffin, or a suitable solvent, and dry it thoroughly. Carry out a visual inspection of the joint.

7 Move the inner splined driving member from side-to-side, to expose each ball in turn at the top of its track. Examine the balls for cracks, flat spots, or signs of surface pitting.

8 Inspect the ball tracks on the inner and outer members. If the tracks have widened, the balls will no longer be a tight fit. At the same time, check the ball cage windows for wear or cracking between the windows.

9 If any of the constant velocity joint components are found to be worn or damaged, it will be necessary to renew the complete joint assembly as the internal parts are not available separately. If the joint is in satisfactory condition, obtain a new gaiter, circlip, retaining clips, and the correct type of

grease. These components are all available individually from Fiat dealers, but may be supplied as a complete repair kit from other sources.

10 Commence reassembly by fitting a new joint retaining circlip to the groove in the end of the shaft.

11 Slide the smaller gaiter securing clip onto the driveshaft, followed by the gaiter and the large securing clip **(see illustrations)**.

12 Pack the CV joint with the specified grease, then twist the joint to ensure that all the recesses are filled **(see illustration)**.

13 Fit the CV joint to the driveshaft, and engage it with the shaft splines. Use a mallet to tap the joint onto the shaft until the circlip

3.4 Remove the circlip from the groove in the driveshaft splines

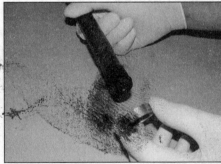

3.11a Slide the smaller gaiter securing clip onto the driveshaft . . .

3.11b . . . followed by the gaiter . . .

3.11c . . . and the large securing clip

3.12 Pack the joint with the specified grease, then twist the joint to ensure all recesses are filled

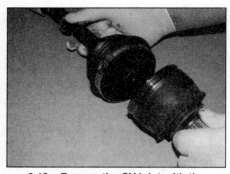

3.13a Engage the CV joint with the driveshaft splines . . .

3.13b . . . then tap the joint onto the shaft until the circlip engages

3.15 Locate the large securing clip over the gaiter and secure the clip by compressing the raised portion

engages correctly behind the joint cage **(see illustrations)**.
14 Fill the gaiter with any remaining grease then slide the large end of the gaiter into position over the joint, ensuring that it is seated squarely over the joint body.
15 Locate the large securing clip over the gaiter and secure the clip in place by compressing the raised portion **(see illustration)**.
16 Check that the smaller end of the gaiter is located in the driveshaft groove then, using a small screwdriver, lift the lip of the gaiter to expel any air trapped inside **(see illustration)**.
17 Slide the smaller securing clip over the gaiter, and secure it as described previously **(see illustration)**.
18 Refit the driveshaft as described in Section 2.

Inner joint

19 Remove the driveshaft as described in Section 2.
20 Release the gaiter smaller clip by cutting it off with a pair of side-cutters **(see illustration)**.
21 Wipe off the excess grease from the tripod and the end of the driveshaft.
22 Using circlip pliers, remove the circlip securing the tripod to the end of the driveshaft **(see illustration)**. Discard the circlip – a new one should be used on refitting.
23 Withdraw the tripod and the gaiter from the end of the driveshaft.
24 Thoroughly clean the tripod and rollers, and the end of the driveshaft using paraffin, or a suitable solvent, and dry thoroughly. Carry out a visual inspection of the joint and renew any components as necessary. If the joint is in satisfactory condition, obtain a new gaiter, circlip, retaining clips, and the correct type of grease. These components are all available individually from Fiat dealers, but may be

supplied as a complete repair kit from other sources.
25 Commence reassembly by sliding the smaller gaiter securing clip onto the driveshaft, followed by the gaiter.
26 Check that the gaiter is located in the driveshaft groove, then fit the securing clip over the gaiter and secure the clip in

place by compressing the raised portion.
27 Refit the tripod and fit a new circlip to secure the tripod to the driveshaft.
28 Pack the specified grease around the tripod rollers and into the joint body, filling the gaiter with any remaining grease.
29 Refit the driveshaft as described in Section 2.

3.16 Lift the lip of the gaiter to expel any air trapped inside

3.17 Slide the smaller clip over the gaiter, and secure it by compressing the raised portion

3.20 Release the smaller clip on the inner joint gaiter by cutting it off with side-cutters

3.22 Using circlip pliers, remove the circlip securing the tripod to the end of the driveshaft

Chapter 9
Braking system

Contents

Degrees of difficulty

Easy, suitable for novice with little experience 	Fairly easy, suitable for beginner with some experience	Fairly difficult, suitable for competent DIY mechanic	Difficult, suitable for experienced DIY mechanic	Very difficult, suitable for expert DIY or professional

Specifications

Front disc brakes

Type	Disc with single-piston sliding calipers
Disc diameter:	
SOHC (8-valve) engine models	240.0 mm
DOHC (16-valve) engine models	257.0 mm
Disc thickness (new):	
SOHC (8-valve) engine models	10.8 to 11.1 mm
DOHC (16-valve) engine models	11.8 to 12.1 mm
Minimum disc thickness (wear limit):	
SOHC (8-valve) engine models	9.2 mm
DOHC (16-valve) engine models	10.2 mm
Maximum disc runout	0.15 mm
Brake pad friction material minimum thickness	1.5 mm

Rear drum brakes

Drum inner diameter (new)	180.0 to 180.2 mm
Maximum drum diameter (wear limit)	181.3 mm
Minimum brake shoe lining thickness	2.0 mm

Torque wrench settings

	Nm	lbf ft
Bleed screw	6	4
Brake disc locating studs	12	9
Brake drum locating studs	12	9
Brake pipe and hose unions	14	10
Front caliper guide pin bolts	27	20
Front caliper mounting bracket-to-swivel hub bolts	53	39
Rear wheel cylinder mounting bolts	10	7
Roadwheel bolts	85	63

1 General information

The braking system is of the vacuum servo-assisted, dual-circuit hydraulic type. The arrangement of the hydraulic system is such that each circuit operates one front and one rear brake from a tandem master cylinder. Under normal circumstances, both circuits operate in unison. However, in the event of hydraulic failure in one circuit, full braking force will still be available at two diagonally-opposite wheels.

All models covered in this manual are fitted with front disc brakes and rear drum brakes. An Anti-lock Braking System (ABS) is fitted as standard to certain models and is offered as an option on all other models (refer to Section 17 for further information on ABS operation).

The front disc brakes are actuated by single-piston sliding type calipers, which ensure that equal pressure is applied to each brake pad.

The rear drum brakes incorporate leading and trailing shoes, which are actuated by twin-piston wheel cylinders. A self-adjust mechanism is incorporated, to automatically compensate for brake shoe wear. As the brake shoe linings wear, the footbrake operation automatically operates the adjuster mechanism to reduce the lining-to-drum clearance.

The mechanical handbrake linkage operates the brake shoes via a lever attached to the trailing brake shoe.

On models without ABS, load-sensitive proportioning valves operate on the rear brake hydraulic circuits, to prevent the possibility of the rear wheels locking before the front wheels under heavy braking. On models equipped with ABS, the hydraulic pressure applied to the rear brakes is regulated by the ABS hydraulic modulator under all braking conditions. On these models, the load-sensitive proportioning valves are not used.

Note: *When servicing any part of the system, work carefully and methodically; also observe scrupulous cleanliness when overhauling any part of the hydraulic system. Always renew components (in axle sets, where applicable) if in doubt about their condition, and use only genuine Fiat replacement parts, or at least those of known good quality. Note the warnings given in 'Safety first!' and at relevant points in this Chapter concerning the dangers of asbestos dust and hydraulic fluid.*

2 Hydraulic system – bleeding

⚠️ *Warning: Hydraulic fluid is poisonous; wash off immediately and thoroughly in the case of skin contact, and seek immediate medical advice if any fluid is swallowed, or gets into the eyes. Certain types of hydraulic fluid are inflammable, and may ignite when allowed into contact with hot components. When servicing any hydraulic system, it is safest to assume that the fluid IS inflammable, and to take precautions against the risk of fire as though it is petrol that is being handled. Hydraulic fluid is also an effective paint stripper, and will attack plastics; if any is spilt, it should be washed off immediately, using copious quantities of fresh water. Finally, it is hygroscopic (it absorbs moisture from the air) – old fluid may be contaminated and unfit for further use. When topping-up or renewing the fluid, always use the recommended type, and ensure that it comes from a freshly-opened sealed container.*

Models without ABS

General

1 The correct operation of any hydraulic system is only possible after removing all air from the components and circuit; and this is achieved by bleeding the system.

2 During the bleeding procedure, add only clean, unused hydraulic fluid of the recommended type; never re-use fluid that has already been bled from the system. Ensure that sufficient fluid is available before starting work.

3 If there is any possibility of incorrect fluid being already in the system, the brake components and circuit must be flushed completely with uncontaminated, correct fluid, and new seals should be fitted throughout the system.

4 If hydraulic fluid has been lost from the system, or air has entered because of a leak, ensure that the fault is cured before proceeding further.

5 Park the car on level ground, switch off the engine and select first or reverse gear (or P), then chock the wheels and release the handbrake.

6 Check that all pipes and hoses are secure, unions tight and bleed screws closed. Remove the dust caps (where applicable), and clean any dirt from around the bleed screws.

7 Unscrew the master cylinder reservoir cap, and top the master cylinder reservoir up to the MAX level line; refit the cap loosely. Remember to maintain the fluid level at least above the MIN level line throughout the procedure, otherwise there is a risk of further air entering the system.

8 There are a number of one-man, do-it-yourself brake bleeding kits currently available from motor accessory shops. It is recommended that one of these kits is used whenever possible, as they greatly simplify the bleeding operation, and also reduce the risk of expelled air and fluid being drawn back into the system. If such a kit is not available, the basic (two-man) method must be used, which is described in detail below.

9 If a kit is to be used, prepare the vehicle as described previously, and follow the kit manufacturer's instructions, as the procedure may vary slightly according to the type being used; generally, they are as outlined below in the relevant sub-section.

10 Whichever method is used, the same sequence must be followed (paragraphs 11 and 12) to ensure the removal of all air from the system.

Bleeding sequence

11 If the system has been only partially disconnected, and suitable precautions were taken to minimise fluid loss, it should be necessary to bleed only that part of the system (ie, the primary or secondary circuit).

12 If the complete system is to be bled, then it should be done working in the following sequence:
   a) *Left-hand rear wheel.*
   b) *Right-hand front wheel.*
   c) *Right-hand rear wheel.*
   d) *Left-hand front wheel.*

Basic (two-man) bleeding method

13 Collect a clean glass jar, a suitable length of plastic or rubber tubing which is a tight fit over the bleed screw, and a ring spanner to fit the screw. The help of an assistant will also be required.

14 Remove the dust cap from the first screw in the sequence if not already done. Fit a suitable spanner to the screw, place the other end of the tube in the jar, and pour in sufficient fluid to cover the end of the tube.

15 Ensure that the master cylinder reservoir fluid level is maintained at least above the MIN level line throughout the procedure.

16 Have the assistant fully depress the brake pedal several times to build-up pressure, then maintain it on the final downstroke.

17 While pedal pressure is maintained, unscrew the bleed screw (approximately one turn) and allow the compressed fluid and air to flow into the jar. The assistant should maintain pedal pressure, following the pedal down to the floor if necessary, and should not release the pedal until instructed to do so. When the flow stops, tighten the bleed screw again, have the assistant release the pedal slowly, and recheck the reservoir fluid level.

18 Repeat the steps given in paragraphs 16 and 17 until the fluid emerging from the bleed screw is free from air bubbles. If the master cylinder has been drained and refilled, and air is being bled from the first screw in the sequence, allow approximately five seconds between cycles for the master cylinder passages to refill.

19 When no more air bubbles appear, tighten the bleed screw securely, remove the tube and spanner, and refit the dust cap (where applicable). Do not overtighten the bleed screw.

20 Repeat the procedure on the remaining screws in the sequence, until all air is removed from the system, and the brake pedal feels firm again.

Bleeding using a one-way valve kit

21 As their name implies, these kits consist of a length of tubing with a one-way valve fitted to prevent expelled air and fluid being drawn back into the system; some kits include a translucent container, which can be positioned so that the air bubbles can be more easily seen flowing from the end of the tube.

22 The kit is connected to the bleed screw, which is then opened. The user returns to the driver's seat, depresses the brake pedal with a smooth, steady stroke, and slowly releases it; this is repeated until the expelled fluid is clear of air bubbles.

23 Note that these kits simplify work so much that it is easy to forget the master cylinder reservoir fluid level; ensure that this is maintained at least above the MIN level line at all times.

Bleeding using a pressure-bleeding kit

24 These kits are usually operated by the reservoir of pressurised air contained in the spare tyre. However, note that it will probably be necessary to reduce the pressure to a lower level than normal; refer to the instructions supplied with the kit.

25 By connecting a pressurised, fluid-filled container to the master cylinder reservoir, bleeding can be carried out simply by opening each screw in turn (in the specified sequence), and allowing the fluid to flow out until no more air bubbles can be seen in the expelled fluid.

26 This method has the advantage that the large reservoir of fluid provides an additional safeguard against air being drawn into the system during bleeding.

27 Pressure-bleeding is particularly effective when bleeding 'difficult' systems, or when bleeding the complete system at the time of routine fluid renewal.

All methods

28 When bleeding is complete, and firm pedal feel is restored, wash off any spilt fluid, tighten the bleed screws securely, and refit their dust caps (where applicable).

29 Check the hydraulic fluid level in the master cylinder reservoir, and top-up if necessary.

30 Discard any hydraulic fluid that has been bled from the system; it will not be fit for re-use.

31 Check the feel of the brake pedal. If it feels at all spongy, air must still be present in the system, and further bleeding is required. Failure to bleed satisfactorily after a reasonable repetition of the bleeding procedure may be due to worn master cylinder seals.

Models with ABS

 Warning: On models equipped with ABS, ensure that the ignition is switched off before starting the bleeding procedure,

to avoid any possibility of voltage being applied to the hydraulic modulator before the bleeding procedure is completed. Ideally, the battery should be disconnected. If voltage is applied to the modulator before the bleeding procedure is complete, this will effectively drain the hydraulic fluid in the modulator, rendering the unit unserviceable. Do not, therefore, attempt to 'run' the modulator in order to bleed the brakes.

32 A pressure-bleeding kit must be used for bleeding the hydraulic system on ABS models – see paragraphs 24 to 27.

33 Following the sequence given in paragraph 12, bleed each brake in turn until clean fluid, free of air bubbles, is seen to emerge. Pause between bleeding each brake to ensure that the fluid level in the reservoir is above the MIN level.

34 When bleeding is complete, and firm pedal feel is restored, wash off any spilt fluid, tighten the bleed screws, and refit their dust caps.

35 Check the hydraulic fluid level in the master cylinder reservoir, and top-up if necessary.

36 Discard any fluid that has been bled from the system; it will not be fit for re-use.

37 Check the feel of the brake pedal. If it feels at all spongy, air must still be present in the system, and further bleeding is required.

 Warning: Do not operate the vehicle if you are in doubt about the effectiveness of the braking system. If considerable air was present in the system prior to bleeding, it is possible for some of this air to remain trapped in the hydraulic modulator. If the pedal continues to feel spongy after repeated bleedings, or if any of the brake system warning lights remain on, have the vehicle towed to a Fiat dealer to be bled with the use of Fiat diagnostic equipment.

---

3 Hydraulic pipes and hoses – renewal

 Warning: Before starting work, refer to the warning at the beginning of Section 2 concerning the dangers of hydraulic fluid.

1 If any pipe or hose is to be renewed, minimise fluid loss by first removing the master cylinder reservoir cap, then tighten the cap down onto a piece of polythene to obtain an airtight seal. Alternatively, flexible hoses can be sealed, if required, using a proprietary brake hose clamp; metal brake pipe unions can be plugged (if care is taken not to allow dirt into the system) or capped immediately they are disconnected. Place a wad of rag under any union that is to be disconnected, to catch any spilt fluid.

2 If a flexible hose is to be disconnected, unscrew the brake pipe union nut before removing the spring clip which secures the hose to its mounting bracket.

3 To unscrew the union nuts, it is preferable to obtain a brake pipe spanner of the correct size; these are available from most large motor accessory shops. Failing this, a close-fitting open-ended spanner will be required, though if the nuts are tight or corroded, their flats may be rounded-off if the spanner slips. In such a case, a self-locking wrench is often the only way to unscrew a stubborn union, but it follows that the pipe and the damaged nuts must be renewed on reassembly. Always clean a union and surrounding area before disconnecting it. If disconnecting a component with more than one union, make a careful note of the connections before disturbing any of them.

4 If a brake pipe is to be renewed, it can be obtained, cut to length and with the union nuts and end flares in place, from Fiat dealers. All that is then necessary is to bend it to shape, following the line of the original, before fitting it to the vehicle. Alternatively, most motor accessory shops can make up brake pipes from kits, but this requires very careful measurement of the original, to ensure that the replacement is of the correct length. The safest answer is usually to take the original to the shop as a pattern.

5 On refitting, do not overtighten the union nuts. It is not necessary to exercise brute force to obtain a sound joint.

6 Ensure that the pipes and hoses are correctly routed, with no kinks, and that they are secured in the clips or brackets provided. After fitting, remove the polythene from the reservoir, and bleed the hydraulic system as described in Section 2. Wash off any spilt fluid, and check carefully for fluid leaks.

---

4 Front brake pads – renewal

 Warning: Renew BOTH sets of front brake pads at the same time – NEVER renew the pads on only one wheel, as uneven braking may result.

 Warning: Note that the dust created by wear of the pads may contain asbestos, which is a health hazard. Never blow it out with compressed air, and don't inhale any of it. An approved filtering mask should be worn when working on the brakes. DO NOT use petrol or petroleum-based solvents to clean brake parts; use proprietary brake cleaner or methylated spirit only.

1 Firmly apply the handbrake, then jack up the front of the car and support it securely on axle stands (see *Jacking and vehicle support*). Remove the front roadwheels.

4.3a Remove the locking clip . . .

4.3b . . . and extract the lower guide pin from the caliper – SOHC (8-valve) engine models

4.4a Pivot the caliper body upwards and withdraw the outer brake pad . . .

2 Release the brake caliper hydraulic hose from the bracket at the base of the suspension strut.

SOHC (8-valve) engine models

3 Remove the locking clip and extract the lower guide pin from the caliper (see illustrations).
4 Pivot the caliper body upwards and withdraw the brake pads from the caliper mounting bracket (see illustrations).

DOHC (16-valve) engine models

5 Using a large screwdriver, prise the lower end of the pad retaining spring clip from the locating hole in the caliper body (see illustration).
6 Disengage the upper end of the retaining spring clip from the caliper and remove the clip (see illustration).
7 Prise out the protective covers over the caliper upper and lower guide pin bolts (see illustration).
8 Using an Allen key, unscrew the upper and lower guide pin bolts to free the caliper from the mounting bracket (see illustration).
9 Lift off the caliper and withdraw the outer brake pad from the mounting bracket (see illustrations).
10 Withdraw the inner brake pad from the caliper piston, noting that the pad is secured

4.4b . . . and inner brake pad from the caliper mounting bracket – SOHC (8-valve) engine models

4.5 Prise the lower end of the pad retaining spring clip from the caliper body – DOHC (16-valve) engine models

4.6 Disengage the ends and remove the spring clip from the caliper – DOHC (16-valve) engine models

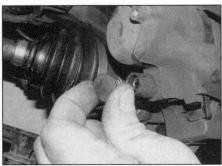

4.7 Prise out the protective covers over the caliper guide pin bolts – DOHC (16-valve) engine models

4.8 Unscrew the caliper upper and lower guide pin bolts – DOHC (16-valve) engine models

4.9a Lift off the brake caliper . . .

4.9b . . . and withdraw the outer brake pad from the mounting bracket – DOHC (16-valve) engine models

4.10 Withdraw the inner brake pad from the caliper piston – DOHC (16-valve) engine models

4.18 Sparingly apply high-temperature brake grease to the brake pad backing plates

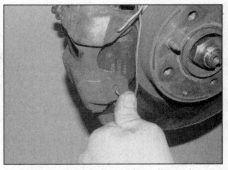

4.26 Ensure that the spring clip ends are correctly located in the caliper holes – DOHC (16-valve) engine models

to the piston by a clip attached to the pad backing plate (see illustration).

11 With the brake pads removed, tie the caliper to the suspension strut using string or a cable tie.

Caution: Do not allow the caliper to hang unsupported on the flexible hydraulic hose.

All models

12 Measure the thickness of each brake pad's friction material. If either pad is worn at any point to the specified minimum thickness or less, all four pads must be renewed. Also, the pads should be renewed if any are fouled with oil or grease; there is no satisfactory way of degreasing friction material, once contaminated. If any of the brake pads are worn unevenly, or are fouled with oil or grease, trace and rectify the cause before reassembly.

13 If the brake pads are still serviceable, carefully clean them using a clean, fine wire brush or similar and brake cleaning fluid. Pay particular attention to the sides and back of the metal backing. Where applicable, clean out the grooves in the friction material, and pick out any large embedded particles of dirt or debris.

14 Clean the surfaces of the brake pad contact points in the caliper body and caliper mounting bracket.

15 Prior to fitting the pads, check that the guide pins can slide freely in the caliper body, and check that the rubber guide pin gaiters are undamaged. Brush the dust and dirt from the caliper and piston, but do not inhale it, as it may contain asbestos.

16 Inspect the dust seal and the area around the piston for signs of damage, corrosion or brake fluid leaks. If evident, refer to Section 5 and overhaul the caliper assembly.

17 If new brake pads are to be fitted, the caliper piston must be pushed back into the cylinder, to allow for the extra depth of the friction material. Either use a G-clamp or similar tool, or use suitable pieces of wood as levers. Provided that the master cylinder reservoir has not been overfilled with hydraulic fluid, there should be no spillage,

but keep a careful watch on the fluid level while retracting the piston. If the fluid level rises above the MAX level line at any time, the surplus should be syphoned off.

 Warning: Do not syphon the fluid by mouth, as it is poisonous; use a syringe or an old poultry baster.

18 Apply a little high-temperature brake grease to the contact surfaces of the pad backing plates; take great care not to allow any grease onto the pad friction linings (see illustration). Similarly, apply brake grease to the pad contact points on the caliper bracket – again take care not to apply excess grease, which may contaminate the pads.

SOHC (8-valve) engine models

19 Place the brake pads in position on the caliper mounting bracket, with the friction material facing the surfaces of the brake disc.

20 Pivot the caliper body down over the brake pads, then refit the lower guide pin and retaining clip.

DOHC (16-valve) engine models

21 Fit the inner pad to the caliper, ensuring that its retaining clip is fully engaged with the caliper piston.

22 Locate the outer pad on the caliper mounting bracket with the pad friction material against the brake disc.

23 Slide the caliper and inner pad into position over the outer pad and locate it in the mounting bracket.

24 Install the caliper guide pin bolts and tighten them to the specified torque.

25 Refit the guide pin bolt protective covers to the caliper.

26 Refit the pad retaining spring to the caliper, ensuring that its ends are correctly located in the caliper holes (see illustration).

All models

27 Check that the caliper body can slide freely on the guide pins. Ensure that the flexible hydraulic hose is not twisted or kinked in any way then refit the hose to the suspension strut bracket. Turn the steering from lock-to-lock and check that the hose

does not chafe against the suspension or steering gear.

28 Repeat the above procedure on the remaining front caliper.

29 With both sets of front brake pads fitted, depress the brake pedal repeatedly until the pads are pressed into firm contact with the brake disc, and normal pedal pressure is restored. Any sponginess felt when depressing the pedal is most probably due to air trapped in the hydraulic system – refer to Section 2 and bleed the brake hydraulic system before progressing any further.

30 Refit the roadwheels, and lower the car to the ground.

31 Check the hydraulic fluid level as described in Weekly checks.

32 Check the operation of the braking system thoroughly.

33 Note that new brake pads will not give full braking efficiency until they have bedded-in. Be prepared for this, and avoid hard braking as far as possible for the first hundred miles or so after pad renewal.

---

5 Front brake caliper – removal, overhaul and refitting

⚠ **Warning: Before starting work, refer to the warnings at the beginning of Sections 2 and 4 concerning the dangers of hydraulic fluid and asbestos dust.**

Removal

1 Firmly apply the handbrake, then jack up the front of the car and support it securely on axle stands (see Jacking and vehicle support). Remove the appropriate front roadwheel.

2 Remove the brake pads as described in Section 4.

3 To minimise fluid loss during the following operations, remove the master cylinder reservoir filler cap, then tighten it down onto a piece of polythene, to obtain an airtight seal. Alternatively, use a brake hose clamp to seal off the flexible hydraulic hose running to the caliper.

Warning: Do not use an ordinary G-clamp or mole grips for this purpose, as these can easily damage the hydraulic hose internally, possibly leading to failure.

4 Clean the area surrounding the brake hose union, then slacken the union half a turn. It won't be possible to separate the union completely without twisting the hose at this stage.

5 On SOHC (8-valve) engine models, unscrew the caliper upper guide pin bolt using a hex bit or Allen key and remove the caliper body from the mounting bracket **(see illustration)**.

6 Hold the brake hose and rotate the caliper to unscrew the hose union from the caliper body. Cover the open ends of the union and the caliper fluid inlet, to prevent dirt ingress. Alternatively, the flexible brake hose may be separated from the rigid brake pipe at the bracket mounted on the inner wheel arch.

7 If desired, the caliper mounting bracket can be removed from the swivel hub after unscrewing the two securing bolts **(see illustration)**.

Overhaul

Note: *Before commencing work, ensure that the appropriate caliper overhaul kit is obtained.*

8 With the caliper on the bench, wipe away all traces of dust and dirt, but *avoid inhaling the dust, as it is a health hazard.*

9 Place a small block of wood between the caliper body and the piston, to act as padding. Remove the piston by applying a jet of low pressure compressed air (such as that produced by a tyre foot pump) to the fluid inlet port.

 Warning: Protect your hands and eyes when using compressed air in this manner – brake fluid may be ejected under pressure when the piston is released.

10 Peel the dust seal from the piston, then use a soft, blunt instrument (such as a knitting needle) to extract the piston seal from the caliper bore.

11 Thoroughly clean all components, using only methylated spirit or clean hydraulic fluid. Never use mineral-based solvents such as petrol or paraffin, which will attack the hydraulic system rubber components.

12 The caliper piston seal, the dust seal and the bleed nipple dust cap are only available as part of a seal kit. Since the manufacturers recommend that the piston seal and dust seal are renewed whenever they are disturbed, all of these components should be discarded on disassembly and new ones fitted on reassembly as a matter of course.

13 Carefully examine all parts of the caliper assembly, looking for signs of wear or damage. In particular, the cylinder bore and piston must be free from any signs of scratches, corrosion or wear. If there is any doubt about the condition of any part of the caliper, the relevant part should be renewed. Note that the piston surface is plated, and **must not** be polished with emery or similar abrasives to remove corrosion or scratches. In addition, the pistons are matched to the caliper bores and can only be renewed as a part of a complete caliper assembly.

14 Check that the threads in the caliper body and the mounting bracket are in good condition. Check that the guide pin(s) are undamaged, and (when cleaned) a reasonably tight sliding fit in the mounting bracket bores.

15 Use compressed air to blow clear the fluid passages.

 Warning: Wear eye protection when using compressed air.

16 Before commencing reassembly, ensure that all components are spotlessly-clean and dry.

17 Soak the new piston seal in clean hydraulic fluid, and fit it to the groove in the cylinder bore, using your fingers only (no tools) to manipulate it into place.

18 Fit the new dust seal inner lip to the cylinder groove, smear clean hydraulic fluid over the piston and caliper cylinder bore, and twist the piston into the dust seal. Press the piston squarely into the cylinder, then slide the dust seal outer lip to the groove in the piston.

Refitting

19 Where applicable, refit the caliper mounting bracket to the hub carrier. Coat the threads of the mounting bolts with thread locking compound, then tighten them to the specified torque.

20 Hold the brake hose and rotate the caliper to screw the hose union back into the caliper body.

21 On SOHC (8-valve) engine models, place the caliper in position on the mounting bracket and tighten the caliper upper guide pin bolt to the specified torque.

22 Refit the brake pads as described in Section 4.

23 On all models, tighten the brake hose-to-caliper union securely.

24 Check that the caliper slides smoothly on its guide pins.

25 Remove the polythene from the master cylinder reservoir filler cap, or remove the clamp from the fluid hose, as applicable.

26 Bleed the hydraulic fluid circuit as described in Section 2. Note that if no other part of the system has been disturbed, it should only be necessary to bleed the relevant front circuit.

27 Depress the brake pedal repeatedly to bring the pads into contact with the brake disc, and ensure that normal pedal pressure is restored.

28 Refit the roadwheel, and lower the car to the ground.

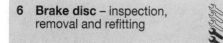

6   Brake disc – inspection, removal and refitting

Inspection

1 Firmly apply the handbrake, then jack up the front of the car and support it securely on axle stands (see *Jacking and vehicle support*). Remove the front roadwheels.

2 Rotate the brake disc by hand and examine the whole of the surface area swept by the brake pads, on both sides of the disc. **Note:** *It will be necessary to remove the front brake pads to allow an adequate inspection of the disc's inner surface; refer to Section 4 for details.*

3 Typically, the disc surface will have a polished appearance and should be free from heavy scoring. Smooth rippling is produced by normal operation and does not indicate excessive wear. Deep scoring and cracks, however, are indications of more serious damage in need of correction.

4 If deep scoring is discovered, it may be possible to have the disc reground to restore the surface, depending on the extent of the damage. To determine whether this is a feasible course of action, it will be necessary to measure the thickness of the disc, as described later.

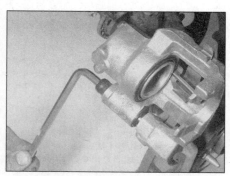

5.5 Unscrew the upper guide pin bolt and remove the caliper from the mounting bracket – SOHC (8-valve) engine models

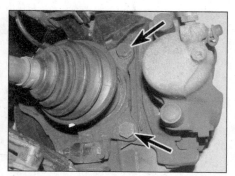

5.7 Caliper mounting bracket retaining bolts (arrowed)

6.8 Measuring brake disc thickness with a micrometer

6.11 Using a dial test indicator to measure brake disc runout

5 Check the whole surface of the disc for cracks, particularly around the roadwheel bolt holes. A cracked disc must be renewed.

6 A ridge of rust and brake dust at the inner and outer edges of the disc, beyond the pad contact area, is normal – this can be scraped away quite easily.

7 Raised ridges caused by the brake pads eroding the disc material, however, are an indication of excessive wear. If close examination reveals such ridges, the thickness of the disc must be measured, to assess whether it is still fit for use.

8 To measure the thickness of the disc, take readings at several points on the surface using a micrometer, in the area swept by the brake pads **(see illustration)**. Include any points where the disc has been scored; align the jaws of the micrometer with the deepest area of scoring, to get a true indication of the extent of the wear. Compare these measurements with the limits listed in the Specifications. If the disc has worn below its minimum thickness, at any point, it must be renewed.

9 If the discs are suspected of causing brake judder, check the disc runout, using one of the following methods:

DTI gauge runout measurement

10 Refit the four roadwheel bolts, together with one M14 plain washer per bolt – this will ensure adequate disc-to-hub contact. Tighten the bolts securely.

11 Clamp the DTI gauge to a stand and

attach the stand, preferably via a magnetic base, to the strut mounting bracket. Align the gauge so that its pointer rests upon the area of the disc swept by the brake pads, on an arc 2.0 mm from the outer edge of the disc **(see illustration)**.

12 Zero the gauge and slowly rotate the disc through one revolution, observing the pointer movement. Note the maximum deflection recorded and compare the figure with that listed in Specifications.

Feeler blade runout measurement

13 Use the feeler blades to measure the clearance between the disc and a convenient fixed point, such as the caliper mounting bracket. Rotate the disc and measure the variation in clearance at several points around the disc. Compare the maximum figure with that listed in Specifications.

14 If the disc runout is outside of its specified tolerance, first check that the hub is not worn (see *Steering and suspension* check in Chapter 1). If the hub is in good condition, remove the disc (as described later in this Section), rotate it through 180° and refit it. This may improve the seating and eradicate the excessive runout.

15 If the runout is still unacceptable, then it may be possible to restore the disc by regrinding; consult your Fiat dealer or a machine shop for a professional opinion – it may prove more economical to purchase a new disc. If the disc cannot be reground, then it must be renewed.

Removal

16 Mark the relationship between the disc and the hub with chalk or a marker pen, to allow correct refitting.

17 To allow the disc to be removed, undo the two bolts securing the brake caliper mounting bracket to the swivel hub **(see illustration 5.7)**. Withdraw the brake caliper and mounting bracket assembly, complete with brake pads, from the swivel hub, and suspend it from a rigid point on the suspension, using wire or a cable tie. Do not allow it to hang unsupported as this will strain the brake hose.

18 Slacken and remove the disc locating studs. Support the disc as you do this and lift it off as it becomes free **(see illustrations)**.

19 Remove the polished glaze from the surface of the disc with sand/emery paper. Use small, circular motions to avoid producing a directional finish on the surface.

Refitting

20 If a new disc is being fitted, remove the protective coating from the surface using an appropriate solvent.

21 Locate the disc on the hub so that the roadwheel bolt and locating stud holes are all correctly lined up; use the alignment marks made during removal. If the disc is being removed in an attempt to improve seating and hence runout, turn the disc through 180° and then refit it.

22 Refit the locating studs and tighten them securely.

23 Recheck the disc runout, using one of the methods described earlier in this Section.

24 Refit the brake caliper and mounting bracket assembly to the swivel hub. Coat the threads of the mounting bolts with thread locking compound, then tighten them to the specified torque.

25 Depress the brake pedal several times to bring the brake pads into contact with the disc.

26 Refit the roadwheel and lower the car to the ground.

27 Check the hydraulic fluid level as described in *Weekly checks*.

---

7 Rear brake drums – removal, inspection and refitting

> ⚠ **Warning: Before starting work, refer to the warning at the beginning of Section 4 concerning the dangers of asbestos dust.**

Removal

1 Chock the front wheels then jack up the rear of the car and securely support it on axle stands (see *Jacking and vehicle support*). Remove the appropriate rear roadwheel and fully release the handbrake.

2 If the original drum is to be refitted, mark the relationship between the drum and the

6.18a Remove the disc locating studs . . .

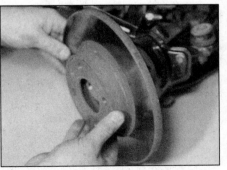

6.18b . . . and lift the disc off the wheel hub

7.2 Slacken and remove the two brake drum locating studs (arrowed)

hub. Slacken and remove the two locating studs and pull the drum from the hub **(see illustration)**.

3 If the drum is binding on the brake shoes, it can be drawn off as follows. Hold the drum still and turn the hub so that the drum and hub flange bolt holes no longer line up. Screw two bolts into the locating stud threaded holes in the drum, and progressively tighten them against the hub flange to push the drum from the hub.

Inspection

Note: *If either drum requires renewal, BOTH should be renewed at the same time, to* ensure even and consistent braking. New brake shoes should also be fitted.

4 Working carefully, remove all traces of brake dust from the drum, but *avoid inhaling the dust, as it is a health hazard.*

5 Clean the outside of the drum, and check it for obvious signs of wear or damage, such as cracks around the roadwheel stud holes; renew the drum if necessary.

6 Carefully examine the inside of the drum. Light scoring of the friction surface is normal, but if heavy scoring is found, the drum must be renewed.

7 It is usual to find a lip on the drum's inboard edge which consists of a mixture of rust and brake dust; this should be carefully scraped away, to leave a smooth surface which can be polished with fine (120- to 150-grade) emery paper. If, however, the lip is due to the friction surface being recessed by excessive wear, then the drum must be renewed.

8 If the drum is thought to be excessively worn, or oval, its internal diameter must be measured at several points using an internal micrometer. Take measurements in pairs, the second at right-angles to the first, and compare the two, to check for signs of ovality. Provided that it does not enlarge the drum to beyond the specified maximum diameter, it may be possible to have the drum refinished by skimming or grinding; if this is not possible, the drums on both sides must be renewed. Note that if the drum is to be skimmed, BOTH

drums must be refinished, to maintain a consistent internal diameter on both sides.

Refitting

9 If a new brake drum is to be installed, use a suitable solvent to remove any preservative coating that may have been applied to its internal friction surfaces. Note that it may also be necessary to shorten the adjuster strut length, by rotating the serrated strut wheel, to allow the drum to pass over the brake shoes – see Section 8 for details.

10 If the original drum is being refitted, align the marks made on the drum and hub before removal, then fit the drum over the hub. Refit the locating studs and tighten them to the specified torque.

11 Depress the footbrake repeatedly to expand the brake shoes against the drum, and ensure that normal pedal pressure is restored.

12 Check and if necessary adjust the handbrake as described in Section 12.

13 Refit the roadwheels, and lower the car to the ground.

8 Rear brake shoes – renewal

⚠️ *Warning: Renew BOTH sets of rear brake shoes at the same time – NEVER renew the shoes on only one wheel, as uneven braking may result.*

⚠️ *Warning: Before starting work, refer to the warning given at the beginning of Section 4, concerning the dangers of asbestos dust.*

1 Remove the rear brake drums, as described in Section 7.

2 Working carefully, and taking the necessary precautions, remove all traces of brake dust from the brake drum, backplate and shoes.

3 Measure the thickness of the friction material of each brake shoe at several points; if either shoe is worn at any point to the specified minimum thickness or less, all four shoes must be renewed as a set. The shoes should also be renewed if any are fouled with hydraulic fluid, oil or grease; there is no satisfactory way of degreasing friction material, once contaminated.

4 If any of the brake shoes are worn unevenly, or contaminated, trace and rectify the cause before reassembly.

5 Note the position of each shoe, and the location of the return springs and self-adjuster mechanism to aid refitting later, **(see illustrations)**.

6 Detach the upper and lower return springs from both brake shoes **(see illustrations)**.

7 Depress the leading brake shoe hold-down spring clip and slide the clip out from under the pin head, while holding the pin from the

8.5a Correct fitted position of the brake shoe upper return spring . . .

8.5b . . . and lower return spring

8.6a Detach the upper return spring . . .

8.6b . . . and lower return spring from both brake shoes

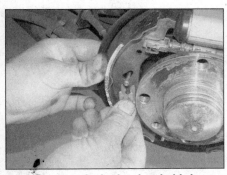

8.7 Depress the brake shoe hold-down spring clip and slide the clip out from under the pin head

8.8a Remove the leading brake shoe from the backplate . . .

8.8b . . . then lift out the self-adjuster mechanism

rear **(see illustration)**. Remove the pin from the rear of the backplate.

8 Remove the leading brake shoe from the backplate then lift out the self-adjuster mechanism **(see illustrations)**.

9 Remove the hold-down spring clip and pin from the trailing brake shoe, then withdraw the shoe from the backplate **(see illustrations)**.

10 Lift the locking catch on the trailing shoe handbrake lever, and slide the handbrake cable end out of the lever **(see illustration)**. Remove the trailing brake shoe.

11 Retain the wheel cylinder pistons in the wheel cylinder using a cable tie or a strong elastic band. Do not depress the brake pedal until the brakes are reassembled.

12 Carefully examine the self-adjuster mechanism for signs of wear or damage. Pay particular attention to the threads and the toothed adjuster wheel, and renew if necessary.

13 Check the condition of all return springs and renew any that show signs of distortion or other damage.

14 Peel back the rubber protective caps, and check the wheel cylinder for fluid leaks or other damage; check that both cylinder pistons are free to move easily. Refer to Section 9, if necessary, for information on wheel cylinder overhaul.

15 Prior to installation, clean the backplate, and apply a thin smear of high-temperature

brake grease or anti-seize compound to all those surfaces of the backplate which bear on the shoes, particularly the wheel cylinder pistons and lower pivot point. Do not allow the lubricant to foul the friction material.

16 Connect the handbrake cable to the lever on the trailing brake shoe, locate the trailing shoe on the backplate and secure in position with the pin and hold-down spring clip.

17 Fit the self-adjuster mechanism into the recess in the trailing brake shoe, then engage the leading shoe with the other end of the adjuster mechanism.

18 Secure the leading shoe in position with the hold-down pin and spring clip.

19 Fit the upper and lower brake shoe return springs, engaging them with the slots in the shoes. Remove the elastic band or cable tie from the wheel cylinder.

20 Turn the serrated wheel at the end of the self-adjuster mechanism, to retract the brake shoes – this will give additional clearance to allow the drum to pass over the shoes during refitting.

21 Refit the brake drum as described in Section 7.

22 Repeat the above procedure on the remaining rear brake.

23 Apply the brake pedal and handbrake lever several times to settle the self-adjusting mechanism. With both rear roadwheels refitted and the rear of the car still raised, turn the wheels by hand to check that the brake

shoes are not binding. Check and if necessary adjust the operation of the handbrake, as described in Section 12.

24 On completion, check the brake hydraulic fluid level in the master cylinder reservoir as described in *Weekly checks*.

25 Note that new shoes will not give full braking efficiency until they have bedded-in. Be prepared for this, and avoid hard braking as far as possible for the first hundred miles or so after shoe renewal.

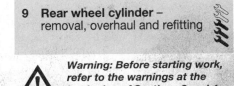

9 Rear wheel cylinder – removal, overhaul and refitting

⚠ *Warning: Before starting work, refer to the warnings at the beginning of Sections 2 and 4 concerning the dangers of hydraulic fluid and asbestos dust.*

Removal

1 Remove the brake drum as described in Section 7.

2 Remove the brake shoes as described in Section 8.

3 To minimise fluid loss during the following operations, remove the master cylinder reservoir filler cap, then tighten it down onto a piece of polythene, to obtain an airtight seal.

4 Clean the brake backplate around the

8.9a Remove the hold-down spring clip and pin from the trailing brake shoe . . .

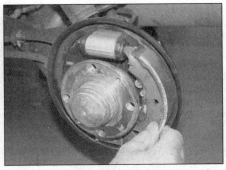

8.9b . . . then withdraw the shoe from the backplate

8.10 Lift the locking catch on the trailing shoe handbrake lever, and slide out the handbrake cable end

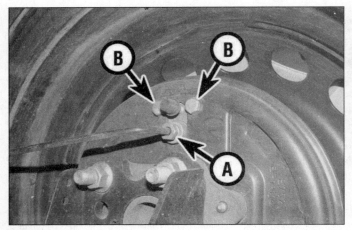

9.4 Wheel cylinder hydraulic pipe union (A) and retaining bolts (B)

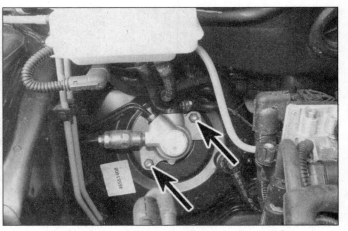

10.5 Master cylinder retaining nuts (arrowed)

wheel cylinder mounting bolts and the hydraulic pipe union, then unscrew the union nut and disconnect the hydraulic pipe **(see illustration)**. Cover the open ends of the pipe and the wheel cylinder to prevent dirt ingress.
5 Remove the two securing bolts, then withdraw the wheel cylinder from the backplate.

Overhaul

Note: *Before commencing work, ensure that the appropriate wheel cylinder overhaul kit is obtained.*
6 Clean the assembly thoroughly, using only methylated spirit or clean brake fluid.
7 Peel off both rubber dust covers, then use paint or similar to mark one of the pistons so that the pistons are not interchanged on reassembly.
8 Withdraw both pistons and the spring.
9 Discard the rubber piston cups and the dust covers. These components should be renewed as a matter of course, and are available as part of an overhaul kit, which also includes the bleed screw dust cap.
10 Check the condition of the cylinder bore and the pistons – the surfaces must be perfect and free from scratches, scoring and corrosion. It is advisable to renew the complete wheel cylinder if there is any doubt as to the condition of the cylinder bore or pistons.
11 Ensure that all components are clean and dry. The pistons, spring and cups should be fitted wet, using hydraulic fluid as a lubricant – soak them in clean fluid before installation.
12 Fit the cups to the pistons, ensuring that they are the correct way round. Use only your fingers (no tools) to manipulate the cups into position.
13 Fit the first piston to the cylinder, taking care not to distort the cup. If the original pistons are being re-used, the marks made on dismantling should be used to ensure that the pistons are refitted to their original bores.
14 Refit the spring and the second piston.
15 Apply a smear of rubber grease to the exposed end of each piston and to the dust cover sealing lips, then fit the dust covers to each end of the wheel cylinder.

Refitting

16 Refitting is a reversal of removal, bearing in mind the following points:
 a) *Tighten the mounting bolts to the specified torque.*
 b) *Refit the brake shoes as described in Section 8, and the brake drum as described in Section 7.*
 c) *Before refitting the roadwheel and lowering the car to the ground, remove the polythene from the fluid reservoir, and bleed the hydraulic system as described in Section 2. Note that if no other part of the system has been disturbed, it should only be necessary to bleed the relevant rear circuit.*

10 Master cylinder – emoval and refitting

 Warning: Before starting work, refer to the warning at the beginning of Section 2 concerning the dangers of hydraulic fluid.

Removal

1 Remove the master cylinder fluid reservoir filler cap, and syphon the hydraulic fluid from the reservoir. **Note:** *Do not syphon the fluid by mouth, as it is poisonous; use a syringe or an old poultry baster.* Alternatively, open any convenient bleed screw in the system, and gently pump the brake pedal to expel the fluid through a tube connected to the screw (see Section 2). Disconnect the wiring connector from the brake fluid level sender unit.
2 Place absorbent rags beneath the fluid reservoir and be prepared for fluid spillage.
3 Release the retaining clips and disconnect the reservoir hydraulic hoses from the master cylinder.

4 Wipe clean the area around the brake pipe unions on the side of the master cylinder, and place absorbent rags beneath the pipe unions to catch any surplus fluid. Make a note of the correct fitted positions of the unions, then unscrew the union nuts and carefully withdraw the pipes. Plug or tape over the pipe ends and master cylinder orifices to minimise the loss of brake fluid, and to prevent the entry of dirt into the system. Wash off any spilt fluid immediately with cold water.

> **HAYNES HiNT** *Cut the finger tips from an old rubber glove and secure them over the open ends of the brake pipes with elastic bands – this will help to minimise fluid loss and prevent the ingress of contaminants.*

5 Slacken and remove the two nuts securing the master cylinder to the vacuum servo unit, then withdraw the unit from the engine compartment **(see illustration)**.

Refitting

6 Remove all traces of dirt from the master cylinder and servo unit mating surfaces and, where applicable, fit a new seal between the master cylinder body and the servo.
7 Fit the master cylinder to the servo unit, ensuring that the servo unit pushrod enters the master cylinder bore centrally. Refit the master cylinder mounting nuts, and tighten them securely.
8 Wipe clean the brake pipe unions, then refit them to the correct master cylinder ports, as noted before removal, and tighten the union nuts securely.
9 Reconnect the reservoir fluid hoses to the master cylinder and secure with new clips.
10 Refill the master cylinder reservoir with fresh hydraulic fluid of the specified type (see *Lubricants and fluids*), and bleed the complete hydraulic system as described in Section 2. Note that it will also be necessary to bleed the

11.4 Stop-light switch wiring connector (arrowed)

12.8 lift out the ashtray from the rear of the centre console

12.9 Undo the retaining screw and remove the ashtray surround

clutch hydraulic system as described in Chapter 6.
11 On completion, thoroughly check the operation of the brake and clutch systems.

11 Stop-light switch –
adjustment, removal and refitting

Adjustment

1 The switch plunger operates on a ratchet.
2 If adjustment is required, pull the plunger fully out – the switch then self-adjusts as the brake pedal is applied and released.

Removal

3 Ensure that the ignition is switched off.
4 Disconnect the wiring connector from the switch **(see illustration)**.
5 Twist the switch anti-clockwise through about half a turn, and withdraw the switch from the pedal bracket. Note the position of the spacer and fitting bush.

Refitting

6 Depress the brake pedal and hold it in this position.
7 Fit the bush and spacer over the end of the switch, then insert the switch into its mounting bracket. Rotate the switch body clockwise through 60° until the locating lug is felt to engage in its recess.
8 Release the brake pedal and allow it to rest

against the switch spacer tab – this adjusts the position of the switch body inside the bush.
9 Now depress the brake pedal again – this has the effect of breaking off the spacer tab and fixes the position of the switch inside the bush.
10 Reconnect the wiring connector, then switch on the ignition and test the operation of the brake lights.

12 Handbrake –
checking and adjustment

Checking

1 The handbrake should be capable of holding the parked vehicle stationary, even on steep slopes, when applied with moderate force. The mechanism should be firm and positive in feel, with no trace of stiffness or sponginess from the cables, and the mechanism should release immediately the handbrake lever is released. If the mechanism does not operate satisfactorily, it should be checked immediately.
2 To check the operation of the handbrake, chock the front wheels then jack up the rear of the car and securely support it on axle stands (see *Jacking and vehicle support*). Release the handbrake lever.
3 Depress the brake pedal several times to establish the correct shoe-to-drum clearance.

4 With the pedal released, check that the rear roadwheels can be rotated – slight dragging is acceptable, but it should be possible to turn each wheel easily.
5 Apply the handbrake lever and check that the rear roadwheels start to drag after one click of the ratchet mechanism, and are fully locked within five clicks of the ratchet.
6 Fully release the handbrake, and check that the rear roadwheels can again be rotated by hand.
7 If the handbrake does not operate as described, carry out the adjustment procedure as follows.

Adjustment

8 From inside the car, lift out the ashtray from the rear of the centre console **(see illustration)**.
9 Undo the retaining screw and remove the ashtray surround from the console **(see illustration)**.
10 The adjustment mechanism is located underneath the handbrake lever. Using a spanner or suitable socket, turn the adjuster bolt clockwise to apply tension to the cables, or anti-clockwise to release the tension on the cables, as necessary **(see illustration)**. Check the operation of the handbrake as described previously and repeat the adjustment procedure as required.
11 On completion, refit the ashtray and lower the car to the ground.

13 Handbrake cables –
removal and refitting

Removal

1 There are two rear handbrake cables, one on each side of the car. To renew either rear cable, proceed as follows.
2 Remove the centre console as described in Chapter 11, then release the handbrake lever.
3 At the base of the handbrake lever, fully slacken the handbrake adjuster bolt, to remove all tension from the cable draw bar, then disconnect the relevant handbrake inner cable from the draw bar **(see illustration)**.

12.10 Handbrake adjuster bolt location (arrowed)

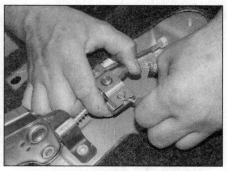

13.3 Disconnect the handbrake inner cable from the draw bar

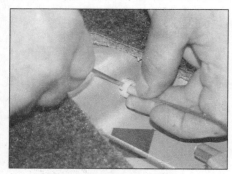

13.4 Depress the retaining tabs and release the handbrake cable grommet from the floorpan

13.7a Release the handbrake cables from their clips on the rear axle mountings (arrowed) . . .

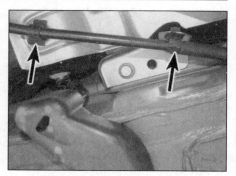

13.7b . . . exhaust heat shields and support brackets (arrowed) . . .

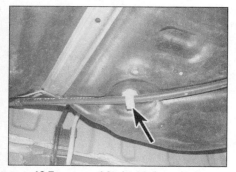

13.7c . . . and fuel tank (arrowed)

4 Depress the retaining tabs and release the cable grommet from the floorpan **(see illustration)**. Withdraw the cable from the vehicle interior.
5 Chock the front wheels then jack up the rear of the car and securely support it on axle stands (see *Jacking and vehicle support*).
6 Remove the rear brake shoes and disconnect the end of the handbrake cable from the lever on the trailing shoe as described in Section 8. Withdraw the cable from the brake backplate.
7 Release the handbrake cable from the retaining clips on the rear axle mounting, exhaust heat shield, fuel tank support bracket

and fuel tank, then remove the cable from under the car **(see illustrations)**.

Refitting

8 Refitting is a reversal of removal, bearing in mind the following points:
a) Ensure that the cable is securely fastened to the clips on the rear axle, heat shield, fuel tank and support bracket.
b) Connect the cable to the trailing brake shoe then refit the brake shoes as described in Section 8.
c) Refit the centre console as described in Chapter 11.
d) On completion, adjust the handbrake as described in Section 12.

14 Handbrake lever – removal and refitting

Removal

1 Remove the centre console as described in Chapter 11, then release the handbrake lever.
2 At the base of the handbrake lever, fully slacken the handbrake adjuster bolt, to remove all tension from the cable draw bar, then disconnect both handbrake inner cables from the draw bar.

3 Disconnect the wiring connector from the handbrake 'on' warning light switch located at the front of the handbrake lever base.
4 Undo the bolts securing the handbrake lever to the floor and remove the lever from the car.

Refitting

5 Refitting is a reversal of removal, bearing in mind the following points:
a) Refit the centre console as described in Chapter 11.
b) On completion, adjust the handbrake as described in Section 12.

15 Handbrake 'on' warning light switch – removal and refitting

Removal

1 Remove the centre console as described in Chapter 11.
2 Disconnect the wiring connector from the switch located at the front of the handbrake lever base **(see illustration)**.
3 Release the retaining clip and remove the switch from its location.

Refitting

4 Refitting is a reversal of removal.

15.2 Disconnect the wiring connector from the handbrake 'on' warning light switch

16.3 Extract the retaining clip (arrowed) and withdraw the servo unit clevis pin

16 Vacuum servo unit – removal and refitting

Removal

1 Remove the master cylinder as described in Section 10.
2 Prise out the grommet and disconnect the vacuum hose from the front of the servo unit.
3 From inside the car, extract the retaining clip and withdraw the clevis pin securing the brake pedal reaction link to the servo unit pushrod **(see illustration)**.
4 Undo the two nuts securing the servo unit

16.4 Servo unit retaining nuts (arrowed)

to the bulkhead and withdraw the unit from within the engine compartment **(see illustration)**.

Refitting

5 Refitting is a reversal of removal.

17 Anti-lock braking system (ABS) – general information

ABS is available as an option on certain models covered by this manual, and is fitted as standard equipment on others. The purpose of the system is to prevent the wheels locking during heavy braking. This is achieved by automatic release of the brake on the relevant wheel, followed by modulated re-application of the brake. The system comprises an electronic control unit, a hydraulic modulator, hydraulic solenoid valves (located in the modulator unit), an electrically-driven fluid return pump, and four wheel speed sensors.

The solenoids (which control the fluid pressure to the calipers/wheel cylinders) are controlled by the electronic control unit, which itself receives signals from the wheel speed sensors. The wheel speed sensors monitor the speed of rotation of each wheel. By comparing the speed signals from the four wheels, the control unit can determine when a wheel is decelerating at an abnormal rate, compared to the speed of the of the other wheels. Using this information, the control unit can predict when a wheel is about to lock, and is able to reduce the fluid pressure to the brake on the relevant wheel to prevent it locking. Once the rotational speed of the monitored wheel returns to approximately that of the other wheels, the hydraulic fluid pressure is increased in stages, to enable braking to continue.

During normal operation, the system functions in the same way as a conventional non-ABS braking system.

18 Anti-lock braking system (ABS) components – removal and refitting

Hydraulic modulator

⚠️ **Warning: Before starting work, refer to the warning at the beginning of Section 2 concerning the dangers of hydraulic fluid.**

Removal

1 Remove the air cleaner assembly as described in Chapter 4A.
2 Remove the battery and battery tray as described in Chapter 5A.
3 Release the locking clip and disconnect the ECU wiring harness connector.
4 Minimise hydraulic fluid loss by first removing the master cylinder reservoir filler cap, then tightening it down onto a piece of polythene, to obtain an airtight seal.
5 Wipe clean the area around the brake pipe unions on the side of the modulator, and place absorbent rags beneath the pipe unions to catch any surplus fluid. Make a note of the correct fitted positions of the unions, then unscrew the union nuts and carefully withdraw the pipes. Plug or tape over the pipe ends and modulator orifices to minimise the loss of fluid, and to prevent the entry of dirt into the system.
6 Undo the two retaining nuts, one on each side of the modulator, and remove the unit from the engine compartment.

Refitting

7 If a new modulator assembly is being fitted, it will be supplied prefilled with hydraulic fluid, and sealed with blanking plugs. Leave the plugs in position until just before connecting the brake pipes.
8 Locate the modulator in position and refit the two retaining nuts. Tighten the nuts securely.
9 Reconnect the brake pipes to their correct locations as noted during removal and tighten the union nuts securely.
10 Reconnect the ECU wiring connector.
11 Refit the air cleaner assembly as described in Chapter 4A.
12 Refit the battery tray and battery as described in Chapter 5A.
13 Remove the polythene from the master cylinder reservoir and bleed the complete brake hydraulic system as described in Section 2. Note that it may also be necessary to bleed the clutch hydraulic system as described in Chapter 6.

Electronic control unit

14 The electronic control unit is removed with the modulator assembly as described previously. The ECU is an integral part of the modulator and the two components cannot be separated.

Front wheel speed sensor

Removal

15 Firmly apply the handbrake, then jack up the front of the car and support it securely on axle stands (see *Jacking and vehicle support*). Remove the relevant front roadwheel.
16 Trace the wiring back from the sensor, and separate the two halves of the wiring connector in the engine compartment. Note the routing of the wiring to aid correct refitting.
17 Unclip the wheel speed sensor wiring from the brackets on the suspension strut **(see illustration)**.
18 Unscrew the retaining bolt and withdraw the sensor from the swivel hub **(see illustration)**.

18.17 Unclip the wheel speed sensor wiring from the brackets on the suspension strut

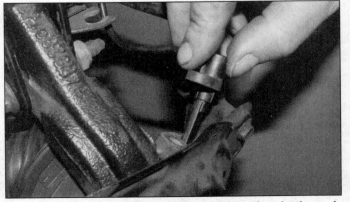

18.18 Unscrew the retaining bolt and withdraw the wheel speed sensor from the swivel hub

Refitting

19 Refitting is a reversal of removal, noting the following points:

  a) *Ensure that the mating faces of the sensor and the swivel hub are clean, and apply a smear of high melting-point brake grease to the sensor location in the swivel hub before refitting.*

  b) *Ensure that the end face of the sensor is clean.*

  c) *Route the wiring as noted before removal.*

Rear wheel speed sensor

Removal

20 Chock the front wheels then jack up the rear of the car and securely support it on axle stands (see *Jacking and vehicle support*). Remove the appropriate rear roadwheel.

21 Refer to Chapter 11, Section 25, and remove the interior lower side trim panel adjacent to the rear seat for access to the wiring connector.

22 Trace the wiring back from the sensor to its wiring connector. Free the connector from its retaining clip, and disconnect the wiring from the main wiring loom.

23 Work back along the sensor wiring, and release it from the retaining clips. Note the routing of the wiring to aid correct refitting.

24 Slacken and remove the bolt securing the sensor unit to the rear stub axle, and remove the sensor and lead assembly.

Refitting

25 Refitting is a reversal of removal, noting the following points:

  a) *Ensure that the mating faces of the sensor and the stub axle are clean, and apply a smear of high melting-point brake grease to the sensor location in the stub axle before refitting.*

  b) *Ensure that the end face of the sensor is clean.*

  c) *Route the wiring as noted before removal.*

Chapter 10
Suspension and steering

Contents

Degrees of difficulty

Easy, suitable for novice with little experience		**Fairly easy,** suitable for beginner with some experience		**Fairly difficult,** suitable for competent DIY mechanic		**Difficult,** suitable for experienced DIY mechanic		**Very difficult,** suitable for expert DIY or professional	

Specifications

Front suspension
Type . . . .   Independent, with MacPherson struts and transverse lower suspension arms. Anti-roll bar fitted to all models

Rear suspension
Type . . . .   Semi-independent torsion beam axle, with coil springs and telescopic shock absorbers

Steering
Type . . . .   Rack-and-pinion with electrically-operated power assistance
Toe setting (front) . . . .   0° (parallel) ± 1°

Torque wrench settings

	Nm	lbf ft
Front suspension		
Anti-roll bar mounting bolts	35	26
Driveshaft nut*	240	177
Lower arm balljoint to swivel hub	32	24
Lower arm front mounting securing bolt	90	66
Lower arm rear mounting securing bolt	110	81
Suspension strut piston rod top nut	60	44
Suspension strut-to-swivel hub bolts	75	55
Suspension strut upper mounting cup-to-piston rod nut	60	44
Rear suspension		
Hub nut*	280	207
Rear axle mounting brackets to axle	90	66
Rear axle mounting brackets to body	60	44
Shock absorber lower securing bolt	100	74
Shock absorber upper securing bolt	80	59
Stub axle to rear axle bracket	25	18
Steering		
Steering column mounting nuts	15	11
Steering gear mounting bolts	70	52
Steering wheel nut*	50	37
Track rod end-to-swivel hub nut	40	30
Universal joint clamp bolt nut	33	24
Roadwheels		
Roadwheel bolts	85	63

* Use a new nut

1 General information

Front suspension

The front suspension is independent, comprising transverse lower wishbones, coil spring-over-damper MacPherson strut units and an anti-roll bar. The swivel hubs are bolted to the base of the strut units and are linked to the lower arms by means of balljoints. The entire front suspension assembly is mounted on a subframe, which is in turn bolted to the vehicle body.

Rear suspension

The rear suspension incorporates a torsion beam axle with trailing arms, coil springs and separate double-acting telescopic shock absorbers. The components form a discrete sub-assembly which can be unbolted from the underside of the vehicle separately or as a complete unit.

Steering

The two-piece steering shaft runs in a tubular column assembly, which is bolted to a bracket mounted on the vehicle bulkhead. The upper shaft is attached to the intermediate shaft by means of a universal joint and the intermediate shaft is similarly connected to the steering gear pinion by a second universal joint.

The rack-and-pinion steering gear is mounted on the front subframe, and is connected by means of track rods to the steering arms projecting rearwards from the swivel hubs. The track rods are fitted with balljoints at their inner and outer ends, to allow for suspension movement, and are threaded to facilitate adjustment.

Dualdrive electrically-operated power steering is fitted to all models. The power assistance is provided by an electric motor and gearbox assembly which is integral with the steering column. The system is controlled by an electronic control unit and provides the driver with two operating strategies – one for normal driving and one for 'city' driving. A control button on the facia is used to switch between the two functions. When the 'city' function is activated, a greater degree of power assistance is provided for ease of town driving and parking manoeuvres.

2 Front swivel hub assembly – removal and refitting

Note: A balljoint separator tool will be required for this operation and a new driveshaft retaining nut will be required for refitting.

Removal

1 Firmly apply the handbrake, then jack up the front of the car and support it securely on axle stands (see Jacking and vehicle support). Remove the appropriate front roadwheel.
2 Using a hammer and chisel or similar tool, tap up the staking securing the driveshaft retaining nut in position.
3 The front wheel hub must be held stationary in order to loosen the driveshaft nut. Ideally, the hub should be held by a suitable tool bolted into place using two of the roadwheel bolts (see Tool Tip). Alternatively, have an assistant firmly apply the foot brake to prevent the hub from rotating. Using a socket and extension bar, slacken and remove the driveshaft retaining nut.

> ⚠️ **Warning: The nut is extremely tight. Discard the nut – a new one must be used on refitting.**

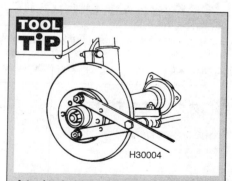

A tool to hold the front hub stationary whilst the driveshaft nut is slackened can be fabricated from two lengths of steel strip (one long, one short) and a nut and bolt; the nut and bolt forming the pivot of a forked tool.

2.5a Undo the brake caliper mounting bracket retaining bolts (arrowed) . . .

2.5b . . . and withdraw the caliper and mounting bracket assembly off the disc

2.7a On models with ABS, release the wheel speed sensor cable from the suspension strut brackets . . .

4 Release the brake caliper hydraulic hose from the bracket at the base of the suspension strut.

5 Undo the two bolts securing the brake caliper mounting bracket to the swivel hub. Withdraw the caliper and mounting bracket assembly, complete with brake pads, off the disc **(see illustrations)**. Suspend the caliper from a convenient place under the wheel arch using string or a cable tie. Do not allow the caliper to hang unsupported from the brake hydraulic hose.

6 If the swivel hub is being removed for renewal of the bearing, mark the relationship between the brake disc and the hub with chalk or a marker pen, to allow correct refitting. Slacken and remove the disc locating studs, then remove the disc from the wheel hub.

7 On models with ABS, release the wheel speed sensor cable from the brackets at the base of the suspension strut. Undo the sensor retaining bolt, withdraw the sensor from the swivel hub and suspend it away from the working area, to avoid the possibility of damage **(see illustrations)**.

8 Unscrew the nut securing the track rod end to the swivel hub. Release the track rod end tapered shank using a balljoint separator tool.

9 Unscrew the two nuts and remove the bolts securing the top of the swivel hub to the base of the suspension strut **(see illustrations)**.

10 Pull the swivel hub outwards at the top to

release the driveshaft outer constant velocity joint from the wheel hub. If necessary, the joint can be tapped free using a soft-faced mallet.

11 Slacken and remove the nut, then withdraw the suspension lower arm balljoint clamp bolt from the swivel hub **(see illustrations)**.

12 Tap a small chisel into the split on the swivel hub to spread the hub slightly, then lift the swivel hub assembly up and off the balljoint shank.

Refitting

13 Locate the swivel hub over the suspension lower arm balljoint, pushing it fully

2.7b . . . then undo the retaining bolt (arrowed) and remove the sensor

into engagement with the balljoint shank. Refit the clamp bolt and secure with the nut tightened to the specified torque.

14 Engage the outer CV joint into the wheel hub, then pivot the top of the swivel hub back towards the car. Screw on the new driveshaft retaining nut, but do not tighten it at this stage.

15 Refit the suspension strut-to-swivel hub bolts, screw on the two nuts and tighten them to the specified torque.

16 Engage the track rod end with the swivel hub, refit the retaining nut and tighten the nut to the specified torque.

17 On models with ABS, ensure that the mating faces of the wheel speed sensor and

2.9a Unscrew the two nuts . . .

2.9b . . . and remove the bolts securing the swivel hub to the suspension strut

2.11a Slacken and remove the retaining nut . . .

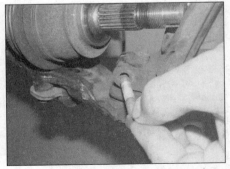

2.11b . . . then withdraw the suspension lower arm balljoint clamp bolt from the swivel hub

the swivel hub are clean, and apply a smear of high melting point brake grease to the sensor location in the swivel hub. Ensure that the end face of the sensor is clean, then locate it in position and secure with the retaining bolt. Refit the sensor cable to the brackets on the suspension strut.

18 If previously removed, locate the brake disc on the hub so that the roadwheel bolt and locating stud holes are all correctly lined up; use the alignment marks made during removal. Refit the locating studs and tighten them securely.

19 Refit the brake caliper and mounting bracket assembly to the swivel hub. Coat the threads of the mounting bolts with thread locking compound, then tighten them to the specified torque (see Chapter 9).

20 Refit the brake caliper hydraulic hose to the bracket at the base of the suspension strut.

21 Using the method employed on removal to prevent rotation of the hub, tighten the driveshaft retaining nut to the specified torque. Secure the nut by tapping the staking into the two grooves in the end of the CV joint using a hammer and chisel.

22 Refit the roadwheel, and lower the car to the ground. Depress the brake pedal several times to bring the brake pads into contact with the disc.

23 It is advisable to have the front wheel toe setting checked at the earliest opportunity.

3 Front hub bearings – renewal

Note: *Various special tools, including a hydraulic press will be required for this operation (see text). If the necessary tools are not available, the swivel hub assembly should be removed as described in Section 2 and taken to a suitably-equipped engineering works for renewal of the bearing.*

1 Remove the swivel hub assembly as described in Section 2.

2 Mount the swivel hub firmly in a bench vice. Attach a slide hammer to the wheel hub flange

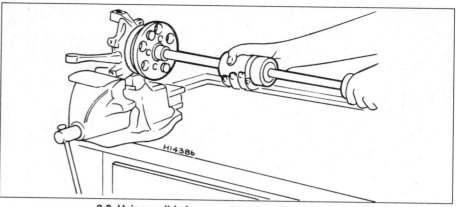

3.2 Using a slide hammer to extract the hub flange

and extract the hub, together with the bearing inner race **(see illustration)**.

3 The bearing inner race must now be removed from the wheel hub using a suitable puller. To provide sufficient clearance for the puller legs, force the inner race away from the hub flange using a hammer and small chisel inserted between the inner race and the hub flange. When sufficient clearance exists, engage the puller legs behind the inner race and draw the race off the wheel hub.

4 Undo the bolt and remove the dust shield from the swivel hub **(see illustrations)**.

5 Using a large screwdriver, extract the bearing retaining circlip from the swivel hub **(see illustration)**.

6 Mount the swivel hub on the press bed and press the bearing out of the hub. Note that a flange on the outboard side of the swivel hub means that the bearing can only be removed in one direction.

7 Before installing the new bearing, thoroughly clean the bearing location in the swivel hub.

8 Fit the new bearing from the inboard side the swivel hub and press it fully into position, applying pressure only to the bearing outer race.

9 Fit the bearing retaining circlip to its groove in the swivel hub so that the circlip's gap is aligned with the aperture for the ABS wheel speed sensor (otherwise the sensor will not function correctly and the ABS failure warning

lamp will illuminate). Refit the dust shield and tighten the retaining bolt securely.

10 Suitably support the bearing inner race on the press bed and press the wheel hub into the bearing.

11 On completion, check that the wheel hub rotates freely in the bearing without resistance or roughness.

12 Refit the swivel hub assembly as described in Section 2.

4 Front suspension strut – removal and refitting

Removal

1 Firmly apply the handbrake, then jack up the front of the car and support it securely on axle stands (see *Jacking and vehicle support*). Remove the appropriate roadwheel(s).

2 Release the brake caliper hydraulic hose (and, where applicable, the ABS wheel speed sensor cable) from the brackets at the base of the suspension strut.

3 Unscrew the two nuts and remove the bolts securing the base of the suspension strut to the top of the swivel hub.

4 Pull the swivel hub outwards at the top to release it from the suspension strut.

5 Have an assistant support the strut from underneath the wheel arch. Working in the

3.4a Undo the retaining bolt . . .

3.4b . . . and remove the dust shield from the swivel hub

3.5 Extract the bearing retaining circlip from the swivel hub

engine compartment, unscrew the nut securing the upper mounting cup to the strut piston rod while counterholding the piston rod with a suitable Allen key. Lift off the upper mounting cup and withdraw the assembly from under the wheel arch (see illustrations).

Refitting

6 Manoeuvre the strut assembly into position under the wheel arch and locate the upper mounting cup over the strut piston. Refit the retaining nut and moderately tighten it at this stage. Final tightening of this nut is carried out with the car resting on its roadwheels.

7 Engage the lower end of the strut with the swivel hub, then fit the securing bolts and nuts. Tighten the nuts to the specified torque.

8 Refit the brake caliper hydraulic hose (and where applicable, the ABS wheel speed sensor cable) to the bracket at the base of the suspension strut.

9 Refit the roadwheel, and lower the car to the ground.

10 With the car resting on its roadwheels, tighten the suspension strut upper mounting cup retaining nut to the specified torque.

5   Front suspension strut – overhaul

Note: *Suitable coil spring compressor tools will be required for this operation.*

1 Remove the front suspension strut as described in Section 4.

2 Fit suitable spring compressors to the coil spring, and compress the spring sufficiently to enable the upper mounting to be turned by hand (see illustration).

⚠️ *Warning: Ensure that the coil spring is compressed sufficiently to remove all the tension from the upper mounting, before attempting to remove the piston rod nut.*

3 Unscrew the nut securing the strut piston rod to the upper mounting, while counterholding the piston with a suitable Allen key (see illustration).

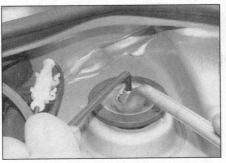

4.5a Unscrew the nut securing the suspension strut upper mounting cup to the piston rod . . .

4 Withdraw the upper mounting and upper spring seat, then withdraw the spring, complete with the compressors (see illustrations).

5 Release the lower end of the dust cover from the strut body, then withdraw the dust cover and bump rubber (see illustration).

6 With the strut assembly now dismantled, examine all the components for wear, damage or deformation. Renew any components as necessary.

7 Examine the strut body for signs of fluid leakage or damage and the piston rod for signs of pitting or scoring. While holding it in an upright position, test the operation of the strut by moving the piston rod through a full stroke, and then through short strokes of 50 to 100 mm. In both cases, the resistance felt

4.5b . . . lift off the mounting cup and withdraw the strut from under the wheel arch

should be smooth and continuous. If the resistance is jerky, or uneven, or if there is any visible sign of wear or damage to the strut, renewal is necessary.

8 If any doubt exists about the condition of the coil spring, carefully remove the spring compressors, and check the spring for distortion and signs of cracking. Renew the spring if it is damaged or distorted, or if there is any doubt about its condition.

⚠️ *Warning: Coil springs are classified by their height when under load – this is indicated by a coloured paint marking on the side of the coil windings. All coil springs fitted to the vehicle must be of the same classification to ensure the correct ride height.*

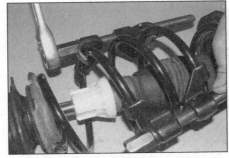

5.2 Compress the coil spring sufficiently to enable the upper mounting to be turned by hand

5.3 Unscrew the nut securing the strut piston rod to the upper mounting

5.4a Withdraw the upper mounting and upper spring seat . . .

5.4b . . . then withdraw the coil spring

5.5 Release the dust cover from the strut body, then withdraw the dust cover and bump rubber

5.10 Fit the spring ensuring that the lower end locates in the spring seat recess (arrowed)

5.11b . . . is on the same side as the swivel hub mounting bracket (arrowed)

6.2a Unscrew the bolts (arrowed) securing the anti-roll bar mountings to the suspension lower arms . . .

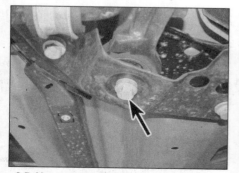

6.5 Unscrew the bolt (arrowed) securing the suspension lower arm rear mounting to the subframe

5.11a Locate the upper spring seat over the piston rod, ensuring that the raised projection (arrowed) . . .

5.12 Refit the upper spring seat so that the pointer (arrowed) will be facing the rear of the car with the strut installed

6.2b . . . and front subframe

6.6 Slacken and remove the nut (arrowed) from the through-bolt at the lower arm front mounting

9 Begin reassembly by refitting the dust cover and bump rubber.

10 Ensure that the coil spring is compressed sufficiently to enable the upper mounting components to be fitted, then fit the spring over the piston rod, ensuring that the lower end of the spring is correctly located in the recess on the lower spring seat (see illustration).

11 Locate the upper spring seat over the piston rod, ensuring that the raised projection on the spring seat is on the same side as the swivel hub mounting bracket at the base of the strut (see illustrations).

12 Refit the upper spring seat and position it so that the pointer on the seat flange will be facing the rear of the car when the strut is installed (see illustration).

13 Fit the piston rod top nut, then tighten the nut to the specified torque, counterholding the piston rod in a manner similar to that used during dismantling. Note that a suitable crows-foot adapter will be required to tighten the piston rod top nut to the specified torque.

14 Remove the spring compressors and refit the strut to the car as described in Section 4.

6 Front suspension lower arm – removal and refitting

Removal

1 Firmly apply the handbrake, then jack up the front of the car and support it securely on axle stands (see *Jacking and vehicle support*). Remove the relevant roadwheel.

2 Unscrew the bolts securing the anti-roll bar mountings to the suspension lower arms on each side of the car. Similarly, unscrew the bolts securing the anti-roll bar mountings to the front subframe (see illustrations). Allow the ends of the anti-roll bar to pivot away from the suspension lower arms.

3 Slacken and remove the nut, then withdraw the suspension lower arm balljoint clamp bolt from the swivel hub.

4 Tap a small chisel into the split on the swivel hub to spread the hub slightly, then lever the end of the suspension lower arm down to release it from the base of the swivel hub.

5 Unscrew the bolt securing the suspension lower arm rear mounting to the subframe (see illustration).

6 Slacken and remove the nut from the through-bolt at the lower arm front mounting (see illustration). Withdraw the bolt.

7 Manoeuvre the suspension lower arm from its mounting locations and remove it from under the car.

8 With the lower arm removed, examine the arm itself, and the mounting bushes, for wear, cracks or damage.

9 Check the balljoint for wear, excessive play, or stiffness. Also check the balljoint dust boot for cracks or damage.

10 The mounting bushes and balljoint assembly are integral with the suspension lower arm, and cannot be renewed independently. If either the bushes or the balljoint are worn or damaged, the complete suspension lower arm assembly must be renewed.

Refitting

Caution: Final tightening of the suspension lower arm and anti-roll bar attachments must be carried out with the car resting on its roadwheels, or damage to the rubber bushes will result.

11 Locate the suspension lower arm in its mountings. Fit the through-bolt to the front mounting bracket and engage it with the lower arm bush. Fit the securing nut, but do not fully tighten it at this stage.

12 Refit the rear mounting bolt, but do not fully tighten the bolt at this stage.

13 Engage the lower arm balljoint with the swivel hub, then refit the balljoint clamp bolt and nut. Tighten the clamp bolt nut to the specified torque.

14 Raise the anti-roll bar into position, then bolt the mounting brackets to the subframe. The anti-roll bar must be preloaded before its outer mounting brackets can be bolted to the suspension arms. Do this by raising the ends of the anti-roll bar with a trolley jack and holding them in this position whilst the bracket mounting bolts are inserted and hand tightened. Do not fully tighten the bolts at this stage.

15 Refit the roadwheel, and lower the car to the ground.

16 Make sure that the car is parked on level ground, then release the handbrake. Roll the vehicle backwards and forwards, and bounce the front of the vehicle to settle the suspension components.

17 Chock the wheels, then tighten all the anti-roll bar and suspension arm mounting nuts and bolts to the specified torque.

18 On completion, have the front wheel toe setting checked at the earliest opportunity.

7 Front suspension lower arm balljoint – renewal

The balljoint is integral with the suspension lower arm. If the balljoint is worn or damaged, the complete lower arm must be renewed, as described in Section 6.

8 Front suspension anti-roll bar – removal and refitting

Removal

1 Firmly apply the handbrake, then jack up the front of the car and support it securely on axle stands (see *Jacking and vehicle support*). Remove both front roadwheels.

2 Unscrew the nuts and disconnect the exhaust front pipe flange from the manifold downpipe. Recover the gasket.

3 Undo the bolt securing the exhaust system front mounting bracket to the subframe. Lower the system and suitably support it.

4 Unscrew the bolts securing the anti-roll bar mountings to the suspension lower arms on either side of the vehicle. Similarly, unscrew the bolts securing the anti-roll bar mountings to the subframe (refer to the illustrations in Section 6).

5 Lower the anti-roll bar and remove it from under the car.

6 Inspect the rubber bushes for cracks or deterioration. If renewal is necessary, slide the old bushes from the bar, and fit the new items, using soapy water as a lubricant. Do not apply grease or oil as this will attack the rubber.

7 Check the anti-roll bar for signs of damage, wear or serious corrosion.

Refitting

8 Refitting is a reversal of removal, bearing in mind the following points:

a) *Moderately tighten the anti-roll bar mountings initially, then tighten them all to the specified torque after the car has been lowered to the ground and is resting on its roadwheels.*

b) *Refit the exhaust system front pipe flange using a new gasket and tighten the nuts to the specified torque (see Chapter 4A).*

9 Rear hub assembly – removal and refitting

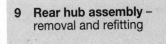

Note: *A new rear hub retaining nut must be used on refitting.*

Removal

1 The rear hub bearings are integral with the hubs themselves, and cannot be renewed separately. If the bearings require renewal, the complete hub assembly must be renewed.

2 Chock the front wheels, then jack up the rear of the vehicle and support securely on axle stands (see *Jacking and vehicle support*). Remove the appropriate rear roadwheel.

3 Remove the brake drum as described in Chapter 9. **Do not** depress the brake pedal whilst the brake drum is removed.

4 Prise the dust cap from the hub, using a mallet and punch.

5 Slacken and remove the hub nut and recover the spacer.

Caution: The nut is tightened to a very high torque. Use a long extension bar to remove the nut and ensure that you have access to torque wrench capable of tightening the new nut to the specified torque before removing the existing nut.

6 Withdraw the hub and bearing assembly from the stub axle, and recover the inner

spacer. Discard the hub nut – a new one must be used on refitting.

7 Thoroughly clean the stub axle, then slide the inner spacer and the hub assembly into position.

8 Fit the outer spacer, then thread a new hub nut onto the end of the stub axle.

9 Tighten the hub nut to the specified torque, then check that the hub spins smoothly and freely. Carefully tap the dust cap into position over the nut.

10 Refit the brake drum as described in Chapter 9.

11 Refit the roadwheel and lower the car to the ground.

10 Rear suspension components – removal and refitting

1 Chock the front wheels then jack up the rear of the car and securely support it on axle stands (see *Jacking and vehicle support*). Remove the relevant rear roadwheel(s).

Shock absorber

Removal

2 Using a trolley jack positioned under the rear axle trailing arm, raise the trailing arm to take the strain from the shock absorber.

3 Slacken and withdraw the shock absorber lower retaining bolt **(see illustration)**.

4 Lower the jack and allow the shock absorber to separate from the trailing arm. Take care to avoid displacing the coil spring.

5 Slacken and withdraw the shock absorber upper retaining bolt.

6 Withdraw the shock absorber from its upper mounting and remove it from under the car.

7 Examine the shock absorber for signs of fluid leakage or damage. While holding it in an upright position, test the operation of the shock absorber by moving the piston through a full stroke, and then through short strokes of 50 to 100 mm. In both cases, the resistance felt should be smooth and continuous. If the resistance is jerky, or uneven, or if there is any visible sign of wear or damage, renewal is necessary.

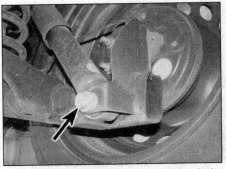

10.3 Shock absorber lower retaining bolt (arrowed)

10.19 Stub axle retaining bolt nuts (arrowed)

Refitting

8 Refitting is a reversal of removal. Tighten the shock absorber upper and lower retaining bolts to the specified torque, but delay this operation until the full weight of the car is resting on its roadwheels.

Coil spring

Removal

9 Using a trolley jack positioned under the rear axle trailing arm, raise the trailing arm to take the strain from the shock absorbers.
10 Slacken and withdraw the shock absorber upper retaining bolts on both sides.
11 Lower the trailing arm gradually using a trolley jack, until the coil spring is released from its lower seat on the trailing arm and its upper seat on the underbody. Make a note of the orientation of the coil spring, to aid correct refitting later.

Refitting

12 Refitting is a reversal of removal. Tighten the shock absorber upper retaining bolts to the specified torque, but delay this operation until the full weight of the car is resting on its roadwheels.

Stub axle

Removal

13 Remove the rear hub assembly as described in Section 9.
14 Remove the rear brake shoes as described in Chapter 9.
15 Using a brake hose clamp, clamp the brake flexible hydraulic hose located adjacent to the rear axle mounting.
16 Clean the brake backplate around the wheel cylinder hydraulic pipe union, then unscrew the union nut and disconnect the hydraulic pipe. Cover the open ends of the pipe and the wheel cylinder to prevent dirt ingress.
17 On models with ABS, slacken and remove the bolt securing the rear wheel speed sensor to the rear of the stub axle and withdraw the sensor from its location. Suspend the sensor away from the working area, to avoid the possibility of damage.
18 Undo the two bolts and remove the brake backplate from the stub axle.

19 Undo the four nuts, withdraw the bolts and remove the stub axle from the rear axle bracket (see illustration).

Refitting

20 Ensure that the stub axle and rear axle bracket mating faces are clean, then locate the stub axle in position. Refit the retaining bolts and nuts and tighten the nuts to the specified torque.
21 Locate the brake backplate on the stub axle, refit the bolts and tighten them securely. Connect the brake pipe to the wheel cylinder and securely tighten the union nut. Remove the brake hose clamp from the flexible hydraulic hose.
22 Refit the rear brake shoes as described in Chapter 9.
23 Refit the rear hub assembly as described in Section 9.
24 Ensure that the mating faces of the wheel speed sensor and the stub axle are clean, and apply a smear of high melting-point brake grease to the sensor location in the stub axle. Clean the end face of the sensor, locate it in place and secure with the retaining bolt.
25 On completion, bleed the brake hydraulic system as described in Chapter 9. Note that if no other part of the system has been disturbed, it should only be necessary to bleed the relevant rear circuit.

Rear axle assembly

Note: *The rubber-in-torsion pivot bushes at the front end of the rear axle assembly are not available separately. If either is worn or damaged, the complete rear axle assembly must be replaced.*

Removal

26 Remove the rear brake shoes on both sides as described in Chapter 9.
27 Using brake hose clamps, clamp the brake flexible hydraulic hoses located adjacent to each rear axle mounting.
28 Clean the area around the brake pipe-to-flexible hose union nuts, and unscrew the pipe unions on each side. Extract the retaining clips and detach the flexible hoses from the brackets on the rear axle. Cover the open ends of the pipes and hoses to prevent dirt ingress.
29 On models with ABS, slacken and remove the bolts securing the rear wheel speed sensors to the rear of the stub axles and withdraw the sensors from their location. Suspend the sensors away from the working area, to avoid the possibility of damage.
30 Release the handbrake cables, and where applicable, the rear wheel speed sensor cables from their clips on the rear axle.
31 Remove both rear coil springs as described previously in this Section.
32 Suitably support the rear axle assembly on a trolley jack and engage the help of an assistant.
33 Undo the bolts securing the rear axle mounting brackets to the underbody on both sides. Slowly lower the jack and guide the axle assembly down and out from under the car.

Refitting

34 Guide the axle assembly into position, refit the mounting bracket retaining bolts and tighten them to the specified torque.
35 Refit the rear coil springs as described previously in this Section.
36 Ensure that the mating faces of the wheel speed sensors and the stub axles are clean, and apply a smear of high melting-point brake grease to the sensor locations in the stub axles. Clean the end face of the sensors, locate them place and secure with the retaining bolts.
37 Refit the flexible brake hydraulic hoses to their mounting brackets and secure with the retaining clips. Reconnect the brake pipe union to each hose and tighten the union nut securely. Remove the brake hose clamps from the hoses.
38 Secure the handbrake cables, and where applicable, the rear wheel speed sensor cables in their clips on the rear axle.
39 Refer to Chapter 9 and refit the rear brake shoes then bleed the brake hydraulic system. Note that if no other part of the system has been disturbed, it should only be necessary to bleed the rear circuits.

11 Steering wheel – removal and refitting

Removal

1 Remove the airbag unit from the steering wheel as described in Chapter 12.
2 Turn the steering wheel to its centre position, so that the roadwheels are pointing straight-ahead.
3 Lift off the protective seal over the steering wheel retaining nut (see illustration).
4 Slacken and remove the steering wheel retaining nut. Discard the nut as a new item must used on refitting.
5 Make alignment marks between the steering wheel and the end of the steering column shaft, to aid correct refitting later.
6 Disconnect the horn switch wiring connector and lift the steering wheel off the column splines. If it is tight, twist it from side-to-side, whilst pulling upwards to release it

11.3 Lift off the protective seal over the steering wheel retaining nut

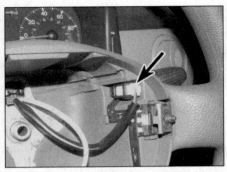

11.6a Disconnect the horn switch wiring connector (arrowed) . . .

11.6b . . . and withdraw the steering wheel from the column splines

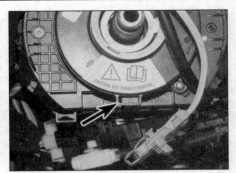

11.7 Check that the clock spring centre position indicator window (arrowed) is centred over the red indicator tab

from the shaft splines **(see illustrations)**. Once the wheel is free, feed the airbag and horn switch wiring through the aperture in the steering wheel and remove the wheel from the car.

7 Check that the centre position indicator window on the outer moving portion of the airbag clock spring is centred over the red indicator tab on the fixed portion **(see illustration)**. It is advisable to secure the moving and fixed portions of the clock spring together using tape to prevent rotation with the steering wheel removed.

Refitting

8 Check that the airbag clock spring is still centred correctly as described in paragraph 7.

12.4a Depress the release button with a small screwdriver . . .

12.4b . . . and withdraw the lock cylinder from its bracket

Remove the tape used to secure the clock spring moving and fixed portions together.

9 Feed the airbag and horn switch wiring through the steering wheel and locate the wheel on the column splines. Ensure that the marks made on the steering wheel and column shaft are aligned.

10 Screw on a new steering wheel retaining nut and tighten the nut to the specified torque. Refit the protective seal over the retaining nut.

11 Reconnect the horn switch wiring connector.

12 Refit the airbag unit as described in Chapter 12.

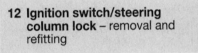

12 Ignition switch/steering column lock – removal and refitting

Removal

1 Disconnect the battery negative terminal (refer to *Disconnecting the battery* in the Reference Chapter).

2 Remove the upper and lower steering column shrouds (see *Facia panels – removal and refitting* in Chapter 11).

3 Insert the key into the ignition switch and turn it to the ON position.

4 Working underneath the steering column, insert a small flat-bladed screwdriver into the access slot in the base of the lock assembly bracket. Depress the release button and

13.4 Disconnect the two main wiring harness connectors from the power steering ECU

withdraw the lock assembly from its bracket, complete with the key **(see illustrations)**.

Refitting

5 To refit the lock, first insert the key and turn it to the ON position. Depress the release button slide the assembly into the retaining bracket until the release button clicks into the access slot.

6 Turn the key back to the OFF position.

7 Refit the steering column shrouds as described in Chapter 11.

8 Reconnect the battery negative terminal.

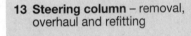

13 Steering column – removal, overhaul and refitting

Removal

1 Remove the steering wheel as described in Section 11.

2 Remove the airbag clock spring and steering column stalk switches as described in Chapter 12.

3 Where fitted, undo the retaining bolts and remove the metal guard plate beneath the power steering electric motor.

4 Disconnect the two main wiring harness connectors from the power steering electric motor ECU **(see illustration)**.

5 Disconnect the wiring connector from the rear of the ignition switch/column lock **(see illustration)**.

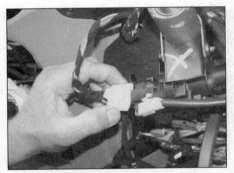

13.5 Disconnect the wiring connector from the ignition switch/column lock

13.6 Unscrew the clamp bolt retaining nut (arrowed) on the intermediate shaft lower universal joint

13.7 Steering column retaining nuts (arrowed)

a) Ensure that the roadwheels are in the straight-ahead position then engage the universal joint with the steering gear pinion, aligning the marks made on removal.
b) Tighten all retaining nuts and bolts to the specified torque.
c) Refit the steering column stalk switches and airbag clock spring as described in Chapter 12.
d) Refit the steering wheel as described in Section 11.

6 Working in the driver's footwell, unscrew the clamp bolt retaining nut on the intermediate shaft lower universal joint **(see illustration)**. Remove the clamp bolt from the retaining clip on the universal joint. Make suitable alignment marks on the steering gear pinion and universal joint to ensure correct orientation when refitting.
7 Undo the four steering column retaining nuts and lower the assembly away from the bulkhead bracket studs **(see illustration)**.
8 Disconnect the universal joint from the steering gear pinion, and remove the steering column from the car.

Overhaul

9 The height adjustment mechanism can be removed by removing the nut from the end of the pivot shaft and withdrawing it.

10 The upper and lower bushes are held in position by staking at the ends of the column tube. Relieve the staking using a mallet and punch to extract the bushes.
11 Check for excessive radial and axial play in the universal joints at both ends of the steering column intermediate shaft. The intermediate shaft may be renewed separately, if required, by slackening the clamp bolt and detaching it from the column upper section.
12 If the vehicle has been involved in an accident, check for deformation in all of the steering column components, particularly the mounting bracket and centre tube. Renew as required.

Refitting

13 Refitting is a reversal of removal, bearing in mind the following points.

14 Power steering electric motor – removal and refitting

Note: If the motor assembly is being renewed, it will be necessary to have the motor torque and position sensors calibrated using Fiat diagnostic test equipment on completion. Full and effective power assistance may not be available until the calibration procedures have been carried out.

Removal

1 Remove the steering column as described in Section 13.
2 Disconnect the motor wiring plugs from the ECU, then undo the three bolts and remove the motor from the gearbox **(see illustrations)**.
3 Remove the drive coupling from the gearbox **(see illustration)**.
4 If necessary, the mounting bushes can be removed from the motor flange by withdrawing the centre inserts and sliding out the rubber bushes **(see illustrations)**.
5 Inspect the motor components for wear or damage and renew as necessary.

Refitting

6 If removed, locate the rubber bushes in the motor flange and refit the centre inserts.
7 Refit the drive coupling to the gearbox, ensuring that it engages fully with the worm gear splines.
8 Engage the motor armature splines with the drive coupling and locate the motor on the gearbox. Refit the three retaining bolts and tighten them securely.
9 Reconnect the motor wiring connectors to the ECU ensuring that the cables are correctly routed.
10 Refit the steering column as described in Section 13.

14.2a Undo the three bolts (arrowed) . . .

14.2b . . . and remove the power steering electric motor from the gearbox

14.3 Remove the drive coupling from the gearbox

14.4a Withdraw the motor mounting bush centre inserts . . .

14.4b . . . and slide out the rubber bushes

15 Rack-and-pinion steering gear assembly – removal and refitting

Note: *A balljoint separator tool will be required for this operation.*

Removal

1 Turn the steering wheel to its centre position, so that the roadwheels are pointing straight-ahead.
2 Remove the battery and battery tray as described in Chapter 5A.
3 Working in the driver's footwell, unscrew the clamp bolt retaining nut on the intermediate shaft lower universal joint. Remove the clamp bolt from the retaining clip on the universal joint. Make suitable alignment marks on the steering gear pinion and universal joint to ensure correct orientation when refitting.
4 On manual transmission models, disconnect the selector cable end fittings from their attachments at the transmission selector levers. Extract the retaining clip securing each selector cable to the transmission support bracket, then withdraw both cables from the bracket.
5 Firmly apply the handbrake, then jack up the front of the car and support it securely on axle stands (see *Jacking and vehicle support*). Remove the front roadwheels.
6 Unscrew the nut securing the track rod end to the swivel hub. Release the track rod end tapered shank using a balljoint separator tool.
7 Unscrew the nuts and disconnect the exhaust front pipe flange from the manifold downpipe. Recover the gasket.
8 Undo the bolt securing the exhaust system front mounting bracket to the subframe. Lower the system and suitably support it.
9 Undo the bolt securing the rear engine/ transmission mounting to the subframe.
10 Slacken and remove the two steering gear-to-subframe bolts.
11 Rotate the steering gear downwards to release it from the bulkhead, then withdraw the steering gear through the wheel arch.

Refitting

12 Refitting is a reversal of removal, bearing in mind the following points.
 a) *Centralise the steering gear by turning the pinion so that the rack moves to full left lock. Now move the rack to full right lock, counting the number of turns of the pinion. Turn the pinion back by half the number of turns counted.*
 b) *Ensure that the roadwheels are in the straight-ahead position then engage steering gear pinion with the universal joint, aligning the marks made on removal.*
 c) *Refit the exhaust system front pipe flange using a new gasket and tighten the nuts to the specified torque (see Chapter 4A).*
 d) *Tighten all retaining nuts and bolts to the specified torque.*
 e) *Tighten the rear engine/transmission*

mounting bolt to the specified torque (see Chapter 2A or 2B as applicable).
 f) *Have the front wheel toe setting checked at the earliest opportunity.*

16 Steering gear rubber gaiters – renewal

Note: *New gaiter retaining clips should be used on refitting.*

1 Remove the relevant track rod end as described in Section 17.
2 Make an alignment mark between the track rod end locknut and the track rod, to allow the locknut to be accurately positioned when refitting. Unscrew the locknut from the end of the track rod.
3 Mark the correct fitted position of the gaiter on the track rod, then release the gaiter securing clips. Slide the gaiter from the steering gear, and off the end of the track rod.
4 Thoroughly clean the track rod and the steering gear housing, using fine abrasive paper to polish off any corrosion, burrs or sharp edges which might damage the new gaiter sealing lips on installation. Scrape off all the grease from the old gaiter, and apply it to the track rod inner balljoint. (This assumes that grease has not been lost or contaminated as a result of damage to the old gaiter. Use fresh grease if in doubt.)
5 Carefully slide the new gaiter onto the track rod, and locate it on the steering gear housing. Align the outer edge of the gaiter with the mark made on the track rod prior to removal, then secure it in position with new retaining clips.
6 Screw the track rod end locknut onto the end of the track rod and position it accurately in accordance with the mark made on removal.
7 Refit the track rod end as described in Section 17.

17 Track rod end – removal and refitting

Note: *A balljoint separator tool will be required for this operation.*

Removal

1 Firmly apply the handbrake, then jack up the front of the car and support it securely on axle stands (see *Jacking and vehicle support*). Remove the relevant front roadwheel.
2 Hold the track rod, and unscrew the track rod end locknut by a quarter of a turn. Do not move the locknut from this position, as it will serve as a handy reference mark on refitting.
3 Partially unscrew the nut securing the track rod end to the steering arm. Using a balljoint separator tool, separate the track rod end from the steering arm **(see illustration)**. Remove the nut and lift the track rod end from the arm.
4 Counting the **exact** number of turns

17.3 Using a balljoint separator tool to separate the track rod end from the steering arm

necessary to do so, unscrew the track rod end from the track rod.

Refitting

5 Carefully clean the track rod end and the track rod threads.
6 Renew the track rod end if the rubber dust cover is cracked, split or perished, or if the movement of the balljoint is either sloppy or too stiff. Also check for other signs of damage such as worn threads.
7 Screw the track rod end onto the track rod by the number of turns noted during removal. This should bring it to within a quarter of a turn from the locknut. Hold the track rod and securely tighten the locknut.
8 Ensure that the ballpin taper is clean, then engage the taper with the steering arm on the swivel hub.
9 Refit the track rod end retaining nut, and tighten the nut to the specified torque.
10 Refit the roadwheel, and lower the car to the ground.
11 Have the front wheel toe setting checked at the earliest opportunity.

18 Wheel alignment and steering angles – general information

General information

A car's steering and suspension geometry is defined in four basic settings – camber, castor, steering axis inclination and toe-setting. With the exception of front wheel toe-setting, none of these settings is adjustable and, in all cases, special equipment is required to check them. Note that front wheel toe-setting is often referred to as 'tracking' or 'front wheel alignment'.

Checking

Due to the special measuring equipment necessary to check the front wheel toe-setting, and the skill required to use it properly, the checking and adjustment of toe-setting is best left to a Fiat dealer or similar expert. Note that most tyre fitting shops now possess sophisticated checking equipment.

Notes

Chapter 11
Bodywork and fittings

Contents

Degrees of difficulty

Easy, suitable for novice with little experience	Fairly easy, suitable for beginner with some experience	Fairly difficult, suitable for competent DIY mechanic	Difficult, suitable for experienced DIY mechanic	Very difficult, suitable for expert DIY or professional

Specifications

Torque wrench settings	Nm	lbf ft
Bonnet-to-hinge bolts	10	7
Door hinge-to-body bolts	55	41
Seat belt inertia reel and anchor bolts	50	37
Towbar attachments:		
Bumper mounting bracket to cross-bar	95	70
Cross-bar to sidearms	95	70
Cross-bar upper mountings	53	39
Fixed towball to towball neck	214	158
Sidearms to captive straps	27	20
Towball neck to cross-bar (fixed towball arrangement)	95	70
Towball receptor unit to cross-bar (detachable towball arrangement)	95	70

1 General information

The bodyshell is composed of pressed-steel sections which are welded together, although some use of structural adhesives is made. In addition, the front wings are bolted on.

The bonnet, door and some other panels vulnerable to corrosion are fabricated from zinc-coated metal. A coating of anti-chip primer, applied prior to paint spraying provides further protection.

Extensive use is made of plastic materials, mainly in the interior, but also in exterior components. The outer sections of the front and rear bumpers are injection-moulded from a synthetic material which is very strong, and yet light. Plastic components such as wheel arch liners are fitted to the underside of the vehicle, to improve the body's resistance to corrosion.

2 Maintenance – bodywork and underframe

The general condition of a vehicle's bodywork is the one thing that significantly affects its value. Maintenance is easy, but needs to be regular. Neglect, particularly after minor damage, can lead quickly to further deterioration and costly repair bills. It is important also to keep watch on those parts of the vehicle not immediately visible, for instance the underside, inside all the wheel arches, and the lower part of the engine compartment.

The basic maintenance routine for the bodywork is washing – preferably with a lot of water, from a hose. This will remove all the loose solids which may have stuck to the vehicle. It is important to flush these off in such a way as to prevent grit from scratching the finish. The wheel arches and underframe need washing in the same way, to remove any accumulated mud, which will retain moisture and tend to encourage rust. Paradoxically enough, the best time to clean the underframe and wheel arches is in wet weather, when the mud is thoroughly wet and soft. In very wet weather, the underframe is usually cleaned of large accumulations automatically, and this is a good time for inspection.

Periodically, except on vehicles with a wax-based underbody protective coating, it is a good idea to have the whole of the underframe of the vehicle steam-cleaned, engine compartment included, so that a thorough inspection can be carried out to see what minor repairs and renovations are necessary. Steam-cleaning is available at many garages, and is necessary for the removal of the accumulation of oily grime, which sometimes is allowed to become thick in certain areas. If steam-cleaning facilities are not available, there are some excellent grease solvents available which can be brush-applied; the dirt can then be simply hosed off. Note that these methods should not be used on vehicles with wax-based underbody protective coating, or the coating will be removed. Such vehicles should be inspected annually, preferably just prior to Winter, when the underbody should be washed down, and any damage to the wax coating repaired. Ideally, a completely fresh coat should be applied. It would also be worth considering the use of such wax-based protection for injection into door panels, sills, box sections, etc, as an additional safeguard against rust damage, where such protection is not provided by the vehicle manufacturer.

After washing paintwork, wipe off with a chamois leather to give an unspotted clear finish. A coat of clear protective wax polish will give added protection against chemical pollutants in the air. If the paintwork sheen has dulled or oxidised, use a cleaner/polisher combination to restore the brilliance of the shine. This requires a little effort, but such dulling is usually caused because regular washing has been neglected. Care needs to be taken with metallic paintwork, as special non-abrasive cleaner/polisher is required to avoid damage to the finish. Always check that the door and ventilator opening drain holes and pipes are completely clear, so that water can be drained out. Brightwork should be treated in the same way as paintwork. Windscreens and windows can be kept clear of the smeary film which often appears, by the use of proprietary glass cleaner. Never use any form of wax or other body or chromium polish on glass.

3 Maintenance – upholstery and carpets

Mats and carpets should be brushed or vacuum-cleaned regularly, to keep them free of grit. If they are badly stained, remove them from the vehicle for scrubbing or sponging, and make quite sure they are dry before refitting. Seats and interior trim panels can be kept clean by wiping with a damp cloth. If they do become stained (which can be more apparent on light-coloured upholstery), use a little liquid detergent and a soft nail brush to scour the grime out of the grain of the material. Do not forget to keep the headlining clean in the same way as the upholstery. When using liquid cleaners inside the vehicle, do not over-wet the surfaces being cleaned. Excessive damp could get into the seams and padded interior, causing stains, offensive odours or even rot.

> **HAYNES HINT**
> *If the inside of the vehicle gets wet accidentally, it is worthwhile taking some trouble to dry it out properly, particularly where carpets are involved. Do not leave oil or electric heaters inside the vehicle for this purpose.*

4 Minor body damage – repair

Minor scratches

If the scratch is very superficial, and does not penetrate to the metal of the bodywork, repair is very simple. Lightly rub the area of the scratch with a paintwork renovator, or a very fine cutting paste, to remove loose paint from the scratch, and to clear the surrounding bodywork of wax polish. Rinse the area with clean water.

Apply touch-up paint to the scratch using a fine paint brush; continue to apply fine layers of paint until the surface of the paint in the scratch is level with the surrounding paintwork. Allow the new paint at least two weeks to harden, then blend it into the surrounding paintwork by rubbing the scratch area with a paintwork renovator or a very fine cutting paste. Finally, apply wax polish.

Where the scratch has penetrated right through to the metal of the bodywork, causing the metal to rust, a different repair technique is required. Remove any loose rust from the bottom of the scratch with a penknife, then apply rust-inhibiting paint to prevent the formation of rust in the future. Using a rubber or nylon applicator, fill the scratch with bodystopper paste. If required, this paste can be mixed with cellulose thinners to provide a very thin paste which is ideal for filling narrow scratches. Before the stopper-paste in the scratch hardens, wrap a piece of smooth cotton rag around the top of a finger. Dip the finger in cellulose thinners, and quickly sweep it across the surface of the stopper-paste in the scratch; this will ensure that the surface of the stopper-paste is slightly hollowed. The scratch can now be painted over as described earlier in this Section.

Dents

When deep denting of the vehicle's bodywork has taken place, the first task is to pull the dent out, until the affected bodywork almost attains its original shape. There is little point in trying to restore the original shape completely, as the metal in the damaged area will have stretched on impact, and cannot be reshaped fully to its original contour. It is better to bring the level of the dent up to a point which is about 3 mm below the level of the surrounding bodywork. In cases where the dent is very shallow anyway, it is not worth trying to pull it out at all. If the underside of the dent is accessible, it can be hammered out gently from behind, using a mallet with a wooden or plastic head. Whilst doing this, hold a suitable block of wood firmly against the outside of the panel, to absorb the impact from the hammer blows and thus prevent a large area of the bodywork from being 'belled-out'.

Should the dent be in a section of the bodywork which has a double skin, or some other factor making it inaccessible from behind, a different technique is called for. Drill several small holes through the metal inside the area – particularly in the deeper section. Then screw long self-tapping screws into the holes, just sufficiently for them to gain a good purchase in the metal. Now the dent can be pulled out by pulling on the protruding heads of the screws with a pair of pliers.

The next stage of the repair is the removal of the paint from the damaged area, and from an inch or so of the surrounding 'sound' bodywork. This is accomplished most easily by using a wire brush or abrasive pad on a power drill, although it can be done just as effectively by hand, using sheets of abrasive paper. To complete the preparation for filling, score the surface of the bare metal with a screwdriver or the tang of a file, or alternatively, drill small holes in the affected area. This will provide a really good 'key' for the filler paste.

To complete the repair, see the Section on filling and respraying.

Rust holes or gashes

Remove all paint from the affected area, and from an inch or so of the surrounding 'sound' bodywork, using an abrasive pad or a wire brush on a power drill. If these are not available, a few sheets of abrasive paper will do the job most effectively. With the paint removed, you will be able to judge the severity of the corrosion, and therefore decide whether to renew the whole panel (if this is possible) or to repair the affected area. New body panels are not as expensive as most people think, and it is often quicker and more satisfactory to fit a new panel than to attempt to repair large areas of corrosion.

Remove all fittings from the affected area, except those which will act as a guide to the original shape of the damaged bodywork (eg headlight shells etc). Then, using tin snips or a hacksaw blade, remove all loose metal and any other metal badly affected by corrosion. Hammer the edges of the hole inwards, in order to create a slight depression for the filler paste.

Wire-brush the affected area to remove the powdery rust from the surface of the remaining metal. Paint the affected area with rust-inhibiting paint, if the back of the rusted area is accessible, treat this also.

Before filling can take place, it will be necessary to block the hole in some way. This can be achieved by the use of aluminium or plastic mesh, or aluminium tape.

Aluminium or plastic mesh, or glass-fibre matting, is probably the best material to use for a large hole. Cut a piece to the approximate size and shape of the hole to be filled, then position it in the hole so that its edges are below the level of the surrounding bodywork. It can be retained in position by several blobs of filler paste around its periphery.

Aluminium tape should be used for small or very narrow holes. Pull a piece off the roll, trim it to the approximate size and shape required, then pull off the backing paper (if used) and stick the tape over the hole; it can be overlapped if the thickness of one piece is insufficient. Burnish down the edges of the tape with the handle of a screwdriver or similar, to ensure that the tape is securely attached to the metal underneath.

Filling and respraying

Before using this Section, see the Sections on dent, deep scratch, rust holes and gash repairs.

Many types of bodyfiller are available, but generally speaking, those proprietary kits which contain a tin of filler paste and a tube of resin hardener are best for this type of repair. A wide, flexible plastic or nylon applicator will be found invaluable for imparting a smooth and well-contoured finish to the surface of the filler.

Mix up a little filler on a clean piece of card or board – measure the hardener carefully (follow the maker's instructions on the pack), otherwise the filler will set too rapidly or too slowly. Using the applicator, apply the filler paste to the prepared area; draw the applicator across the surface of the filler to achieve the correct contour and to level the surface. As soon as a contour that approximates to the correct one is achieved, stop working the paste – if you carry on too long, the paste will become sticky and begin to 'pick-up' on the applicator. Continue to add thin layers of filler paste at 20-minute intervals, until the level of the filler is just proud of the surrounding bodywork.

Once the filler has hardened, the excess can be removed using a metal plane or file. From then on, progressively-finer grades of abrasive paper should be used, starting with a 40-grade production paper, and finishing with a 400-grade wet-and-dry paper. Always wrap the abrasive paper around a flat rubber, cork, or wooden block – otherwise the surface of the filler will not be completely flat. During the smoothing of the filler surface, the wet-and-dry paper should be periodically rinsed in water. This will ensure that a very smooth finish is imparted to the filler at the final stage.

At this stage, the dent should be surrounded by a ring of bare metal, which in turn should be encircled by the finely 'feathered' edge of the good paintwork. Rinse the repair area with clean water, until all of the dust produced by the rubbing-down operation has gone.

Spray the whole area with a light coat of primer – this will show up any imperfections in the surface of the filler. Repair these imperfections with fresh filler paste or bodystopper, and once more smooth the surface with abrasive paper. Repeat this spray-and-repair procedure until you are satisfied that the surface of the filler, and the feathered edge of the paintwork, are perfect. Clean the repair area with clean water, and allow to dry fully.

HAYNES HiNT *If bodystopper is used, it can be mixed with cellulose thinners to form a really thin paste which is ideal for filling small holes.*

The repair area is now ready for final spraying. Paint spraying must be carried out in a warm, dry, windless and dust-free atmosphere. This condition can be created artificially if you have access to a large indoor working area, but if you are forced to work in the open, you will have to pick your day very carefully. If you are working indoors, dousing the floor in the work area with water will help to settle the dust which would otherwise be in the atmosphere. If the repair area is confined to one body panel, mask off the surrounding panels; this will help to minimise the effects of a slight mis-match in paint colours. Bodywork fittings (eg chrome strips, door handles etc) will also need to be masked off. Use genuine masking tape, and several thicknesses of newspaper, for the masking operations.

Before commencing to spray, agitate the aerosol can thoroughly, then spray a test area (an old tin, or similar) until the technique is mastered. Cover the repair area with a thick coat of primer; the thickness should be built up using several thin layers of paint, rather than one thick one. Using 400-grade wet-and-dry paper, rub down the surface of the primer until it is really smooth. While doing this, the work area should be thoroughly doused with water, and the wet-and-dry paper periodically rinsed in water. Allow to dry before spraying on more paint.

Spray on the top coat, again building up the thickness by using several thin layers of paint. Start spraying at one edge of the repair area, and then, using a side-to-side motion, work until the whole repair area and about 2 inches of the surrounding original paintwork is covered. Remove all masking material 10 to 15 minutes after spraying on the final coat of paint.

Allow the new paint at least two weeks to harden, then, using a paintwork renovator, or a very fine cutting paste, blend the edges of the paint into the existing paintwork. Finally, apply wax polish.

Plastic components

With the use of more and more plastic body components by the vehicle manufacturers (eg bumpers. spoilers, and in some cases major body panels), rectification of more serious damage to such items has become a matter of either entrusting repair work to a specialist in this field, or renewing complete components. Repair of such damage by the DIY owner is not really feasible, owing to the cost of the equipment and materials required for effecting such repairs. The basic technique involves making a groove along the line of the

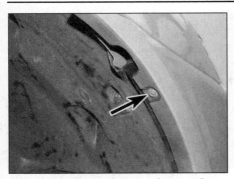

6.2a Undo the upper screw (arrowed) . . .

6.2b . . . and lower screw (arrowed) each side, securing the edge of the bumper to the wheel arch liner

6.3a Undo the two bolts each side securing the upper edge of the bumper to the front wing . . .

crack in the plastic, using a rotary burr in a power drill. The damaged part is then welded back together, using a hot-air gun to heat up and fuse a plastic filler rod into the groove. Any excess plastic is then removed, and the area rubbed down to a smooth finish. It is important that a filler rod of the correct plastic is used, as body components can be made of a variety of different types (eg polycarbonate, ABS, polypropylene).

Damage of a less serious nature (abrasions, minor cracks etc) can be repaired by the DIY owner using a two-part epoxy filler repair material. Once mixed in equal proportions, this is used in similar fashion to the bodywork filler used on metal panels. The filler is usually cured in twenty to thirty minutes, ready for sanding and painting.

If the owner is renewing a complete component himself, or if he has repaired it with epoxy filler, he will be left with the problem of finding a suitable paint for finishing which is compatible with the type of plastic used. At one time, the use of a universal paint was not possible, owing to the complex range of plastics encountered in body component applications. Standard paints, generally speaking, will not bond to plastic or rubber satisfactorily. However, it is now possible to obtain a plastic body parts finishing kit which consists of a pre-primer treatment, a primer and coloured top coat. Full instructions are

normally supplied with a kit, but basically, the method of use is to first apply the pre-primer to the component concerned, and allow it to dry for up to 30 minutes. Then the primer is applied, and left to dry for about an hour before finally applying the special-coloured top coat. The result is a correctly-coloured component, where the paint will flex with the plastic or rubber, a property that standard paint does not normally possess.

5 Major body damage – repair

Where serious damage has occurred, or large areas need renewal due to neglect, it means that complete new panels will need welding-in, and this is best left to professionals. If the damage is due to impact, it will also be necessary to check completely the alignment of the bodyshell, and this can only be carried out accurately by a Fiat dealer using special jigs. If the alignment of the bodyshell is not corrected, the car's handling may be seriously affected. In addition, excessive stress may be imposed on the steering, suspension, tyres or transmission, causing abnormal wear or even complete failure.

6 Front bumper – removal and refitting

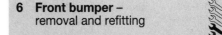

Removal

1 For improved access, firmly apply the handbrake, then jack up the front of the car and support it securely on axle stands (see *Jacking and vehicle support*).
2 Undo the two screws each side securing the edge of the bumper to the wheel arch liner **(see illustrations)**.
3 Undo the two bolts securing the upper edge of the bumper to the front wing on each side. Reach up behind the wheel arch liner to gain access to the front bolt **(see illustrations)**.
4 From below, undo the bolt securing the bumper lower outer edge to the crossmember on each side.
5 Undo the two centre bolts securing the front underside of the bumper to the crossmember **(see illustration)**.
6 Support the bumper, then undo the remaining two bolts from the upper edge of the bumper **(see illustration)**.
7 Where applicable, unplug the wiring from the rear of the foglight units.
8 Unclip any electrical cabling secured to the rear side of the bumper then, with the help of

6.3b . . . reaching up behind the wheel arch liner to access the front bolt (arrowed)

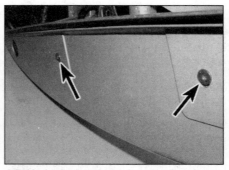

6.5 Undo the two bolts (arrowed) securing the front underside of the bumper to the crossmember

6.6 Undo the remaining two bolts (arrowed) from the upper edge of the bumper

6.8 Carefully withdraw the bumper from the car

7.4 Undo the screws securing the rear bumper lower mountings to the brackets on the underbody

7.5 Undo the four retaining bolts from the upper edge of the bumper

an assistant, carefully draw the bumper away from the front of the car **(see illustration)**.

Refitting

9 Refitting is a reversal of removal.

7 Rear bumper –
removal and refitting

Removal

1 For improved access, firmly apply the handbrake, then jack up the front of the car and support it securely on axle stands (see *Jacking and vehicle support*).
2 Undo the screws each side securing the edge of the bumper to the wheel arch liner.
3 Reach up behind the wheel arch liner and undo the two screws securing the upper edge of the bumper to the rear wing on each side.
4 From below, undo the screws securing the rear bumper lower mountings to the brackets on the vehicle underbody **(see illustration)**.
5 Support the bumper, then undo the four retaining bolts from the upper edge of the bumper **(see illustration)**.
6 With the help of an assistant, carefully draw the bumper away from the car. When sufficient clearance exists, remove the number plate light bulbholder from the light unit by twisting the bulbholder anti-clockwise to release the bayonet fitting **(see illustrations)**.

7 Unclip any electrical cabling that may be secured to the inside of the bumper, then remove the bumper from the car.

Refitting

8 Refitting is a reversal of removal.

8 Tailgate –
removal and refitting

Removal

1 Disconnect the battery negative terminal (refer to *Disconnecting the battery* in the Reference Chapter).
2 Remove the tailgate inner trim panel as described in Section 25.
3 Undo the two screws and withdraw the high-level stop-light from the tailgate. Disconnect the stop-light wiring connector.
4 Disconnect the wiring connectors for the tailgate lock and tailgate wiper motor and unbolt the earth leads. Check for any other wiring connectors which must be disconnected to facilitate tailgate removal. **Note:** *Carefully label each wiring harness connector to aid correct refitting.*
5 Tie a length of cord to the wiring harness, then bind the loose ends of the cabling together using PVC tape. Prise the wiring harness grommet from the upper edge of the tailgate, then feed the wiring through the

aperture in the tailgate. Untie the cord from the harness, but leave it in place in the tailgate, to aid refitting later.
6 Disconnect the fluid hose from the tailgate washer nozzle, then tie a length of cord to the hose and draw it out of the tailgate, using the same procedure carried out on the wiring harness.
7 Have an assistant support the tailgate in the open position.
8 Detach the upper ends of the support struts from the tailgate as described in Section 9.
9 Slacken and unscrew the bolts securing the hinges to the tailgate, then lift the tailgate from the vehicle **(see illustration)**.

Refitting

10 Refitting is a reversal of removal, bearing in mind the following points.
  a) *Tie the cord to the wiring harness and use it to pull the harness through the aperture and into the tailgate. Repeat the procedure on the washer fluid hose.*
  b) *Do not fully tighten the hinge bolts until the tailgate adjustment has been checked, as described in the following paragraphs.*

Adjustment

11 Close the tailgate **carefully**, in case the alignment is incorrect, which may cause scratching on the tailgate or the body as the tailgate is closed, and check for alignment with the adjacent panels. If necessary,

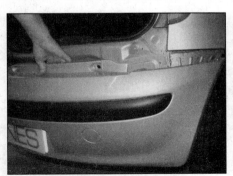

7.6a Withdraw the bumper from the car . . .

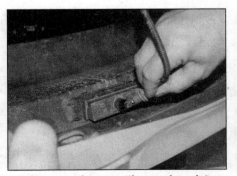

7.6b . . . and remove the number plate light bulbholder from the light unit

8.9 Tailgate hinge retaining bolts (arrowed)

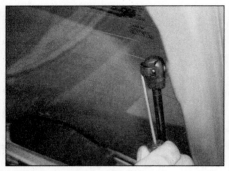

9.2 Using a small screwdriver, lever off the tailgate strut balljoint spring clips

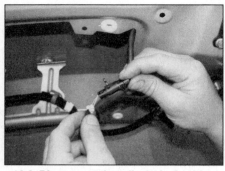

10.2 Disconnect the tailgate lock wiring connector . . .

10.3 . . . unscrew the two securing bolts (arrowed) . . .

slacken the bolts that secure the hinges to the bodywork and re-align the tailgate to suit. Once the tailgate is correctly aligned, tighten the hinge bolts securely.

12 Check that the tailgate fastens and releases in a satisfactory manner. If adjustment is necessary, slacken the striker plate retaining bolts, and adjust the position of the striker to suit. Once the lock is operating correctly, securely tighten the striker plate retaining bolts.

13 If necessary, adjust the protrusion of the rubber buffers at the lower edge of the tailgate by screwing them in or out, as appropriate.

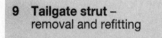

9 Tailgate strut – removal and refitting

Removal

1 Open the tailgate and support it using suitable wooden props.

2 At the upper end of each strut, lever off the balljoint spring clip. Compress the strut slightly by hand and then prise the strut balljoint from the stud on the tailgate **(see illustration)**.

 Warning: The strut may still be under tension and could extend suddenly once detached from its mountings.

3 Release the lower end of each strut from the studs on the rear wings in the same way.

Refitting

4 Refitting is a reversal of removal.

10 Tailgate lock components – removal and refitting

Lock and cylinder assembly

Removal

1 Remove the tailgate inner trim panel as described in Section 25.

2 Unclip the tailgate lock wiring harness from the tailgate, then disconnect the wiring connector **(see illustration)**.

3 Slacken and unscrew the two bolts securing the lock assembly to the lower edge of the tailgate **(see illustration)**.

4 Carefully withdraw the lock assembly, together with the lock cylinder **(see illustration)**.

Refitting

5 Refitting is the reversal of removal.

Lock barrel

Removal

6 Remove the lock assembly as described previously.

7 Insert the key into the lock barrel, then undo the screw securing the lock cylinder to the rear of the lock body **(see illustration)**.

8 Using a hooked tool, extract the lock barrel retaining clip, then withdraw the lock barrel from the lock cylinder **(see illustrations)**.

10.4 . . . and withdraw the tailgate lock assembly, together with the lock cylinder

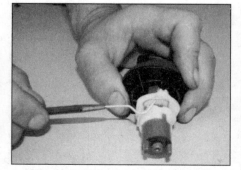

10.8a Using a hooked tool, extract the lock barrel retaining clip . . .

Refitting

9 Refitting is the reversal of removal.

Striker plate

Removal

10 With the tailgate open, mark the position of the striker plate in relation to the bodywork using a pencil or marker pen, to aid accurate refitting.

11 Slacken and unscrew the bolts securing the striker plate to the body.

12 Remove the striker plate from its aperture, disconnect the remote release cable and remove the striker.

Refitting

13 Refitting is a reversal of removal. Use the markings made during removal to give the correct alignment.

14 Check that the tailgate fastens and releases

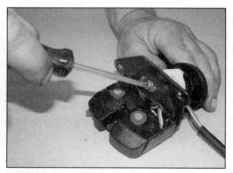

10.7 Undo the screw securing the lock cylinder to the tailgate lock body

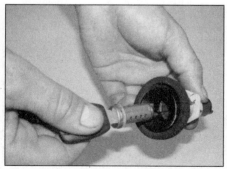

10.8b . . . then withdraw the lock barrel from the lock cylinder

12.3 Bonnet lock assembly retaining nuts (arrowed)

in a satisfactory manner. If adjustment is necessary, slacken the striker plate retaining bolts, and adjust the position of the plate to suit. Once the lock is operating correctly, securely tighten the striker plate retaining bolts.

11 Bonnet – removal and refitting
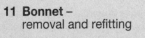

Removal

1 Open the bonnet and prop it up with a stout pole.
2 Disconnect the washer jet hose at the bonnet connector.
3 Mark the relationship between the hinges and the edge of the bonnet using a soft pencil or marker pen. Slacken and unscrew the bolts; have an assistant support the bonnet as the last bolts are removed.
4 With the help of an assistant, lift off the bonnet and set it down on its edge, using a dust sheet to protect the paintwork.

Refitting

5 Refit the bonnet and retaining bolts, using the markings made during removal to achieve the correct alignment. Note that the bolt mounting holes are slotted to allow adjustment if required. On completion, tighten the bolts to the specified torque.
6 Reconnect the washer hose, then check that the bonnet fastens and releases in a satisfactory manner. If necessary, adjust the bonnet lock assembly, as described in Section 12.

12 Bonnet lock assembly – removal and refitting

Removal

1 Open the bonnet and mark the relationship between the lock assembly and the front body panel using a soft pencil or marker pen.
2 Disconnect the lock sensor wiring connector located behind the lock assembly.
3 Slacken and unscrew the two nuts and withdraw the lock assembly from its location (see illustration).

4 Disconnect the lock release cable and remove the lock assembly.

Refitting

5 Refitting is a reversal of removal. Use the alignment markings made during removal to aid accurate refitting. Check that the bonnet fastens and releases in a satisfactory manner, noting that the mounting holes are slotted to allow adjustment of the lock, if required. On completion, tighten the bolts securely.
6 If necessary, adjust the protrusion of the rubber buffers on the front body panel (located above each headlamp unit) by screwing them in or out, as appropriate. When the rubber buffers are correctly adjusted, there should be just enough free movement to allow the bonnet to be closed and locked easily, without using excessive force, but not enough to allow the bonnet to rattle when secured in the locked position.

13 Bonnet release cable – removal and refitting
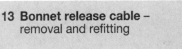

Removal

1 Disconnect the release cable from the bonnet lock assembly as described in Section 12.
2 Working around the engine bay, extract the release cable from its securing clips.

14.1a Prise out the trim cap . . .

14.2a On manually-adjustable mirrors, prise the rubber cover off the adjustment lever

3 In the driver's footwell, undo the two nuts securing the release handle mounting bracket to the body.
4 Tie a length of string to the end of the cable in the engine compartment, then carefully pull the cable through the bulkhead grommet into the passenger's compartment. Untie the string from the cable, but leave it in place in the bulkhead, to aid refitting.

Refitting

5 Refitting is a reversal of removal, using the string to draw the cable through the bulkhead into the engine compartment. Reconnect the cable to the bonnet lock and adjust the lock position as described in Section 12.

14 Door inner trim panel – removal and refitting

Front door
Removal

1 Prise out the trim cap and undo the screw securing the exterior mirror inner trim panel (see illustrations).
2 Where a manually-adjustable exterior mirror is fitted, prise the rubber cover off the adjustment lever, then unscrew and remove the locking collar using pointed-nose pliers (see illustrations).
3 Pull the panel from its location to disengage

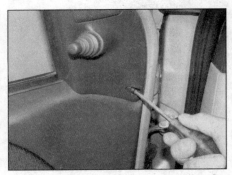

14.1b . . . and undo the screw securing the exterior mirror inner trim panel to the front door

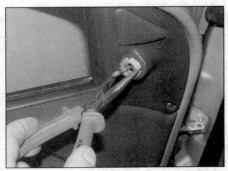

14.2b Using pointed-nose pliers, unscrew and remove the locking collar

14.3 Pull the mirror trim panel from its location and disconnect the loudspeaker wiring connector

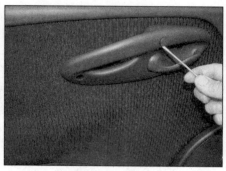

14.4a Lift off the trim caps . . .

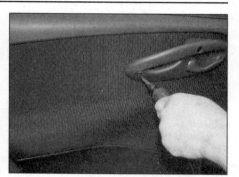

14.4b . . . undo the retaining screws . . .

14.4c . . . then remove the door interior handle surround

14.5a Prise off the loudspeaker grille . . .

the retaining clips. Disconnect the loudspeaker wiring connector and remove the panel **(see illustration)**.

4 Lift off the trim caps, undo the retaining screws, then remove the door interior handle surround **(see illustrations)**.

5 Carefully prise off the loudspeaker grille, then undo the three loudspeaker retaining screws. Withdraw the speaker from the door and disconnect the wiring connectors **(see illustrations)**.

6 Undo the three retaining screws in the loudspeaker aperture, and the single screw in the oddments pocket just below the aperture **(see illustration)**.

7 Lift out the loudspeaker protective cover and withdraw the loudspeaker wiring from the base of the cover **(see illustration)**.

8 Prise out the trim cap and undo the screw securing the rear of the trim panel to the door frame **(see illustrations)**.

9 Undo the screw at the upper front corner of the panel, and the remaining four screws securing the lower edge of the panel to the door frame **(see illustration)**.

10 Using a suitable forked tool inserted between the door and the trim panel, release the press-stud clips located around the edge of the panel, then lift the trim panel upwards **(see illustration)**.

11 Pull the panel from the door, noting that the lower window aperture weatherstrip is integral

14.5b . . . then undo the three loudspeaker retaining screws (arrowed)

14.6 Undo the three retaining screws in the loudspeaker aperture, and the single screw (arrowed) in the oddments pocket

14.7 Lift out the loudspeaker protective cover and withdraw the wiring from the base of the cover

14.8a Prise out the trim cap . . .

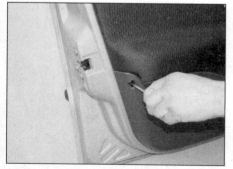

14.8b . . . and undo the screw securing the rear of the trim panel to the door frame

14.9 Undo the screw (arrowed) at the upper front corner of the panel, and the remaining screws securing the lower edge

14.10 Using a forked tool, release the press-stud clips, then lift the trim panel from the door

14.12 Carefully remove the plastic sealing sheet from the inside of the door

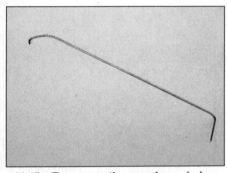

14.15a To remove the rear door window regulator handle retaining clip, bend a length of welding rod

14.15b Slide the hooked end of the rod behind the regulator handle . . .

14.15c . . . and pull the clip off the handle

with the trim panel and must be released from the door as the panel is withdrawn.

12 If work is to be carried out on the door internal components, it will be necessary to remove the plastic sealing sheet from the inside of the door. Start at one corner of the sheet and carefully peel it away, using a sharp blade to split the sealant bead, if necessary **(see illustration)**.

13 Store the detached sealing sheet such that it cannot become contaminated with dust; this will allow it to be re-used later.

Refitting

14 Refitting is a reversal of removal, bearing in mind the following points:
a) *Ensure that the sealing sheet is correctly refitted, press it on firmly to ensure that it is adequately sealed around its edges. It should be possible to use the original sealant, but if necessary, new sealant can be obtained from a Fiat dealer.*
b) *Make sure that the weatherstrip engages securely with the edge of the door as the panel is refitted.*

Rear door

Removal

15 Using a length of welding rod or similar, bent at one end to form a hook, extract the window regulator handle retaining clip and pull the handle from the regulator shaft **(see illustrations)**.

16 Lift off the trim caps, undo the retaining screws, then remove the door interior handle surround **(see illustrations)**.

17 Prise out the trim cap and undo the screw

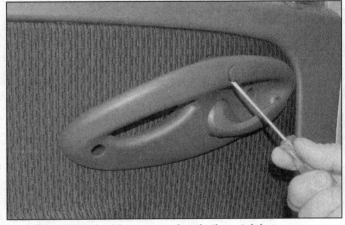

14.16a Lift off the trim caps and undo the retaining screws . . .

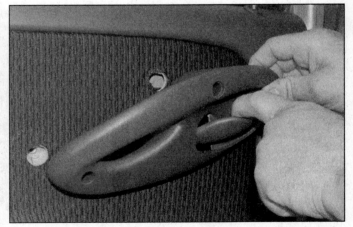

14.16b . . . then remove the rear door interior handle surround

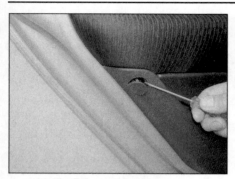

14.17a Prise out the trim cap . . .

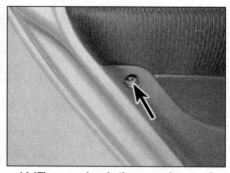

14.17b . . . and undo the screw (arrowed) securing the rear of the trim panel to the door

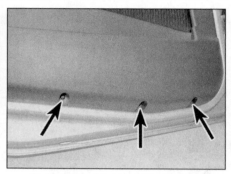

14.18 Undo the remaining screws (arrowed) securing the lower edge of the panel to the door

securing the rear of the trim panel to the door frame **(see illustrations)**.

18 Undo the remaining three screws securing the lower edge of the panel to the door frame **(see illustration)**.

19 Using a suitable forked tool inserted between the door and the trim panel, release the press-stud clips located around the edge of the panel, then lift the trim panel upwards **(see illustration)**.

20 Pull the panel from the door, noting that the lower window aperture weatherstrip is integral with the trim panel and must be released from the door as the panel is withdrawn.

21 If work is to be carried out on the door internal components, remove the plastic sealing sheet as described in paragraphs 12 and 13 **(see illustration)**.

Refitting

22 Refitting is a reversal of removal, bearing in mind the following points:
a) *Ensure that the sealing sheet is correctly refitted, press it on firmly to ensure that it is adequately sealed around its edges. It should be possible to use the original sealant, but if necessary, new sealant can be obtained from a Fiat dealer.*
b) *Make sure that the weatherstrip engages securely with the edge of the door as the panel is refitted.*

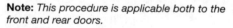

15 Door – removal and refitting

Note: *This procedure is applicable both to the front and rear doors.*

Removal

1 Unplug the multi-way electrical connector from the inner edge of the door.
2 Undo the two bolts and release the check strap attachment on the door pillar.
3 Have an assistant support the door, then unscrew the door hinge retaining bolts, and lift the door from the car.

Refitting

4 Refitting is a reversal of removal. On completion, tighten the hinge bolts securely.

14.19 Using a forked tool, release the press-stud clips, then lift the trim panel from the door

Adjustment

5 Close the door **carefully**, in case the alignment is incorrect, which may cause scratching on the door or the body as the door is closed, and check the fit of the door with the surrounding panels.

6 If adjustment is required, loosen the hinge-to-body securing bolts (the bolt holes are elongated to allow for adjustment) and move the hinges as required to achieve satisfactory alignment. Tighten the securing bolts securely on completion.

7 Check the operation of the door lock. If necessary, slacken the securing bolts, and adjust the position of the lock striker on the body pillar to achieve satisfactory alignment. Tighten the bolts securely on completion.

16.3 Drill out the pop rivets securing the anti-theft partition to the front door panel

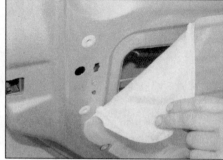

14.21 Carefully remove the plastic sealing sheet from the inside of the door

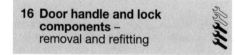

16 Door handle and lock components – removal and refitting

Front door exterior handle

Removal

1 Ensure that the door window glass is in the fully closed position.
2 Remove the door inner trim panel and sealing sheet as described in Section 14.
3 Drill out the four pop rivets securing the anti-theft partition to the door panel **(see illustration)**. Manipulate the partition out through the door panel aperture.
4 Working inside the door space, unbolt and

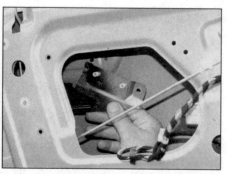

16.4 Unbolt and remove the lock shield from the rear of the door handle

16.8 Refit the anti-theft partition and secure with new pop rivets

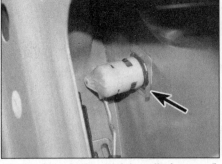

16.12a Extract the retaining clip (arrowed) from the rear of the front door lock cylinder . . .

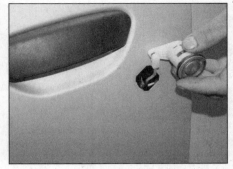

16.12b . . . then remove the cylinder from the door

remove the lock shield from the rear of the door handle **(see illustration)**.

5 Detach the link rod from the door lock mechanism, then lift the handle assembly from the door.

Refitting

6 Locate the handle in position and connect the link rod to the door lock mechanism.

7 Place the lock shield in position then refit and securely tighten the handle retaining bolts.

8 Refit the anti-theft partition and secure with new pop rivets **(see illustration)**.

9 Refit the door inner trim panel and sealing sheet as described in Section 14.

Front door lock cylinder

Removal

10 Carry out the operations described previously in paragraphs 1 to 3.

11 Detach the lock cylinder link rod from the door lock mechanism.

12 Working inside the door space, release the metal retaining clip from the rear of the cylinder using a pair of pliers. Extract the lock cylinder from the door **(see illustrations)**.

Refitting

13 Locate the lock cylinder in the door and secure with the retaining clip.

14 Connect the lock cylinder link rod to the door lock mechanism.

15 Refit the anti-theft partition and secure with new pop rivets.

16 Refit the door inner trim panel and sealing sheet as described in Section 14.

Front door interior handle

Removal

17 Remove the door inner trim panel and sealing sheet as described in Section 14.

18 Undo the three retaining screws and withdraw the handle from the door **(see illustration)**.

19 Detach the lock mechanism link rod from the handle lever and remove the handle **(see illustration)**.

Refitting

20 Refitting is a reversal of removal. Refit the

door inner trim panel and sealing sheet as described in Section 14.

Front door lock mechanism

Removal

21 Carry out the operations described previously in paragraphs 1 to 3.

22 Detach the lock mechanism link rod from the interior handle lever, then release the rod from the guide clip.

23 Detach the lock cylinder link rod from the door lock mechanism.

24 Disconnect the central locking wiring connectors from the base of the lock motor.

25 At the trailing edge of the door, remove

16.18 Undo the retaining screws and withdraw the interior handle from the door

16.25 Undo the three screws (arrowed) securing the lock mechanism to the door

the three screws that secure the lock mechanism to the door **(see illustration)**.

26 Manoeuvre the lock mechanism, complete with locking knob link rod out through the door aperture **(see illustration)**.

Refitting

27 Refitting is a reversal of removal. On completion, refit the anti-theft partition and secure with new pop rivets, then refit the door inner trim panel and sealing sheet as described in Section 14.

Rear door exterior handle

Removal

28 Ensure that the door window glass is in the fully closed position.

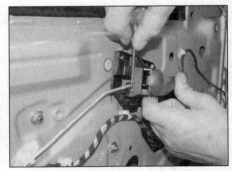

16.19 Detach the lock mechanism link rod and remove the handle

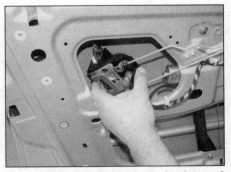

16.26 Manoeuvre the lock mechanism and locking knob link rod out through the door aperture

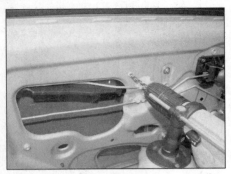

16.30 Drill out the pop rivets securing the anti-theft partition to the rear door panel

16.31 Undo the two exterior handle retaining bolts (arrowed) and withdraw the handle from the door

16.33 Refit the anti-theft partition and secure with new pop rivets

29 Remove the door inner trim panel and sealing sheet as described in Section 14.
30 Drill out the two pop rivets securing the anti-theft partition to the door panel (see illustration). Manipulate the partition out through the door panel aperture.
31 Working inside the door space, undo the two exterior handle retaining bolts and withdraw the handle from the door (see illustration).

Refitting

32 Locate the handle in position and secure with the two retaining bolts.

33 Refit the anti-theft partition and secure with new pop rivets (see illustration).
34 Refit the door inner trim panel and sealing sheet as described in Section 14.

Rear door interior handle

Removal

35 Remove the door inner trim panel and sealing sheet as described in Section 14.
36 Undo the two retaining screws and withdraw the handle from the door (see illustration).
37 Detach the lock mechanism link rod from the handle lever and remove the handle.

Refitting

38 Refitting is a reversal of removal. Refit the door inner trim panel and sealing sheet as described in Section 14.

Rear door lock mechanism

Removal

39 Carry out the operations described previously in paragraphs 28 to 30.
40 Undo the two retaining bolts and remove the window glass lower rear guide channel (see illustrations).
41 Detach the lock mechanism link rod from the interior handle lever, then release the rod from the guide clip.
42 Similarly detach the locking knob link rod from the bellcrank, then release the rod from the guide clip.
43 Disconnect the central locking wiring connectors from the base of the lock motor.
44 At the trailing edge of the door, remove the three screws that secure the lock mechanism to the door (see illustration).
45 Manoeuvre the lock mechanism, complete with link rods, out through the door aperture (see illustration).

Refitting

46 Refitting is a reversal of removal. On completion, refit the anti-theft partition and secure with new pop rivets, then refit the door

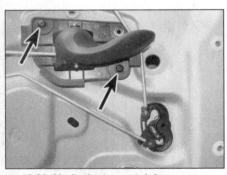

16.36 Undo the two retaining screws (arrowed) and withdraw the rear door interior handle

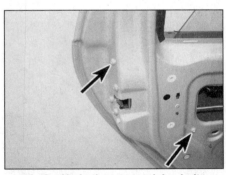

16.40a Undo the two retaining bolts (arrowed) . . .

16.40b . . . and remove the window glass lower rear guide channel

16.44 Undo the three screws (arrowed) securing the rear door lock mechanism to the door

16.45 Manoeuvre the lock mechanism and link rods out through the door aperture

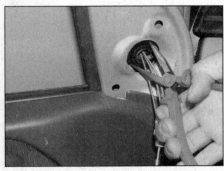

17.4 Using pointed-nose pliers, unscrew the retaining nut and withdraw the mirror from the door

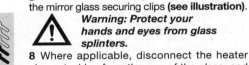

17.7 Using a small screwdriver, carefully release the mirror glass securing clips

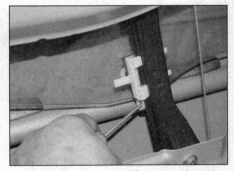

18.3a Engage a screwdriver over the strap at the base of the window glass fastener and push downwards . . .

inner trim panel and sealing sheet as described in Section 14.

17 Exterior mirror components – removal and refitting

Mirror assembly

Removal

1 Remove the mirror inner trim panel as described in Section 14, paragraphs 1 to 3.
2 On models with electrically-adjustable mirrors, disconnect the mirror wiring connector.
3 Remove the foam insulation for access to the mirror retaining nut.
4 Using pointed-nose pliers engaged with the slots in the mirror retaining nut, unscrew the nut and withdraw the mirror from the door **(see illustration)**.

Refitting

5 Refitting is a reversal of removal.

Mirror glass

Removal

6 Push the inner edge of the glass inwards to create an opening between the outer edge of the glass and the mirror body.

7 Insert a small screwdriver between the mirror glass and the mirror body, and carefully release the mirror glass securing clips **(see illustration)**.

⚠️ *Warning: Protect your hands and eyes from glass splinters.*

8 Where applicable, disconnect the heater element wiring from the rear of the glass, and withdraw the glass from the mirror assembly.

Refitting

9 Where applicable, reconnect the wires to the rear of the mirror glass, then push the glass into position to engage the securing clips.

18 Door window glass and regulator – removal and refitting

Front window glass

Removal

1 Remove the door inner trim panel and the plastic sealing sheet, as described in Section 14.
2 Operate the window regulator mechanism, such that the glass-to-regulator retaining clip is accessible through the door aperture.
3 Support the glass, then unclip the plastic fastener that secures the window glass to the

regulator mechanism. To do this, engage a screwdriver over the strap at the base of the fastener and push downwards. This will release the fastener from its retaining peg **(see illustrations)**.
4 With the plastic fastener released, disengage the regulator mechanism from the hole at the base of the window glass.
5 Lower the glass to the bottom of the guide channels, and disengage the front edge of the glass from the front guide channel.
6 Pull the glass out of the rear guide channel to disengage the plastic slider **(see illustration)**.
7 Lift the glass upwards at the rear and remove it from the inside of the door frame **(see illustration)**.

Refitting

8 Locate the glass in the door and engage the plastic slider with the rear guide channel. Push the glass rearwards until the slider is heard to engage with the channel.
9 Engage the front edge of the glass with the front guide channel, then move the glass upwards to its mid position.
10 Engage the regulator mechanism with the hole at the base of the glass, then reach up behind and reconnect the plastic fastener.
11 Check the operation of the glass and regulator then refit the door inner trim panel and plastic sheet as described in Section 14.

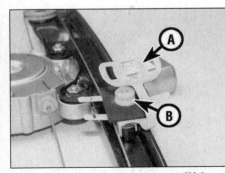

18.3b . . . to release the fastener (A) from the retaining peg (B)

18.6 Pull the glass out of the rear guide channel to disengage the plastic slider (arrowed)

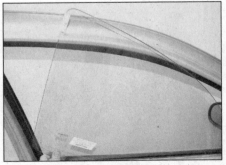

18.7 Lift the glass upwards at the rear and remove it from the inside of the door frame

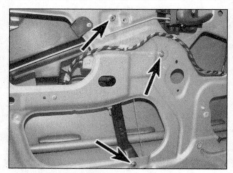

18.14 Unscrew the three nuts (arrowed) securing the regulator assembly to the front door

18.15 Lower the regulator assembly and disconnect the motor wiring connector

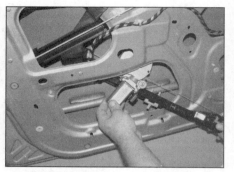

18.16 Manipulate the regulator assembly out through the door aperture

Front window regulator

Removal

12 Separate the window glass from the regulator mechanism, as described in paragraphs 1 to 4.

13 Fully raise the window glass, and secure the glass in position using suitable tape, or by wedging the glass in position using rags between the glass and the edge of the door – ensure that the glass cannot drop into the door. Alternatively, lift the glass panel out through the window aperture.

14 Unscrew the three nuts securing the regulator assembly to the door **(see illustration)**.

15 Lower the assembly down to the bottom

of the door and disconnect the motor wiring connector **(see illustration)**.

16 Manipulate the complete regulator assembly out through the aperture in the door **(see illustration)**.

Refitting

17 Refitting is a reversal of removal, bearing in mind the following points:

a) *Attach the window glass to the regulator as described previously, before tightening the regulator retaining nuts.*

b) *Check the operation of the window mechanism before refitting the door inner trim panel.*

c) *Refit the door inner trim panel and plastic sheet as described in Section 14.*

Rear window glass

Removal

18 Remove the door inner trim panel and the plastic sealing sheet, as described in Section 14.

19 Carefully prise the lower window aperture outer weatherstrip upwards from its location, and remove it from the door frame **(see illustration)**.

20 Operate the window regulator mechanism to move the glass to the fully closed position.

21 Undo the two retaining bolts and remove the window glass lower rear guide channel **(see illustrations 16.40a and 16.40b)**.

22 Operate the window regulator mechanism, such that the glass-to-regulator retaining clip is accessible through the door aperture.

23 Support the glass, then unclip the plastic fastener that secures the window glass to the regulator mechanism. To do this, pull the strap at the base of the fastener downwards. This will release the fastener from its retaining peg **(see illustrations 18.3a and 18.3b)**.

24 With the plastic fastener released, disengage the regulator mechanism from the hole at the base of the window glass.

25 Lower the glass to the bottom of the guide channels, and pull the rear channel out of the door aperture **(see illustration)**.

26 Move the glass rearwards to disengage the plastic slider from the front guide channel, then pull the front channel out of the door aperture **(see illustrations)**.

27 Lift the glass upwards at the rear and remove it from the outside of the door frame **(see illustration)**.

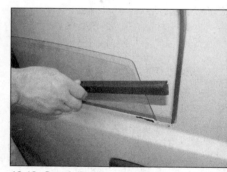

18.19 Carefully prise the rear door window aperture weatherstrip upwards and remove it from the door

18.25 Lower the glass to the bottom of the guide channels, and pull the rear channel out of the door aperture

18.26a Move the glass rearwards to disengage the plastic slider (arrowed) from the front guide channel . . .

18.26b . . . then pull the front channel out of the door aperture

18.27 Lift the glass upwards at the rear and remove it from the outside of the door frame

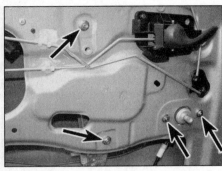

18.36 Unscrew the four nuts (arrowed) securing the rear window regulator assembly to the door

Refitting

28 Locate the glass in the door and refit the front guide channel.

29 Engage the plastic slider with the front guide channel and push the glass forwards until the slider is heard to engage with the channel.

30 Locate the rear guide channel over the glass and push the channel down into its location in the door aperture.

31 Engage the regulator mechanism with the hole at the base of the glass, then reach up behind and reconnect the plastic fastener.

32 Refit the window aperture outer weatherstrip.

33 Check the operation of the glass and regulator then refit the door inner trim panel and plastic sheet as described in Section 14.

Rear window regulator

Removal

34 Separate the window glass from the regulator mechanism, as described in paragraphs 18 and 22 to 24.

35 Fully raise the window glass, and secure the glass in position using suitable tape, or by wedging the glass in position using rags between the glass and the edge of the door – ensure that the glass cannot drop into the door. Alternatively, lift the glass panel out through the window aperture.

36 Unscrew the four nuts securing the regulator assembly to the door **(see illustration)**.

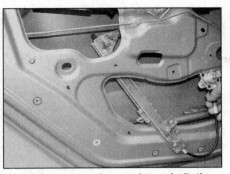

18.37 Disengage the regulator shaft, then manipulate the regulator assembly out through the door aperture

37 Disengage the regulator shaft from the door, then lower the assembly and manipulate it out through the door aperture **(see illustration)**.

Refitting

38 Refitting is a reversal of removal, bearing in mind the following points:
 a) *Attach the window glass to the regulator as described previously, before tightening the regulator retaining nuts.*
 b) *Check the operation of the window mechanism before refitting the door inner trim panel.*
 c) *Refit the door inner trim panel and plastic sheet as described in Section 14.*

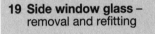

19 Side window glass – removal and refitting

Removal

1 Prise off the trim cover and undo the two bolts securing the locking catch to the body.

2 Undo the upper and lower retaining screws and lift off the outer trim over the window hinges **(see illustrations)**.

3 With an assistant supporting the window glass, undo the hinge retaining bolts and withdraw the glass from the window aperture **(see illustration)**.

Refitting

4 Refitting is a reversal of removal.

20 Windscreen and tailgate glass – general information

These areas of glass are secured by the tight fit of the weatherstrip in the body aperture, and are bonded in position with a special adhesive. Renewal of such fixed glass is a difficult, messy and time-consuming task, which is considered beyond the scope of the home mechanic. It is difficult, unless one has plenty of practice, to obtain a secure, waterproof fit. Furthermore, the task carries a high risk of breakage; this applies especially to the laminated glass windscreen. In view of this, owners are strongly advised to have this sort of work carried out by one of the many specialist windscreen fitters.

For those possessing the necessary skills and equipment to carry out this task, some preliminary removal of the vehicle interior trim and associated components is necessary, as follows, referring to the procedures contained in the Sections and Chapters indicated.

Windscreen

 a) *Remove both wiper arms (Chapter 12).*
 b) *Remove the windscreen scuttle grille panel (Section 22 of this Chapter).*
 c) *Remove the front pillar trim on both sides (Section 25 of this Chapter).*
 d) *Remove the sun visors.*

Tailgate window glass

 a) *Remove the tailgate trim panel (Section 25 of this Chapter).*

21 Sunroof – general information

1 Due to the complexity of the sunroof mechanism, considerable expertise is needed to repair, renew or adjust the sunroof components successfully. Removal of the roof first requires the headlining to be removed, which is a complex and tedious operation, and not a task to be undertaken lightly.

19.2a Undo the upper and lower retaining screws . . .

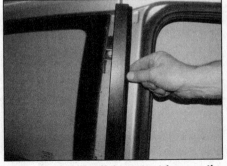

19.2b . . . and lift off the outer trim over the side window hinges

19.3 Undo the hinge retaining bolts (arrowed) and withdraw the glass from the window aperture

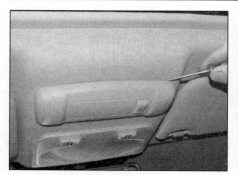

21.3a Carefully prise the overhead console from its location . . .

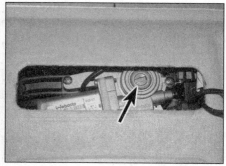

21.3b . . . to gain access to the sunroof motor spindle (arrowed)

22.3 Undo the windscreen scuttle panel centre and outer retaining screws . . .

Therefore, any problems with the sunroof should be referred to a Fiat dealer.

2 If the sunroof motor fails to operate, first check the relevant fuse. If the fault cannot be traced and rectified, the sunroof can be opened and closed manually, using the special crank handle supplied in the vehicle toolkit to turn the motor spindle.

3 To gain access to the motor spindle, ensure that the ignition key is in the 'off' position, then carefully prise the overhead console from its location. Engage the crank handle with the spindle, and turn the handle to open or close the sunroof **(see illustrations)**.

4 Once the roof is closed, remove the crank handle, and clip the overhead console back into place.

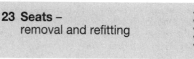

22 Body exterior fittings –
removal and refitting

Windscreen scuttle grille panel

1 Open and support the bonnet.

2 Remove the windscreen wiper arms as described in Chapter 12.

3 Undo the centre retaining screw and the two outer screws securing the panel to the scuttle **(see illustration)**.

4 Release the end of weatherstrip from its location at each side of the panel **(see illustration)**.

5 Lift the panel up at the front then move it forward to disengage the rear locating clips **(see illustration)**.

6 Refitting is a reversal of removal.

Wheel arch liners

7 The wheel arch liners are secured by self-tapping screws and removal is self-evident and straightforward. Multiple liner panels are used which overlap each other at their edges. In some instances it may be necessary to move aside adjoining panels for access to a specific panel.

Body trim strips and badges

8 The various body trim strips and badges are held in position with a special adhesive tape. Removal requires the trim/badge to be heated, to soften the adhesive, and then cut

away from the surface. Due to the high risk of damage to the vehicle paintwork during this operation, it is recommended that this task should be entrusted to a Fiat dealer.

23 Seats –
removal and refitting

Front seat

> ⚠ **Warning: Certain models are equipped with side airbags built into the outer sides of the front seats. Refer to Chapter 12 for the precautions which should be observed when dealing with an airbag system. Do not tamper with the airbag unit in any way,**

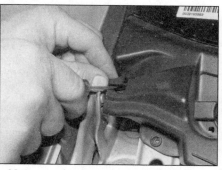

22.4 . . . release the end of weatherstrip from its location each side . . .

23.3 Front seat rail front securing bolt (arrowed) . . .

and do not attempt to test any airbag system components. Note that the airbag is triggered if the mechanism is supplied with an electrical current (including via an ohmmeter), or if the assembly is subjected to a temperature of greater than 100°C.

Removal

1 On models with side airbags in the front seats, de-activate the airbag system, as described in Chapter 12, before attempting to remove the seat.

2 The front seats rails are secured to the floorpan by four bolts.

3 Slide the seat towards the rear of the car to gain access to the two bolts at the front, then slacken and remove them **(see illustration)**.

4 Slide the seat fully forwards and remove the two rearmost bolts **(see illustration)**. Where

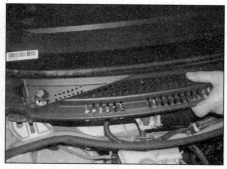

22.5 . . . then lift the panel up at the front and move it forward to disengage the rear clips

23.4 . . . and rear securing bolt (arrowed)

23.7a Undo the retaining bolt and lift up the rear seat back centre hinge locking cover . . .

23.7b . . . then disengage the seat pivot from the centre mounting

23.8 Undo the two side hinge securing bolts and remove the seat back from the car

applicable, disconnect the airbag, and/or seat heater wiring connectors, then remove the seat from the car

Refitting

5 Refitting is a reversal of removal.

Rear seat back

Removal

6 Raise the seat cushion and tilt it fully forward. Release the seat back from its locking catches and tip it forward slightly.
7 On models with split rear seat backs, undo the retaining bolt and lift up the centre hinge locking cover. Disengage the seat pivot from the centre mounting (see illustrations).
8 Undo the two bolts securing the side hinges to the body and remove the seat back from the car (see illustration).

Refitting

9 Refitting is a reversal of removal.

Rear seat cushion

Removal

10 Raise the seat cushion and tilt it fully forward.
11 Undo the bolts securing the hinged brackets to the floorpan, then lift out the cushion (see illustration).

Refitting

12 Refitting is a reversal of removal.

---

24 Seat belt components – removal and refitting

Note: *Record the positions of the washers and spacers on the seat belt anchors, and ensure they are refitted in their original positions.*

Front seat belt

Warning: On certain models, the front seat belt inertia reels are equipped with a pyrotechnic pretensioner mechanism. Refer to the airbag system precautions contained in Chapter 12 which apply equally to the seat belt pretensioners. Do not tamper with the inertia reel pretensioner unit in any way, and do not attempt to test the unit.

Removal – 3-door models

1 De-activate the airbag system (which will also de-activate the pyrotechnic pretensioner mechanism, where fitted), as described in Chapter 12, before attempting to remove the seatbelt.
2 Remove the side trim panel as described in Section 25.
3 Lift up the trim cap over the seat belt upper anchor nut. Undo the upper anchor nut and release the seat belt from the height adjuster (see illustration).

4 Undo the inertia reel retaining bolt and withdraw the inertia reel from the centre pillar (see illustration). Where applicable, disconnect the pretensioner wiring connector and remove the seat belt assembly from the car.

Removal – 5-door models

5 De-activate the airbag system (which will also de-activate the pyrotechnic pretensioner mechanism, where fitted), as described in Chapter 12, before attempting to remove the seatbelt.
6 Remove the centre pillar trim panels as described in Section 25.
7 Extract the retaining clip and remove the seat belt upper guide pin from the centre pillar.
8 Undo the inertia reel retaining bolt and withdraw the inertia reel from the centre pillar. Where applicable, disconnect the pretensioner wiring connector and remove the seat belt assembly from the car.

Refitting

9 Refitting is a reversal of removal, ensuring that all mounting bolts are tightened to the specified torque.

Front seat belt stalk

Removal

10 Unscrew the anchor bolt and withdraw the stalk assembly from the side of the seat.

23.11 Rear seat cushion hinged bracket retaining bolt (arrowed)

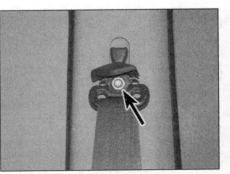

24.3 Front seat belt upper anchor nut (arrowed)

24.4 Front seat belt inertia reel retaining bolt (arrowed)

24.17 Rear seat belt inertia reel retaining bolt (arrowed) – 3-door models

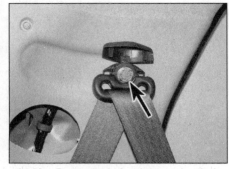

24.22a Rear seat belt upper anchor bolt (arrowed) . . .

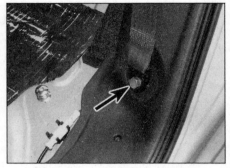

24.22b . . . and lower anchor bolt (arrowed) – 5-door models

Refitting

11 Refit the stalk and tighten the anchor bolt to the specified torque.

Rear seat belt and buckles

Removal – 3-door models

12 Remove the parcel shelf from the luggage compartment.

13 Raise the seat cushion and tilt it fully forward.

14 Remove the rear loudspeaker from the parcel shelf support as described in Chapter 12.

15 Lift up the trim caps and undo the seat belt upper and lower anchor bolts.

16 Withdraw the seat belt through the incision in the loudspeaker housing.

17 Undo the inertia reel retaining bolt and remove the seat belt assembly from the car (see illustration).

18 Undo the seat belt buckle anchor bolt(s) and remove the relevant seat belt buckles.

Removal – 5-door models

19 Remove the parcel shelf from the luggage compartment.

20 Raise the seat cushion and tilt it fully forward.

21 Where fitted, disconnect the wiring connector, undo the retaining screws and remove the audio amplifier/loudspeaker unit from the luggage compartment.

22 Lift up the trim caps and undo the seat belt upper and lower anchor bolts (see illustrations).

23 Withdraw the seat belt through the incision in the parcel shelf support.

24 Where applicable, undo the retaining bolts and remove the audio amplifier/loudspeaker unit mounting bracket from around the inertia reel (see illustration).

25 Undo the inertia reel retaining bolt and remove the seat belt assembly from the car (see illustration).

26 Undo the seat belt buckle anchor bolt(s) and remove the relevant seat belt buckles (see illustration).

Refitting

27 Refitting is a reversal of removal, but tighten the seat belt anchor bolts to the specified torque.

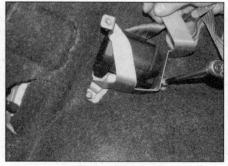

24.24 Undo the bolts and remove the audio amplifier/loudspeaker unit mounting bracket – 5-door models

24.25 Rear seat belt inertia reel retaining bolt (arrowed) – 5-door models

24.26 Rear seat belt buckle anchor bolts (arrowed) – 5-door models

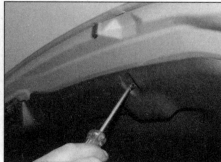

25.3 Undo the retaining screws securing the lower edge of the tailgate inner trim panel

25 Interior trim panels – removal and refitting

General

1 The interior trim panels are secured by a combination of metal and plastic clips and screws. When releasing certain types of securing clips, a suitable forked tool will prove invaluable to avoid damage to the panel and clips. A degree of force will be necessary to pull some of the panels from their locations, especially where numerous internal retaining clips are used. Be prepared for some of the plastic clips to break when their relevant panel is being removed.

Door inner trim panels

2 Refer to Section 14.

Tailgate inner trim panel

3 Undo the retaining screws securing the lower edge of the panel to the tailgate (see illustration).

4 Starting at the lower rear corner, pull the panel downwards to release the securing

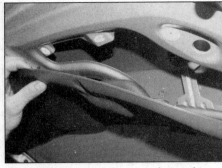

25.4 Pull the panel downwards to release the securing clips, then remove the panel from the tailgate

25.6a Undo the retaining screw at the front . . .

25.6b . . . and rear of the sill trim panel

clips, then remove the panel from the tailgate **(see illustration)**.

5 To refit the panel, locate it in position, ensuring that the retaining clips engage, and secure with the lower retaining screws.

Sill trim panels

6 Undo the retaining screws at each end of the panel **(see illustrations)**.

7 Carefully pull the panel away from the sill to release the securing clips **(see illustration)**.

8 To refit the panel, locate it in position, ensuring that the retaining clips engage, and secure with the two screws.

Front pillar trim panels

9 Locally remove the front door weatherstrip from the edge of the panel.

10 Carefully pull the panel away from the pillar to release the securing clips **(see illustration)**.

11 Refitting is a reversal of removal, ensuring the weatherstrip is correctly seated.

Centre pillar trim panels

3-door models

12 Locally remove the front door weatherstrip from the edge of the centre pillar.

13 Lift up the trim cap over the seat belt upper anchor bolt. Undo the upper anchor bolt and release the seat belt from the height adjuster. Record the positions of the washers

and spacers on the upper anchor bolt to ensure correct refitting.

14 Using a small screwdriver, carefully prise off the seat belt height adjuster knob.

15 Undo the screw securing the side trim panel to the base of the centre pillar trim panel **(see illustration)**.

16 Carefully pull the centre pillar trim panel and the upper part of the side trim panel away from the pillar to release the securing clips.

17 Disengage the centre pillar trim from the side trim panel and remove the trim.

18 Refitting is a reversal of removal, ensuring that all retaining clips are fully engaged. Refit the seat belt upper anchor bolt with the washers and spacers correctly positioned as

noted during removal. Tighten the upper anchor bolt to the specified torque.

5-door models

19 Remove the sill trim panel as described previously.

20 Locally remove the front and rear door weatherstrip from the edges of the centre pillar.

21 Undo the screw securing the side trim panel to the base of the centre pillar trim panel **(see illustration)**.

22 Lift up the trim cap over the seat belt upper anchor bolt. Undo the upper anchor bolt and release the seat belt from the height adjuster **(see illustration)**. Record the

25.7 Carefully pull the panel away from the sill to release the securing clips

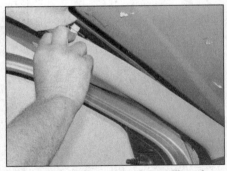

25.10 Carefully pull the front pillar trim panel away from the pillar to release the securing clips

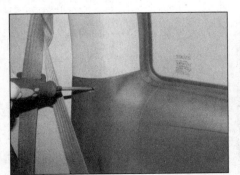

25.15 Undo the screw securing the side trim panel to the centre pillar trim panel – 3-door models

25.21 Undo the screw securing the side trim panel to the base of the centre pillar trim panel – 5-door models

25.22 Undo the front seat belt upper anchor bolt . . .

25.23 . . . and lower anchor bolt – 5-door models

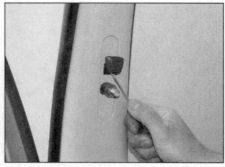

25.24 Carefully prise off the seat belt height adjuster knob – 5-door models

25.25 Undo the retaining screw at the base of the centre pillar trim panel upper section – 5-door models

positions of the washers and spacers on the upper anchor bolt to ensure correct refitting.

23 Similarly, undo the seat belt lower anchor bolt, recording the positions of the washers and spacers **(see illustration)**.

24 Using a small screwdriver, carefully prise off the seat belt height adjuster knob **(see illustration)**.

25 Undo the retaining screw at the base of the centre pillar trim panel upper section **(see illustration)**.

26 Carefully pull the panel away from the pillar to release the securing clips **(see illustration)**.

27 Separate the upper section of the panel from the lower section and disengage the seat

belt **(see illustration)**. Remove the two sections of the panel from the car.

28 Refitting is a reversal of removal, ensuring that all retaining clips are fully engaged. Refit the seat belt anchor bolts with the washers and spacers correctly positioned as noted during removal. Tighten the anchor bolts to the specified torque.

Side trim panels

3-door models

29 Remove the sill trim panel as described previously.

30 Locally remove the front door weatherstrip from the edge of the centre pillar.

31 Remove the rear seat cushion and seat back as described in Section 23.

32 Undo the bolt securing the front seat belt lower anchor rail to the base of the sill **(see illustration)**. Slide the seat belt off the anchor rail then disengage the anchor rail rear mounting.

33 Undo the rear seat belt lower anchor bolt **(see illustration)**. Record the positions of the washers and spacers on the lower anchor bolt to ensure correct refitting.

34 Undo the screw securing the side trim panel to the base of the centre pillar trim panel.

35 Carefully pull the panel away from the body to release the securing clips **(see illustration)**.

36 Slide the seat belt out through the incision in the panel **(see illustration)**.

25.26 Carefully pull the panel away from the pillar to release the securing clips – 5-door models

25.27 Separate the upper section of the panel from the lower section and disengage the seat belt – 5-door models

25.32 Undo the bolt securing the front seat belt lower anchor rail to the base of the sill – 3-door models

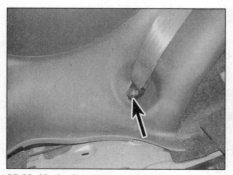

25.33 Undo the rear seat belt lower anchor bolt (arrowed) – 3-door models

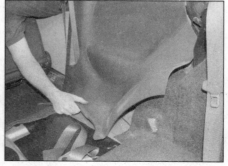

25.35 Carefully pull the side trim panel away from the body to release the securing clips – 3-door models

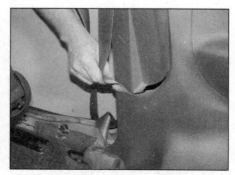

25.36 Slide the seat belt out through the incision in the panel – 3-door models

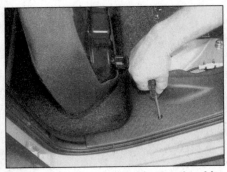

25.42 Undo the screws securing the side trim panel to the sill in the rear door aperture – 5-door models

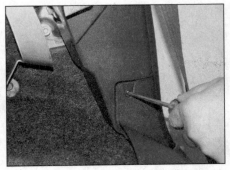

25.43 Undo the screw securing the upper corner of the panel above the wheel arch – 5-door models

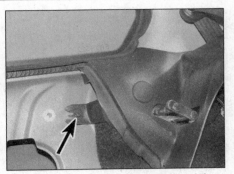

25.50 Parcel shelf support side retaining screw (arrowed) – 3-door models

37 Refitting is a reversal of removal, ensuring that all retaining clips are fully engaged. Refit the seat belt anchor bolts with the washers and spacers correctly positioned as noted during removal. Tighten the anchor bolts to the specified torque.

5-door models

38 Remove the rear seat back as described in Section 23.
39 Locally remove the rear door weatherstrip from the edge of the side trim panel.
40 Undo the rear seat belt lower anchor bolt. Record the positions of the washers and spacers on the lower anchor bolt to ensure correct refitting.

41 Undo the screw securing the lower front corner of the side trim panel to the base of the centre pillar trim panel.
42 Undo the two screws securing the upper edge of the panel to the sill in the rear door aperture **(see illustration)**.
43 Undo the screw securing the upper rear corner of the panel to the body above the inner wheel arch **(see illustration)**.
44 Carefully pull the panel away from the body to release the securing clips.
45 Refitting is a reversal of removal, ensuring that all retaining clips are fully engaged. Refit the rear seat belt anchor bolt with the washers and spacers correctly positioned as noted during removal.

Tighten the anchor bolt to the specified torque.

Parcel shelf supports

46 Remove the parcel shelf from the luggage compartment.
47 Remove the side trim panel as described previously.
48 Remove the rear loudspeaker as described in Chapter 12.
49 Carefully prise the luggage compartment light from the base of the parcel shelf support and disconnect the wiring connector.
50 On 3-door models, undo the screw securing the parcel shelf support to the body below the side window **(see illustration)**.
51 Undo the screws securing the upper section of the parcel shelf support to the inner wing, and the screw securing the lower section in the luggage compartment **(see illustrations)**.
52 Lift up the trim cap and undo the seat belt upper anchor bolt. Record the positions of the washers and spacers on the anchor bolt to ensure correct refitting.
53 Carefully pull the support away from the body to release the securing clips **(see illustration)**.
54 Withdraw the seat belt through the incision in the loudspeaker housing, and remove the support from the car **(see illustration)**.
55 Refitting is a reversal of removal, ensuring that all retaining clips are fully engaged. Refit the rear seat belt upper anchor bolt with the washers and spacers correctly positioned as noted during removal. Tighten the anchor bolt to the specified torque.

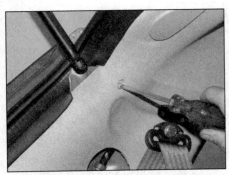

25.51a Undo the screws securing the upper section of the parcel shelf support to the inner wing . . .

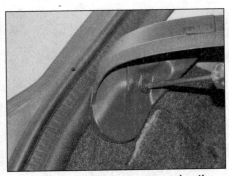

25.51b . . . and the screw securing the lower section in the luggage compartment

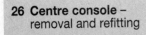

26 Centre console – removal and refitting

Removal

Manual transmission models

1 Disconnect the battery negative terminal (refer to *Disconnecting the battery* in the Reference Chapter).
2 Carefully prise the base of the gear lever

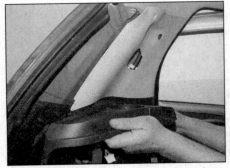

25.53 Carefully pull the support away from the body to release the securing clips . . .

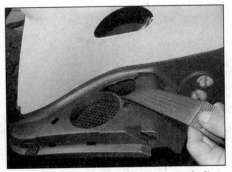

25.54 . . . then withdraw the seat belt through the incision in the loudspeaker housing

26.2a Carefully prise the base of the gear lever boot from its location . . .

26.2b . . . then undo the screws (arrowed) securing the console to the gear lever housing – manual transmission models

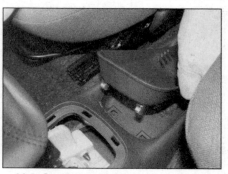

26.3 Carefully prise up the front of the oddments tray to release the two retaining clips – manual transmission models

boot from its location, then undo the two screws securing the console to the gear lever housing (see illustrations).

3 Carefully prise up the front edge of the oddments tray to release the two retaining clips (see illustration). Disengage the rear edge of the oddments tray from the base of the handbrake lever and remove the tray.

4 Undo the two retaining nuts located in the oddments tray aperture (see illustration).

5 Lift out the ashtray from the rear of the centre console.

6 Undo the retaining screw and remove the

ashtray surround from the console (see illustrations).

7 Undo the nut, now exposed, securing the rear of the console to the floor (see illustration).

8 Pull up the handbrake lever as far as it will go.

9 Lift the console up at the rear and manipulate it over the handbrake lever.

10 Disconnect the wiring connectors from the console switches as applicable.

11 Feed the gear lever boot through the console aperture and remove the console from the car (see illustration).

Automatic transmission models

12 Disconnect the battery negative terminal (refer to *Disconnecting the battery* in the Reference Chapter).

13 Remove the selector lever cover from the gear selector lever assembly as described in Chapter 7B.

14 Undo the two screws securing the console to the gear selector lever housing (see illustration).

15 Carefully prise up the lower edge of the

26.4 Undo the two retaining nuts (arrowed) in the oddments tray aperture – manual transmission models

26.6a Undo the retaining screw (arrowed) . . .

26.6b . . . and remove the ashtray surround from the console – manual transmission models

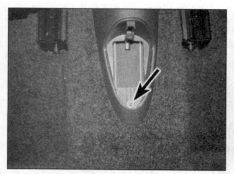

26.7 Undo the nut (arrowed) securing the rear of the console to the floor – manual transmission models

26.11 Feed the gear lever boot through the aperture and remove the console – manual transmission models

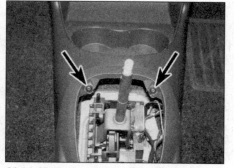

26.14 Undo the screws (arrowed) securing the console to the gear selector lever housing – automatic transmission models

26.15 Carefully prise up and remove the coin holder from the console – automatic transmission models

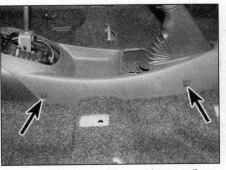

26.16 Undo the two screws (arrowed) on each side of the console – automatic transmission models

26.18 Lift the console from its location and remove it from the car – automatic transmission models

coin holder and remove the holder from the console (see illustration).

16 Undo the two retaining screws located on each side of the console (see illustration).

17 Remove the rear ashtray housing and undo the console rear retaining nut as described in paragraphs 5 to 7.

18 Lift the console from its location, disconnect the wiring connectors from the console switches as applicable, and remove the console from the car (see illustration).

Refitting

19 Refitting is a reversal of removal. On

automatic transmission models, refit the selector lever cover as described in Chapter 7B.

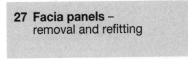

27 Facia panels –
removal and refitting

⚠ *Warning: All models are equipped with an airbag system. The driver's airbag is mounted in the steering wheel centre pad and, where fitted, the*

passenger's airbag is mounted in the passenger's side of the facia. Make sure that the safety precautions given in Chapter 12 are followed, to prevent personal injury.

Glovebox

Removal

1 Open the glovebox and use a small screwdriver to push the two plastic hinge pins inwards (see illustration).

2 With the hinge pins released, withdraw the glovebox from the facia.

Refitting

3 Refitting is a reversal of removal.

Driver's side lower panel

Removal

4 Release the two plastic screws located at the top of the panel, then lift the panel from the facia.

Refitting

5 Refitting is a reversal of removal.

Steering column shrouds

Removal

6 Undo the four retaining screws and remove the lower shroud from the underside of the steering column (see illustration).

7 Remove the steering wheel as described in Chapter 10.

8 Undo the two screws securing the front of the upper shroud to the steering column switch assembly. Manipulate the shroud out from under the instrument panel and remove the shroud from the column (see illustrations).

Refitting

9 Refitting is a reversal of removal, referring to Chapter 10 for steering wheel refitting procedures.

Instrument panel surround

Removal

10 Undo the two lower retaining screws, one

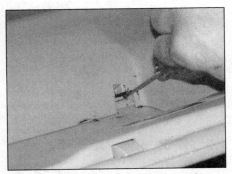

27.1 Push the two plastic hinge pins inwards and remove the glovebox from the facia

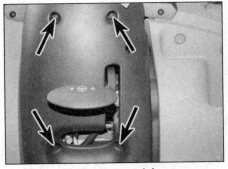

27.6 Undo the four retaining screws (arrowed) and remove the lower steering column shroud

27.8a Undo the two screws securing the front of the upper shroud to the switch assembly . . .

27.8b . . . then manipulate the shroud out from under the instrument panel

27.10 Undo the two instrument panel surround lower retaining screws

27.11a Undo the two upper screws . . .

27.11b . . . then withdraw the surround from the facia

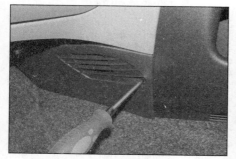

27.14a Undo the retaining screws securing the vent panels to the lower centre panel . . .

27.14b . . . withdraw the panels to disengage the rear retaining clips

27.15 Undo the two lower centre panel retaining screws (arrowed) located beneath the ashtray

27.16 Carefully prise free the upper edge of the panel to disengage the four retaining clips

27.17 Disconnect the wiring connector, then withdraw the panel from the facia

27.20 Undo the two lower screws (arrowed) securing the centre switch panel to the facia

on each side of the surround (see illustration).
11 Undo the two upper screws in the centre of the surround, then withdraw the surround from the facia (see illustrations).

Refitting

12 Refitting is a reversal of removal.

Lower centre panel

Removal

13 Remove the centre console as described in Section 26.
14 Undo the retaining screws securing the vent panels to the lower centre panel. Withdraw the panels from their location to disengage the rear retaining clips (see illustrations).
15 Undo the two lower centre panel retaining

screws located beneath the ashtray (see illustration).
16 Carefully prise free the upper edge of the panel to disengage the four retaining clips (see illustration).
17 Disconnect the wiring connector at the rear of the panel, then withdraw the panel from the facia (see illustration).

Refitting

18 Refitting is a reversal of removal.

Centre switch panel

Removal

19 Remove the lower centre panel as described previously.
20 Undo the two lower screws securing the switch panel to the facia (see illustration).
21 Lower the panel from its location to free

the upper retaining tags, disconnect the wiring connectors and remove the panel (see illustration).

27.21 Lower the panel to free the upper retaining tags, then disconnect the wiring connectors

27.25 Undo the two screws (arrowed) in the centre switch panel aperture

27.26 Undo the four screws (arrowed) in the radio/cassette player aperture and remove the centre vent panel

27.34 Lift up the locking catch and disconnect the wiring connector from the body computer

Refitting

22 Refitting is a reversal of removal.

Centre vent panel

Removal

23 Remove the radio/cassette player as described in Chapter 12.
24 Remove the centre switch panel as described previously.
25 Undo the two retaining screws located in the centre switch panel aperture **(see illustration)**.
26 Undo the four retaining screws located in the radio/cassette player aperture and remove the centre vent panel from the facia **(see illustration)**.

Refitting

27 Refitting is a reversal of removal.

Complete facia assembly

Note: *This is an involved operation entailing the removal of numerous components and assemblies, and the disconnection of a multitude of wiring connectors. Make notes on the location of all disconnected wiring, or attach labels to the connectors, to avoid confusion when refitting.*

Removal

28 Disconnect the battery negative terminal

(refer to *Disconnecting the battery* in the Reference Chapter).
29 Remove the front pillar trim panels on both sides as described in Section 25.
30 Remove all the facia panels described previously in this Section.
31 Remove the steering column as described in Chapter 10.
32 Remove the instrument panel as described in Chapter 12.
33 Where fitted, remove the passenger's airbag as described in Chapter 12.
34 Lift up the locking catch and disconnect the wiring connector from the body computer **(see illustration)**.

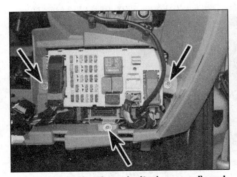

27.35 Undo the three bolts (arrowed) and release the fuse/relay box

35 Undo the three bolts and release the fuse/relay box from the facia **(see illustration)**.
36 Carefully prise out the retaining bolt access covers from the top of the facia at the centre, and on each side **(see illustration)**.
37 Undo the three bolts now accessible, securing the upper edge of the facia to the body **(see illustration)**.
38 Prise out the lower retaining bolt access cover on the passenger's side **(see illustration)**.
39 Undo the bolts securing the lower part of the facia to the body **(see illustrations)**.
40 Carefully pull the whole facia moulding

27.36 Carefully prise out the retaining bolt access covers from the top of the facia

27.37 Undo the three bolts securing the upper edge of the facia to the body

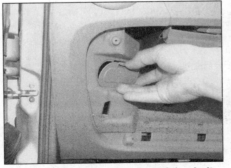

27.38 Prise out the lower retaining bolt access cover on the passenger's side

27.39a Undo the facia centre bolts (arrowed) . . .

27.39b . . . the side bolt (arrowed) on the passenger's side . . .

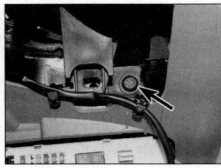

27.39c . . . and driver's side (arrowed) . . .

27.39d . . . and the lower bolt (arrowed) on each side

27.40 Carefully pull the facia moulding away from the bulkhead

away from the bulkhead slightly **(see illustration)**. Label all remaining wiring connectors to aid correct refitting later, then disconnect them. Check that nothing remains connected between the facia and bulkhead then draw the facia moulding away and remove it from the car.

Refitting

41 Refitting is a reversal of removal, noting the following points:

a) Reinstate all electrical connections according to the labels made during

removal and ensure that cables are secured in their clips, using the original routing.

b) Refer to the Chapters indicated and refit all components disturbed during the removal process.

c) On completion, reconnect the battery negative terminal and check the operation of all controls, gauges and instruments disturbed during the removal process, including the heating/air conditioning system.

28 Witter towbar installation

Caution: *On certain Punto models, it may be necessary to fit additional strengthening braces (supplied as a kit by Fiat dealers) to the rear chassis members before installation of the towbar. Consult a Fiat dealer for further information and, where applicable, ensure that the strengthening braces are fitted in accordance with the manufacturer's instructions before proceeding with the towbar installation.*

General information

1 Although the following information specifically depicts the fitting of a Witter towbar, the procedures can be used as a general guide for other towbar types.
2 Prior to starting, read through the entire procedure to familiarise yourself with the work involved and ensure that all necessary tools and equipment are available.
3 On completion of the installation, refer to Chapter 12 for towbar electrical socket installation and wiring connection details.
4 Refer to *Dimensions and weights* in the Reference Chapter for maximum towing weights and trailer nose weight which must be strictly observed.

Materials

5 Unpack the towbar and check that all the following parts are contained in the kit **(see illustration)**. The illustration shows the component arrangement when a fixed towball is being used. If the optional detachable towball is to be used, items 5, 6, 7, 8 and 12 will not be required. The installation procedures contained in this Section cover both towball types.

1) Cross-bar.
2) Left-hand sidearm.
3) Right-hand sidearm.
4) Captive straps (2).
5) Neck – for use with fixed towball.
6) Spacing bushes (2) – for use with fixed towball.
7) M12 x 90 x 1.75 mm bolts (2) – for use with fixed towball.
8) Disc spring washers (2) – for use with fixed towball.
9) M8 x 40 x 1.25 mm bolts (2), nuts (2), lockwashers (4) and flat washers (4).
10) M12 x 35 x 1.75 mm bolts (4), nuts (2), lockwashers (4) and flat washers (2).
11) M10 x 30 x 1.5 mm bolts (2), nuts (2), lockwashers (2) and flat washers (4).
12) M16 x 50 x 2.0 mm bolts (2), nuts (2) and lockwashers (2) – for use with fixed towball.

Towbar installation

Note: *Refer to illustration 28.5 for details of the components and mounting points described in the following procedure.*
6 Chock the front wheels then jack up the rear of the car and securely support it on axle

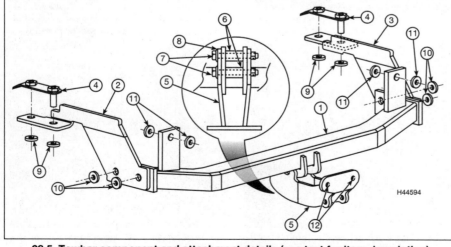

28.5 Towbar component and attachment details (see text for item description)

28.7 Undo the screws securing the rear bumper lower mountings to the brackets on the underbody

28.11 Mark the chassis side rail 35.0 mm forward from the centre of the forward-most mounting hole

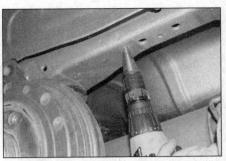

28.12a Drill a pilot hole at the position marked, then enlarge the hole using a conical hole cutter . . .

28.12b . . . until it is possible to insert the captive strap

28.12c . . . Feed the strap through the chassis side rail, allowing the mounting stud to protrude through the existing hole

28.13a Locate the left-hand sidearm in position . . .

stands (see *Jacking and Vehicle Support*). Remove the rear roadwheels.

7 Undo the screws securing the rear bumper lower mountings to the brackets on the vehicle underbody **(see illustration)**.

8 Release the exhaust rear silencer from the rubber mounting, then undo the retaining bolt and remove the rubber mounting support bracket from the chassis side rail.

9 Undo the remaining bolts and remove the exhaust system rear heat shield.

10 Prise out the plastic blanking plugs from the holes in the chassis side rails at position 9.

11 Working on the left-hand side, make a mark on the chassis side rail 35.0 mm forward (towards the front of the car) from the centre of the forward-most mounting hole at position 9 **(see illustration)**.

12 Drill a pilot hole at the position marked,

then enlarge the hole using a conical hole cutter until it is possible to insert the captive strap (4). Feed the strap through the hole and into the chassis side rail, allowing the mounting stud to protrude through the rearmost existing hole **(see illustrations)**.

13 With the captive strap in place, locate the left-hand sidearm (2) in position, followed by the previously removed exhaust heat shield and exhaust mounting support bracket **(see illustrations)**. Secure the assembly with the bolt, nut, flat washers and lockwashers (9), tightened finger tight only at this stage.

14 Repeat paragraphs 11 and 12 on the right-hand side of the car, then place the remaining captive strap (4) in position. Fit the right-hand sidearm (3) and secure the sidearm with the bolt, nut, flat washers and lockwashers (9), tightened finger tight only at this stage.

15 Engage the cross-bar (1) with the two sidearms, and loosely attach the two upper mountings with the bolts, nuts, flat washers and lockwashers (11) **(see illustrations)**. Note

28.13b . . . followed by the previously removed exhaust heat shield . . .

28.13c . . . and exhaust mounting support bracket

28.15a Engage the cross-bar with the two sidearms . . .

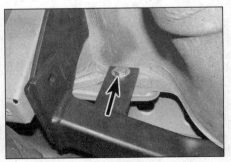

28.15b . . . and attach the upper mountings (arrowed) with the bolts, nuts, flat washers and lockwashers

28.16 Attach the cross-bar to the rearmost holes in the sidearms using the bolts and lockwashers

28.17a If the fixed towball is to be used, locate the two spacing bushes between the mounting flanges in the cross-bar

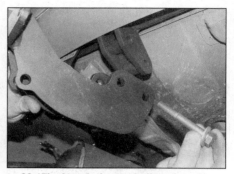

28.17b Attach the towball neck to the cross-bar and secure with the bolts and disc spring washers

that on 3-door models it will be necessary to cut off the left-hand inner mounting flange from the bumper to provide clearance for the towbar electrical socket mounting plate on the cross-bar.

16 Loosely attach the cross-bar (1) to the rearmost holes in the left-hand and right-hand sidearms (2 and 3), using the bolts and lockwashers (10) **(see illustration)**.

17 If the standard fixed towball arrangement is to be used, locate the two spacing bushes (6) between the mounting flanges in the cross-bar (1) **(see illustration)**. Attach the towball neck (5) to the cross-bar and secure

with the bolts (7) and disc spring washers (8) **(see illustration)**. Tighten the bolts to the torque setting given in the Specifications at the start of this Chapter.

18 If the optional detachable towball is being fitted, position the towball receptor unit between the mounting flanges in the cross-bar (1). Insert the two bolts supplied with the kit through the mounting holes, place the safety chain plate in position and secure the assembly with the two Nyloc nuts **(see illustrations)**. Tighten the nuts to the torque setting given in the Specifications at the start of this Chapter.

19 Using the forward-most mounting bolt holes in the cross-bar (1) as a guide, drill a 12.5 mm diameter hole through the bumper mounting bracket on each side **(see illustration)**. Fit the remaining mounting bolts (10), with a flat washer under the bolt head and secure with the nuts and lockwashers moderately tightened **(see illustration)**.

20 Check the fit and alignment of the towbar components, then tighten all mountings and attachments to the torque settings given in the Specifications at the start of this Chapter.

21 On completion, re-attach the exhaust rear silencer to the rubber mounting and refit the bumper lower mounting screws. Refit the roadwheels and lower the car to the ground.

Towball attachment

Fixed towball type

Note: *To avoid obscuring the number plate, the towball should be removed when not in use.*

22 Position the towball on the towball neck flange and insert the two retaining bolts (12). Fit the lockwashers and retaining nuts and tighten the nuts to the torque settings given in the Specifications at the start of this Chapter **(see illustration)**.

Detachable towball type

23 Insert the locking handle into the towball

28.18a If the detachable towball is being fitted, position the receptor unit in the cross-bar, fit the bolts and safety chain plate . . .

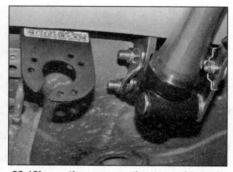

28.18b . . . then secure the assembly with the two Nyloc nuts

28.19a Drill a 12.5 mm diameter hole through the bumper mounting brackets each side . . .

28.19b . . . fit the mounting bolts with a flat washer under the bolt head and secure with the nuts and lockwashers

28.22 Secure the fixed towball to the towbar neck flange with the two bolts nuts and lockwashers

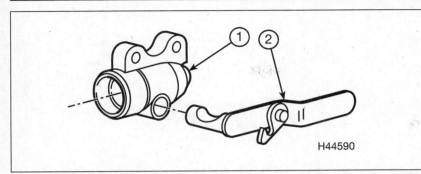

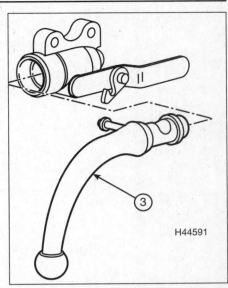

28.23 To fit the detachable towball, insert the locking handle (2) into the receptor unit (1) with the pivot cut-out portion upwards

receptor unit with the cut-out portion of the pivot facing upwards **(see illustration)**.

24 Hold the locking handle as described and insert the towball neck into the receptor unit with the towball facing downwards **(see illustration)**.

25 Rotate the towball neck anti-clockwise through 180°, then pivot the locking handle upwards until the spring-loaded catch engages with the peg on the towball neck **(see illustrations)**.

26 Removal of the towball neck and handle is a reverse of the attachment procedure. After removal, store the components in the bag provided and cover the aperture in the receptor unit with the weather cover.

28.24 Hold the locking handle and insert the towball neck (3) into the receptor unit with the towball facing downwards

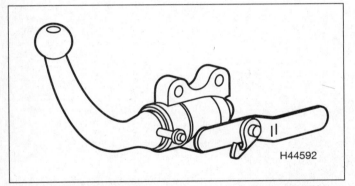

28.25a Rotate the towball neck anti-clockwise through 180° . . .

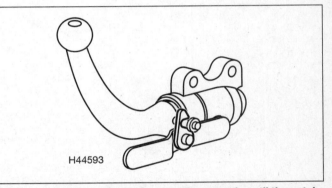

28.25b . . . then pivot the locking handle upwards until the catch engages with the towball neck peg

Notes

Chapter 12
Body electrical systems

Contents

Degrees of difficulty

Easy, suitable for novice with little experience	**Fairly easy,** suitable for beginner with some experience	**Fairly difficult,** suitable for competent DIY mechanic	**Difficult,** suitable for experienced DIY mechanic	**Very difficult,** suitable for expert DIY or professional

Specifications

Bulb ratings	Watts
Courtesy light	10
Front direction indicator light	21
Front direction indicator repeater light	5
Front foglight	55
Front sidelight	5
Headlights	55
High-level stop-light	5
Luggage compartment light	5
Number plate light	5
Rear direction indicator light	21
Rear foglight	21
Reversing light	21
Stop-light	21
Tail light	5

1 General information and precautions

The electrical system is of 12 volt negative earth type. Power for the lights and all electrical accessories is supplied by a lead-acid type battery, which is charged by the alternator.

This Chapter covers repair and service procedures for the various electrical components not associated with the engine. Information on the battery, alternator and starter motor can be found in Chapter 5A.

It should be noted that, prior to working on any component in the electrical system, the battery negative terminal should first be disconnected, to prevent the possibility of electrical short-circuits and/or fires (refer to refer to *Disconnecting the battery* in the Reference Chapter).

 Warning: Before carrying out any work on the electrical system, read through the precautions given in 'Safety first!' at the beginning of this manual, and in Chapter 5A.

 Warning: Certain models are equipped with an airbag system and may also have pyrotechnic seat belt pretensioners. When working on the electrical system, refer to the precautions given in Section 19, to avoid the possibility of personal injury.

2 Electrical fault finding – general information

Note: *Refer to the precautions given in 'Safety first!' and in Section 1 of this Chapter before starting work. The following tests relate to testing of the main electrical circuits, and should not be used to test delicate electronic circuits (such as engine management systems and anti-lock braking systems), particularly where an electronic control unit is used.*

General

1 A typical electrical circuit consists of an electrical component, any switches, relays, motors, fuses, fusible links or circuit breakers related to that component, and the wiring and connectors which link the component to both the battery and the chassis. To help to pinpoint a problem in an electrical circuit, wiring diagrams are included at the end of this Chapter.

2 Before attempting to diagnose an electrical fault, first study the appropriate wiring diagram, to obtain a more complete understanding of the components included in the particular circuit concerned. The possible sources of a fault can be narrowed down by noting whether other components related to the circuit are operating properly. If several components or circuits fail at one time, the problem is likely to be related to a shared fuse or earth connection.

3 Electrical problems usually stem from simple causes, such as loose or corroded connections, a faulty earth connection, a blown fuse, a melted fusible link, or a faulty relay (refer to Section 3 for details of testing relays). Visually inspect the condition of all fuses, wires and connections in a problem circuit before testing the components. Use the wiring diagrams to determine which terminal connections will need to be checked, in order to pinpoint the trouble-spot.

4 The basic tools required for electrical fault-finding include a circuit tester or voltmeter (a 12 volt bulb with a set of test leads can also be used for certain tests); a self-powered test light (sometimes known as a continuity tester); an ohmmeter (to measure resistance); a battery and set of test leads; and a jumper wire, preferably with a circuit breaker or fuse incorporated, which can be used to bypass suspect wires or electrical components. Before attempting to locate a problem with test instruments, use the wiring diagram to determine where to make the connections.

5 To find the source of an intermittent wiring fault (usually due to a poor or dirty connection, or damaged wiring insulation), a wiggle test can be performed on the wiring. This involves wiggling the wiring by hand, to see if the fault occurs as the wiring is moved. It should be possible to narrow down the source of the fault to a particular section of wiring. This method of testing can be used in conjunction with any of the tests described in the following sub-Sections.

6 Apart from problems due to poor connections, two basic types of fault can occur in an electrical circuit – open-circuit or short-circuit.

7 Open-circuit faults are caused by a break somewhere in the circuit, which prevents current from flowing. An open-circuit fault will prevent a component from working, but will not cause the relevant circuit fuse to blow.

8 Short-circuit faults are normally caused by a breakdown in wiring insulation, which allows a feed wire to touch either another wire, or an earthed component such as the bodyshell. This allows the current flowing in the circuit to 'escape' along an alternative route, usually to earth. As the circuit does not now follow its original complete path, it is known as a 'short' circuit. A short-circuit fault will normally cause the relevant circuit fuse to blow.

Finding an open-circuit

9 To check for an open-circuit, connect one lead of a circuit tester or voltmeter to either the negative battery terminal or a known good earth.

10 Connect the other lead to a connector in the circuit being tested, preferably nearest to the battery or fuse.

11 Switch on the circuit, bearing in mind that some circuits are live only when the ignition switch is moved to a particular position.

12 If voltage is present (indicated either by the tester bulb lighting or a voltmeter reading, as applicable), this means that the section of the circuit between the relevant connector and the battery is problem-free.

13 Continue to check the remainder of the circuit in the same fashion.

14 When a point is reached at which no voltage is present, the problem must lie between that point and the previous test point with voltage. Most problems can be traced to a broken, corroded or loose connection.

Finding a short-circuit

15 To check for a short-circuit, first disconnect the load(s) from the circuit (loads are the components which draw current from a circuit, such as bulbs, motors, heating elements, etc).

16 Remove the relevant fuse from the circuit, and connect a circuit tester or voltmeter to the fuse connections.

17 Switch on the circuit, bearing in mind that some circuits are live only when the ignition switch is moved to a particular position.

18 If voltage is present (indicated either by the tester bulb lighting or a voltmeter reading, as applicable), this means that there is a short-circuit.

19 If no voltage is present, but the fuse still blows with the load(s) connected, this indicates an internal fault in the load(s).

Finding an earth fault

20 The battery negative terminal is connected to 'earth' – the metal of the engine/transmission and the car body – and most systems are wired so that they only receive a positive feed, the current returning via the metal of the car body. This means that the component mounting and the body form part of that circuit. Loose or corroded mountings can therefore cause a range of electrical faults, ranging from total failure of a circuit, to a puzzling partial fault. In particular, lights may shine dimly (especially when another circuit sharing the same earth point is in operation), motors (eg wiper motors or the radiator cooling fan motor) may run slowly, and the operation of one circuit may have an apparently-unrelated effect on another. Note that on many vehicles, earth straps are used between certain components, such as the engine/transmission and the body, usually where there is no metal-to-metal contact between components, due to flexible rubber mountings, etc.

21 To check whether a component is properly earthed, disconnect the battery, and connect one lead of an ohmmeter to a known good earth point. Connect the other lead to the wire or earth connection being tested. The resistance reading should be zero; if not, check the connection as follows.

22 If an earth connection is thought to be faulty, dismantle the connection, and clean back to bare metal both the bodyshell and the

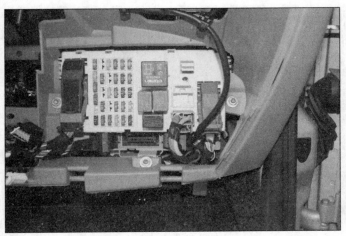

3.2 The main fuses are located in the fusebox under the facia on the driver's side

3.4 Additional fuses and circuit breakers are located in the engine compartment fuse/relay box

wire terminal or the component earth connection mating surface. Be careful to remove all traces of dirt and corrosion, then use a knife to trim away any paint, so that a clean metal-to-metal joint is made. On reassembly, tighten the joint fasteners securely; if a wire terminal is being refitted, use serrated washers between the terminal and the bodyshell, to ensure a clean and secure connection. When the connection is remade, prevent the onset of corrosion in the future by applying a coat of petroleum jelly or silicone-based grease, or by spraying on (at regular intervals) a proprietary ignition sealer.

3 Fuses and relays – general information

Fuses

1 Fuses are designed to break a circuit when a predetermined current is reached, in order to protect the components and wiring which could be damaged by excessive current flow. Any excessive current flow will be due to a fault in the circuit, usually a short-circuit (see Section 2).

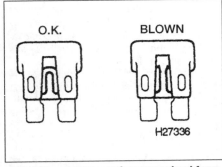

3.5 A blown fuse can be recognised from its melted or broken wire

2 The main fuses are located in the fusebox under the facia on the driver's side **(see illustration)**.
3 To gain access to the fuses, release the two plastic screws located at the top of the facia lower panel, then lift the panel from the facia.
4 Additional fuses and circuit breakers are located in the fuse/relay box in the engine compartment; release the clips and lift off the cover to gain access **(see illustration)**.
5 A blown fuse can be recognised from its melted or broken wire **(see illustration)**.
6 To remove a fuse, first ensure that the relevant circuit is switched off.
7 Using the plastic tool clipped to the main fusebox, pull the fuse from its location.
8 Spare fuses are provided in the main fusebox.
9 Before renewing a blown fuse, trace and rectify the cause, and always use a fuse of the correct rating (fuse ratings are specified on the inside of the fusebox cover panel). Never substitute a fuse of a higher rating, or make temporary repairs using wire or metal foil; more serious damage, or even fire, could result.
10 Note that the fuses are colour-coded as follows. Refer to the wiring diagrams for details of the fuse ratings used and the circuits protected.

Colour	Rating
Orange	5A
Red	10A
Blue	15A
Yellow	20A
Clear or White	25A
Green	30A

11 The radio/cassette player fuse is located in the rear of the unit, and can be accessed after removing the radio/cassette player – refer to Section 12 for greater detail.

Relays

12 A relay is an electrically-operated switch, which is used for the following reasons:
a) A relay can switch a heavy current remotely from the circuit in which the current is flowing, therefore allowing the use of lighter-gauge wiring and switch contacts.
b) A relay can receive more than one control input, unlike a mechanical switch.
c) A relay can have a timer function – for example, the intermittent wiper relay.

13 The main and optional equipment relays are primarily located in the engine compartment fuse/relay box (see *Fuses*). Additional relays may be fitted, depending on model and specification and these are generally mounted adjacent to the component being controlled.
14 If a circuit or system controlled by a relay develops a fault, and the relay is suspect, operate the system. If the relay is functioning, it should be possible to hear it click as it is energised. If this is the case, the fault lies with the components or wiring of the system. If the relay is not being energised, then either the relay is not receiving a main supply or a switching voltage, or the relay itself is faulty. Testing is by the substitution of a known good unit, but be careful – while some relays are identical in appearance and in operation, others look similar but perform different functions.
15 To remove a relay, first ensure that the relevant circuit is switched off. The relay can then simply be pulled out from the socket, and pushed back into position.

4 Bulbs (exterior lights) – renewal

General

1 Whenever a bulb is renewed, note the following points:
a) Ensure that the relevant electrical circuit is isolated before removing a bulb. If in doubt, disconnect the battery negative

4.3a Release the spring clip . . .

4.3b . . . and lift off the plastic cover from the rear outer corner of the headlight unit

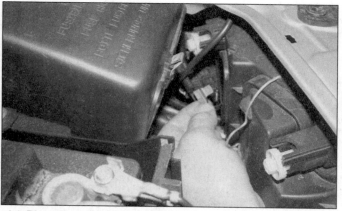

4.4 Disconnect the wiring connector from the rear of the dipped beam bulb

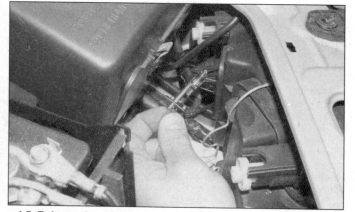

4.5 Release the retaining spring clip and remove the bulb from the headlight unit

terminal (refer to Disconnecting the battery in the Reference Chapter) before starting work.

b) Remember that, if the circuit has just been in use, the bulb may be extremely hot.

c) Always check the bulb contacts and holder, ensuring that there is clean metal-to-metal contact between the bulb and its live contact(s) and earth. Clean off any corrosion or dirt before fitting a new bulb.

d) Wherever bayonet-type bulbs are fitted, ensure that the live contact(s) bear firmly against the bulb contact.

e) Always ensure that the new bulb is of the correct rating (see Specifications), and that it is completely clean before fitting it; this applies particularly to headlight/foglight bulbs (see following paragraphs).

Headlight

2 Open and support the bonnet.

Dipped beam bulb

3 Release the spring clip and lift off the plastic cover from the rear outer corner of the headlight unit (see illustrations).

4 Disconnect the wiring connector from the rear of the bulb (see illustration).

5 Release the retaining spring clip and remove the bulb from the headlight unit (see illustration).

6 When handling the new bulb, use a tissue or clean cloth to avoid touching the glass with the fingers; moisture and grease from the skin can cause blackening and rapid failure of this type of bulb. If the glass is accidentally touched, wipe it clean using methylated spirit. Avoid knocking or shaking the bulb as this may weaken the filament.

7 Install the new bulb, using a reversal of the removal procedure, ensuring that its locating tabs are correctly located in the light unit cut-outs. Secure the bulb in position with the retaining clip.

Main beam bulb

8 Release the two spring clips and lift off the plastic cover from the rear inner corner of the headlight unit (see illustrations).

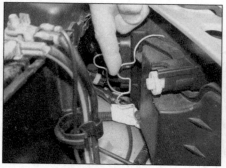

4.8a Release the two spring clips . . .

4.8b . . . and lift off the plastic cover from the rear inner corner of the headlight unit

4.9 Disconnect the wiring connector from the rear of the main beam bulb

4.10a Release the retaining spring clip . . .

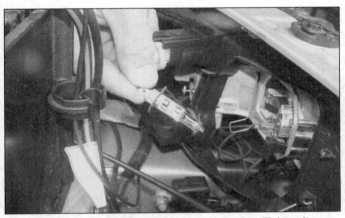

4.10b . . . and remove the bulb from the headlight unit

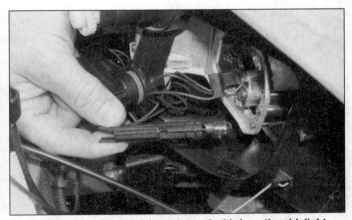

4.15 Depress the retaining tabs and withdraw the sidelight bulbholder from the headlight unit

9 Disconnect the wiring connector from the rear of the bulb **(see illustration)**.

10 Release the retaining spring clip and remove the bulb from the headlight unit **(see illustrations)**.

11 When handling the new bulb, use a tissue or clean cloth to avoid touching the glass with the fingers; moisture and grease from the skin can cause blackening and rapid failure of this type of bulb. If the glass is accidentally touched, wipe it clean using methylated spirit. Avoid knocking or shaking the bulb as this may weaken the filament.

12 Install the new bulb, using a reversal of the removal procedure. Ensure that its locating tabs are correctly located in the light unit cut-outs and secure the bulb in position with the retaining clip.

Sidelight

13 Open and support the bonnet.

14 Release the two spring clips and lift off the plastic cover from the rear inner corner of the headlight unit **(see illustrations 4.8a and 4.8b)**.

15 Depress the retaining tabs and withdraw

the sidelight bulbholder from the headlight unit **(see illustration)**.

16 Remove the push-fit bulb from the bulbholder **(see illustration)**.

17 Fit the new bulb using a reversal of the removal procedure.

Front direction indicator

18 Open and support the bonnet.

4.16 Remove the push-fit bulb from the bulbholder

19 Release the two spring clips and lift off the plastic cover from the rear inner corner of the headlight unit **(see illustrations 4.8a and 4.8b)**.

20 Twist the bulbholder anti-clockwise and withdraw it from the light unit **(see illustration)**.

21 The bulb is a bayonet fit in the bulbholder.

22 Fit the new bulb using a reversal of the removal procedure.

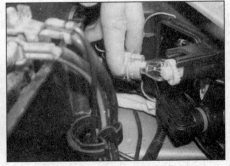

4.20 Twist the direction indicator bulbholder anti-clockwise and withdraw it from the headlight unit

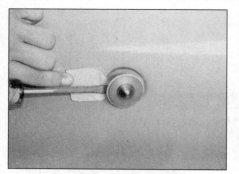

4.23 Push the side repeater light unit rearwards, then lever it out of the wing aperture

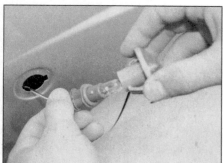

4.24 Twist the bulbholder anti-clockwise to release it from the light unit

Indicator side repeater

23 Push the light unit towards the rear of the vehicle slightly, then insert a screwdriver behind the front edge of the unit and lever it out of the wing aperture **(see illustration)**.
24 Withdraw the light unit, then twist the bulbholder anti-clockwise to release it from the light unit **(see illustration)**.

25 The bulb is a push-fit in the bulbholder.
26 Fit the new bulb using a reversal of the removal procedure.

Front foglight

27 Refer to the headlight dipped beam bulb renewal procedure described previously. Note that, due to the restricted working clearance in the engine compartment, it will be necessary to remove the headlight unit, as described in Section 6, if the left-hand foglight bulb is being renewed.

Rear light cluster bulbs

28 For access to the left-hand light cluster on models equipped with an audio amplifier/loudspeaker unit, undo the retaining screws and move the unit to one side.
29 Working from within the loadspace, prise the plastic cap from the rear pillar trim panel **(see illustration)**.
30 Using the screwdriver and special socket provided with the vehicle's toolkit, unscrew the rear light cluster upper securing bolt **(see illustration)**.
31 Fold back the access flap in the rear carpet and unscrew the lower securing bolt in the same way **(see illustration)**.
32 Pull the light cluster away from the bodywork and disconnect the wiring connector **(see illustration)**.
33 Remove the screws and separate the

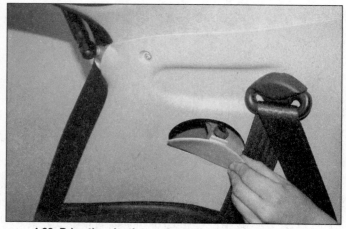

4.29 Prise the plastic cap from the rear pillar trim panel

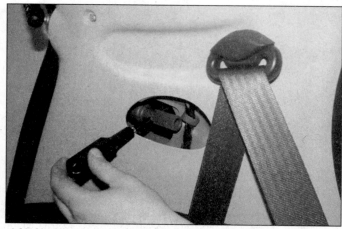

4.30 Unscrew the rear light cluster upper securing bolt using the screwdriver and special socket

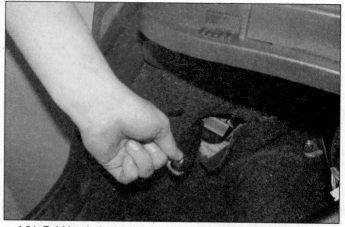

4.31 Fold back the carpet access flap and unscrew the lower securing bolt in the same way

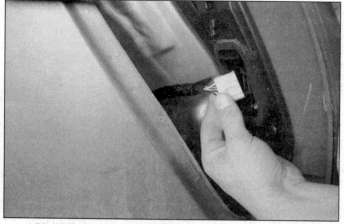

4.32 Withdraw the light cluster and disconnect the wiring connector

4.33a Undo the retaining screws . . .

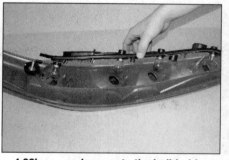

4.33b . . . and separate the bulbholder from the lens unit

4.34 Remove the bayonet fit bulbs from the bulbholder

bulbholder from the lens unit (see illustrations).

34 The bulbs are a bayonet fit in the bulbholder (see illustration).

35 Fit the new bulb using a reversal of the removal procedure.

Rear number plate light

36 Using a small screwdriver, carefully prise the right-hand side of the light unit

from its location in the bumper.

37 Twist the bulbholder anti-clockwise and withdraw it from the light unit.

38 The bulb is a push-fit in the bulbholder.

39 Fit the new bulb using a reversal of the removal procedure.

High-level stop-light

40 Open the tailgate and undo the two stop-light unit retaining screws (see illustration).

41 Withdraw the light unit from the tailgate and disconnect the wiring connector at the bulbholder (see illustration).

42 Release the plastic retaining clip at the end of the bulbholder and lift the bulbholder from the light unit (see illustration).

43 Remove the relevant push-fit bulb from the bulbholder (see illustration).

44 Fit the new bulb using a reversal of the removal procedure.

4.40 Undo the two high-level stop-light unit retaining screws

4.41 Withdraw the light unit and disconnect the bulbholder wiring connector

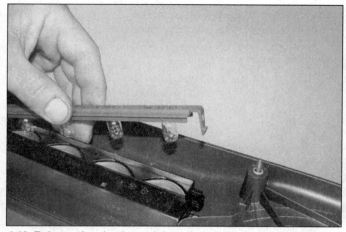

4.42 Release the plastic retaining clip and lift the bulbholder from the light unit

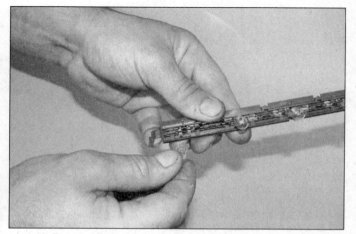

4.43 Remove the relevant push-fit bulb from the bulbholder

5.2 Carefully prise the courtesy light unit from its location

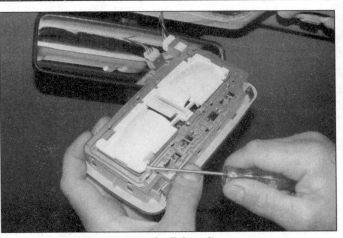

5.3a Lift the tab on the light unit rear cover . . .

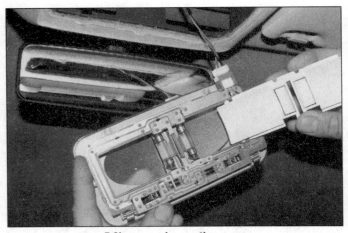

5.3b . . . and open the cover

5.4 Remove the relevant festoon bulb from the bulbholder contacts

5 Bulbs (interior lights) – renewal

General

1 Whenever a bulb is renewed, note the following points:

  a) *Ensure that the relevant electrical circuit is isolated before removing a bulb. If in doubt, disconnect the battery negative terminal (refer to* Disconnecting the battery *in the Reference Chapter) before starting work.*

  b) *Remember that, if the light has just been in use, the bulb may be extremely hot.*

  c) *Always check the bulb contacts and holder, ensuring that there is clean metal-to-metal contact between the bulb and its live contact(s) and earth. Clean off any corrosion or dirt before fitting a new bulb.*

  d) *Wherever bayonet-type bulbs are fitted, ensure that the live contact(s) bear firmly against the bulb contact.*

  e) *Always ensure that the new bulb is of the correct rating (see Specifications), and that it is completely clean before fitting it.*

Courtesy light

2 Using a small screwdriver, carefully prise the light unit from its location **(see illustration)**.

5.7 Carefully prise the luggage compartment light unit from the support panel

3 Insert the screwdriver under the tab on the light unit rear cover and open the cover **(see illustrations)**.

4 Remove the relevant festoon bulb from the bulbholder contacts **(see illustration)**.

5 Fit the new bulb using a reversal of the removal procedure.

Luggage compartment light

6 The light unit is located under the right-hand parcel shelf support panel.

7 Using a small screwdriver, carefully prise the light unit from the support panel **(see illustration)**.

8 Open the bulbholder and remove the push-fit bulb **(see illustrations)**.

9 Fit the new bulb using a reversal of the removal procedure.

Instrument panel illumination

10 The instrument panel illumination and warning light bulbs are an integral part of the instrument panel cluster and cannot be renewed separately.

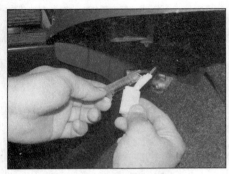

5.8a Open the bulbholder . . .

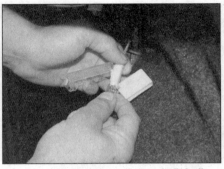

5.8b . . . and remove the push-fit bulb

5.13 Remove the relevant push-fit bulb
from the heater/ventilation control panel

Switch illumination

11 The bulbs that illuminate the facia-mounted switches are integral with the switch body and cannot be renewed separately.

Heater/ventilation control illumination

12 Remove the facia lower centre panel as described in Chapter 12.
13 Remove the relevant push-fit bulb from its location in the ventilation control panel (see illustration).

14 Fit the new bulb using a reversal of the removal procedure.

6 Exterior light units –
removal and refitting

Caution: Ensure that the relevant electrical circuit is isolated before removing a light unit. If in doubt, disconnect the battery negative terminal (refer to Disconnecting the battery in the Reference Chapter).

Headlight

Removal

1 Remove the front bumper as described in Chapter 11.
2 Unscrew the headlight side and upper securing bolts (see illustration).
3 Withdraw the inner edge of the headlight unit from its location then disengage the locating peg from the front wing (see illustrations).
4 Disconnect the wiring connector and remove the headlight unit from the car (see illustration).

Refitting

5 Refitting is a reversal of removal. On completion, it is advisable to have the headlight beam alignment checked with reference to Section 8.

Indicator side repeater light

6 The procedure is described as part of the bulb renewal procedure in Section 4.

Rear light cluster

7 The procedure is described as part of the bulb renewal procedure in Section 4.

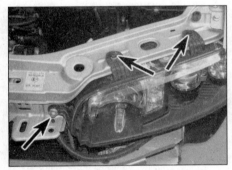

6.2 Unscrew the headlight side and upper securing bolts (arrowed)

6.3a Withdraw the inner edge of the headlight unit from its location . . .

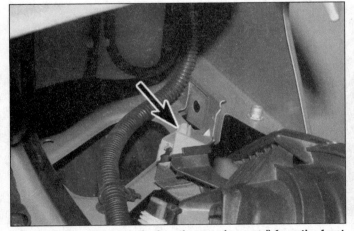

6.3b . . . then disengage the locating peg (arrowed) from the front wing

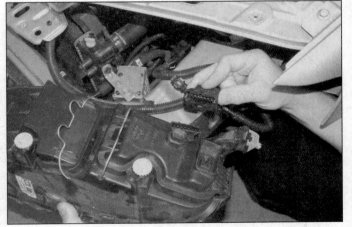

6.4 Disconnect the wiring connector and remove the headlight unit

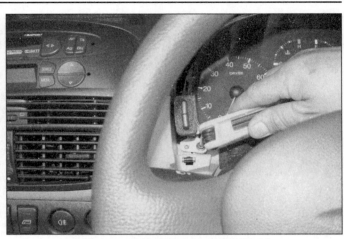

7.3a Undo the instrument panel upper retaining screw . . .

7.3b . . . and the single screw each side

Rear number plate light

8 The procedure is described as part of the bulb renewal procedure in Section 4.

High-level stop-light

9 The procedure is described as part of the bulb renewal procedure in Section 4.

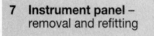

7 Instrument panel –
removal and refitting

Removal

1 Disconnect the battery negative terminal (refer to *Disconnecting the battery* in the Reference Chapter).
2 Remove the instrument panel surround from the facia as described in Chapter 11, Section 27.
3 Undo the upper screw, and the single screw each side securing the instrument panel to the facia (see illustrations).
4 Tip the instrument panel down at the top and carefully pull the it away from the facia slightly (see illustration).
5 Reach behind the panel, lift up the wiring connector locking catch and disconnect the connector (see illustration). Remove the instrument panel from the car.
6 The instrument panel cannot be dismantled and the individual components are not available separately.

Refitting

7 Refitting is a reversal of removal.

8 Headlight beam alignment –
general information

Accurate adjustment of the headlight beam is only possible using optical beam-setting equipment, and this work should therefore be carried out by a Fiat dealer or suitably-equipped workshop. Incorrectly adjusted headlamps can dazzle other drivers and cause accidents.

Certain models are equipped with a headlight aim adjustment system, operated by a switch located on the instrument panel. The system allows the aim of the headlights to be adjusted to compensate for the varying loads carried in the vehicle. The system should be positioned according to the load being carried in the vehicle as follows:

Position 0	Front seats occupied (1 or 2 people).
Position 1	Front and rear seats occupied (5 people).
Position 2	Front and rear seats occupied and luggage compartment loaded.
Position 3	Driver's seat occupied and luggage compartment fully-loaded.

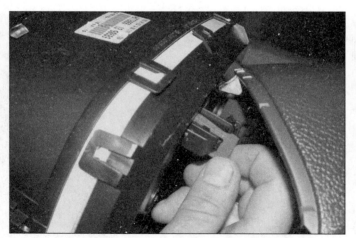

7.4 Tip the panel down at the top and pull the it away from the facia slightly

7.5 Lift up the wiring connector locking catch and disconnect the connector

9.2 Undo the bolt securing the horn mounting bracket to the front body panel

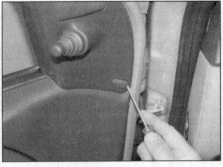

10.2a Prise out the trim cap . . .

10.2b . . . and undo the screw securing the exterior mirror inner trim panel to the front door

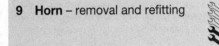

9 Horn – removal and refitting

Removal

1 The horn is located at the front right-hand side of the engine compartment.
2 Undo the bolt securing the horn mounting bracket to the front body panel (see illustration). Disconnect the wiring connectors and remove the horn and bracket.
3 Undo the securing nut and separate the horn from the bracket.

Refitting

4 Refitting is a reversal of removal.

10 Loudspeakers – removal and refitting

Removal

1 Ensure that the radio/cassette unit is switched off.

Front door tweeter speaker

2 Prise out the trim cap and undo the screw securing the exterior mirror inner trim panel (see illustrations).
3 Where a manually-adjustable exterior mirror is fitted, prise the rubber cover off the adjustment lever, then unscrew and remove

the locking collar using pointed-nose pliers (see illustrations).
4 Pull the panel from its location to disengage the retaining clips. Disconnect the loudspeaker wiring connector and lift the speaker from the panel bracket (see illustrations).

Front door main speaker

5 Carefully prise off the loudspeaker grille, then undo the three loudspeaker retaining screws (see illustrations). Withdraw the speaker from the door and disconnect the wiring connectors.

Rear parcel shelf speakers

6 Working in the luggage compartment, disconnect the wiring connector at the relevant loudspeaker.

10.3a On manually-adjustable mirrors, prise the rubber cover off the adjustment lever

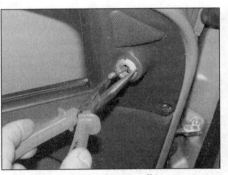

10.3b Using pointed-nose pliers, unscrew and remove the locking collar

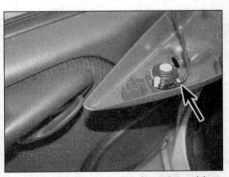

10.4a Disconnect the loudspeaker wiring connector (arrowed) . . .

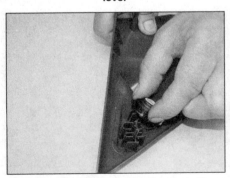

10.4b . . . and lift the speaker from the panel bracket

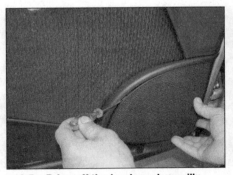

10.5a Prise off the loudspeaker grille . . .

10.5b . . . then undo the three loudspeaker retaining screws (arrowed)

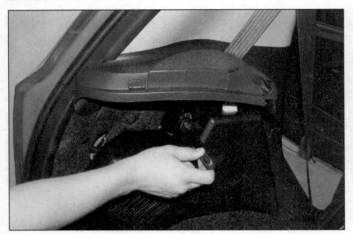

10.8 Undo the retaining screws, and remove the audio amplifier/loudspeaker unit

10.9 Undo the retaining screws and separate the two halves of the unit

7 Undo the two screws securing the loudspeaker to the parcel shelf support bracket and remove the speaker.

Sub-woofer

8 Disconnect the wiring connector, undo the retaining screws, and remove the audio amplifier/loudspeaker unit from the luggage compartment **(see illustration)**.
9 Undo the retaining screws and separate the two halves of the unit **(see illustration)**.
10 Disconnect the wiring connectors, undo the four screws and remove the speaker **(see illustration)**.

Refitting

11 Refitting is a reversal of removal.

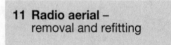

11 Radio aerial – removal and refitting

Removal

1 Using a small screwdriver, carefully prise the interior courtesy light unit from its location.
2 Undo the bolt securing the aerial base to

the roof panel. Withdraw the aerial base and disconnect the co-axial cable.

Refitting

3 Refitting is a reversal of removal, but ensure that seal between the aerial housing and the roof panel is in good condition.

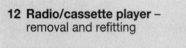

12 Radio/cassette player – removal and refitting

Note: *Once the battery has been disconnected, the radio/cassette unit cannot be re-activated until the appropriate security code has been entered. Do not remove the unit unless the appropriate code is known.*

Removal

1 Disconnect the battery negative terminal (refer to *Disconnecting the battery* in the Reference Chapter).
2 Insert the special extraction tools supplied with the vehicle into the holes on either side of the radio/cassette unit. Press them home until

10.10 Disconnect the wiring connectors, undo the screws and remove the speaker

the internal clips can be felt to release **(see illustration)**. Note that if the original extraction tools are not available, new ones can be obtained from motor accessory outlets.
3 Pull the unit from the facia, then disconnect the aerial lead and wiring connector from the rear of the unit **(see illustrations)**.

Refitting

4 Refitting is a reversal of removal, ensuring that the wiring is routed freely behind the unit.

12.2 Remove the radio/cassette player using the special extraction tools

12.3a Disconnect the aerial lead . . .

12.3b . . . and wiring connector from the rear of the unit

13.4 Slacken the clamp ring bolt (arrowed) at the rear of the stalk switch unit

13.5 Withdraw the stalk switch unit and disconnect the wiring connectors

13 Switches – removal and refitting

Steering column switches

Removal

1 Remove the steering wheel as described in Chapter 10.
2 Remove the steering column shrouds as described in Chapter 11, Section 27.
3 Remove the airbag clockspring as described in Section 20 of this Chapter.
4 Using an Allen key, slacken the clamp ring bolt at the rear of the switch unit **(see illustration)**.
5 Withdraw the stalk switch unit off the steering column and disconnect the switch wiring connectors **(see illustration)**.

Refitting

6 Refitting is a reversal of removal. Refit the airbag clockspring, steering column shrouds and steering wheel with reference to the Chapters and Sections indicated.

Facia switches

7 The switches mounted in the centre of the facia and around the instrument panel are sealed units and cannot be individually removed.
8 Removal and refitting procedures for the centre switch panel in the facia are contained in Chapter 11, Section 27; instrument panel removal and refitting procedures are given in Section 7 of this Chapter.

Stop-light switch

9 Refer to the information contained in Chapter 9.

Centre console switches

10 Carefully prise the switch control panel from the centre console.
11 Disconnect the wiring connectors from

the rear of the switches and remove the control panel. Note that the individual switches cannot be removed separately from the panel.
12 Refitting is a reversal of removal.

14 Tailgate wiper motor – removal and refitting

Removal

1 Disconnect the battery negative terminal (refer to *Disconnecting the battery* in the Reference Chapter).
2 Remove the tailgate inner trim panel as described in Chapter 11, Section 25.
3 Remove the wiper arm with reference to Section 17.
4 Working inside the tailgate, disconnect the tailgate wiper motor wiring connector.
5 Unscrew the three bolts securing the motor to the tailgate and remove the motor assembly **(see illustration)**.

Refitting

6 Refitting is a reversal of removal. Refit the wiper arm with reference to Section 17.

15 Windscreen/tailgate washer system components – removal and refitting

Washer fluid reservoir

Removal

1 Firmly apply the handbrake, then jack up the front of the car and support it securely on axle stands (see *Jacking and vehicle support*). Remove the left-hand front roadwheel.
2 Undo the retaining screws and remove the wheel arch liner.
3 From under the wheel arch undo the two reservoir retaining bolts.

4 Lower the reservoir from its location and disconnect the washer pump wiring connectors and the fluid hoses. Remove the reservoir from under the wheel arch.

Refitting

5 Refitting is a reversal of removal.

Washer pump(s)

Removal

6 Remove the washer fluid reservoir, as described in the previous sub-Section.
7 Release the spring clip, then pull the washer pump from the reservoir. Where applicable, recover the grommet.

Refitting

8 Refitting is a reversal of removal.

Windscreen washer nozzles

Removal

9 Open the bonnet.
10 Working under the bonnet, depress the securing tabs and push the relevant nozzle from the bonnet. Disconnect the fluid hose, and withdraw the nozzle.

Refitting

11 Refitting is a reversal of removal.

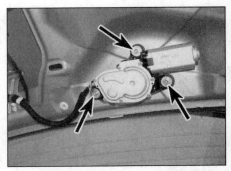

14.5 Tailgate wiper motor retaining bolts (arrowed)

16.4a Lift off the wiper motor protective cover . . .

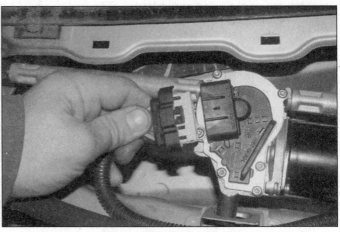

16.4b . . . and disconnect the motor wiring connector

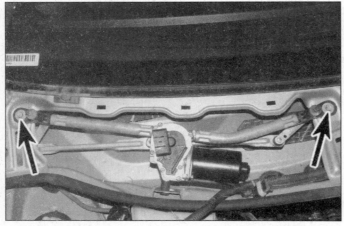

16.5a Undo the two wiper motor and linkage retaining bolts (arrowed) . . .

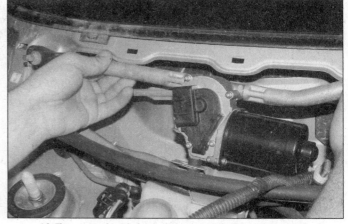

16.5b . . . and withdraw the assembly from the scuttle

Tailgate washer nozzle

Removal

12 Remove the high-level stop-light as described in Section 4.
13 Working in the tailgate aperture behind the high-level stop-light, disconnect the washer fluid hose from the nozzle.
14 Depress the securing tabs and push the nozzle from the tailgate.

Refitting

15 Refitting is a reversal of removal.

16 Windscreen wiper motor and linkage – removal and refitting

Removal

1 Disconnect the battery negative terminal (refer to *Disconnecting the battery* in the Reference Chapter).
2 Refer to Section 17 and remove both wiper arms.

3 Remove the windscreen scuttle grille panel as described in Chapter 11, Section 22.
4 Lift off the wiper motor protective cover and disconnect the motor wiring connector **(see illustrations)**.
5 Undo the two wiper motor and linkage retaining bolts and withdraw the assembly from the scuttle **(see illustrations)**.

Refitting

6 Refitting is a reversal of removal.

17 Wiper arm – removal and refitting

Removal

1 Operate the wiper motor, then switch it off so that the wiper arm returns to the at-rest/parked position.
2 Stick a length of masking tape on the glass below the edge of the wiper blade, to use as an alignment aid on refitting.

3 Prise off the wiper arm spindle nut cover, then slacken and remove the spindle nut **(see illustration)**.
4 Lift the blade off the glass, and pull the wiper arm off its spindle. If necessary, the arm can be carefully levered off the spindle using a suitable flat-bladed screwdriver. If both windscreen wiper arms are removed, note

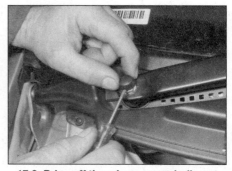

17.3 Prise off the wiper arm spindle nut cover, then slacken and remove the spindle nut

their locations, as different arms are fitted to the driver's and passenger's sides.

Refitting

5 Ensure that the wiper arm and spindle splines are clean and dry.

6 When refitting a wiper arm, refit the arm to the spindle, aligning the wiper blade with the tape fitted before removal. If both windscreen wiper arms have been removed, ensure that the arms are refitted to their correct positions as noted before removal.

7 Refit the spindle nut, tighten it securely, and refit the nut cover.

18 Anti-theft system and engine immobiliser – general information

All models in the range are equipped as standard with a central locking system incorporating an electronic engine immobiliser function.

The electronic engine immobiliser is operated by a transponder fitted to the ignition key, in conjunction with an analogue module fitted around the ignition switch.

When the ignition key is inserted in the switch and turned to the ignition 'on' position, the control module sends a preprogrammed recognition code signal to the module on the ignition switch. If the recognition code signal matches that of the transponder on the ignition key, an unlocking request signal is sent to the engine management ECU allowing the engine to be started. If the ignition key signal is not recognised, the engine management system remains immobilised.

When the ignition is switched off, a locking signal is sent to the ECU and the engine is immobilised until the unlocking request signal is again received.

19 Airbag system – general information, precautions and system de-activation

General information

A driver's airbag is fitted as standard on all models, with passenger's airbag, side airbags, and side window airbags available as optional equipment on most models. The driver's airbag is located in the steering wheel centre pad and the passenger's airbag is located above the glovebox in the facia. The side airbags are located in the front seat backs, and the side window airbags are located in the roof headlining on both sides of the car. In addition, pyrotechnic seat belt pretensioners are fitted to the inertia reels of the front seat belts.

The airbag and seat belt pyrotechnic safety systems are armed only when the ignition is switched on, however, a reserve power source maintains a power supply to the systems in the event of a break in the main electrical supply. The airbags are activated by a 'g' sensor (deceleration sensor), and controlled by an electronic control unit located under the centre of the facia. The side airbags and side window airbags are activated by severe side impact and operate in conjunction with the main system. The pyrotechnic seat belt pretensioners operate independently of the main system.

The airbags are inflated by a gas generator, which forces the bag out from its location in the steering wheel, facia, seat back frame or roof headlining.

Precautions

 Warning: The following precautions must be observed when working on vehicles equipped with an airbag system, to prevent the possibility of personal injury. Many of the precautions are equally applicable to the pyrotechnic seat belt pretensioners and should be similarly observed.

General

The following precautions **must** be observed when carrying out work on a vehicle equipped with an airbag:

a) *Do not disconnect the battery with the engine running.*

b) *Before carrying out any work in the vicinity of the airbag, removal of any of the airbag components, or any welding work on the vehicle, de-activate the system as described in the following sub-Section.*

c) *Do not attempt to test any of the airbag system circuits using test meters or any other test equipment.*

d) *If the airbag warning light comes on, or any fault in the system is suspected, consult a Fiat dealer without delay. Do not attempt to carry out fault diagnosis, or any dismantling of the components.*

When handling an airbag

a) *Transport the airbag by itself, bag upward.*

b) *Do not put your arms around the airbag.*

c) *Carry the airbag close to the body, bag outward.*

d) *Do not drop the airbag or expose it to impacts.*

e) *Do not attempt to dismantle the airbag unit.*

f) *Do not connect any form of electrical equipment to any part of the airbag circuit.*

When storing an airbag unit

a) *Store the unit in a cupboard with the airbag upward.*

b) *Do not expose the airbag to temperatures above 80°C.*

c) *Do not expose the airbag to flames.*

d) *Do not attempt to dispose of the airbag – consult a Fiat dealer.*

e) *Never refit an airbag which is known to be faulty or damaged.*

De-activation of airbag system

The system must be de-activated before carrying out any work on the airbag components or surrounding area:

a) *Switch on the ignition and check the operation of the airbag warning light on the instrument panel. The light should illuminate when the ignition is switched on, then extinguish.*

b) *Switch off the ignition.*

c) *Remove the ignition key.*

d) *Switch off all electrical equipment.*

e) *Disconnect the battery negative terminal (refer to Disconnecting the battery in the Reference Chapter).*

f) *Insulate the battery negative terminal and the end of the battery negative lead to prevent any possibility of contact.*

g) *Wait for at least ten minutes before carrying out any further work.*

Activation of airbag system

To activate the system on completion of any work, proceed as follows:

a) *Ensure that there are no occupants in the vehicle, and that there are no loose objects around the vicinity of the steering wheel. Close the vehicle doors and windows.*

b) *Ensure that the ignition is switched off then reconnect the battery negative terminal.*

c) *Open the driver's door and switch on the ignition, without reaching in front of the steering wheel. Check that the airbag warning light illuminates briefly then extinguishes.*

d) *Switch off the ignition.*

e) *If the airbag warning light does not operate as described in paragraph c), consult a Fiat dealer before driving the vehicle.*

20 Airbag system components – removal and refitting

 Warning: Refer to the precautions given in Section 19 before attempting to carry out work on any of the airbag components. Any suspected faults with the airbag system should be referred to a Fiat dealer – under no circumstances attempt to carry out any work other than removal and refitting of the front airbag unit(s) and/or the airbag clockspring, as described in the following paragraphs.

Electronic control unit

1 The airbag ECU is located under the centre of the facia and is accessible after removal of the lower centre side vent panels beneath the facia.

20.5 Lift the airbag unit from the steering wheel and disconnect the wiring connector

20.12 Disconnect the wiring connector from the top of the airbag clockspring

Driver's airbag unit

Removal

2 De-activate the airbag system as described in Section 19.

3 Turn the steering wheel as necessary for access to the airbag retaining bolts at the rear of the wheel.

4 Undo the three airbag retaining bolts.

5 Carefully lift the airbag unit from the steering wheel and disconnect the wiring connector **(see illustration)**.

6 If the airbag unit is to be stored for any length of time, refer to the storage precautions given in Section 19.

Refitting

7 Refitting is a reversal of removal, bearing in mind the following points:

a) *Do not strike the airbag unit, or expose it to impacts during refitting.*

b) *On completion of refitting, activate the airbag system as described in Section 19.*

Airbag clockspring

Removal

8 Remove the driver's airbag unit, as described previously in this Section.

9 Remove the steering wheel as described in Chapter 10.

10 Remove the steering column shrouds as described in Chapter 11, Section 27.

11 Check that the centre position indicator window on the outer moving portion of the airbag clock spring is centred over the red indicator tab on the fixed portion. If not already done, it is advisable to secure the moving and fixed portions of the clock spring together using tape to prevent rotation with the steering wheel removed.

12 Disconnect the wiring connector from the top of the clockspring **(see illustration)**.

13 Unscrew the three securing screws, and withdraw the clockspring from the steering column **(see illustrations)**.

Refitting

14 Refitting is a reversal of removal, bearing in mind the following points:

a) *Ensure that the centre position indicator window on the outer moving portion of the clockspring is centred over the red indicator tab on the fixed portion.*

b) *Ensure that the roadwheels are in the straight-ahead position before refitting the clockspring and steering wheel.*

c) *Refit the steering wheel as described in Chapter 10, and refit the airbag unit as described previously in this Section.*

Passenger's airbag unit

Removal

15 The passenger's airbag is fitted to the upper part of the facia, above the glovebox.

16 De-activate the airbag system as described in Section 19.

17 Remove the glovebox as described in Chapter 11, Section 27.

20.13a Unscrew the three securing screws . . .

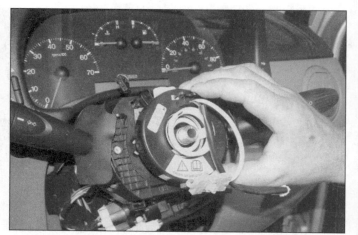

20.13b . . . and withdraw the clockspring from the steering column

20.18a Prise out the passenger's airbag immobiliser switch from the facia . . .

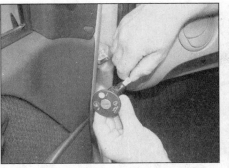

20.18b . . . and disconnect the switch wiring connector

20.19 Undo the bolts (arrowed) securing the airbag assembly to the facia rail

18 Carefully prise out the immobiliser switch from the side of the facia and disconnect the switch wiring connector **(see illustrations)**.

19 Working in the glovebox aperture, undo the bolts securing the airbag assembly to the facia support rail **(see illustration)**. Carefully withdraw the airbag from the facia and disconnect the wiring connector.

20 If the airbag unit is to be stored for any length of time, refer to the storage precautions given in Section 19.

Refitting

21 Refitting is a reversal of removal, bearing in mind the following points:
  a) *Do not strike the airbag unit, or expose it to impacts during refitting.*
  b) *On completion of refitting, activate the airbag system as described in Section 19.*

Side and side window airbags

22 The side, and side window, airbags are located respectively within the front seat backs and roof headlining, and no attempt should be made to remove them. Any suspected problems with the side airbag system should be referred to a Fiat dealer.

---

21 Towbar electrical socket – installation and wiring connection

General information

1 Refer to Chapter 11 for towbar installation details (specifically detailing the installation of a Witter towbar).

2 Although the following information depicts the installation and connection of a specific make of electrical socket, the procedures can be used as a general guide for all installations.

3 Prior to starting, read through the entire procedure to familiarise yourself with the work involved and ensure that all necessary tools and equipment are available.

4 Check that all rear lights are working correctly prior to installation, then ensure that all electrical circuits are switched off.

Materials

5 Unpack the installation kit and check that all the following parts are contained:
  a) *Pre-wired electrical socket.*

  b) *Socket mounting plate.*
  c) *Audible warning unit.*
  d) *Cable snap connectors.*

Socket installation

6 Remove the rear bumper as described in Chapter 11.

7 If the towbar is not fitted with an electrical socket mounting plate, fit the plate supplied with the kit, using the existing towbar mounting bolts.

8 Where a mounting plate is incorporated in the towbar, locate the electrical socket on the mounting plate, insert the screws and secure with the retaining nuts **(see illustrations)**.

9 From within the luggage compartment, extract the rubber grommet for the number plate wiring harness from the inner body panel.

10 Feed the socket wiring loom up through the outer hole in the body rear panel, then through the inner hole and into the luggage compartment **(see illustration overleaf)**.

11 Suitably enlarge the hole in the rubber grommet using a sharp knife, or by careful use of a drill. Take care not to damage the number

21.8a Locate the electrical socket on the mounting plate and insert the retaining screws . . .

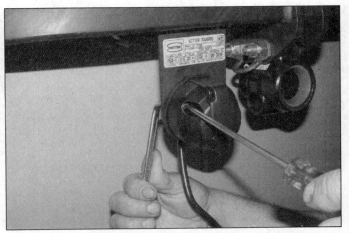

21.8b . . . then secure the screws with the retaining nuts

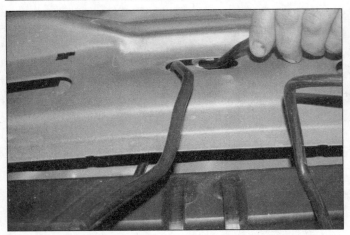

21.10 Feed the socket wiring loom through the hole in the body rear panel into the luggage compartment

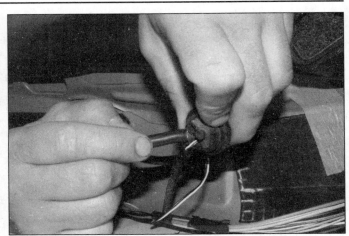

21.12 Insert the wiring loom through the rubber grommet

plate wiring harness insulation when enlarging the hole.

12 Feed the electrical socket wiring loom through the rubber grommet and into the left-hand side of the luggage compartment **(see illustration)**. Refit the grommet to its location, then refit the rear bumper as described in Chapter 11.

Wiring connections

Note: *All Punto models have bulb failure monitoring. If a tow bar is wired without including a "smart" relay the failure warning light will be illuminated when the trailer is connected.*

13 The electrical socket pin connections, wiring cable colours and vehicle connections are as follows:

Towbar electrical socket	Cable colour	Vehicle connection
Pin 1	Yellow	Yellow of audible warning unit.
Pin 2	Blue	Rear foglight wiring in vehicle harness.
Pin 3	White	Earth connection.
Pin 4	Green	Green of audible warning unit.
Pin 5	Brown	Right-hand tail lights in vehicle wiring harness.
Pin 6	Red	Stop-lights in vehicle wiring harness.
Pin 7	Black	Left-hand tail lights in vehicle wiring harness.

14 The audible warning unit wiring cable colours and vehicle connections are as follows:

Wire colour	Vehicle connection
Orange	Left-hand direction indicator in vehicle wiring harness.
Slate	Right-hand direction indicator in vehicle wiring harness.
Black	Earth connection.
Green	To pin 4 of towbar electrical socket.
Yellow	To pin 1 of towbar electrical socket.

15 Using a sharp knife, carefully cut off approximately 150 mm of the black cable sheath from the end of the electrical socket wiring loom **(see illustrations)**. Take great care not to cut through the insulation of the wires inside.

16 Strip off approximately 10 mm of insulation from the end of the audible warning unit and towbar socket yellow wires.

17 Connect the two yellow wires together using an in-line connector and crimp the connector securely using a crimping tool **(see illustrations)**.

18 Repeat paragraphs 16 and 17 to connect the two green wires together.

19 Strip off the insulation from the end of the towbar socket white (earth) wire, and the audible warning unit black (earth) wire. Join the two wires together using a tag connector and securely crimp the connector **(see illustration)**.

20 Undo the nut securing the vehicle wiring junction box to the rear body panel on the left-hand side. Slide the tag connector with the two earth wires over the stud and secure with the retaining nut **(see illustrations)**.

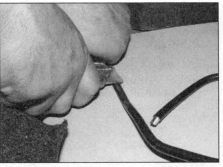

21.15a Cut the socket wiring cable sheath approximately 150 mm from the end . . .

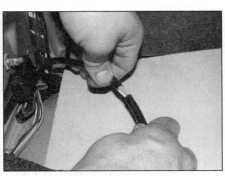

21.15b . . . then remove the cut portion from the loom

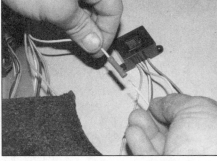

21.17a Connect the two yellow wires together using an in-line connector . . .

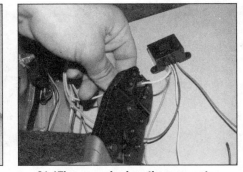

21.17b . . . and crimp the connector securely using a crimping tool

21.19 Join the two earth wires together using a tag connector

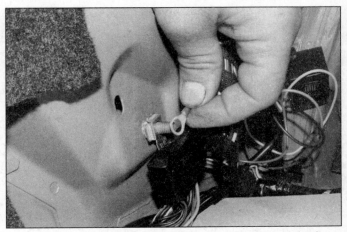

21.20a Slide the earth wire tag connector over the junction box mounting stud . . .

21 Remove the rear light cluster on the left-hand side as described in Section 6.

22 Trace the vehicle wiring harness back from the rear light cluster to the lower left-hand corner of the luggage compartment. Peel back the outer covering of the harness sufficiently to attach the cable snap connectors to the relevant wires in the harness.

23 Using the wiring diagrams at the end of this Chapter, and with reference to the rear light cluster bulbholder and wiring connector, identify the supply wire for the left-hand rear direction indicator bulb.

24 Using a snap connector, connect the orange wire of the audible warning unit to the direction indicator supply wire **(see illustration)**.

25 Continue this procedure to connect the towbar socket red and black wires to the left-hand stop-light and tail light supply wires respectively.

26 To connect the remaining wires from the towbar socket and audible warning unit, remove the rear light cluster on the right-hand side.

27 Trace the vehicle wiring harness from the right-hand rear light cluster back towards the left-hand side of the car. Identify the relevant wires in the harness and make the connections using the same procedure as for the left-hand side wiring.

28 When all the connections have been made, attach the audible warning unit to the rear body panel (or a similar location) using foam adhesive pads or similar **(see illustration)**.

29 Check that all connections have been securely made then neatly arrange the wiring. If necessary, use insulation tape to bind the new wiring to the vehicle harness.

30 Refit the rear light clusters and check the operation of the towbar socket and audible warning unit. The trailer direction indicator lights should flash in unison with those on the car, and the audible warning unit should buzz. If the audible warning unit does not buzz, this indicates a bulb failure on the trailer.

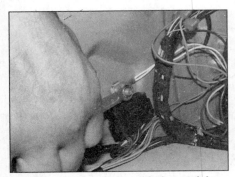

21.20b . . . and secure with the retaining nut

21.24 Connect the towbar socket and audible warning unit wiring to the vehicle harness using snap connectors

21.28 Attach the audible warning unit to a suitable place on the rear body panel

Punto wiring diagrams

Diagram 1

Key to symbols

Bulb	⊗
Flashing bulb	⊗
Switch	
Multiple contact switch (ganged)	
Fuse/fusible link and current rating	F5 30A
Resistor	
Variable resistor	
Variable resistor	
Wire splice or soldered joint	
Connecting wires	

Item no.	**2**
Single speed pump/motor	M
Twin speed pump/motor	M
Gauge/meter	
Earth point	
Diode	
Light emitting diode (LED)	
Solenoid actuator	
Heating element	

Wire colour
(brown with black tracer) ▬▬ M/N ▬▬

Screened cable

Dashed outline denotes part of a
larger item, containing in this case
an electronic or solid state device.
e.g. connector A, pin 2.

Key to circuits

Diagram 1	Information for wiring diagrams.
Diagram 2	Starting, charging, engine cooling fan, horn, electric power steering.
Diagram 3	Side, tail & number plate lights, headlights.
Diagram 4	Stop & reversing lights, direction indicators & hazard warning lights, front & rear fog lights.
Diagram 5	Cigar lighter & accessory socket, electric sunroof, electric mirrors, heated rear window.
Diagram 6	Wash/wipe.
Diagram 7	Instrument cluster.
Diagram 8	Interior lighting, heater blower (without A/C), safety restraint system, audio system (low spec).
Diagram 9	Audio system (high spec), air conditioning.
Diagram 10	Central locking, electric windows, ABS.

Earth locations

E1	At battery terminal
E2	LH inner wing
E3	LH inner wing
E4	LH inner wing
E5	RH footwell
E6	LH side of luggage compartment
E7	On gearbox
E8	LH inner wing

Fuses

Fuse	Rating	Circuit protected
F1	60A	Maxi fuse, dashboard power: standard functions
F2	40A	Maxi fuse, dashboard power: optional functions
F3	20A	Maxi fuse, ignition switch
F4	50A	Maxi fuse, ABS power
F5	60A	Maxi fuse, electric power steering
F6	30A	Maxi fuse, low speed engine cooling fan
F7	50A	Maxi fuse, high speed engine cooling fan
F8	30A	Heater blower
F9	20A	Headlight washer
F10	15A	Horn
F11	10A	Glow plug control unit, tachometer, canister purge solenoid, lambda sensor
F12	10A	RH dip beam headlight
F13	10A	LH dip beam headlight, headlight levelling
F14	10A	RH main beam headlight
F15	10A	LH main beam headlight
F16	7.5A	Engine management control unit, engine cooling system relay
F17	7.5A	Engine management control unit, fuel pump solenoid valve unit
F18	7.5A	Engine management control unit
F19	7.5A	Air conditioning compressor
F20	20A	Heated Diesel fuel filter
F21	15A	Engine stop solenoid (Diesel), fuel pump
F22	20A	Fuel injectors, fuel pump, ignition coils
F23	10A	Automatic transmission control unit
F30	15A	Fog lights
F31	7.5A	Air conditioning, reversing light, heater blower fan relay
F32	15A	Lighting system
F35	10A	Electric power steering, automatic transmission
F36	15A	Subwoofer
F37	10A	Instrument cluster, brake lights
F38	20A	Central locking
F39	10A	Luggage compartment light, interior light, audio system, diagnostic socket
F40	30A	Heated rear window
F41	7.5A	Heated mirrors
F42	7.5A	ABS control unit
F43	30A	Wash/wipe
F44	20A	Cigar lighter
F45	15A	Heated seats
F46	15A	Sunroof
F47	20A	LH electric window
F48	20A	RH electric window
F49	7.5A	Audio system, instrument cluster, electric mirrors
F50	7.5A	Airbag
F51	7.5A	Instrument panel illumination, number plate lights
F52	15A	Rear window wiper
F53	10A	Hazard warning lights, direction indicators, instrument cluster
F54	60A	Maxi fuse, glow plug system
F55	7.5A	Automatic transmission

Engine fusebox

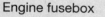

Passenger fusebox

H32814

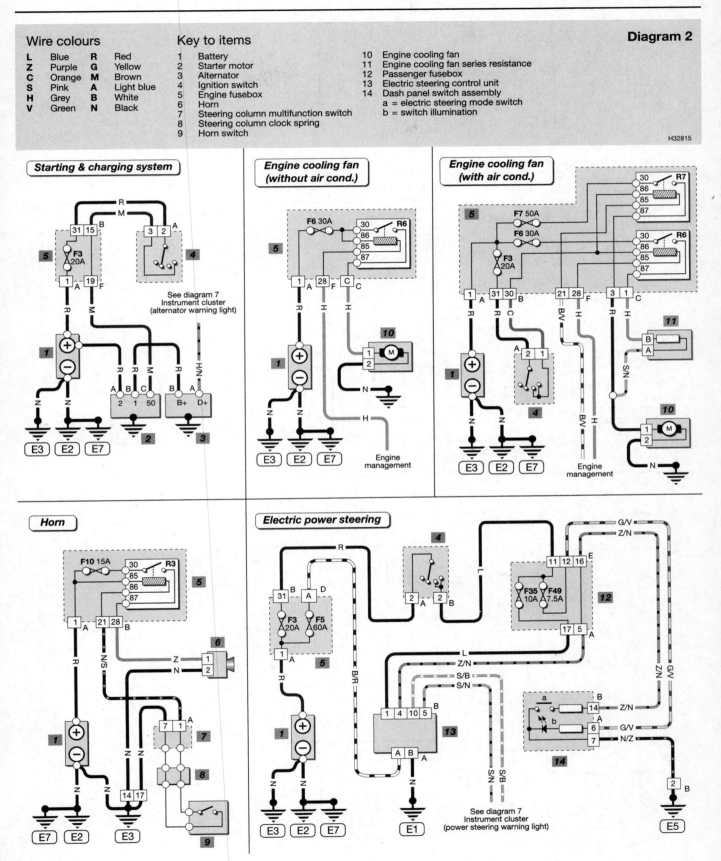

Diagram 2

Wire colours
L	Blue	R	Red
Z	Purple	G	Yellow
C	Orange	M	Brown
S	Pink	A	Light blue
H	Grey	B	White
V	Green	N	Black

Key to items
1 Battery
2 Starter motor
3 Alternator
4 Ignition switch
5 Engine fusebox
6 Horn
7 Steering column multifunction switch
8 Steering column clock spring
9 Horn switch
10 Engine cooling fan
11 Engine cooling fan series resistance
12 Passenger fusebox
13 Electric steering control unit
14 Dash panel switch assembly
a = electric steering mode switch
b = switch illumination

H32815

Starting & charging system

See diagram 7
Instrument cluster
(alternator warning light)

Engine cooling fan (without air cond.)

Engine cooling fan (with air cond.)

Engine management

Engine management

Horn

Electric power steering

See diagram 7
Instrument cluster
(power steering warning light)

Wire colours

L	Blue	**R**	Red
Z	Purple	**G**	Yellow
C	Orange	**M**	Brown
S	Pink	**A**	Light blue
H	Grey	**B**	White
V	Green	**N**	Black

Key to items

1   Battery
4   Ignition switch
5   Engine fusebox
7   Steering column multifunction switch
   a = side/headlight switch
   b = dip/main beam switch
   c = headlight flasher switch
12 Passenger fusebox

17 Multi-timer unit
18 LH headlight unit
   a = sidelight
   b = dip/main beam
19 RH headlight unit
   a =sidelight
   b = dip/main beam

20 LH rear light unit
   a = tail light
21 RH rear light unit
   a = tail light
22 Number plate light

Diagram 3

H32816

Side, tail & number plate lights

Headlights

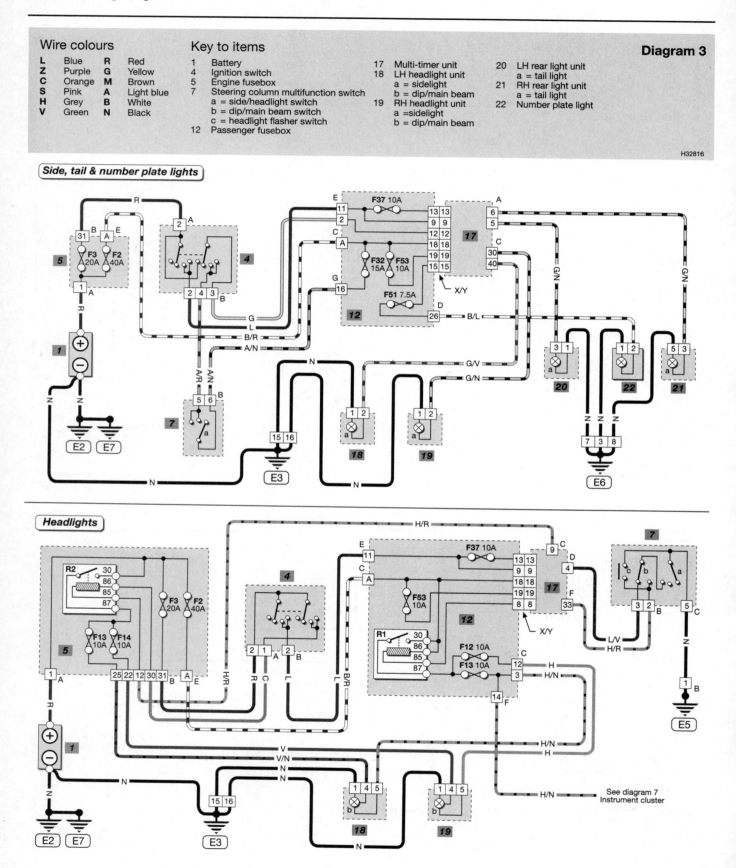

See diagram 7
Instrument cluster

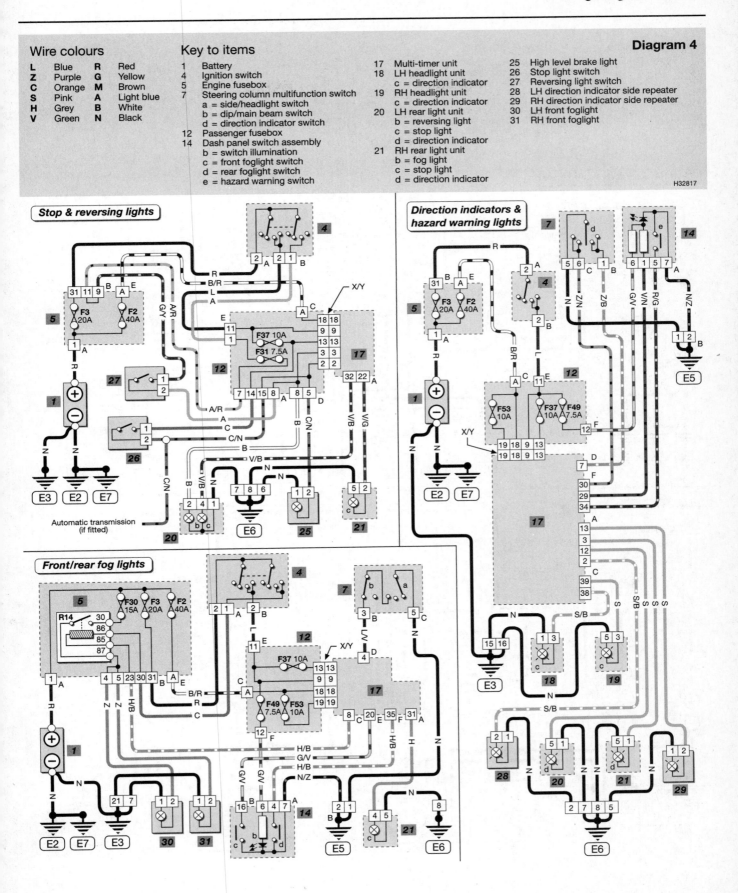

Wire colours

L	Blue	R	Red
Z	Purple	G	Yellow
C	Orange	M	Brown
S	Pink	A	Light blue
H	Grey	B	White
V	Green	N	Black

Key to items

1   Battery
4   Ignition switch
5   Engine fusebox
7   Steering column multifunction switch
    a = side/headlight switch
    b = dip/main beam switch
    d = direction indicator switch
12   Passenger fusebox
14   Dash panel switch assembly
    b = switch illumination
    c = front foglight switch
    d = rear foglight switch
    e = hazard warning switch

17   Multi-timer unit
18   LH headlight unit
    c = direction indicator
19   RH headlight unit
    c = direction indicator
20   LH rear light unit
    b = reversing light
    c = stop light
    d = direction indicator
21   RH rear light unit
    b = fog light
    c = stop light
    d = direction indicator

25   High level brake light
26   Stop light switch
27   Reversing light switch
28   LH direction indicator side repeater
29   RH direction indicator side repeater
30   LH front foglight
31   RH front foglight

Diagram 4

H32817

Stop & reversing lights

Direction indicators & hazard warning lights

Front/rear fog lights

Wire colours

L	Blue	R	Red
Z	Purple	G	Yellow
C	Orange	M	Brown
S	Pink	A	Light blue
H	Grey	B	White
V	Green	N	Black

Key to items

1 Battery
4 Ignition switch
5 Engine fusebox
7 Steering column multifunction switch
  a = side/headlight switch
12 Passenger fusebox
14 Dash panel switch assembly
  b = switch illumination
  f = heated rear window/mirror switch

17 Multi-timer unit
33 Cigar lighter/accessory socket
34 Sunroof assembly
35 LH mirror assembly
36 RH mirror assembly
37 Mirror control switch
38 Heated rear window

Diagram 5

H32818

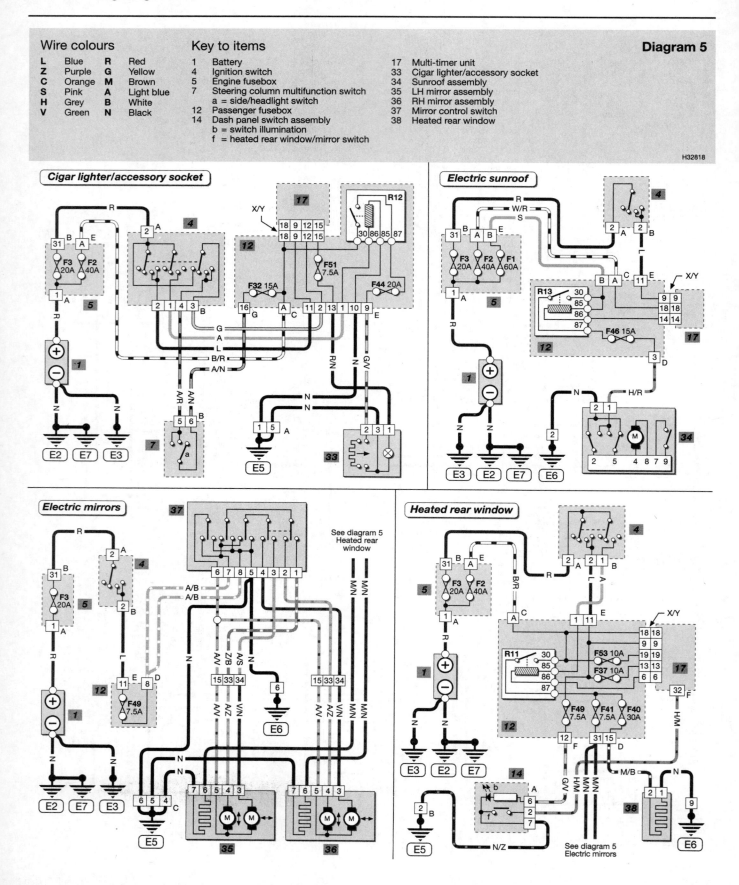

Cigar lighter/accessory socket

Electric sunroof

Electric mirrors

Heated rear window

Wire colours

L	Blue	**R**	Red
Z	Purple	**G**	Yellow
C	Orange	**M**	Brown
S	Pink	**A**	Light blue
H	Grey	**B**	White
V	Green	**N**	Black

Key to items

1   Battery
4   Ignition switch
5   Engine fusebox
7   Steering column multifunction switch
   a = side/headlight switch
   e = washer switch
   f = front wiper switch
   g = rear wiper switch
12 Passenger fusebox

17 Multi-timer unit
45 Front/rear washer pump
46 Headlight washer pump
47 Front wiper motor
48 Rear wiper motor

Diagram 6

H32819

Wash/wipe

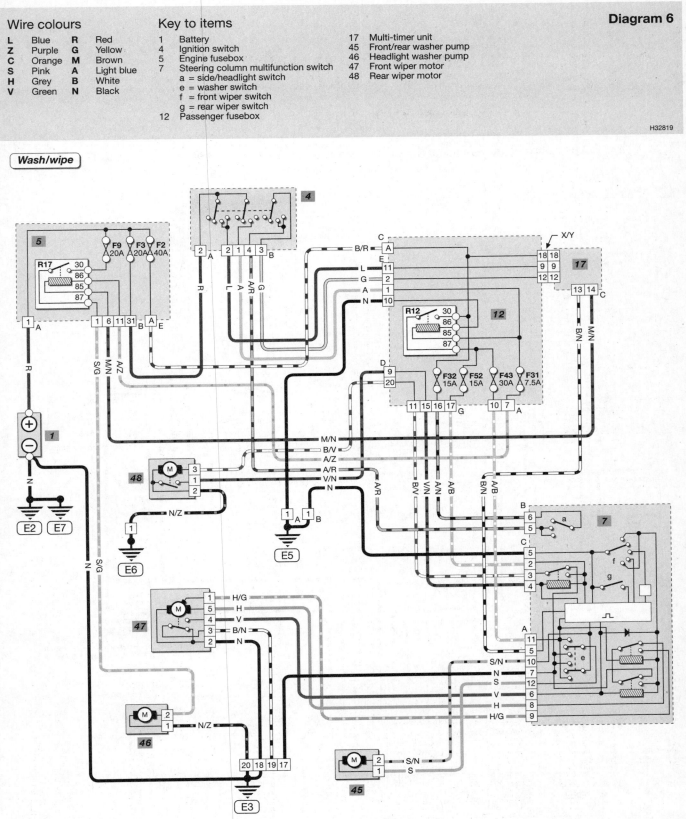

Wire colours

L	Blue	**R**	Red
Z	Purple	**G**	Yellow
C	Orange	**M**	Brown
S	Pink	**A**	Light blue
H	Grey	**B**	White
V	Green	**N**	Black

Key to items

1 Battery
4 Ignition switch
5 Engine fusebox
12 Passenger fusebox
17 Multi-timer unit
50 Handbrake switch
51 Low brake fluid switch
52 Fuel gauge sender/fuel pump
53 Instrument cluster
  a = tachometer
  b = speedometer
  c = coolant temp. gauge
  d = high temperature warning light

e = fuel gauge
f = low fuel warning light
g = passenger airbag disabled
h = airbag fault warning light
i = digital display
j = handbrake/brake warning light
k = low oil pressure warning light
l = alternator warning light
m = engine management warning light
n = sidelight warning light
o = main beam warning light
p = direction indicator warning light
q = rear foglight warning light

r = heated rear window warning light
s = CODE warning light
t = front foglight warning light
u = alarm warning light
v = ABS warning light
w = power steering function warning light
x = power steering failure warning light
y = door ajar warning light
z = bulb failure warning light
a1= instrument illumination

Diagram 7

H32820

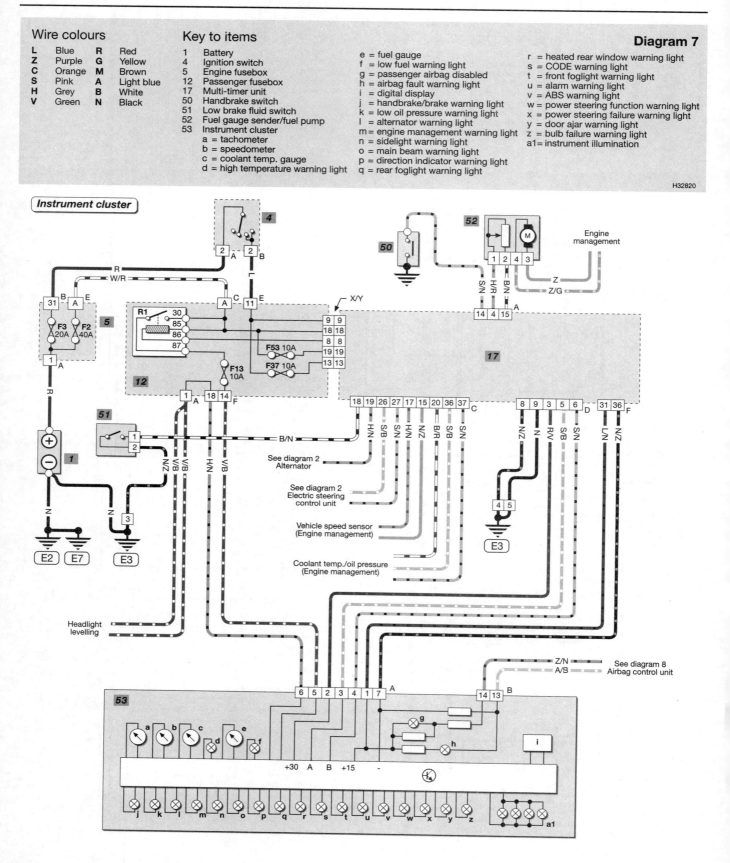

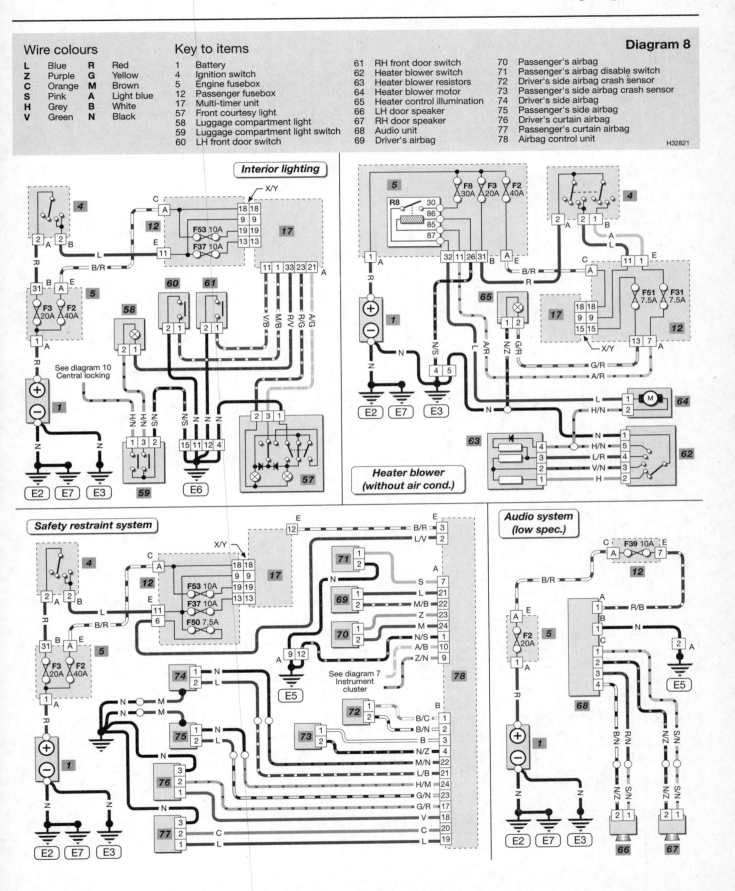

Wire colours

L	Blue	**R**	Red
Z	Purple	**G**	Yellow
C	Orange	**M**	Brown
S	Pink	**A**	Light blue
H	Grey	**B**	White
V	Green	**N**	Black

Key to items

1 Battery
4 Ignition switch
5 Engine fusebox
12 Passenger fusebox
17 Multi-timer unit
57 Front courtesy light
58 Luggage compartment light
59 Luggage compartment light switch
60 LH front door switch

61 RH front door switch
62 Heater blower switch
63 Heater blower resistors
64 Heater blower motor
65 Heater control illumination
66 LH door speaker
67 RH door speaker
68 Audio unit
69 Driver's airbag

70 Passenger's airbag
71 Passenger's airbag disable switch
72 Driver's side airbag crash sensor
73 Passenger's side airbag crash sensor
74 Driver's side airbag
75 Passenger's side airbag
76 Driver's curtain airbag
77 Passenger's curtain airbag
78 Airbag control unit

Diagram 8

H32821

Interior lighting

Heater blower (without air cond.)

Safety restraint system

Audio system (low spec.)

Wire colours

L	Blue	R	Red
Z	Purple	G	Yellow
C	Orange	M	Brown
S	Pink	A	Light blue
H	Grey	B	White
V	Green	N	Black

Key to items

1	Battery
4	Ignition switch
5	Engine fusebox
12	Passenger fusebox
17	Multi-timer unit
62	Heater blower switch/AC switch
63	Heater blower resistors
64	Heater blower motor
65	Heater control illumination
80	Connector block
81	Subwoofer
82	Electric aerial
83	LH front tweeter
84	RH front tweeter
85	LH rear speaker
86	RH rear speaker
88	LH door speaker
89	RH door speaker
90	Audio unit
91	Pressure switch
92	Thermostat
93	Compressor clutch

Diagram 9

H32822

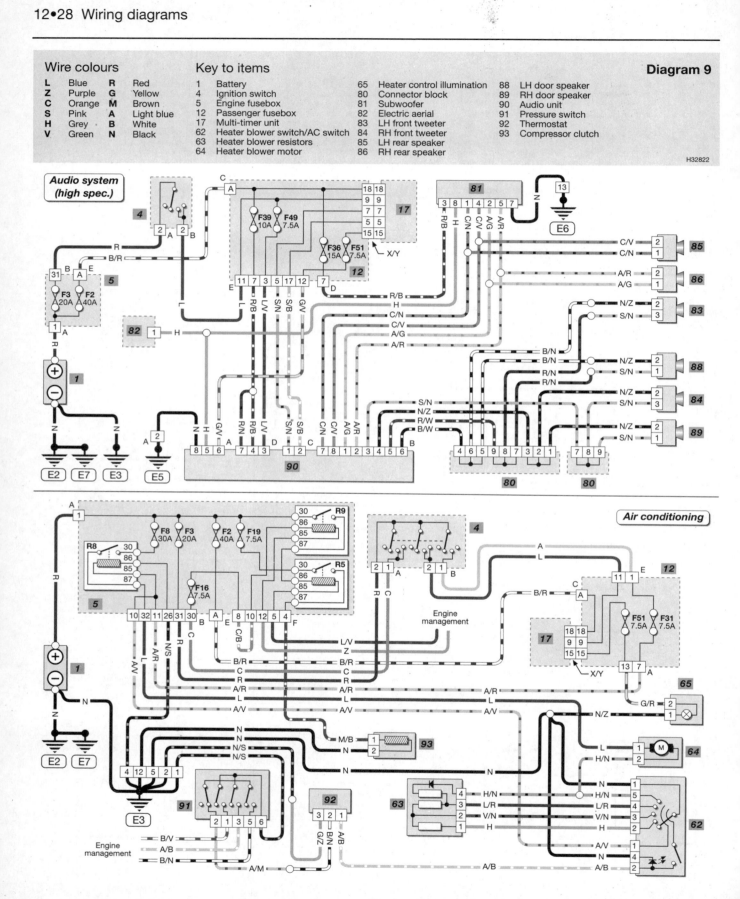

Audio system (high spec.)

Air conditioning

Wire colours

L	Blue	**R**	Red
Z	Purple	**G**	Yellow
C	Orange	**M**	Brown
S	Pink	**A**	Light blue
H	Grey	**B**	White
V	Green	**N**	Black

Key to items

1   Battery
4   Ignition switch
5   Engine fusebox
12 Passenger fusebox
14 Dash panel switch assembly
    b = switch illumination
    g = electric window switch
17 Multi-timer unit

26 Stop light switch
80 Connector block
95 LH front locking motor
96 LH rear locking motor
97 RH front locking motor
98 RH rear locking motor
99 LH electric window motor
100 RH electric window motor

101 ABS control unit
102 LH front wheel sensor
103 LH rear wheel sensor
104 RH front wheel sensor
105 RH rear wheel sensor

Diagram 10

H32823

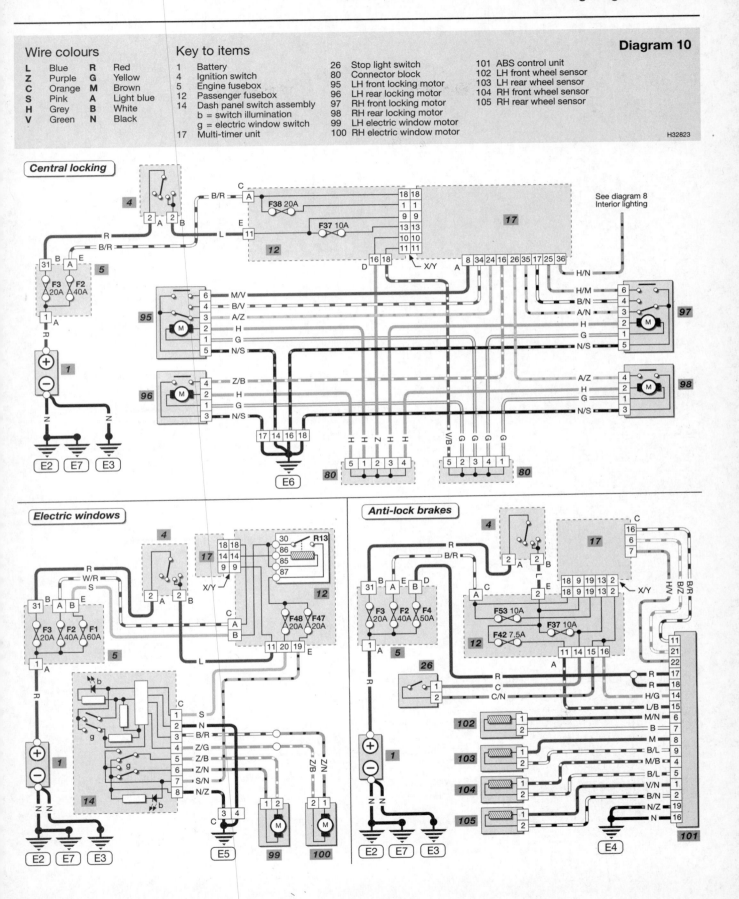

Central locking

See diagram 8
Interior lighting

Electric windows

Anti-lock brakes

Notes

Dimensions and weights

Note: *All figures are approximate, and may vary according to model. Refer to manufacturer's data for exact figures.*

Dimensions

Overall length	3835 mm
Overall width (excluding mirrors)	1660 mm
Overall height (unladen)	1480 mm
Wheelbase	2460 mm
Front track	1398 mm
Rear track	1392 mm

Weights

Kerb weight*	860 to 975 kg
Maximum gross vehicle weight*	1370 to 1485 kg
Maximum roof rack load	75 kg
Maximum towing weight*:	
Braked trailer	1000 kg
Unbraked trailer	400 kg
Maximum trailer nose weight (braked trailer)	60 kg

Depending on model and specification.

Length (distance)

Inches (in)	x 25.4	= Millimetres (mm)	x 0.0394	=	Inches (in)
Feet (ft)	x 0.305	= Metres (m)	x 3.281	=	Feet (ft)
Miles	x 1.609	= Kilometres (km)	x 0.621	=	Miles

Volume (capacity)

Cubic inches (cu in; in³)	x 16.387	= Cubic centimetres (cc; cm³)	x 0.061	=	Cubic inches (cu in; in³)
Imperial pints (Imp pt)	x 0.568	= Litres (l)	x 1.76	=	Imperial pints (Imp pt)
Imperial quarts (Imp qt)	x 1.137	= Litres (l)	x 0.88	=	Imperial quarts (Imp qt)
Imperial quarts (Imp qt)	x 1.201	= US quarts (US qt)	x 0.833	=	Imperial quarts (Imp qt)
US quarts (US qt)	x 0.946	= Litres (l)	x 1.057	=	US quarts (US qt)
Imperial gallons (Imp gal)	x 4.546	= Litres (l)	x 0.22	=	Imperial gallons (Imp gal)
Imperial gallons (Imp gal)	x 1.201	= US gallons (US gal)	x 0.833	=	Imperial gallons (Imp gal)
US gallons (US gal)	x 3.785	= Litres (l)	x 0.264	=	US gallons (US gal)

Mass (weight)

Ounces (oz)	x 28.35	= Grams (g)	x 0.035	=	Ounces (oz)
Pounds (lb)	x 0.454	= Kilograms (kg)	x 2.205	=	Pounds (lb)

Force

Ounces-force (ozf; oz)	x 0.278	= Newtons (N)	x 3.6	=	Ounces-force (ozf; oz)
Pounds-force (lbf; lb)	x 4.448	= Newtons (N)	x 0.225	=	Pounds-force (lbf; lb)
Newtons (N)	x 0.1	= Kilograms-force (kgf; kg)	x 9.81	=	Newtons (N)

Pressure

Pounds-force per square inch (psi; lbf/in²; lb/in²)	x 0.070	= Kilograms-force per square centimetre (kgf/cm²; kg/cm²)	x 14.223	=	Pounds-force per square inch (psi; lbf/in²; lb/in²)
Pounds-force per square inch (psi; lbf/in²; lb/in²)	x 0.068	= Atmospheres (atm)	x 14.696	=	Pounds-force per square inch (psi; lbf/in²; lb/in²)
Pounds-force per square inch (psi; lbf/in²; lb/in²)	x 0.069	= Bars	x 14.5	=	Pounds-force per square inch (psi; lbf/in²; lb/in²)
Pounds-force per square inch (psi; lbf/in²; lb/in²)	x 6.895	= Kilopascals (kPa)	x 0.145	=	Pounds-force per square inch (psi; lbf/in²; lb/in²)
Kilopascals (kPa)	x 0.01	= Kilograms-force per square centimetre (kgf/cm²; kg/cm²)	x 98.1	=	Kilopascals (kPa)
Millibar (mbar)	x 100	= Pascals (Pa)	x 0.01	=	Millibar (mbar)
Millibar (mbar)	x 0.0145	= Pounds-force per square inch (psi; lbf/in²; lb/in²)	x 68.947	=	Millibar (mbar)
Millibar (mbar)	x 0.75	= Millimetres of mercury (mmHg)	x 1.333	=	Millibar (mbar)
Millibar (mbar)	x 0.401	= Inches of water (inH₂O)	x 2.491	=	Millibar (mbar)
Millimetres of mercury (mmHg)	x 0.535	= Inches of water (inH₂O)	x 1.868	=	Millimetres of mercury (mmHg)
Inches of water (inH₂O)	x 0.036	= Pounds-force per square inch (psi; lbf/in²; lb/in²)	x 27.68	=	Inches of water (inH₂O)

Torque (moment of force)

Pounds-force inches (lbf in; lb in)	x 1.152	= Kilograms-force centimetre (kgf cm; kg cm)	x 0.868	=	Pounds-force inches (lbf in; lb in)
Pounds-force inches (lbf in; lb in)	x 0.113	= Newton metres (Nm)	x 8.85	=	Pounds-force inches (lbf in; lb in)
Pounds-force inches (lbf in; lb in)	x 0.083	= Pounds-force feet (lbf ft; lb ft)	x 12	=	Pounds-force inches (lbf in; lb in)
Pounds-force feet (lbf ft; lb ft)	x 0.138	= Kilograms-force metres (kgf m; kg m)	x 7.233	=	Pounds-force feet (lbf ft; lb ft)
Pounds-force feet (lbf ft; lb ft)	x 1.356	= Newton metres (Nm)	x 0.738	=	Pounds-force feet (lbf ft; lb ft)
Newton metres (Nm)	x 0.102	= Kilograms-force metres (kgf m; kg m)	x 9.804	=	Newton metres (Nm)

Power

Horsepower (hp)	x 745.7	= Watts (W)	x 0.0013	=	Horsepower (hp)

Velocity (speed)

Miles per hour (miles/hr; mph)	x 1.609	= Kilometres per hour (km/hr; kph)	x 0.621	=	Miles per hour (miles/hr; mph)

Fuel consumption*

Miles per gallon, Imperial (mpg)	x 0.354	= Kilometres per litre (km/l)	x 2.825	=	Miles per gallon, Imperial (mpg)
Miles per gallon, US (mpg)	x 0.425	= Kilometres per litre (km/l)	x 2.352	=	Miles per gallon, US (mpg)

Temperature

Degrees Fahrenheit = (°C x 1.8) + 32   Degrees Celsius (Degrees Centigrade; °C) = (°F - 32) x 0.56

It is common practice to convert from miles per gallon (mpg) to litres/100 kilometres (l/100km), where mpg x l/100 km = 282

Spare parts are available from many sources, including maker's appointed garages, accessory shops, and motor factors. To be sure of obtaining the correct parts, it will sometimes be necessary to quote the vehicle identification number. If possible, it can also be useful to take the old parts along for positive identification. Items such as starter motors and alternators may be available under a service exchange scheme - any parts returned should be clean.

Our advice regarding spare parts is as follows.

Officially appointed garages

This is the best source of parts which are peculiar to your car, and which are not otherwise generally available (eg, badges, interior trim, certain body panels, etc). It is also the only place at which you should buy parts if the vehicle is still under warranty.

Accessory shops

These are very good places to buy materials and components needed for the maintenance of your car (oil, air and fuel filters, light bulbs, drivebelts, greases, brake pads, tough-up paint, etc). Components of this nature sold by a reputable shop are of the same standard as those used by the car manufacturer.

Besides components, these shops also sell tools and general accessories, usually have convenient opening hours, charge lower prices, and can often be found close to home. Some accessory shops have parts counters where components needed for almost any repair job can be purchased or ordered.

Motor factors

Good factors will stock all the more important components which wear out comparatively quickly, and can sometimes supply individual components needed for the overhaul of a larger assembly (eg, brake seals and hydraulic parts, bearing shells, pistons, valves). They may also handle work such as cylinder block reboring, crankshaft regrinding, etc.

Tyre and exhaust specialists

These outlets may be independent, or members of a local or national chain. They frequently offer competitive prices when compared with a main dealer or local garage, but it will pay to obtain several quotes before making a decision. When researching prices, also ask what 'extras' may be added - for instance fitting a new valve and balancing the wheel are both commonly charged on top of the price of a new tyre.

Other sources

Beware of parts or materials obtained from market stalls, car boot sales or similar outlets. Such items are not invariably sub-standard, but there is little chance of compensation if they do prove unsatisfactory. In the case of safety-critical components such as brake pads, there is the risk not only of financial loss, but also of an accident causing injury or death.

Second-hand components or assemblies obtained from a car breaker can be a good buy in some circumstances, but his sort of purchase is best made by the experienced DIY mechanic.

Vehicle identification

Modifications are a continuing and unpublicised process in vehicle manufacture, quite apart from major model changes. Spare parts manuals and lists are compiled upon a numerical basis, the individual vehicle identification numbers being essential to correct identification of the component concerned.

When ordering spare parts, always give as much information as possible. Quote the car model, year of manufacture and registration, VIN and engine numbers as appropriate.

The *Vehicle Identification Number (VIN)* plate is riveted to the front of the engine compartment, behind and above the right hand headlamp unit. The vehicle identification number is also stamped into the floorpan, beneath the carpet between the driver's door and seat **(see illustration)**.

The engine number is stamped on the cylinder block, just below the cylinder head joint at the timing belt end.

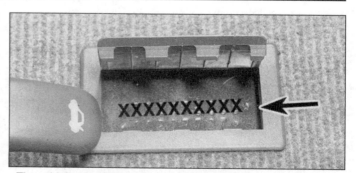

The vehicle identification number (arrowed) is stamped into the floorpan, beneath the carpet between the driver's door and seat

Whenever servicing, repair or overhaul work is carried out on the car or its components, observe the following procedures and instructions. This will assist in carrying out the operation efficiently and to a professional standard of workmanship.

Joint mating faces and gaskets

When separating components at their mating faces, never insert screwdrivers or similar implements into the joint between the faces in order to prise them apart. This can cause severe damage which results in oil leaks, coolant leaks, etc upon reassembly. Separation is usually achieved by tapping along the joint with a soft-faced hammer in order to break the seal. However, note that this method may not be suitable where dowels are used for component location.

Where a gasket is used between the mating faces of two components, a new one must be fitted on reassembly; fit it dry unless otherwise stated in the repair procedure. Make sure that the mating faces are clean and dry, with all traces of old gasket removed. When cleaning a joint face, use a tool which is unlikely to score or damage the face, and remove any burrs or nicks with an oilstone or fine file.

Make sure that tapped holes are cleaned with a pipe cleaner, and keep them free of jointing compound, if this is being used, unless specifically instructed otherwise.

Ensure that all orifices, channels or pipes are clear, and blow through them, preferably using compressed air.

Oil seals

Oil seals can be removed by levering them out with a wide flat-bladed screwdriver or similar implement. Alternatively, a number of self-tapping screws may be screwed into the seal, and these used as a purchase for pliers or some similar device in order to pull the seal free.

Whenever an oil seal is removed from its working location, either individually or as part of an assembly, it should be renewed.

The very fine sealing lip of the seal is easily damaged, and will not seal if the surface it contacts is not completely clean and free from scratches, nicks or grooves. If the original sealing surface of the component cannot be restored, and the manufacturer has not made provision for slight relocation of the seal relative to the sealing surface, the component should be renewed.

Protect the lips of the seal from any surface which may damage them in the course of fitting. Use tape or a conical sleeve where possible. Lubricate the seal lips with oil before fitting and, on dual-lipped seals, fill the space between the lips with grease.

Unless otherwise stated, oil seals must be fitted with their sealing lips toward the lubricant to be sealed.

Use a tubular drift or block of wood of the appropriate size to install the seal and, if the seal housing is shouldered, drive the seal down to the shoulder. If the seal housing is unshouldered, the seal should be fitted with its face flush with the housing top face (unless otherwise instructed).

Screw threads and fastenings

Seized nuts, bolts and screws are quite a common occurrence where corrosion has set in, and the use of penetrating oil or releasing fluid will often overcome this problem if the offending item is soaked for a while before attempting to release it. The use of an impact driver may also provide a means of releasing such stubborn fastening devices, when used in conjunction with the appropriate screwdriver bit or socket. If none of these methods works, it may be necessary to resort to the careful application of heat, or the use of a hacksaw or nut splitter device.

Studs are usually removed by locking two nuts together on the threaded part, and then using a spanner on the lower nut to unscrew the stud. Studs or bolts which have broken off below the surface of the component in which they are mounted can sometimes be removed using a stud extractor. Always ensure that a blind tapped hole is completely free from oil, grease, water or other fluid before installing the bolt or stud. Failure to do this could cause the housing to crack due to the hydraulic action of the bolt or stud as it is screwed in.

When tightening a castellated nut to accept a split pin, tighten the nut to the specified torque, where applicable, and then tighten further to the next split pin hole. Never slacken the nut to align the split pin hole, unless stated in the repair procedure.

When checking or retightening a nut or bolt to a specified torque setting, slacken the nut or bolt by a quarter of a turn, and then retighten to the specified setting. However, this should not be attempted where angular tightening has been used.

For some screw fastenings, notably cylinder head bolts or nuts, torque wrench settings are no longer specified for the latter stages of tightening, "angle-tightening" being called up instead. Typically, a fairly low torque wrench setting will be applied to the bolts/nuts in the correct sequence, followed by one or more stages of tightening through specified angles.

Locknuts, locktabs and washers

Any fastening which will rotate against a component or housing during tightening should always have a washer between it and the relevant component or housing.

Spring or split washers should always be renewed when they are used to lock a critical component such as a big-end bearing retaining bolt or nut. Locktabs which are folded over to retain a nut or bolt should always be renewed.

Self-locking nuts can be re-used in non-critical areas, providing resistance can be felt when the locking portion passes over the bolt or stud thread. However, it should be noted that self-locking stiffnuts tend to lose their effectiveness after long periods of use, and should then be renewed as a matter of course.

Split pins must always be replaced with new ones of the correct size for the hole.

When thread-locking compound is found on the threads of a fastener which is to be re-used, it should be cleaned off with a wire brush and solvent, and fresh compound applied on reassembly.

Special tools

Some repair procedures in this manual entail the use of special tools such as a press, two or three-legged pullers, spring compressors, etc. Wherever possible, suitable readily-available alternatives to the manufacturer's special tools are described, and are shown in use. In some instances, where no alternative is possible, it has been necessary to resort to the use of a manufacturer's tool, and this has been done for reasons of safety as well as the efficient completion of the repair operation. Unless you are highly-skilled and have a thorough understanding of the procedures described, never attempt to bypass the use of any special tool when the procedure described specifies its use. Not only is there a very great risk of personal injury, but expensive damage could be caused to the components involved.

Environmental considerations

When disposing of used engine oil, brake fluid, antifreeze, etc, give due consideration to any detrimental environmental effects. Do not, for instance, pour any of the above liquids down drains into the general sewage system, or onto the ground to soak away. Many local council refuse tips provide a facility for waste oil disposal, as do some garages. If none of these facilities are available, consult your local Environmental Health Department, or the National Rivers Authority, for further advice.

With the universal tightening-up of legislation regarding the emission of environmentally-harmful substances from motor vehicles, most vehicles have tamperproof devices fitted to the main adjustment points of the fuel system. These devices are primarily designed to prevent unqualified persons from adjusting the fuel/air mixture, with the chance of a consequent increase in toxic emissions. If such devices are found during servicing or overhaul, they should, wherever possible, be renewed or refitted in accordance with the manufacturer's requirements or current legislation.

OIL CARE · FOLLOW THE CODE

OIL BANK LINE
0800 66 33 66
www.oilbankline.org.uk

Note: It is antisocial and illegal to dump oil down the drain. To find the location of your local oil recycling bank, call this number free.

The jack supplied with the vehicle tool kit should only be used for changing the roadwheels in an emergency– see *Wheel changing* at the front of this manual. When carrying out any other kind of work, raise the vehicle using a hydraulic (or trolley) jack, and always supplement the jack with axle stands positioned under the reinforced vehicle jack location points on the sills on each side of the car **(see illustration)**.

When using a hydraulic jack to raise the front of the car, position the jack head under the transmission differential housing **(see illustration)**. **Do not** jack the car under the sill, sump, or any of the steering or suspension components. With the car raised, axle stands should be positioned beneath the vehicle jacking points on each side of the car. Position a block of wood with a groove cut in it on the axle stand to prevent the weight of the car resting on the sill edge; align the sill edge with the groove in the wood so that the weight is spread evenly over the surface of the block.

To raise the rear of the car, position the jack head adjacent to one of the rear vehicle jack location points on the sill. Raise one side of the car then position an axle stand beneath the jacking point. Use a grooved block of wood on the jack and axle stand as described in the previous paragraph. The other side of the car can then be raised and supported in the same way. **Do not** attempt to raise the car with the jack positioned underneath the beam axle or suspension components.

⚠ *Warning: Never work under, around, or near a raised vehicle, unless it is adequately supported in at least two places.*

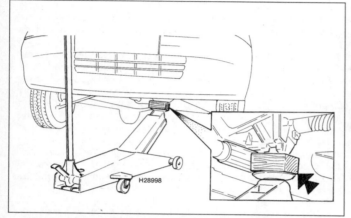

When using a hydraulic jack to raise the front of the vehicle, position the jack head under the transmission differential housing, using an interposed block of wood

Reinforced jack location points (arrowed) are located at the front and rear of the sills on each side of the car

Disconnecting the battery

Several systems fitted to the vehicle require battery power to be available at all times, either to ensure their continued operation (such as the clock) or to maintain control unit memories which would be erased if the battery were to be disconnected. Whenever the battery is to be disconnected therefore, first note the following, to ensure that there are no unforeseen consequences of this action:

a) *First, on any vehicle with central locking, it is a wise precaution to remove the key from the ignition, and to keep it with you, so that it does not get locked in if the central locking should engage accidentally when the battery is reconnected.*

b) *If a security-coded audio unit is fitted, and the unit and/or the battery is disconnected, the unit will not function again on reconnection until the correct security code is entered. Details of this procedure, which varies according to the unit fitted, are given in the vehicle owner's*

handbook. Ensure you have the correct code before you disconnect the battery. If you do not have the code or details of the correct procedure, but can supply proof of ownership and a legitimate reason for wanting this information, a Fiat dealer may be able to help.

c) *The engine management system electronic control unit is of the 'self-learning' type, meaning that as it operates, it also monitors and stores the settings which give optimum engine performance under all operating conditions. When the battery is disconnected, these settings are lost and the ECU reverts to the base settings programmed into its memory at the factory. On restarting, this may lead to the engine running/idling roughly until the ECU has re-learned the optimum settings. This process is best accomplished by taking the vehicle on a road test (for approximately 15 minutes), covering all*

engine speeds and loads, concentrating mainly in the 2,500 to 3,500 rpm region.

Devices known as 'memory-savers' (or 'code-savers') can be used to avoid some of the above problems. Precise details vary according to the device used. Typically, it is plugged into the cigarette lighter, and is connected by its own wires to a spare battery; the vehicle's own battery is then disconnected from the electrical system, leaving the memory-saver to pass sufficient current to maintain audio unit security codes and any other memory values, and also to run permanently-live circuits such as the clock.

⚠ *Warning: Some of these devices allow a considerable amount of current to pass, which can mean that many of the vehicle's systems are still operational when the main battery is disconnected. If a memory saver is used, ensure that the circuit concerned is actually 'dead' before carrying out any work on it!*

Introduction

A selection of good tools is a fundamental requirement for anyone contemplating the maintenance and repair of a motor vehicle. For the owner who does not possess any, their purchase will prove a considerable expense, offsetting some of the savings made by doing-it-yourself. However, provided that the tools purchased meet the relevant national safety standards and are of good quality, they will last for many years and prove an extremely worthwhile investment.

To help the average owner to decide which tools are needed to carry out the various tasks detailed in this manual, we have compiled three lists of tools under the following headings: *Maintenance and minor repair, Repair and overhaul,* and *Special.* Newcomers to practical mechanics should start off with the *Maintenance and minor repair* tool kit, and confine themselves to the simpler jobs around the vehicle. Then, as confidence and experience grow, more difficult tasks can be undertaken, with extra tools being purchased as, and when, they are needed. In this way, a *Maintenance and minor repair* tool kit can be built up into a *Repair and overhaul* tool kit over a considerable period of time, without any major cash outlays. The experienced do-it-yourselfer will have a tool kit good enough for most repair and overhaul procedures, and will add tools from the *Special* category when it is felt that the expense is justified by the amount of use to which these tools will be put.

Maintenance and minor repair tool kit

The tools given in this list should be considered as a minimum requirement if routine maintenance, servicing and minor repair operations are to be undertaken. We recommend the purchase of combination spanners (ring one end, open-ended the other); although more expensive than open-ended ones, they do give the advantages of both types of spanner.

☐ *Combination spanners:*
   Metric - 8 to 19 mm inclusive
☐ *Adjustable spanner - 35 mm jaw (approx.)*
☐ *Spark plug spanner (with rubber insert) - petrol models*
☐ *Spark plug gap adjustment tool - petrol models*
☐ *Set of feeler gauges*
☐ *Brake bleed nipple spanner*
☐ *Screwdrivers:*
   Flat blade - 100 mm long x 6 mm dia
   Cross blade - 100 mm long x 6 mm dia
   Torx - various sizes (not all vehicles)
☐ *Combination pliers*
☐ *Hacksaw (junior)*
☐ *Tyre pump*
☐ *Tyre pressure gauge*
☐ *Oil can*
☐ *Oil filter removal tool*
☐ *Fine emery cloth*
☐ *Wire brush (small)*
☐ *Funnel (medium size)*
☐ *Sump drain plug key (not all vehicles)*

Repair and overhaul tool kit

These tools are virtually essential for anyone undertaking any major repairs to a motor vehicle, and are additional to those given in the *Maintenance and minor repair* list. Included in this list is a comprehensive set of sockets. Although these are expensive, they will be found invaluable as they are so versatile - particularly if various drives are included in the set. We recommend the half-inch square-drive type, as this can be used with most proprietary torque wrenches.

The tools in this list will sometimes need to be supplemented by tools from the *Special* list:

☐ *Sockets (or box spanners) to cover range in previous list (including Torx sockets)*
☐ *Reversible ratchet drive (for use with sockets)*
☐ *Extension piece, 250 mm (for use with sockets)*
☐ *Universal joint (for use with sockets)*
☐ *Flexible handle or sliding T "breaker bar" (for use with sockets)*
☐ *Torque wrench (for use with sockets)*
☐ *Self-locking grips*
☐ *Ball pein hammer*
☐ *Soft-faced mallet (plastic or rubber)*
☐ *Screwdrivers:*
   Flat blade - long & sturdy, short (chubby), and narrow (electrician's) types
   Cross blade – long & sturdy, and short (chubby) types
☐ *Pliers:*
   Long-nosed
   Side cutters (electrician's)
   Circlip (internal and external)
☐ *Cold chisel - 25 mm*
☐ *Scriber*
☐ *Scraper*
☐ *Centre-punch*
☐ *Pin punch*
☐ *Hacksaw*
☐ *Brake hose clamp*
☐ *Brake/clutch bleeding kit*
☐ *Selection of twist drills*
☐ *Steel rule/straight-edge*
☐ *Allen keys (inc. splined/Torx type)*
☐ *Selection of files*
☐ *Wire brush*
☐ *Axle stands*
☐ *Jack (strong trolley or hydraulic type)*
☐ *Light with extension lead*
☐ *Universal electrical multi-meter*

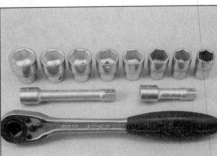

Sockets and reversible ratchet drive

Brake bleeding kit

Torx key, socket and bit

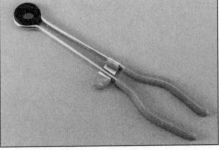

Hose clamp

Angular-tightening gauge

Special tools

The tools in this list are those which are not used regularly, are expensive to buy, or which need to be used in accordance with their manufacturers' instructions. Unless relatively difficult mechanical jobs are undertaken frequently, it will not be economic to buy many of these tools. Where this is the case, you could consider clubbing together with friends (or joining a motorists' club) to make a joint purchase, or borrowing the tools against a deposit from a local garage or tool hire specialist. It is worth noting that many of the larger DIY superstores now carry a large range of special tools for hire at modest rates.

The following list contains only those tools and instruments freely available to the public, and not those special tools produced by the vehicle manufacturer specifically for its dealer network. You will find occasional references to these manufacturers' special tools in the text of this manual. Generally, an alternative method of doing the job without the vehicle manufacturers' special tool is given. However, sometimes there is no alternative to using them. Where this is the case and the relevant tool cannot be bought or borrowed, you will have to entrust the work to a dealer.

- ☐ Angular-tightening gauge
- ☐ Valve spring compressor
- ☐ Valve grinding tool
- ☐ Piston ring compressor
- ☐ Piston ring removal/installation tool
- ☐ Cylinder bore hone
- ☐ Balljoint separator
- ☐ Coil spring compressors (where applicable)
- ☐ Two/three-legged hub and bearing puller
- ☐ Impact screwdriver
- ☐ Micrometer and/or vernier calipers
- ☐ Dial gauge
- ☐ Stroboscopic timing light
- ☐ Dwell angle meter/tachometer
- ☐ Fault code reader
- ☐ Cylinder compression gauge
- ☐ Hand-operated vacuum pump and gauge
- ☐ Clutch plate alignment set
- ☐ Brake shoe steady spring cup removal tool
- ☐ Bush and bearing removal/installation set
- ☐ Stud extractors
- ☐ Tap and die set
- ☐ Lifting tackle
- ☐ Trolley jack

Buying tools

Reputable motor accessory shops and superstores often offer excellent quality tools at discount prices, so it pays to shop around.

Remember, you don't have to buy the most expensive items on the shelf, but it is always advisable to steer clear of the very cheap tools. Beware of 'bargains' offered on market stalls or at car boot sales. There are plenty of good tools around at reasonable prices, but always aim to purchase items which meet the relevant national safety standards. If in doubt, ask the proprietor or manager of the shop for advice before making a purchase.

Care and maintenance of tools

Having purchased a reasonable tool kit, it is necessary to keep the tools in a clean and serviceable condition. After use, always wipe off any dirt, grease and metal particles using a clean, dry cloth, before putting the tools away. Never leave them lying around after they have been used. A simple tool rack on the garage or workshop wall for items such as screwdrivers and pliers is a good idea. Store all normal spanners and sockets in a metal box. Any measuring instruments, gauges, meters, etc, must be carefully stored where they cannot be damaged or become rusty.

Take a little care when tools are used. Hammer heads inevitably become marked, and screwdrivers lose the keen edge on their blades from time to time. A little timely attention with emery cloth or a file will soon restore items like this to a good finish.

Working facilities

Not to be forgotten when discussing tools is the workshop itself. If anything more than routine maintenance is to be carried out, a suitable working area becomes essential.

It is appreciated that many an owner-mechanic is forced by circumstances to remove an engine or similar item without the benefit of a garage or workshop. Having done this, any repairs should always be done under the cover of a roof.

Wherever possible, any dismantling should be done on a clean, flat workbench or table at a suitable working height.

Any workbench needs a vice; one with a jaw opening of 100 mm is suitable for most jobs. As mentioned previously, some clean dry storage space is also required for tools, as well as for any lubricants, cleaning fluids, touch-up paints etc, which become necessary.

Another item which may be required, and which has a much more general usage, is an electric drill with a chuck capacity of at least 8 mm. This, together with a good range of twist drills, is virtually essential for fitting accessories.

Last, but not least, always keep a supply of old newspapers and clean, lint-free rags available, and try to keep any working area as clean as possible.

Micrometers

Dial test indicator ("dial gauge")

Strap wrench

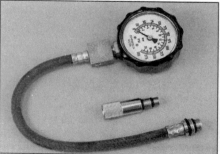
Compression tester

Fault code reader

This is a guide to getting your vehicle through the MOT test. Obviously it will not be possible to examine the vehicle to the same standard as the professional MOT tester. However, working through the following checks will enable you to identify any problem areas before submitting the vehicle for the test.

Where a testable component is in borderline condition, the tester has discretion in deciding whether to pass or fail it. The basis of such discretion is whether the tester would be happy for a close relative or friend to use the vehicle with the component in that condition. If the vehicle presented is clean and evidently well cared for, the tester may be more inclined to pass a borderline component than if the vehicle is scruffy and apparently neglected.

It has only been possible to summarise the test requirements here, based on the regulations in force at the time of printing. Test standards are becoming increasingly stringent, although there are some exemptions for older vehicles.

An assistant will be needed to help carry out some of these checks.

The checks have been sub-divided into four categories, as follows:

1 Checks carried out **FROM THE DRIVER'S SEAT**

2 Checks carried out **WITH THE VEHICLE ON THE GROUND**

3 Checks carried out **WITH THE VEHICLE RAISED AND THE WHEELS FREE TO TURN**

4 Checks carried out on **YOUR VEHICLE'S EXHAUST EMISSION SYSTEM**

---

1 Checks carried out **FROM THE DRIVER'S SEAT**

Handbrake

☐ Test the operation of the handbrake. Excessive travel (too many clicks) indicates incorrect brake or cable adjustment.
☐ Check that the handbrake cannot be released by tapping the lever sideways. Check the security of the lever mountings.

Footbrake

☐ Depress the brake pedal and check that it does not creep down to the floor, indicating a master cylinder fault. Release the pedal, wait a few seconds, then depress it again. If the pedal travels nearly to the floor before firm resistance is felt, brake adjustment or repair is necessary. If the pedal feels spongy, there is air in the hydraulic system which must be removed by bleeding.

☐ Check that the brake pedal is secure and in good condition. Check also for signs of fluid leaks on the pedal, floor or carpets, which would indicate failed seals in the brake master cylinder.
☐ Check the servo unit (when applicable) by operating the brake pedal several times, then keeping the pedal depressed and starting the engine. As the engine starts, the pedal will move down slightly. If not, the vacuum hose or the servo itself may be faulty.

Steering wheel and column

☐ Examine the steering wheel for fractures or looseness of the hub, spokes or rim.
☐ Move the steering wheel from side to side and then up and down. Check that the steering wheel is not loose on the column, indicating wear or a loose retaining nut. Continue moving the steering wheel as before, but also turn it slightly from left to right.
☐ Check that the steering wheel is not loose on the column, and that there is no abnormal

movement of the steering wheel, indicating wear in the column support bearings or couplings.

Windscreen, mirrors and sunvisor

☐ The windscreen must be free of cracks or other significant damage within the driver's field of view. (Small stone chips are acceptable.) Rear view mirrors must be secure, intact, and capable of being adjusted.

290mm

☐ The driver's sunvisor must be capable of being stored in the "up" position.

Seat belts and seats

Note: *The following checks are applicable to all seat belts, front and rear.*

☐ Examine the webbing of all the belts (including rear belts if fitted) for cuts, serious fraying or deterioration. Fasten and unfasten each belt to check the buckles. If applicable, check the retracting mechanism. Check the security of all seat belt mountings accessible from inside the vehicle.

☐ Seat belts with pre-tensioners, once activated, have a "flag" or similar showing on the seat belt stalk. This, in itself, is not a reason for test failure.

☐ The front seats themselves must be securely attached and the backrests must lock in the upright position.

Doors

☐ Both front doors must be able to be opened and closed from outside and inside, and must latch securely when closed.

2 Checks carried out WITH THE VEHICLE ON THE GROUND

Vehicle identification

☐ Number plates must be in good condition, secure and legible, with letters and numbers correctly spaced – spacing at (A) should be at least twice that at (B).

☐ The VIN plate and/or homologation plate must be legible.

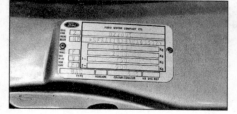

Electrical equipment

☐ Switch on the ignition and check the operation of the horn.

☐ Check the windscreen washers and wipers, examining the wiper blades; renew damaged or perished blades. Also check the operation of the stop-lights.

☐ Check the operation of the sidelights and number plate lights. The lenses and reflectors must be secure, clean and undamaged.

☐ Check the operation and alignment of the headlights. The headlight reflectors must not be tarnished and the lenses must be undamaged.

☐ Switch on the ignition and check the operation of the direction indicators (including the instrument panel tell-tale) and the hazard warning lights. Operation of the sidelights and stop-lights must not affect the indicators - if it does, the cause is usually a bad earth at the rear light cluster.

☐ Check the operation of the rear foglight(s), including the warning light on the instrument panel or in the switch.

☐ The ABS warning light must illuminate in accordance with the manufacturers' design. For most vehicles, the ABS warning light should illuminate when the ignition is switched on, and (if the system is operating properly) extinguish after a few seconds. Refer to the owner's handbook.

Footbrake

☐ Examine the master cylinder, brake pipes and servo unit for leaks, loose mountings, corrosion or other damage.

☐ The fluid reservoir must be secure and the fluid level must be between the upper (A) and lower (B) markings.

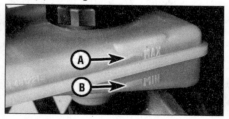

☐ Inspect both front brake flexible hoses for cracks or deterioration of the rubber. Turn the steering from lock to lock, and ensure that the hoses do not contact the wheel, tyre, or any part of the steering or suspension mechanism. With the brake pedal firmly depressed, check the hoses for bulges or leaks under pressure.

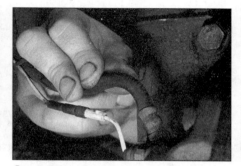

Steering and suspension

☐ Have your assistant turn the steering wheel from side to side slightly, up to the point where the steering gear just begins to transmit this movement to the roadwheels. Check for excessive free play between the steering wheel and the steering gear, indicating wear or insecurity of the steering column joints, the column-to-steering gear coupling, or the steering gear itself.

☐ Have your assistant turn the steering wheel more vigorously in each direction, so that the roadwheels just begin to turn. As this is done, examine all the steering joints, linkages, fittings and attachments. Renew any component that shows signs of wear or damage. On vehicles with power steering, check the security and condition of the steering pump, drivebelt and hoses.

☐ Check that the vehicle is standing level, and at approximately the correct ride height.

Shock absorbers

☐ Depress each corner of the vehicle in turn, then release it. The vehicle should rise and then settle in its normal position. If the vehicle continues to rise and fall, the shock absorber is defective. A shock absorber which has seized will also cause the vehicle to fail.

Exhaust system

☐ Start the engine. With your assistant holding a rag over the tailpipe, check the entire system for leaks. Repair or renew leaking sections.

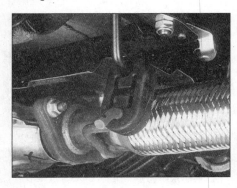

3 Checks carried out **WITH THE VEHICLE RAISED AND THE WHEELS FREE TO TURN**

Jack up the front and rear of the vehicle, and securely support it on axle stands. Position the stands clear of the suspension assemblies. Ensure that the wheels are clear of the ground and that the steering can be turned from lock to lock.

Steering mechanism

☐ Have your assistant turn the steering from lock to lock. Check that the steering turns smoothly, and that no part of the steering mechanism, including a wheel or tyre, fouls any brake hose or pipe or any part of the body structure.
☐ Examine the steering rack rubber gaiters for damage or insecurity of the retaining clips. If power steering is fitted, check for signs of damage or leakage of the fluid hoses, pipes or connections. Also check for excessive stiffness or binding of the steering, a missing split pin or locking device, or severe corrosion of the body structure within 30 cm of any steering component attachment point.

Front and rear suspension and wheel bearings

☐ Starting at the front right-hand side, grasp the roadwheel at the 3 o'clock and 9 o'clock positions and rock gently but firmly. Check for free play or insecurity at the wheel bearings, suspension balljoints, or suspension mountings, pivots and attachments.
☐ Now grasp the wheel at the 12 o'clock and 6 o'clock positions and repeat the previous inspection. Spin the wheel, and check for roughness or tightness of the front wheel bearing.

☐ If excess free play is suspected at a component pivot point, this can be confirmed by using a large screwdriver or similar tool and levering between the mounting and the component attachment. This will confirm whether the wear is in the pivot bush, its retaining bolt, or in the mounting itself (the bolt holes can often become elongated).

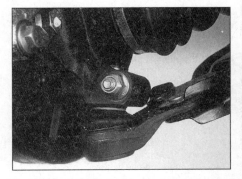

☐ Carry out all the above checks at the other front wheel, and then at both rear wheels.

Springs and shock absorbers

☐ Examine the suspension struts (when applicable) for serious fluid leakage, corrosion, or damage to the casing. Also check the security of the mounting points.
☐ If coil springs are fitted, check that the spring ends locate in their seats, and that the spring is not corroded, cracked or broken.
☐ If leaf springs are fitted, check that all leaves are intact, that the axle is securely attached to each spring, and that there is no deterioration of the spring eye mountings, bushes, and shackles.

☐ The same general checks apply to vehicles fitted with other suspension types, such as torsion bars, hydraulic displacer units, etc. Ensure that all mountings and attachments are secure, that there are no signs of excessive wear, corrosion or damage, and (on hydraulic types) that there are no fluid leaks or damaged pipes.
☐ Inspect the shock absorbers for signs of serious fluid leakage. Check for wear of the mounting bushes or attachments, or damage to the body of the unit.

Driveshafts (fwd vehicles only)

☐ Rotate each front wheel in turn and inspect the constant velocity joint gaiters for splits or damage. Also check that each driveshaft is straight and undamaged.

Braking system

☐ If possible without dismantling, check brake pad wear and disc condition. Ensure that the friction lining material has not worn excessively, (A) and that the discs are not fractured, pitted, scored or badly worn (B).

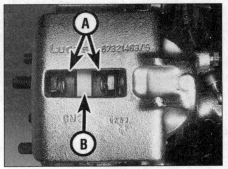

☐ Examine all the rigid brake pipes underneath the vehicle, and the flexible hose(s) at the rear. Look for corrosion, chafing or insecurity of the pipes, and for signs of bulging under pressure, chafing, splits or deterioration of the flexible hoses.
☐ Look for signs of fluid leaks at the brake calipers or on the brake backplates. Repair or renew leaking components.
☐ Slowly spin each wheel, while your assistant depresses and releases the footbrake. Ensure that each brake is operating and does not bind when the pedal is released.

☐ Examine the handbrake mechanism, checking for frayed or broken cables, excessive corrosion, or wear or insecurity of the linkage. Check that the mechanism works on each relevant wheel, and releases fully, without binding.

☐ It is not possible to test brake efficiency without special equipment, but a road test can be carried out later to check that the vehicle pulls up in a straight line.

Fuel and exhaust systems

☐ Inspect the fuel tank (including the filler cap), fuel pipes, hoses and unions. All components must be secure and free from leaks.

☐ Examine the exhaust system over its entire length, checking for any damaged, broken or missing mountings, security of the retaining clamps and rust or corrosion.

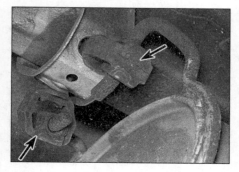

Wheels and tyres

☐ Examine the sidewalls and tread area of each tyre in turn. Check for cuts, tears, lumps, bulges, separation of the tread, and exposure of the ply or cord due to wear or damage. Check that the tyre bead is correctly seated on the wheel rim, that the valve is sound and properly seated, and that the wheel is not distorted or damaged.

☐ Check that the tyres are of the correct size for the vehicle, that they are of the same size and type on each axle, and that the pressures are correct.

☐ Check the tyre tread depth. The legal minimum at the time of writing is 1.6 mm over at least three-quarters of the tread width. Abnormal tread wear may indicate incorrect front wheel alignment.

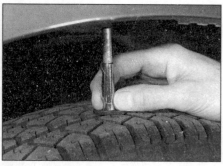

Body corrosion

☐ Check the condition of the entire vehicle structure for signs of corrosion in load-bearing areas. (These include chassis box sections, side sills, cross-members, pillars, and all suspension, steering, braking system and seat belt mountings and anchorages.) Any corrosion which has seriously reduced the thickness of a load-bearing area is likely to cause the vehicle to fail. In this case professional repairs are likely to be needed.

☐ Damage or corrosion which causes sharp or otherwise dangerous edges to be exposed will also cause the vehicle to fail.

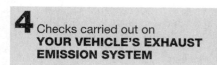

4 Checks carried out on **YOUR VEHICLE'S EXHAUST EMISSION SYSTEM**

Petrol models

☐ Have the engine at normal operating temperature, and make sure that it is in good tune (ignition system in good order, air filter element clean, etc).

☐ Before any measurements are carried out, raise the engine speed to around 2500 rpm, and hold it at this speed for 20 seconds. Allow the engine speed to return to idle, and watch for smoke emissions from the exhaust tailpipe. If the idle speed is obviously much too high, or if dense blue or clearly-visible black smoke comes from the tailpipe for more than 5 seconds, the vehicle will fail. As a rule of thumb, blue smoke signifies oil being burnt (engine wear) while black smoke signifies unburnt fuel (dirty air cleaner element, or other carburettor or fuel system fault).

☐ An exhaust gas analyser capable of measuring carbon monoxide (CO) and hydrocarbons (HC) is now needed. If such an instrument cannot be hired or borrowed, a local garage may agree to perform the check for a small fee.

CO emissions (mixture)

☐ At the time of writing, for vehicles first used between 1st August 1975 and 31st July 1986 (P to C registration), the CO level must not exceed 4.5% by volume. For vehicles first used between 1st August 1986 and 31st July 1992 (D to J registration), the CO level must not exceed 3.5% by volume. Vehicles first

used after 1st August 1992 (K registration) must conform to the manufacturer's specification. The MOT tester has access to a DOT database or emissions handbook, which lists the CO and HC limits for each make and model of vehicle. The CO level is measured with the engine at idle speed, and at "fast idle". The following limits are given as a general guide:

At idle speed -
    CO level no more than 0.5%
At "fast idle" (2500 to 3000 rpm) -
    CO level no more than 0.3%
    (Minimum oil temperature 60ºC)

☐ If the CO level cannot be reduced far enough to pass the test (and the fuel and ignition systems are otherwise in good condition) then the carburettor is badly worn, or there is some problem in the fuel injection system or catalytic converter (as applicable).

HC emissions

☐ With the CO within limits, HC emissions for vehicles first used between 1st August 1975 and 31st July 1992 (P to J registration) must not exceed 1200 ppm. Vehicles first used after 1st August 1992 (K registration) must conform to the manufacturer's specification. The MOT tester has access to a DOT database or emissions handbook, which lists the CO and HC limits for each make and model of vehicle. The HC level is measured with the engine at "fast idle". The following is given as a general guide:

At "fast idle" (2500 to 3000 rpm) -
    HC level no more than 200 ppm
    (Minimum oil temperature 60ºC)

☐ Excessive HC emissions are caused by incomplete combustion, the causes of which can include oil being burnt, mechanical wear and ignition/fuel system malfunction.

Diesel models

☐ The only emission test applicable to Diesel engines is the measuring of exhaust smoke density. The test involves accelerating the engine several times to its maximum unloaded speed.

Note: *It is of the utmost importance that the engine timing belt is in good condition before the test is carried out.*

☐ The limits for Diesel engine exhaust smoke, introduced in September 1995 are:

Vehicles first used before 1st August 1979:
    Exempt from metered smoke testing, but must not emit "dense blue or clearly visible black smoke for a period of more than 5 seconds at idle" or "dense blue or clearly visible black smoke during acceleration which would obscure the view of other road users".

Non-turbocharged vehicles first used after 1st August 1979: 2.5m⁻¹

Turbocharged vehicles first used after 1st August 1979: 3.0m⁻¹

☐ Excessive smoke can be caused by a dirty air cleaner element. Otherwise, professional advice may be needed to find the cause.

Engine

☐ Engine fails to rotate when attempting to start
☐ Engine rotates, but will not start
☐ Engine difficult to start when cold
☐ Engine difficult to start when hot
☐ Starter motor noisy or excessively-rough in engagement
☐ Engine starts, but stops immediately
☐ Engine idles erratically
☐ Engine misfires at idle speed
☐ Engine misfires throughout the driving speed range
☐ Engine hesitates on acceleration
☐ Engine stalls
☐ Engine lacks power
☐ Engine backfires
☐ Oil pressure warning light illuminated with engine running
☐ Engine runs-on after switching off
☐ Engine noises

Cooling system

☐ Overheating
☐ Overcooling
☐ External coolant leakage
☐ Internal coolant leakage
☐ Corrosion

Fuel and exhaust systems

☐ Excessive fuel consumption
☐ Fuel leakage and/or fuel odour
☐ Excessive noise or fumes from exhaust system

Clutch

☐ Pedal travels to floor – no pressure or very little resistance
☐ Clutch fails to disengage (unable to select gears)
☐ Clutch slips (engine speed increases, with no increase in vehicle speed)
☐ Judder as clutch is engaged
☐ Noise when depressing or releasing clutch pedal

Manual transmission

☐ Noisy in neutral with engine running
☐ Noisy in one particular gear
☐ Difficulty engaging gears
☐ Jumps out of gear
☐ Vibration
☐ Lubricant leaks

Automatic transmission

☐ Fluid leakage
☐ Transmission fluid brown, or has burned smell
☐ General gear selection problems
☐ Engine will not start in any gear, or starts in gears other than Park or Neutral
☐ Transmission slips, shifts roughly, is noisy, or has no drive in forward or reverse gears

Driveshafts

☐ Clicking or knocking noise on turns (at slow speed on full-lock)
☐ Vibration when accelerating or decelerating

Braking system

☐ Vehicle pulls to one side under braking
☐ Noise (grinding or high-pitched squeal) when brakes applied
☐ Excessive brake pedal travel
☐ Brake pedal feels spongy when depressed
☐ Excessive brake pedal effort required to stop vehicle
☐ Judder felt through brake pedal or steering wheel when braking
☐ Brakes binding
☐ Rear wheels locking under normal braking

Suspension and steering systems

☐ Vehicle pulls to one side
☐ Wheel wobble and vibration
☐ Excessive pitching and/or rolling around corners, or during braking
☐ Wandering or general instability
☐ Excessively-stiff steering
☐ Excessive play in steering
☐ Lack of power assistance
☐ Tyre wear excessive

Electrical system

☐ Battery will not hold a charge for more than a few days
☐ Ignition/no-charge warning light remains illuminated with engine running
☐ Ignition/no-charge warning light fails to come on
☐ Lights inoperative
☐ Instrument readings inaccurate or erratic
☐ Horn inoperative, or unsatisfactory in operation
☐ Windscreen/tailgate wipers inoperative, or unsatisfactory in operation
☐ Windscreen/tailgate washers inoperative, or unsatisfactory in operation
☐ Electric windows inoperative, or unsatisfactory in operation

Introduction

The vehicle owner who does his or her own maintenance according to the recommended service schedules should not have to use this section of the manual very often. Modern component reliability is such that, provided those items subject to wear or deterioration are inspected or renewed at the specified intervals, sudden failure is comparatively rare. Faults do not usually just happen as a result of sudden failure, but develop over a period of time. Major mechanical failures in particular are usually preceded by characteristic symptoms over hundreds or even thousands of miles. Those components which do occasionally fail without warning are often small and easily carried in the vehicle.

With any fault-finding, the first step is to decide where to begin investigations. Sometimes this is obvious, but on other occasions, a little detective work will be necessary. The owner who makes half a dozen haphazard adjustments or replacements may be successful in curing a fault (or its symptoms), but will be none the wiser if the fault recurs, and ultimately may have spent more time and money than was necessary. A calm and logical approach will be found to be more satisfactory in the long run. Always take into account any warning signs or abnormalities that may have been noticed in the period preceding the fault –

power loss, high or low gauge readings, unusual smells, etc – and remember that failure of components such as fuses or spark plugs may only be pointers to some underlying fault.

The pages which follow provide an easy-reference guide to the more common problems which may occur during the operation of the vehicle. These problems and their possible causes are grouped under headings denoting various components or systems, such as Engine, Cooling system, etc. The Chapter and/or Section which deals with the problem is also shown in brackets. Whatever the fault, certain basic principles apply. These are as follows:

Verify the fault. This is simply a matter of being sure that you know what the symptoms are before starting work. This is particularly important if you are investigating a fault for someone else, who may not have described it very accurately.

Don't overlook the obvious. For example, if the vehicle won't start, is there petrol in the tank? (Don't take anyone else's word on this particular point, and don't trust the fuel gauge either!) If an electrical fault is indicated, look for loose or broken wires before digging out the test gear.

Cure the disease, not the symptom. Substituting a flat battery with a fully-charged one will get you off the hard shoulder, but if the underlying cause is not attended to, the new battery will go the same way. Similarly, changing oil-fouled spark plugs (petrol models) for a new set will get you moving again, but remember that the reason for the fouling (if it wasn't simply an incorrect grade of plug) will have to be established and corrected.

Don't take anything for granted. Particularly, don't forget that a new component may itself be defective (especially if it's been rattling around in the boot for months), and don't leave components out of a fault diagnosis sequence just because they are new or recently-fitted. When you do finally diagnose a difficult fault, you'll probably realise that all the evidence was there from the start.

Engine

Engine fails to rotate when attempting to start

☐ Battery terminal connections loose or corroded (*Weekly Checks*).
☐ Battery discharged or faulty (Chapter 5A).
☐ Broken, loose or disconnected wiring in the starting circuit (Chapter 5A).
☐ Defective starter solenoid or switch (Chapter 5A).
☐ Defective starter motor (Chapter 5A).
☐ Starter pinion or flywheel ring gear teeth loose or broken (Chapter 2A, 2B and 5A).
☐ Engine earth strap broken or disconnected (Chapter 5A).

Engine rotates, but will not start

☐ Fuel tank empty.
☐ Battery discharged (engine rotates slowly) (Chapter 5A).
☐ Battery terminal connections loose or corroded (*Weekly checks*).
☐ Ignition components damp or damaged (Chapter 1 and 5B).
☐ Broken, loose or disconnected wiring in the ignition circuit (Chapter 1 and 5B).
☐ Worn, faulty or incorrectly-gapped spark plugs (Chapter 1).
☐ Fuel injection system fault (Chapter 4A).
☐ Major mechanical failure (eg camshaft drive) (Chapter 2A or 2B).

Engine difficult to start when cold

☐ Battery discharged (Chapter 5A).
☐ Battery terminal connections loose or corroded (*Weekly checks*).
☐ Worn, faulty or incorrectly-gapped spark plugs (Chapter 1).
☐ Fuel injection system fault (Chapter 4A).
☐ Other ignition system fault (Chapter 1 and 5B).
☐ Low cylinder compressions (Chapter 2A or 2B).

Engine difficult to start when hot

☐ Air filter element dirty or clogged (Chapter 1).
☐ Fuel injection system fault (Chapter 4A).
☐ Low cylinder compressions (Chapter 2A or 2B).

Starter motor noisy or excessively-rough in engagement

☐ Starter pinion or flywheel ring gear teeth loose or broken (Chapter 2A, 2B and 5A).
☐ Starter motor mounting bolts loose or missing (Chapter 5A).
☐ Starter motor internal components worn or damaged (Chapter 5A).

Engine starts, but stops immediately

☐ Loose or faulty electrical connections in the ignition circuit (Chapter 1 and 5B).
☐ Vacuum leak at the throttle body or inlet manifold (Chapter 4A).
☐ Blocked injector/fuel injection system fault (Chapter 4A).

Engine idles erratically

☐ Air filter element clogged (Chapter 1).
☐ Vacuum leak at the throttle body, inlet manifold or associated hoses (Chapter 4A or 4B).
☐ Worn, faulty or incorrectly-gapped spark plugs (Chapter 1).
☐ Uneven or low cylinder compressions (Chapter 2A or 2B).
☐ Camshaft lobes worn (Chapter 2A or 2B).
☐ Timing belt incorrectly tensioned (Chapter 2A or 2B).
☐ Blocked injector/fuel injection system fault (Chapter 4A).

Engine misfires at idle speed

☐ Worn, faulty or incorrectly-gapped spark plugs (Chapter 1).
☐ Faulty spark plug HT leads (Chapter 1).
☐ Vacuum leak at the throttle body, inlet manifold or associated hoses (Chapter 4A).
☐ Blocked injector/fuel injection system fault (Chapter 4A).
☐ Uneven or low cylinder compressions (Chapter 2A or 2B).
☐ Disconnected, leaking, or perished crankcase ventilation hoses (Chapter 4B).

Engine misfires throughout the driving speed range

☐ Fuel pump faulty, or delivery pressure low (Chapter 4A).
☐ Fuel tank vent blocked, or fuel pipes restricted (Chapter 4A).
☐ Vacuum leak at the throttle body, inlet manifold or associated hoses (Chapter 4A).
☐ Worn, faulty or incorrectly-gapped spark plugs (Chapter 1).
☐ Faulty spark plug HT leads (Chapter 1).
☐ Faulty ignition coil (Chapter 5B).
☐ Uneven or low cylinder compressions (Chapter 2A or 2B).
☐ Blocked injector/fuel injection system fault (Chapter 4A).

Engine hesitates on acceleration

☐ Worn, faulty or incorrectly-gapped spark plugs (Chapter 1).
☐ Vacuum leak at the throttle body, inlet manifold or associated hoses (Chapter 4A).
☐ Blocked injector/fuel injection system fault (Chapter 4A).

Engine stalls

☐ Vacuum leak at the throttle body, inlet manifold or associated hoses (Chapter 4A).
☐ Fuel pump faulty, or delivery pressure low (Chapter 4A).
☐ Fuel tank vent blocked, or fuel pipes restricted (Chapter 4A).
☐ Blocked injector/fuel injection system fault (Chapter 4A).

Engine (continued)

Engine lacks power

- [ ] Timing belt incorrectly fitted or tensioned (Chapter 2A or 2B).
- [ ] Fuel pump faulty, or delivery pressure low (Chapter 4A).
- [ ] Uneven or low cylinder compressions (Chapter 2A or 2B).
- [ ] Worn, faulty or incorrectly-gapped spark plugs (Chapter 1).
- [ ] Vacuum leak at the throttle body, inlet manifold or associated hoses (Chapter 4A).
- [ ] Blocked injector/fuel injection system fault (Chapter 4A).
- [ ] Brakes binding (Chapter 9).
- [ ] Clutch slipping (Chapter 6).

Engine backfires

- [ ] Timing belt incorrectly fitted or tensioned (Chapter 2A or 2B).
- [ ] Vacuum leak at the throttle body, inlet manifold or associated hoses (Chapter 4A).
- [ ] Blocked injector/fuel injection system fault (Chapter 4A).

Oil pressure warning light illuminated with engine running

- [ ] Low oil level, or incorrect oil grade (*Weekly checks*).
- [ ] Faulty oil pressure warning light switch (Chapter 5A).
- [ ] Worn engine bearings and/or oil pump (Chapter 2C).
- [ ] High engine operating temperature (Chapter 3).
- [ ] Oil pressure relief valve defective (Chapter 2A or 2B).
- [ ] Oil pick-up strainer clogged (Chapter 2A or 2B).

Engine runs-on after switching off

- [ ] Excessive carbon build-up in engine (Chapter 2A or 2B).
- [ ] High engine operating temperature (Chapter 3).
- [ ] Fuel injection system fault (Chapter 4A).

Engine noises

Pre-ignition (pinking) or knocking during accelerat[ion] under load

- [ ] Ignition timing incorrect/ignition system fault (Chapter 1 a[nd])
- [ ] Incorrect grade of spark plug (Chapter 1).
- [ ] Incorrect grade of fuel (Chapter 4A).
- [ ] Vacuum leak at the throttle body, inlet manifold or associa[ted] hoses (Chapter 4A).
- [ ] Excessive carbon build-up in engine (Chapter 2A or 2B).
- [ ] Blocked injector/fuel injection system fault (Chapter 4A).

Whistling or wheezing noises

- [ ] Leaking inlet manifold or throttle body gasket (Chapter 4A).
- [ ] Leaking exhaust manifold gasket or pipe-to-manifold joint (Chapter 4A).
- [ ] Leaking vacuum hose (Chapter 4A, 4B and 9).
- [ ] Blowing cylinder head gasket (Chapter 2A or 2B).

Tapping or rattling noises

- [ ] Worn valve gear or camshaft (Chapter 2A, 2B or 2C).
- [ ] Ancillary component fault (coolant pump, alternator, etc) (Chapter 3, 5A, etc).

Knocking or thumping noises

- [ ] Worn big-end bearings (regular heavy knocking, perhaps less[ening] under load) (Chapter 2C).
- [ ] Worn main bearings (rumbling and knocking, perhaps worsen[ing] under load) (Chapter 2C).
- [ ] Piston slap (most noticeable when cold) (Chapter 2C).
- [ ] Ancillary component fault (coolant pump, alternator, etc) (Chapter 3, 5A, etc).

Cooling system

Overheating

- [ ] Insufficient coolant in system (*Weekly checks*).
- [ ] Thermostat faulty (Chapter 3).
- [ ] Radiator core blocked, or grille restricted (Chapter 3).
- [ ] Electric cooling fan faulty (Chapter 3).
- [ ] Pressure cap faulty (Chapter 3).
- [ ] Ignition timing incorrect/ignition system fault (Chapter 1 and 5B).
- [ ] Inaccurate temperature gauge sender unit (Chapter 3).
- [ ] Airlock in cooling system.

Overcooling

- [ ] Thermostat faulty (Chapter 3).
- [ ] Inaccurate temperature gauge sender unit (Chapter 3).

External coolant leakage

- [ ] Deteriorated or damaged hoses or hose clips (Chapter 1).
- [ ] Radiator core or heater matrix leaking (Chapter 3).
- [ ] Pressure cap faulty (Chapter 3).
- [ ] Coolant pump seal leaking (Chapter 3).
- [ ] Boiling due to overheating (Chapter 3).
- [ ] Core plug leaking (Chapter 2C).

Internal coolant leakage

- [ ] Leaking cylinder head gasket (Chapter 2A or 2B).
- [ ] Cracked cylinder head or cylinder bore (Chapter 2A, 2B or 2C).

Corrosion

- [ ] Infrequent draining and flushing (Chapter 1).
- [ ] Incorrect coolant mixture or inappropriate coolant type (Chapter 1).

Fuel and exhaust systems

Excessive fuel consumption

☐ Air filter element dirty or clogged (Chapter 1).
☐ Fuel injection system fault (Chapter 4A).
☐ Ignition timing incorrect/ignition system fault (Chapter 1 and 5B).
☐ Tyres under-inflated (Weekly checks).

Fuel leakage and/or fuel odour

☐ Damaged fuel tank, pipes or connections (Chapter 4A or 4B).

Excessive noise or fumes from exhaust system

☐ Leaking exhaust system or manifold joints (Chapter 1 and 4A).
☐ Leaking, corroded or damaged silencers or pipe (Chapter 1 and 4A).
☐ Broken mountings causing body or suspension contact (Chapter 1).

Clutch

Pedal travels to floor – no pressure or very little resistance

☐ Hydraulic fluid level low/air in the hydraulic system (Chapter 6).
☐ Broken clutch release bearing or fork (Chapter 6).
☐ Broken diaphragm spring in clutch pressure plate (Chapter 6).

Clutch fails to disengage (unable to select gears).

☐ Hydraulic fluid level low/air in the hydraulic system (Chapter 6).
☐ Clutch friction plate sticking on gearbox input shaft splines (Chapter 6).
☐ Clutch friction plate sticking to flywheel or pressure plate (Chapter 6).
☐ Faulty pressure plate assembly (Chapter 6).
☐ Clutch release mechanism worn or incorrectly assembled (Chapter 6).

Clutch slips (engine speed increases, with no increase in vehicle speed).

☐ Clutch friction plate linings excessively worn (Chapter 6).
☐ Clutch friction plate linings contaminated with oil or grease (Chapter 6).
☐ Faulty pressure plate or weak diaphragm spring (Chapter 6).

Judder as clutch is engaged

☐ Clutch friction plate linings contaminated with oil or grease (Chapter 6).
☐ Clutch friction plate linings excessively worn (Chapter 6).
☐ Faulty or distorted pressure plate or diaphragm spring (Chapter 6).
☐ Worn or loose engine/transmission mountings (Chapter 2A or 2B).
☐ Clutch friction plate hub or gearbox input shaft splines worn (Chapter 6).

Noise when depressing or releasing clutch pedal

☐ Worn clutch release bearing (Chapter 6).
☐ Worn or dry clutch pedal bushes (Chapter 6).
☐ Faulty pressure plate assembly (Chapter 6).
☐ Pressure plate diaphragm spring broken (Chapter 6).
☐ Broken friction plate cushioning springs (Chapter 6).

Manual transmission

Noisy in neutral with engine running

☐ Input shaft bearings worn (noise apparent with clutch pedal released, but not when depressed) (Chapter 7A).*
☐ Clutch release bearing worn (noise apparent with clutch pedal depressed, possibly less when released) (Chapter 6).

Noisy in one particular gear

☐ Worn, damaged or chipped gear teeth (Chapter 7A).*

Difficulty engaging gears

☐ Clutch fault (Chapter 6).
☐ Worn or damaged gearchange linkage/cable (Chapter 7A).
☐ Worn synchroniser units (Chapter 7A).*

Jumps out of gear

☐ Worn or damaged gearchange linkage/cable (Chapter 7A).
☐ Worn synchroniser units (Chapter 7A).*
☐ Worn selector forks (Chapter 7A).*

Vibration

☐ Lack of oil (Chapter 1).
☐ Worn bearings (Chapter 7A).*

Lubricant leaks

☐ Leaking differential output oil seal (Chapter 7A).
☐ Leaking housing joint (Chapter 7A).*
☐ Leaking input shaft oil seal (Chapter 7A).*

* Although the corrective action necessary to remedy the symptoms described is beyond the scope of the home mechanic, the above information should be helpful in isolating the cause of the condition, so that the owner can communicate clearly with a professional mechanic.

Automatic transmission

Note: *Due to the complexity of the automatic transmission, it is difficult for the home mechanic to properly diagnose and service this unit. For problems other than the following, the vehicle should be taken to a dealer service department or automatic transmission specialist. Do not be too hasty in removing the transmission if a fault is suspected, as most of the testing is carried out with the unit still fitted.*

Fluid leakage

☐ Automatic transmission fluid is usually dark in colour. Fluid leaks should not be confused with engine oil, which can easily be blown onto the transmission by airflow.

☐ To determine the source of a leak, first remove all built-up dirt and grime from the transmission housing and surrounding areas using a degreasing agent, or by steam-cleaning. Drive the vehicle at low speed, so airflow will not blow the leak far from its source. Raise and support the vehicle, and determine where the leak is coming from. The following are common areas of leakage:

a) *Oil pan (Chapter 1 and 7B).*
b) *Dipstick tube (Chapter 1 and 7B).*
c) *Transmission-to-fluid cooler pipes/unions (Chapter 7B).*

Transmission fluid brown, or has burned smell

☐ Transmission fluid level low, or fluid in need of renewal (Chapter 1).

General gear selection problems

☐ Chapter 7B deals with checking and adjusting the selector cable on automatic transmissions. The following are common problems which may be caused by a poorly-adjusted cable:
a) *Engine starting in gears other than Park or Neutral.*
b) *Indicator panel indicating a gear other than the one actually being used.*
c) *Vehicle moves when in Park or Neutral.*
☐ Refer to Chapter 7B for the selector cable adjustment procedure.

Engine will not start in any gear, or starts in gears other than Park or Neutral

☐ Incorrect selector cable adjustment (Chapter 7B).

Transmission slips, is noisy, or has no drive in forward or reverse gears

☐ There are many probable causes for the above problems, but the home mechanic should be concerned with only one possibility – fluid level. Before taking the vehicle to a dealer or transmission specialist, check the fluid level and condition of the fluid as described in *Weekly checks* and Chapter 1. Correct the fluid level as necessary, or change the fluid and filter if needed. If the problem persists, professional help will be necessary.

Driveshafts

Clicking or knocking noise on turns (at slow speed on full-lock).

☐ Lack of constant velocity joint lubricant, possibly due to damaged gaiter (Chapter 8).
☐ Worn outer constant velocity joint (Chapter 8).

Vibration when accelerating or decelerating

☐ Worn inner constant velocity joint (Chapter 8).
☐ Bent or distorted driveshaft (Chapter 8).

Braking system

Note: *Before assuming that a brake problem exists, make sure that the tyres are in good condition and correctly inflated, that the front wheel alignment is correct, and that the vehicle is not loaded with weight in an unequal manner. Apart from checking the condition of all pipe and hose connections, any faults occurring on the anti-lock braking system should be referred to a Fiat dealer for diagnosis.*

Vehicle pulls to one side under braking

☐ Worn, defective, damaged or contaminated brake pads/shoes on one side (Chapter 1 and 9).
☐ Seized or partially-seized front brake caliper/wheel cylinder piston (Chapter 1 and 9).
☐ A mixture of brake pad/shoe lining materials fitted between sides (Chapter 1 and 9).
☐ Brake caliper or backplate mounting bolts loose (Chapter 9).
☐ Worn or damaged steering or suspension components (Chapter 1 and 10).

Noise (grinding or high-pitched squeal) when brakes applied

☐ Brake pad or shoe friction lining material worn down to metal backing (Chapter 1 and 9).
☐ Excessive corrosion of brake disc or drum. (May be apparent after the vehicle has been standing for some time (Chapter 1 and 9).
☐ Foreign object (stone chipping, etc) trapped between brake disc and shield (Chapter 1 and 9).

Excessive brake pedal travel

☐ Inoperative rear brake self-adjust mechanism (Chapter 9).
☐ Faulty master cylinder (Chapter 9).
☐ Air in hydraulic system (Chapter 9).

Brake pedal feels spongy when depressed

☐ Air in hydraulic system (Chapter 9).
☐ Deteriorated flexible rubber brake hoses (Chapter 1 and 9).
☐ Master cylinder mounting nuts loose (Chapter 9).
☐ Faulty master cylinder (Chapter 9).

Braking system (continued_

Excessive brake pedal effort required to stop vehicle

- ☐ Faulty vacuum servo unit (Chapter 9).
- ☐ Disconnected, damaged or insecure brake servo vacuum hose (Chapter 9).
- ☐ Primary or secondary hydraulic circuit failure (Chapter 9).
- ☐ Seized brake caliper or wheel cylinder piston(s) (Chapter 9).
- ☐ Brake pads or brake shoes incorrectly fitted (Chapter 9).
- ☐ Incorrect grade of brake pads or brake shoes fitted (Chapter 9).
- ☐ Brake pads or brake shoe linings contaminated (Chapter 9).

Judder felt through brake pedal or steering wheel when braking

- ☐ Excessive run-out or distortion of discs/drums (Chapter 9).

- ☐ Brake pad or brake shoe linings worn (Chapter 1 and 9).
- ☐ Brake caliper or brake backplate mounting bolts loose (Chapter 9).
- ☐ Wear in suspension or steering components or mountings (Chapter 1 and 10).

Brakes binding

- ☐ Seized brake caliper or wheel cylinder piston(s) (Chapter 9).
- ☐ Incorrectly-adjusted handbrake mechanism (Chapter 9).
- ☐ Faulty master cylinder (Chapter 9).

Rear wheels locking under normal braking

- ☐ Rear brake shoe linings contaminated (Chapter 1 and 9).
- ☐ Faulty brake pressure regulator (Chapter 9).

Suspension and steering

Note: *Before diagnosing suspension or steering faults, be sure that the trouble is not due to incorrect tyre pressures, mixtures of tyre types, or binding brakes.*

Vehicle pulls to one side

- ☐ Defective tyre (*Weekly checks*).
- ☐ Excessive wear in suspension or steering components (Chapter 1 and 10).
- ☐ Incorrect front wheel alignment (Chapter 1).
- ☐ Accident damage to steering or suspension components (Chapter 1).

Wheel wobble and vibration

- ☐ Front roadwheels out of balance (vibration felt mainly through the steering wheel) (Chapter 1).
- ☐ Rear roadwheels out of balance (vibration felt throughout the vehicle) (Chapter 1).
- ☐ Roadwheels damaged or distorted (Chapter 1).
- ☐ Faulty or damaged tyre (*Weekly checks*).
- ☐ Worn steering or suspension joints, bushes or components (Chapter 1 and 10).
- ☐ Wheel bolts loose (Chapter 1 and 10).

Excessive pitching and/or rolling around corners, or during braking

- ☐ Defective shock absorbers (Chapter 10).
- ☐ Broken or weak spring and/or suspension component (Chapter 10).
- ☐ Worn or damaged anti-roll bar or mountings (Chapter 10).

Wandering or general instability

- ☐ Incorrect front wheel alignment (Chapter 1).
- ☐ Worn steering or suspension joints, bushes or components (Chapter 1 and 10).
- ☐ Roadwheels out of balance (Chapter 1).
- ☐ Faulty or damaged tyre (*Weekly checks*).
- ☐ Wheel bolts loose (Chapter 1 and 10).
- ☐ Defective shock absorbers (Chapter 10).

Excessively-stiff steering

- ☐ Lack of steering gear lubricant (Chapter 10).
- ☐ Seized track rod end balljoint or suspension balljoint (Chapter 1 and 10).
- ☐ Incorrect front wheel alignment (Chapter 1).
- ☐ Steering rack or column bent or damaged (Chapter 10).

Excessive play in steering

- ☐ Worn steering column intermediate shaft universal joint (Chapter 10).
- ☐ Worn steering track rod end balljoints (Chapter 1 and 10).
- ☐ Worn rack-and-pinion steering gear (Chapter 10).
- ☐ Worn steering or suspension joints, bushes or components (Chapter 1 and 10).

Lack of power assistance

- ☐ Faulty electronic power steering motor or control unit fault (Chapter 10).

Tyre wear excessive

Tyres worn on inside or outside edges

- ☐ Tyres under-inflated (wear on both edges) (*Weekly checks*).
- ☐ Incorrect camber or castor angles (wear on one edge only) (Chapter 1).
- ☐ Worn steering or suspension joints, bushes or components (Chapter 1 and 10).
- ☐ Excessively-hard cornering.
- ☐ Accident damage.

Tyre treads exhibit feathered edges

- ☐ Incorrect toe setting (Chapter 1).

Tyres worn in centre of tread

- ☐ Tyres over-inflated (*Weekly checks*).

Tyres worn on inside and outside edges

- ☐ Tyres under-inflated (*Weekly checks*).

Tyres worn unevenly

- ☐ Tyres/wheels out of balance (Chapter 1).
- ☐ Excessive wheel or tyre run-out (Chapter 1).
- ☐ Worn shock absorbers (Chapter 1 and 10).
- ☐ Faulty tyre (*Weekly checks*).

Electrical system

Note: *For problems associated with the starting system, refer to the faults listed under Engine earlier in this Section.*

Battery will not hold a charge for more than a few days

- [ ] Battery defective internally (Chapter 5A).
- [ ] Battery terminal connections loose or corroded (*Weekly checks*).
- [ ] Auxiliary drivebelt worn or incorrectly adjusted (Chapter 1).
- [ ] Alternator not charging at correct output (Chapter 5A).
- [ ] Alternator or voltage regulator faulty (Chapter 5A).
- [ ] Short-circuit causing continual battery drain (Chapter 5A and 12).

Ignition/no-charge warning light remains illuminated with engine running

- [ ] Auxiliary drivebelt broken, worn, or incorrectly adjusted (Chapter 1).
- [ ] Alternator brushes worn, sticking, or dirty (Chapter 5A).
- [ ] Alternator brush springs weak or broken (Chapter 5A).
- [ ] Internal fault in alternator or voltage regulator (Chapter 5A).
- [ ] Broken, disconnected, or loose wiring in charging circuit (Chapter 5A).

Ignition/no-charge warning light fails to come on

- [ ] Warning light bulb blown (Chapter 12).
- [ ] Broken, disconnected, or loose wiring in warning light circuit (Chapter 12).
- [ ] Alternator faulty (Chapter 5A).

Lights inoperative

- [ ] Bulb blown (Chapter 12).
- [ ] Corrosion of bulb or bulbholder contacts (Chapter 12).
- [ ] Blown fuse (Chapter 12).
- [ ] Faulty relay (Chapter 12).
- [ ] Broken, loose, or disconnected wiring (Chapter 12).
- [ ] Faulty switch (Chapter 12).

Instrument readings inaccurate or erratic

Instrument readings increase with engine speed

- [ ] Faulty voltage regulator (Chapter 12).

Fuel or temperature gauges give no reading

- [ ] Faulty gauge sender unit (Chapter 3 and 4A).
- [ ] Wiring open-circuit (Chapter 12).
- [ ] Faulty gauge (Chapter 12).

Fuel or temperature gauges give continuous maximum reading

- [ ] Faulty gauge sender unit (Chapter 3 and 4A).
- [ ] Wiring short-circuit (Chapter 12).
- [ ] Faulty gauge (Chapter 12).

Horn inoperative, or unsatisfactory in operation

Horn operates all the time

- [ ] Horn push either earthed or stuck down (Chapter 12).
- [ ] Horn cable-to-horn push earthed (Chapter 12).

Horn fails to operate

- [ ] Blown fuse (Chapter 12).
- [ ] Cable or cable connections loose, broken or disconnected (Chapter 12).
- [ ] Faulty horn (Chapter 12).

Horn emits intermittent or unsatisfactory sound

- [ ] Cable connections loose (Chapter 12).
- [ ] Horn mountings loose (Chapter 12).
- [ ] Faulty horn (Chapter 12).

Windscreen/tailgate wipers inoperative, or unsatisfactory in operation

Wipers fail to operate, or operate very slowly

- [ ] Wiper blades stuck to screen, or linkage seized or binding (Chapter 1 and 12).
- [ ] Blown fuse (Chapter 12).
- [ ] Cable or cable connections loose, broken or disconnected (Chapter 12).
- [ ] Faulty relay (Chapter 12).
- [ ] Faulty wiper motor (Chapter 12).

Wiper blades sweep over too large or too small an area of the glass

- [ ] Wiper arms incorrectly positioned on spindles (Chapter 1).
- [ ] Excessive wear of wiper linkage (Chapter 12).
- [ ] Wiper motor or linkage mountings loose or insecure (Chapter 12).

Wiper blades fail to clean the glass effectively

- [ ] Wiper blade rubbers worn or perished (*Weekly checks*).
- [ ] Wiper arm tension springs broken, or arm pivots seized (Chapter 12).
- [ ] Insufficient windscreen washer additive to adequately remove road film (*Weekly checks*).

Windscreen/tailgate washers inoperative, or unsatisfactory in operation

One or more washer jets inoperative

- [ ] Blocked washer jet (Chapter 1).
- [ ] Disconnected, kinked or restricted fluid hose (Chapter 12).
- [ ] Insufficient fluid in washer reservoir (*Weekly checks*).

Washer pump fails to operate

- [ ] Broken or disconnected wiring or connections (Chapter 12).
- [ ] Blown fuse (Chapter 12).
- [ ] Faulty washer switch (Chapter 12).
- [ ] Faulty washer pump (Chapter 12).

Washer pump runs for some time before fluid is emitted from jets

- [ ] Faulty one-way valve in fluid supply hose (Chapter 12).

Electric windows inoperative, or unsatisfactory in operation

Window glass will only move in one direction

- [ ] Faulty switch (Chapter 12).

Window glass slow to move

- [ ] Regulator seized or damaged, or in need of lubrication (Chapter 11).
- [ ] Door internal components or trim fouling regulator (Chapter 11).
- [ ] Faulty motor (Chapter 11).

Window glass fails to move

- [ ] Blown fuse (Chapter 12).
- [ ] Faulty relay (Chapter 12).
- [ ] Broken or disconnected wiring or connections (Chapter 12).
- [ ] Faulty motor (Chapter 11).

A

ABS (Anti-lock brake system) A system, usually electronically controlled, that senses incipient wheel lockup during braking and relieves hydraulic pressure at wheels that are about to skid.

Air bag An inflatable bag hidden in the steering wheel (driver's side) or the dash or glovebox (passenger side). In a head-on collision, the bags inflate, preventing the driver and front passenger from being thrown forward into the steering wheel or windscreen.

Air cleaner A metal or plastic housing, containing a filter element, which removes dust and dirt from the air being drawn into the engine.

Air filter element The actual filter in an air cleaner system, usually manufactured from pleated paper and requiring renewal at regular intervals.

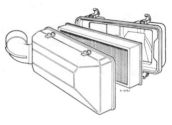

Air filter

Allen key A hexagonal wrench which fits into a recessed hexagonal hole.

Alligator clip A long-nosed spring-loaded metal clip with meshing teeth. Used to make temporary electrical connections.

Alternator A component in the electrical system which converts mechanical energy from a drivebelt into electrical energy to charge the battery and to operate the starting system, ignition system and electrical accessories.

Alternator (exploded view)

Ampere (amp) A unit of measurement for the flow of electric current. One amp is the amount of current produced by one volt acting through a resistance of one ohm.

Anaerobic sealer A substance used to prevent bolts and screws from loosening. Anaerobic means that it does not require oxygen for activation. The Loctite brand is widely used.

Antifreeze A substance (usually ethylene glycol) mixed with water, and added to a vehicle's cooling system, to prevent freezing of the coolant in winter. Antifreeze also contains chemicals to inhibit corrosion and the formation of rust and other deposits that

would tend to clog the radiator and coolant passages and reduce cooling efficiency.

Anti-seize compound A coating that reduces the risk of seizing on fasteners that are subjected to high temperatures, such as exhaust manifold bolts and nuts.

Anti-seize compound

Asbestos A natural fibrous mineral with great heat resistance, commonly used in the composition of brake friction materials. Asbestos is a health hazard and the dust created by brake systems should never be inhaled or ingested.

Axle A shaft on which a wheel revolves, or which revolves with a wheel. Also, a solid beam that connects the two wheels at one end of the vehicle. An axle which also transmits power to the wheels is known as a live axle.

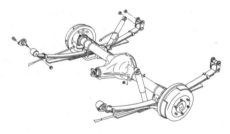

Axle assembly

Axleshaft A single rotating shaft, on either side of the differential, which delivers power from the final drive assembly to the drive wheels. Also called a driveshaft or a halfshaft.

B

Ball bearing An anti-friction bearing consisting of a hardened inner and outer race with hardened steel balls between two races.

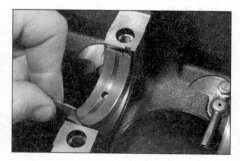

Bearing

Bearing The curved surface on a shaft or in a bore, or the part assembled into either, that permits relative motion between them with minimum wear and friction.

Big-end bearing The bearing in the end of the connecting rod that's attached to the crankshaft.

Bleed nipple A valve on a brake wheel cylinder, caliper or other hydraulic component that is opened to purge the hydraulic system of air. Also called a bleed screw.

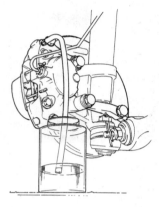

Brake bleeding

Brake bleeding Procedure for removing air from lines of a hydraulic brake system.

Brake disc The component of a disc brake that rotates with the wheels.

Brake drum The component of a drum brake that rotates with the wheels.

Brake linings The friction material which contacts the brake disc or drum to retard the vehicle's speed. The linings are bonded or riveted to the brake pads or shoes.

Brake pads The replaceable friction pads that pinch the brake disc when the brakes are applied. Brake pads consist of a friction material bonded or riveted to a rigid backing plate.

Brake shoe The crescent-shaped carrier to which the brake linings are mounted and which forces the lining against the rotating drum during braking.

Braking systems For more information on braking systems, consult the *Haynes Automotive Brake Manual*.

Breaker bar A long socket wrench handle providing greater leverage.

Bulkhead The insulated partition between the engine and the passenger compartment.

C

Caliper The non-rotating part of a disc-brake assembly that straddles the disc and carries the brake pads. The caliper also contains the hydraulic components that cause the pads to pinch the disc when the brakes are applied. A caliper is also a measuring tool that can be set to measure inside or outside dimensions of an object.

Camshaft A rotating shaft on which a series of cam lobes operate the valve mechanisms. The camshaft may be driven by gears, by sprockets and chain or by sprockets and a belt.

Canister A container in an evaporative emission control system; contains activated charcoal granules to trap vapours from the fuel system.

Canister

Carburettor A device which mixes fuel with air in the proper proportions to provide a desired power output from a spark ignition internal combustion engine.

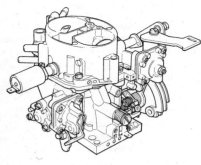

Carburettor

Castellated Resembling the parapets along the top of a castle wall. For example, a castellated balljoint stud nut.

Castellated nut

Castor In wheel alignment, the backward or forward tilt of the steering axis. Castor is positive when the steering axis is inclined rearward at the top.

Catalytic converter A silencer-like device in the exhaust system which converts certain pollutants in the exhaust gases into less harmful substances.

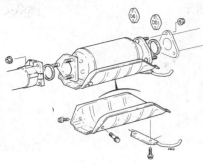

Catalytic converter

Circlip A ring-shaped clip used to prevent endwise movement of cylindrical parts and shafts. An internal circlip is installed in a groove in a housing; an external circlip fits into a groove on the outside of a cylindrical piece such as a shaft.

Clearance The amount of space between two parts. For example, between a piston and a cylinder, between a bearing and a journal, etc.

Coil spring A spiral of elastic steel found in various sizes throughout a vehicle, for example as a springing medium in the suspension and in the valve train.

Compression Reduction in volume, and increase in pressure and temperature, of a gas, caused by squeezing it into a smaller space.

Compression ratio The relationship between cylinder volume when the piston is at top dead centre and cylinder volume when the piston is at bottom dead centre.

Constant velocity (CV) joint A type of universal joint that cancels out vibrations caused by driving power being transmitted through an angle.

Core plug A disc or cup-shaped metal device inserted in a hole in a casting through which core was removed when the casting was formed. Also known as a freeze plug or expansion plug.

Crankcase The lower part of the engine block in which the crankshaft rotates.

Crankshaft The main rotating member, or shaft, running the length of the crankcase, with offset "throws" to which the connecting rods are attached.

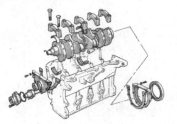

Crankshaft assembly

Crocodile clip See Alligator clip

D

Diagnostic code Code numbers obtained by accessing the diagnostic mode of an engine management computer. This code can be used to determine the area in the system where a malfunction may be located.

Disc brake A brake design incorporating a rotating disc onto which brake pads are squeezed. The resulting friction converts the energy of a moving vehicle into heat.

Double-overhead cam (DOHC) An engine that uses two overhead camshafts, usually one for the intake valves and one for the exhaust valves.

Drivebelt(s) The belt(s) used to drive accessories such as the alternator, water pump, power steering pump, air conditioning compressor, etc. off the crankshaft pulley.

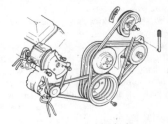

Accessory drivebelts

Driveshaft Any shaft used to transmit motion. Commonly used when referring to the axleshafts on a front wheel drive vehicle.

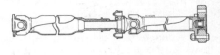

Driveshaft

Drum brake A type of brake using a drum-shaped metal cylinder attached to the inner surface of the wheel. When the brake pedal is pressed, curved brake shoes with friction linings press against the inside of the drum to slow or stop the vehicle.

Drum brake assembly

E

EGR valve A valve used to introduce exhaust gases into the intake air stream.

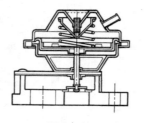

EGR valve

Electronic control unit (ECU) A computer which controls (for instance) ignition and fuel injection systems, or an anti-lock braking system. For more information refer to the *Haynes Automotive Electrical and Electronic Systems Manual*.

Electronic Fuel Injection (EFI) A computer controlled fuel system that distributes fuel through an injector located in each intake port of the engine.

Emergency brake A braking system, independent of the main hydraulic system, that can be used to slow or stop the vehicle if the primary brakes fail, or to hold the vehicle stationary even though the brake pedal isn't depressed. It usually consists of a hand lever that actuates either front or rear brakes mechanically through a series of cables and linkages. Also known as a handbrake or parking brake.

Endfloat The amount of lengthwise movement between two parts. As applied to a crankshaft, the distance that the crankshaft can move forward and back in the cylinder block.

Engine management system (EMS) A computer controlled system which manages the fuel injection and the ignition systems in an integrated fashion.

Exhaust manifold A part with several passages through which exhaust gases leave the engine combustion chambers and enter the exhaust pipe.

Exhaust manifold

F

Fan clutch A viscous (fluid) drive coupling device which permits variable engine fan speeds in relation to engine speeds.

Feeler blade A thin strip or blade of hardened steel, ground to an exact thickness, used to check or measure clearances between parts.

Feeler blade

Firing order The order in which the engine cylinders fire, or deliver their power strokes, beginning with the number one cylinder.

Flywheel A heavy spinning wheel in which energy is absorbed and stored by means of momentum. On cars, the flywheel is attached to the crankshaft to smooth out firing impulses.

Free play The amount of travel before any action takes place. The "looseness" in a linkage, or an assembly of parts, between the initial application of force and actual movement. For example, the distance the brake pedal moves before the pistons in the master cylinder are actuated.

Fuse An electrical device which protects a circuit against accidental overload. The typical fuse contains a soft piece of metal which is calibrated to melt at a predetermined current flow (expressed as amps) and break the circuit.

Fusible link A circuit protection device consisting of a conductor surrounded by heat-resistant insulation. The conductor is smaller than the wire it protects, so it acts as the weakest link in the circuit. Unlike a blown fuse, a failed fusible link must frequently be cut from the wire for replacement.

G

Gap The distance the spark must travel in jumping from the centre electrode to the side

Adjusting spark plug gap

electrode in a spark plug. Also refers to the spacing between the points in a contact breaker assembly in a conventional points-type ignition, or to the distance between the reluctor or rotor and the pickup coil in an electronic ignition.

Gasket Any thin, soft material - usually cork, cardboard, asbestos or soft metal - installed between two metal surfaces to ensure a good seal. For instance, the cylinder head gasket seals the joint between the block and the cylinder head.

Gasket

Gauge An instrument panel display used to monitor engine conditions. A gauge with a movable pointer on a dial or a fixed scale is an analogue gauge. A gauge with a numerical readout is called a digital gauge.

H

Halfshaft A rotating shaft that transmits power from the final drive unit to a drive wheel, usually when referring to a live rear axle.

Harmonic balancer A device designed to reduce torsion or twisting vibration in the crankshaft. May be incorporated in the crankshaft pulley. Also known as a vibration damper.

Hone An abrasive tool for correcting small irregularities or differences in diameter in an engine cylinder, brake cylinder, etc.

Hydraulic tappet A tappet that utilises hydraulic pressure from the engine's lubrication system to maintain zero clearance (constant contact with both camshaft and valve stem). Automatically adjusts to variation in valve stem length. Hydraulic tappets also reduce valve noise.

I

Ignition timing The moment at which the spark plug fires, usually expressed in the number of crankshaft degrees before the piston reaches the top of its stroke.

Inlet manifold A tube or housing with passages through which flows the air-fuel mixture (carburettor vehicles and vehicles with throttle body injection) or air only (port fuel-injected vehicles) to the port openings in the cylinder head.

J

Jump start Starting the engine of a vehicle with a discharged or weak battery by attaching jump leads from the weak battery to a charged or helper battery.

L

Load Sensing Proportioning Valve (LSPV) A brake hydraulic system control valve that works like a proportioning valve, but also takes into consideration the amount of weight carried by the rear axle.

Locknut A nut used to lock an adjustment nut, or other threaded component, in place. For example, a locknut is employed to keep the adjusting nut on the rocker arm in position.

Lockwasher A form of washer designed to prevent an attaching nut from working loose.

M

MacPherson strut A type of front suspension system devised by Earle MacPherson at Ford of England. In its original form, a simple lateral link with the anti-roll bar creates the lower control arm. A long strut - an integral coil spring and shock absorber - is mounted between the body and the steering knuckle. Many modern so-called MacPherson strut systems use a conventional lower A-arm and don't rely on the anti-roll bar for location.

Multimeter An electrical test instrument with the capability to measure voltage, current and resistance.

N

NOx Oxides of Nitrogen. A common toxic pollutant emitted by petrol and diesel engines at higher temperatures.

O

Ohm The unit of electrical resistance. One volt applied to a resistance of one ohm will produce a current of one amp.

Ohmmeter An instrument for measuring electrical resistance.

O-ring A type of sealing ring made of a special rubber-like material; in use, the O-ring is compressed into a groove to provide the sealing action.

O-ring

Overhead cam (ohc) engine An engine with the camshaft(s) located on top of the cylinder head(s).

Overhead valve (ohv) engine An engine with the valves located in the cylinder head, but with the camshaft located in the engine block.

Oxygen sensor A device installed in the engine exhaust manifold, which senses the oxygen content in the exhaust and converts this information into an electric current. Also called a Lambda sensor.

P

Phillips screw A type of screw head having a cross instead of a slot for a corresponding type of screwdriver.

Plastigage A thin strip of plastic thread, available in different sizes, used for measuring clearances. For example, a strip of Plastigage is laid across a bearing journal. The parts are assembled and dismantled; the width of the crushed strip indicates the clearance between journal and bearing.

Plastigage

Propeller shaft The long hollow tube with universal joints at both ends that carries power from the transmission to the differential on front-engined rear wheel drive vehicles.

Proportioning valve A hydraulic control valve which limits the amount of pressure to the rear brakes during panic stops to prevent wheel lock-up.

R

Rack-and-pinion steering A steering system with a pinion gear on the end of the steering shaft that mates with a rack (think of a geared wheel opened up and laid flat). When the steering wheel is turned, the pinion turns, moving the rack to the left or right. This movement is transmitted through the track rods to the steering arms at the wheels.

Radiator A liquid-to-air heat transfer device designed to reduce the temperature of the coolant in an internal combustion engine cooling system.

Refrigerant Any substance used as a heat transfer agent in an air-conditioning system. R-12 has been the principle refrigerant for many years; recently, however, manufacturers have begun using R-134a, a non-CFC substance that is considered less harmful to the ozone in the upper atmosphere.

Rocker arm A lever arm that rocks on a shaft or pivots on a stud. In an overhead valve engine, the rocker arm converts the upward movement of the pushrod into a downward movement to open a valve.

Rotor In a distributor, the rotating device inside the cap that connects the centre electrode and the outer terminals as it turns, distributing the high voltage from the coil secondary winding to the proper spark plug. Also, that part of an alternator which rotates inside the stator. Also, the rotating assembly of a turbocharger, including the compressor wheel, shaft and turbine wheel.

Runout The amount of wobble (in-and-out movement) of a gear or wheel as it's rotated. The amount a shaft rotates "out-of-true." The out-of-round condition of a rotating part.

S

Sealant A liquid or paste used to prevent leakage at a joint. Sometimes used in conjunction with a gasket.

Sealed beam lamp An older headlight design which integrates the reflector, lens and filaments into a hermetically-sealed one-piece unit. When a filament burns out or the lens cracks, the entire unit is simply replaced.

Serpentine drivebelt A single, long, wide accessory drivebelt that's used on some newer vehicles to drive all the accessories, instead of a series of smaller, shorter belts. Serpentine drivebelts are usually tensioned by an automatic tensioner.

Serpentine drivebelt

Shim Thin spacer, commonly used to adjust the clearance or relative positions between two parts. For example, shims inserted into or under bucket tappets control valve clearances. Clearance is adjusted by changing the thickness of the shim.

Slide hammer A special puller that screws into or hooks onto a component such as a shaft or bearing; a heavy sliding handle on the shaft bottoms against the end of the shaft to knock the component free.

Sprocket A tooth or projection on the periphery of a wheel, shaped to engage with a chain or drivebelt. Commonly used to refer to the sprocket wheel itself.

Starter inhibitor switch On vehicles with an automatic transmission, a switch that prevents starting if the vehicle is not in Neutral or Park.

Strut See MacPherson strut.

T

Tappet A cylindrical component which transmits motion from the cam to the valve stem, either directly or via a pushrod and rocker arm. Also called a cam follower.

Thermostat A heat-controlled valve that regulates the flow of coolant between the cylinder block and the radiator, so maintaining optimum engine operating temperature. A thermostat is also used in some air cleaners in which the temperature is regulated.

Thrust bearing The bearing in the clutch assembly that is moved in to the release levers by clutch pedal action to disengage the clutch. Also referred to as a release bearing.

Timing belt A toothed belt which drives the camshaft. Serious engine damage may result if it breaks in service.

Timing chain A chain which drives the camshaft.

Toe-in The amount the front wheels are closer together at the front than at the rear. On rear wheel drive vehicles, a slight amount of toe-in is usually specified to keep the front wheels running parallel on the road by offsetting other forces that tend to spread the wheels apart.

Toe-out The amount the front wheels are closer together at the rear than at the front. On front wheel drive vehicles, a slight amount of toe-out is usually specified.

Tools For full information on choosing and using tools, refer to the *Haynes Automotive Tools Manual.*

Tracer A stripe of a second colour applied to a wire insulator to distinguish that wire from another one with the same colour insulator.

Tune-up A process of accurate and careful adjustments and parts replacement to obtain the best possible engine performance.

Turbocharger A centrifugal device, driven by exhaust gases, that pressurises the intake air. Normally used to increase the power output from a given engine displacement, but can also be used primarily to reduce exhaust emissions (as on VW's "Umwelt" Diesel engine).

U

Universal joint or U-joint A double-pivoted connection for transmitting power from a driving to a driven shaft through an angle. A U-joint consists of two Y-shaped yokes and a cross-shaped member called the spider.

V

Valve A device through which the flow of liquid, gas, vacuum, or loose material in bulk may be started, stopped, or regulated by a movable part that opens, shuts, or partially obstructs one or more ports or passageways. A valve is also the movable part of such a device.

Valve clearance The clearance between the valve tip (the end of the valve stem) and the rocker arm or tappet. The valve clearance is measured when the valve is closed.

Vernier caliper A precision measuring instrument that measures inside and outside dimensions. Not quite as accurate as a micrometer, but more convenient.

Viscosity The thickness of a liquid or its resistance to flow.

Volt A unit for expressing electrical "pressure" in a circuit. One volt that will produce a current of one ampere through a resistance of one ohm.

W

Welding Various processes used to join metal items by heating the areas to be joined to a molten state and fusing them together. For more information refer to the *Haynes Automotive Welding Manual.*

Wiring diagram A drawing portraying the components and wires in a vehicle's electrical system, using standardised symbols. For more information refer to the *Haynes Automotive Electrical and Electronic Systems Manual.*

Note: *References throughout this index are in the form* **"Chapter number"** • **"Page number"**

Haynes Manuals – The Complete UK Car List

Title	Book No.
ALFA ROMEO Alfasud/Sprint (74 - 88) up to F *	0292
Alfa Romeo Alfetta (73 - 87) up to E *	0531
AUDI 80, 90 & Coupe Petrol (79 - Nov 88) up to F	0605
Audi 80, 90 & Coupe Petrol (Oct 86 - 90) D to H	1491
Audi 100 & 200 Petrol (Oct 82 - 90) up to H	0907
Audi 100 & A6 Petrol & Diesel (May 91 - May 97) H to P	3504
Audi A3 Petrol & Diesel (96 - May 03) P to 03	4253
Audi A4 Petrol & Diesel (95 - 00) M to X	3575
Audi A4 Petrol & Diesel (01 - 04) X to 54	4609
AUSTIN A35 & A40 (56 - 67) up to F *	0118
Austin/MG/Rover Maestro 1.3 & 1.6 Petrol (83 - 95) up to M	0922
Austin/MG Metro (80 - May 90) up to G	0718
Austin/Rover Montego 1.3 & 1.6 Petrol (84 - 94) A to L	1066
Austin/MG/Rover Montego 2.0 Petrol (84 - 95) A to M	1067
Mini (59 - 69) up to H *	0527
Mini (69 - 01) up to X	0646
Austin/Rover 2.0 litre Diesel Engine (86 - 93) C to L	1857
Austin Healey 100/6 & 3000 (56 - 68) up to G *	0049
BEDFORD CF Petrol (69 - 87) up to E	0163
Bedford/Vauxhall Rascal & Suzuki Supercarry (86 - Oct 94) C to M	3015
BMW 316, 320 & 320i (4-cyl) (75 - Feb 83) up to Y *	0276
BMW 320, 320i, 323i & 325i (6-cyl) (Oct 77 - Sept 87) up to E	0815
BMW 3- & 5-Series Petrol (81 - 91) up to J	1948
BMW 3-Series Petrol (Apr 91 - 99) H to V	3210
BMW 3-Series Petrol (Sept 98 - 03) S to 53	4067
BMW 520i & 525e (Oct 81 - June 88) up to E	1560
BMW 525, 528 & 528i (73 - Sept 81) up to X *	0632
BMW 5-Series 6-cyl Petrol (April 96 - Aug 03) N to 03	4151
BMW 1500, 1502, 1600, 1602, 2000 & 2002 (59 - 77) up to S *	0240
CHRYSLER PT Cruiser Petrol (00 - 03) W to 53	4058
CITROËN 2CV, Ami & Dyane (67 - 90) up to H	0196
Citroën AX Petrol & Diesel (87 - 97) D to P	3014
Citroën Berlingo & Peugeot Partner Petrol & Diesel (96 - 05) P to 55	4281
Citroën BX Petrol (83 - 94) A to L	0908
Citroën C15 Van Petrol & Diesel (89 - Oct 98) F to S	3509
Citroën C3 Petrol & Diesel (02 - 05) 51 to 05	4197
Citroen C5 Petrol & Diesel (01-08) Y to 08	4745
Citroën CX Petrol (75 - 88) up to F	0528
Citroën Saxo Petrol & Diesel (96 - 04) N to 54	3506
Citroën Visa Petrol (79 - 88) up to F	0620
Citroën Xantia Petrol & Diesel (93 - 01) K to Y	3082
Citroën XM Petrol & Diesel (89 - 00) G to X	3451
Citroën Xsara Petrol & Diesel (97 - Sept 00) R to W	3751
Citroën Xsara Picasso Petrol & Diesel (00 - 02) W to 52	3944
Citroen Xsara Picasso (03-08)	4784
Citroën ZX Diesel (91 - 98) J to S	1922
Citroën ZX Petrol (91 - 98) H to S	1881
Citroën 1.7 & 1.9 litre Diesel Engine (84 - 96) A to N	1379
FIAT 126 (73 - 87) up to E *	0305
Fiat 500 (57 - 73) up to M *	0090
Fiat Bravo & Brava Petrol (95 - 00) N to W	3572
Fiat Cinquecento (93 - 98) K to R	3501
Fiat Panda (81 - 95) up to M	0793
Fiat Punto Petrol & Diesel (94 - Oct 99) L to V	3251
Fiat Punto Petrol (Oct 99 - July 03) V to 03	4066
Fiat Punto Petrol (03-07) 03 to 07	4746
Fiat Regata Petrol (84 - 88) A to F	1167
Fiat Tipo Petrol (88 - 91) E to J	1625
Fiat Uno Petrol (83 - 95) up to M	0923
Fiat X1/9 (74 - 89) up to G *	0273
FORD Anglia (59 - 68) up to G *	0001

Title	Book No.
Ford Capri II (& III) 1.6 & 2.0 (74 - 87) up to E *	0283
Ford Capri II (& III) 2.8 & 3.0 V6 (74 - 87) up to E	1309
Ford Cortina Mk I & Corsair 1500 ('62 - '66) up to D*	0214
Ford Cortina Mk III 1300 & 1600 (70 - 76) up to P *	0070
Ford Escort Mk I 1100 & 1300 (68 - 74) up to N *	0171
Ford Escort Mk I Mexico, RS 1600 & RS 2000 (70 - 74) up to N *	0139
Ford Escort Mk II Mexico, RS 1800 & RS 2000 (75 - 80) up to W *	0735
Ford Escort (75 - Aug 80) up to V *	0280
Ford Escort Petrol (Sept 80 - Sept 90) up to H	0686
Ford Escort & Orion Petrol (Sept 90 - 00) H to X	1737
Ford Escort & Orion Diesel (Sept 90 - 00) H to X	4081
Ford Fiesta (76 - Aug 83) up to Y	0334
Ford Fiesta Petrol (Aug 83 - Feb 89) A to F	1030
Ford Fiesta Petrol (Feb 89 - Oct 95) F to N	1595
Ford Fiesta Petrol & Diesel (Oct 95 - Mar 02) N to 02	3397
Ford Fiesta Petrol & Diesel (Apr 02 - 07) 02 to 57	4170
Ford Focus Petrol & Diesel (98 - 01) S to Y	3759
Ford Focus Petrol & Diesel (Oct 01 - 05) 51 to 05	4167
Ford Galaxy Petrol & Diesel (95 - Aug 00) M to W	3984
Ford Granada Petrol (Sept 77 - Feb 85) up to B *	0481
Ford Granada & Scorpio Petrol (Mar 85 - 94) B to M	1245
Ford Ka (96 - 02) P to 52	3570
Ford Mondeo Petrol (93 - Sept 00) K to X	1923
Ford Mondeo Petrol & Diesel (Oct 00 - Jul 03) X to 03	3990
Ford Mondeo Petrol & Diesel (July 03 - 07) 03 to 56	4619
Ford Mondeo Diesel (93 - 96) L to N	3465
Ford Orion Petrol (83 - Sept 90) up to H	1009
Ford Sierra 4-cyl Petrol (82 - 93) up to K	0903
Ford Sierra V6 Petrol (82 - 91) up to J	0904
Ford Transit Petrol (Mk 2) (78 - Jan 86) up to C	0719
Ford Transit Petrol (Mk 3) (Feb 86 - 89) C to G	1468
Ford Transit Diesel (Feb 86 - 99) C to T	3019
Ford Transit Diesel (00-06)	4775
Ford 1.6 & 1.8 litre Diesel Engine (84 - 96) A to N	1172
Ford 2.1, 2.3 & 2.5 litre Diesel Engine (77 - 90) up to H	1606
FREIGHT ROVER Sherpa Petrol (74 - 87) up to E	0463
HILLMAN Avenger (70 - 82) up to Y	0037
Hillman Imp (63 - 76) up to R *	0022
HONDA Civic (Feb 84 - Oct 87) A to E	1226
Honda Civic (Nov 91 - 96) J to N	3199
Honda Civic Petrol (Mar 95 - 00) M to X	4050
Honda Civic Petrol & Diesel (01 - 05) X to 55	4611
Honda CR-V Petrol & Diesel (01-06)	4747
Honda Jazz (01 - Feb 08) 51 - 57	4735
HYUNDAI Pony (85 - 94) C to M	3398
JAGUAR E Type (61 - 72) up to L *	0140
Jaguar MkI & II, 240 & 340 (55 - 69) up to H *	0098
Jaguar XJ6, XJ & Sovereign; Daimler Sovereign (68 - Oct 86) up to D	0242
Jaguar XJ6 & Sovereign (Oct 86 - Sept 94) D to M	3261
Jaguar XJ12, XJS & Sovereign; Daimler Double Six (72 - 88) up to F	0478
JEEP Cherokee Petrol (93 - 96) K to N	1943
LADA 1200, 1300, 1500 & 1600 (74 - 91) up to J	0413
Lada Samara (87 - 91) D to J	1610
LAND ROVER 90, 110 & Defender Diesel (83 - 07) up to 56	3017
Land Rover Discovery Petrol & Diesel (89 - 98) G to S	3016
Land Rover Discovery Diesel (Nov 98 - Jul 04) S to 04	4606
Land Rover Freelander Petrol & Diesel (97 - Sept 03) R to 53	3929
Land Rover Freelander Petrol & Diesel (Oct 03 - Oct 06) 53 to 56	4623

Title	Book No.
Land Rover Series IIA & III Diesel (58 - 85) up to C	0529
Land Rover Series II, IIA & III 4-cyl Petrol (58 - 85) up to C	0314
MAZDA 323 (Mar 81 - Oct 89) up to G	1608
Mazda 323 (Oct 89 - 98) G to R	3455
Mazda 626 (May 83 - Sept 87) up to E	0929
Mazda B1600, B1800 & B2000 Pick-up Petrol (72 - 88) up to F	0267
Mazda RX-7 (79 - 85) up to C *	0460
MERCEDES-BENZ 190, 190E & 190D Petrol & Diesel (83 - 93) A to L	3450
Mercedes-Benz 200D, 240D, 240TD, 300D & 300TD 123 Series Diesel (Oct 76 - 85)	1114
Mercedes-Benz 250 & 280 (68 - 72) up to L *	0346
Mercedes-Benz 250 & 280 123 Series Petrol (Oct 76 - 84) up to B *	0677
Mercedes-Benz 124 Series Petrol & Diesel (85 - Aug 93) C to K	3253
Mercedes-Benz A-Class Petrol & Diesel (98-04) S to 54	4748
Mercedes-Benz C-Class Petrol & Diesel (93 - Aug 00) L to W	3511
Mercedes-Benz C-Class (00-06)	4780
MGA (55 - 62) *	0475
MGB (62 - 80) up to W	0111
MG Midget & Austin-Healey Sprite (58 - 80) up to W *	0265
MINI Petrol (July 01 - 05) Y to 05	4273
MITSUBISHI Shogun & L200 Pick-Ups Petrol (83 - 94) up to M	1944
MORRIS Ital 1.3 (80 - 84) up to B	0705
Morris Minor 1000 (56 - 71) up to K	0024
NISSAN Almera Petrol (95 - Feb 00) N to V	4053
Nissan Almera & Tino Petrol (Feb 00 - 07) V to 56	4612
Nissan Bluebird (May 84 - Mar 86) A to C	1223
Nissan Bluebird Petrol (Mar 86 - 90) C to H	1473
Nissan Cherry (Sept 82 - 86) up to D	1031
Nissan Micra (83 - Jan 93) up to K	0931
Nissan Micra (93 - 02) K to 52	3254
Nissan Micra Petrol (03-07) 52 to 57	4734
Nissan Primera Petrol (90 - Aug 99) H to T	1851
Nissan Stanza (82 - 86) up to D	0824
Nissan Sunny Petrol (May 82 - Oct 86) up to D	0895
Nissan Sunny Petrol (Oct 86 - Mar 91) D to H	1378
Nissan Sunny Petrol (Apr 91 - 95) H to N	3219
OPEL Ascona & Manta (B Series) (Sept 75 - 88) up to F *	0316
Opel Ascona Petrol (81 - 88)	3215
Opel Astra Petrol (Oct 91 - Feb 98)	3156
Opel Corsa Petrol (83 - Mar 93)	3160
Opel Corsa Petrol (Mar 93 - 97)	3159
Opel Kadett Petrol (Nov 79 - Oct 84) up to B	0634
Opel Kadett Petrol (Oct 84 - Oct 91)	3196
Opel Omega & Senator Petrol (Nov 86 - 94)	3157
Opel Rekord Petrol (Feb 78 - Oct 86) up to D	0543
Opel Vectra Petrol (Oct 88 - Oct 95)	3158
PEUGEOT 106 Petrol & Diesel (91 - 04) J to 53	1882
Peugeot 205 Petrol (83 - 97) A to P	0932
Peugeot 206 Petrol & Diesel (98 - 01) S to X	3757
Peugeot 206 Petrol & Diesel (02 - 06) 51 to 06	4613
Peugeot 306 Petrol & Diesel (93 - 02) K to 02	3073
Peugeot 307 Petrol & Diesel (01 - 04) Y to 54	4147
Peugeot 309 Petrol (86 - 93) C to K	1266
Peugeot 405 Petrol (88 - 97) E to P	1559
Peugeot 405 Diesel (88 - 97) E to P	3198
Peugeot 406 Petrol & Diesel (96 - Mar 99) N to T	3394
Peugeot 406 Petrol & Diesel (Mar 99 - 02) T to 52	3982

* Classic reprint

Title	Book No.
Peugeot 505 Petrol (79 - 89) up to G	0762
Peugeot 1.7/1.8 & 1.9 litre Diesel Engine (82 - 96) up to N	0950
Peugeot 2.0, 2.1, 2.3 & 2.5 litre Diesel Engines (74 - 90) up to H	1607
PORSCHE 911 (65 - 85) up to C	0264
Porsche 924 & 924 Turbo (76 - 85) up to C	0397
PROTON (89 - 97) F to P	3255
RANGE ROVER V8 Petrol (70 - Oct 92) up to K	0606
RELIANT Robin & Kitten (73 - 83) up to A *	0436
RENAULT 4 (61 - 86) up to D *	0072
Renault 5 Petrol (Feb 85 - 96) B to N	1219
Renault 9 & 11 Petrol (82 - 89) up to F	0822
Renault 18 Petrol (79 - 86) up to D	0598
Renault 19 Petrol (89 - 96) F to N	1646
Renault 19 Diesel (89 - 96) F to N	1946
Renault 21 Petrol (86 - 94) C to M	1397
Renault 25 Petrol & Diesel (84 - 92) B to K	1228
Renault Clio Petrol (91 - May 98) H to R	1853
Renault Clio Diesel (91 - June 96) H to N	3031
Renault Clio Petrol & Diesel (May 98 - May 01) R to Y	3906
Renault Clio Petrol & Diesel (June '01 - '05) Y to 55	4168
Renault Espace Petrol & Diesel (85 - 96) C to N	3197
Renault Laguna Petrol & Diesel (94 - 00) L to W	3252
Renault Laguna Petrol & Diesel (Feb 01 - Feb 05) X to 54	4283
Renault Mégane & Scénic Petrol & Diesel (96 - 99) N to T	3395
Renault Mégane & Scénic Petrol & Diesel (Apr 99 - 02) T to 52	3916
Renault Megane Petrol & Diesel (Oct 02 - 05) 52 to 55	4284
Renault Scenic Petrol & Diesel (Sept 03 - 06) 53 to 06	4297
ROVER 213 & 216 (84 - 89) A to G	1116
Rover 214 & 414 Petrol (89 - 96) G to N	1689
Rover 216 & 416 Petrol (89 - 96) G to N	1830
Rover 211, 214, 216, 218 & 220 Petrol & Diesel (Dec 95 - 99) N to V	3399
Rover 25 & MG ZR Petrol & Diesel (Oct 99 - 04) V to 54	4145
Rover 414, 416 & 420 Petrol & Diesel (May 95 - 98) M to R	3453
Rover 45 / MG ZS Petrol & Diesel (99 - 05) V to 55	4384
Rover 618, 620 & 623 Petrol (93 - 97) K to P	3257
Rover 75 / MG ZT Petrol & Diesel (99 - 06) S to 06	4292
Rover 820, 825 & 827 Petrol (86 - 95) D to N	1380
Rover 3500 (76 - 87) up to E *	0365
Rover Metro, 111 & 114 Petrol (May 90 - 98) G to S	1711
SAAB 95 & 96 (66 - 76) up to R *	0198
Saab 90, 99 & 900 (79 - Oct 93) up to L	0765
Saab 900 (Oct 93 - 98) L to R	3512
Saab 9000 (4-cyl) (85 - 98) C to S	1686
Saab 9-3 Petrol & Diesel (98 - Aug 02) R to 02	4614
Saab 9-3 Petrol & Diesel (02-07) 52 to 57	4749
Saab 9-5 4-cyl Petrol (97 - 04) R to 54	4156
SEAT Ibiza & Cordoba Petrol & Diesel (Oct 93 - Oct 99) L to V	3571
Seat Ibiza & Malaga Petrol (85 - 92) B to K	1609
SKODA Estelle (77 - 89) up to G	0604
Skoda Fabia Petrol & Diesel (00 - 06) W to 06	4376
Skoda Favorit (89 - 96) F to N	1801
Skoda Felicia Petrol & Diesel (95 - 01) M to X	3505
Skoda Octavia Petrol & Diesel (98 - Apr 04) R to 04	4285
SUBARU 1600 & 1800 (Nov 79 - 90) up to H *	0995

Title	Book No.
SUNBEAM Alpine, Rapier & H120 (67 - 74) up to N *	0051
SUZUKI SJ Series, Samurai & Vitara (4-cyl) Petrol (82 - 97) up to P	1942
Suzuki Supercarry & Bedford/Vauxhall Rascal (86 - Oct 94) C to M	3015
TALBOT Alpine, Solara, Minx & Rapier (75 - 86) up to D	0337
Talbot Horizon Petrol (78 - 86) up to D	0473
Talbot Samba (82 - 86) up to D	0823
TOYOTA Avensis Petrol (98 - Jan 03) R to 52	4264
Toyota Carina E Petrol (May 92 - 97) J to P	3256
Toyota Corolla (80 - 85) up to C	0683
Toyota Corolla (Sept 83 - Sept 87) A to E	1024
Toyota Corolla (Sept 87 - Aug 92) E to K	1683
Toyota Corolla Petrol (Aug 92 - 97) K to P	3259
Toyota Corolla Petrol (July 97 - Feb 02) P to 51	4286
Toyota Hi-Ace & Hi-Lux Petrol (69 - Oct 83) up to A	0304
Toyota RAV4 Petrol & Diesel (94-06) L to 55	4750
Toyota Yaris Petrol (99 - 05) T to 05	4265
TRIUMPH GT6 & Vitesse (62 - 74) up to N *	0112
Triumph Herald (59 - 71) up to K *	0010
Triumph Spitfire (62 - 81) up to X	0113
Triumph Stag (70 - 78) up to T *	0441
Triumph TR2, TR3, TR3A, TR4 & TR4A (52 - 67) up to F *	0028
Triumph TR5 & 6 (67 - 75) up to P *	0031
Triumph TR7 (75 - 82) up to Y *	0322
VAUXHALL Astra Petrol (80 - Oct 84) up to B	0635
Vauxhall Astra & Belmont Petrol (Oct 84 - Oct 91) B to J	1136
Vauxhall Astra Petrol (Oct 91 - Feb 98) J to R	1832
Vauxhall/Opel Astra & Zafira Petrol (Feb 98 - Apr 04) R to 04	3758
Vauxhall/Opel Astra & Zafira Diesel (Feb 98 - Apr 04) R to 04	3797
Vauxhall/Opel Astra Petrol (04 - 08)	4732
Vauxhall/Opel Astra Diesel (04 - 08)	4733
Vauxhall/Opel Calibra (90 - 98) G to S	3502
Vauxhall Carlton Petrol (Oct 78 - Oct 86) up to D	0480
Vauxhall Carlton & Senator Petrol (Nov 86 - 94) D to L	1469
Vauxhall Cavalier Petrol (81 - Oct 88) up to F	0812
Vauxhall Cavalier Petrol (Oct 88 - 95) F to N	1570
Vauxhall Chevette (75 - 84) up to B	0285
Vauxhall/Opel Corsa Diesel (Mar 93 - Oct 00) K to X	4087
Vauxhall Corsa Petrol (Mar 93 - 97) K to R	1985
Vauxhall/Opel Corsa Petrol (Apr 97 - Oct 00) P to X	3921
Vauxhall/Opel Corsa Petrol & Diesel (Oct 00 - Sept 03) X to 53	4079
Vauxhall/Opel Corsa Petrol & Diesel (Oct 03 - Aug 06) 53 to 06	4617
Vauxhall/Opel Frontera Petrol & Diesel (91 - Sept 98) J to S	3454
Vauxhall Nova Petrol (83 - 93) up to K	0909
Vauxhall/Opel Omega Petrol (94 - 99) L to T	3510
Vauxhall/Opel Vectra Petrol & Diesel (95 - Feb 99) N to S	3396
Vauxhall/Opel Vectra Petrol & Diesel (Mar 99 - May 02) T to 02	3930
Vauxhall/Opel Vectra Petrol & Diesel (June 02 - Sept 05) 02 to 55	4618
Vauxhall/Opel 1.5, 1.6 & 1.7 litre Diesel Engine (82 - 96) up to N	1222
VW 411 & 412 (68 - 75) up to P *	0091
VW Beetle 1200 (54 - 77) up to S	0036
VW Beetle 1300 & 1500 (65 - 75) up to P	0039

Title	Book No.
VW 1302 & 1302S (70 - 72) up to L *	0110
VW Beetle 1303, 1303S & GT (72 - 75) up to P	0159
VW Beetle Petrol & Diesel (Apr 99 - 07) T to 57	3798
VW Golf & Jetta Mk 1 Petrol 1.1 & 1.3 (74 - 84) up to A	0716
VW Golf, Jetta & Scirocco Mk 1 Petrol 1.5, 1.6 & 1.8 (74 - 84) up to A	0726
VW Golf & Jetta Mk 1 Diesel (78 - 84) up to A	0451
VW Golf & Jetta Mk 2 Petrol (Mar 84 - Feb 92) A to J	1081
VW Golf & Vento Petrol & Diesel (Feb 92 - Mar 98) J to R	3097
VW Golf & Bora Petrol & Diesel (April 98 - 00) R to X	3727
VW Golf & Bora 4-cyl Petrol & Diesel (01 - 03) X to 53	4169
VW Golf & Jetta Petrol & Diesel (04 - 07) 53 to 07	4610
VW LT Petrol Vans & Light Trucks (76 - 87) up to E	0637
VW Passat & Santana Petrol (Sept 81 - May 88) up to E	0814
VW Passat 4-cyl Petrol & Diesel (May 88 - 96) E to P	3498
VW Passat 4-cyl Petrol & Diesel (Dec 96 - Nov 00) P to X	3917
VW Passat Petrol & Diesel (Dec 00 - May 05) X to 05	4279
VW Polo & Derby (76 - Jan 82) up to X	0335
VW Polo (82 - Oct 90) up to H	0813
VW Polo Petrol (Nov 90 - Aug 94) H to L	3245
VW Polo Hatchback Petrol & Diesel (94 - 99) M to S	3500
VW Polo Hatchback Petrol (00 - Jan 02) V to 51	4150
VW Polo Petrol & Diesel (02 - May 05) 51 to 05	4608
VW Scirocco (82 - 90) up to H *	1224
VW Transporter 1600 (68 - 79) up to V	0082
VW Transporter 1700, 1800 & 2000 (72 - 79) up to V *	0226
VW Transporter (air-cooled) Petrol (79 - 82) up to Y *	0638
VW Transporter (water-cooled) Petrol (82 - 90) up to H	3452
VW Type 3 (63 - 73) up to M *	0084
VOLVO 120 & 130 Series (& P1800) (61 - 73) up to M *	0203
Volvo 142, 144 & 145 (66 - 74) up to N *	0129
Volvo 240 Series Petrol (74 - 93) up to K	0270
Volvo 262, 264 & 260/265 (75 - 85) up to C *	0400
Volvo 340, 343, 345 & 360 (76 - 91) up to J	0715
Volvo 440, 460 & 480 Petrol (87 - 97) D to P	1691
Volvo 740 & 760 Petrol (82 - 91) up to J	1258
Volvo 850 Petrol (92 - 96) J to P	3260
Volvo 940 petrol (90 - 98) H to R	3249
Volvo S40 & V40 Petrol (96 - Mar 04) N to 04	3569
Volvo S40 & V50 Petrol & Diesel (Mar 04 - Jun 07) 04 to 07	4731
Volvo S60 Petrol & Diesel (01-08)	4793
Volvo S70, V70 & C70 Petrol (96 - 99) P to V	3573
Volvo V70 / S80 Petrol & Diesel (98 - 05) S to 55	4263

DIY MANUAL SERIES

The Haynes Air Conditioning Manual	4192
The Haynes Car Electrical Systems Manual	4251
The Haynes Manual on Bodywork	4198
The Haynes Manual on Brakes	4178
The Haynes Manual on Carburettors	4177
The Haynes Manual on Diesel Engines	4174
The Haynes Manual on Engine Management	4199
The Haynes Manual on Fault Codes	4175
The Haynes Manual on Practical Electrical Systems	4267
The Haynes Manual on Small Engines	4250
The Haynes Manual on Welding	4176

* Classic reprint

CL24.08/09

Preserving Our Motoring Heritage

< *The Model J Duesenberg Derham Tourster. Only eight of these magnificent cars were ever built – this is the only example to be found outside the United States of America*

Almost every car you've ever loved, loathed or desired is gathered under one roof at the Haynes Motor Museum. Over 300 immaculately presented cars and motorbikes represent every aspect of our motoring heritage, from elegant reminders of bygone days, such as the superb Model J Duesenberg to curiosities like the bug-eyed BMW Isetta. There are also many old friends and flames. Perhaps you remember the 1959 Ford Popular that you did your courting in? The magnificent 'Red Collection' is a spectacle of classic sports cars including AC, Alfa Romeo, Austin Healey, Ferrari, Lamborghini, Maserati, MG, Riley, Porsche and Triumph.

A Perfect Day Out

Each and every vehicle at the Haynes Motor Museum has played its part in the history and culture of Motoring. Today, they make a wonderful spectacle and a great day out for all the family. Bring the kids, bring Mum and Dad, but above all bring your camera to capture those golden memories for ever. You will also find an impressive array of motoring memorabilia, a comfortable 70 seat video cinema and one of the most extensive transport book shops in Britain. The Pit Stop Cafe serves everything from a cup of tea to wholesome, home-made meals or, if you prefer, you can enjoy the large picnic area nestled in the beautiful rural surroundings of Somerset.

John Haynes O.B.E., Founder and Chairman of the museum at the wheel of a Haynes Light 12.

< *Graham Hill's Lola Cosworth Formula 1 car next to a 1934 Riley Sports.*

The Museum is situated on the A359 Yeovil to Frome road at Sparkford, just off the A303 in Somerset. It is about 40 miles south of Bristol, and 25 minutes drive from the M5 intersection at Taunton.
Open 9.30am - 5.30pm (10.00am - 4.00pm Winter) 7 days a week, *except Christmas Day, Boxing Day and New Years Day*
Special rates available for schools, coach parties and outings Charitable Trust No. 292048